MASTER VISUALLY®

by Joe Kraynak

Visual™

Creating Web Pages

Master VISUALLY® Creating Web Pages

Published by
Wiley Publishing, Inc.
111 River Street
Hoboken, NJ 07030-5774

Published simultaneously in Canada

Library of Congress Control Number: 2004112341

ISBN: 0-7645-7726-3

Manufactured in the United States of America

10 9 8 7 6 5 4 3 2 1

1VH/SX/RQ/QU/IN

Trademark Acknowledgments

Contact Us

For general information on our other products and services please contact our Customer Care Department within the U.S. at 800-762-2974, outside the U.S. at 317-572-3993 or fax 317-572-4002.

For technical support please visit www.wiley.com/techsupport.

WILEY

U.S. Sales

Contact Wiley
at (800) 762-2974 or
fax (317) 572-4002.

Praise for Visual Books...

"If you have to see it to believe it, this is the book for you!"
—PC World

"A master tutorial/reference — from the leaders in visual learning!"
—Infoworld

"A publishing concept whose time has come!"
—The Globe and Mail

"Just wanted to say THANK YOU to your company for providing books which make learning fast, easy, and exciting! I learn visually so your books have helped me greatly – from Windows instruction to Web development. Best wishes for continued success."
— Angela J. Barker (Springfield, MO)

"I have over the last 10-15 years purchased thousands of dollars worth of computer books but find your books the most easily read, best set out, and most helpful and easily understood books on software and computers I have ever read. Please keep up the good work."
—John Gatt (Adamstown Heights, Australia)

"You're marvelous! I am greatly in your debt."
—Patrick Baird (Lacey, WA)

"I am an avid fan of your Visual books. If I need to learn anything, I just buy one of your books and learn the topic it in no time. Wonders! I have even trained my friends to give me Visual books as gifts."
—Illona Bergstrom (Aventura, FL)

"I have quite a few of your Visual books and have been very pleased with all of them. I love the way the lessons are presented!"
—Mary Jane Newman (Yorba Linda, CA)

"Like a lot of other people, I understand things best when I see them visually. Your books really make learning easy and life more fun."
—John T. Frey (Cadillac, MI)

"Your Visual books have been a great help to me. I now have a number of your books and they are all great. My friends always ask to borrow my Visual books - trouble is, I always have to ask for them back!"
— John Robson
(Brampton, Ontario, Canada)

"I write to extend my thanks and appreciation for your books. They are clear, easy to follow, and straight to the point. Keep up the good work! I bought several of your books and they are just right! No regrets! I will always buy your books because they are the best."
—Seward Kollie (Dakar, Senegal)

"What fantastic teaching books you have produced! Congratulations to you and your staff."
—Bruno Tonon (Melbourne, Australia)

"Thank you for the wonderful books you produce. It wasn't until I was an adult that I discovered how I learn—visually. Although a few publishers claim to present the materially visually, nothing compares to Visual books. I love the simple layout. Everything is easy to follow. I can just grab a book and use it at my computer, lesson by lesson. And I understand the material! You really know the way I think and learn. Thanks so much!"
—Stacey Han (Avondale, AZ)

"The Greatest. This whole series is the best computer-learning tool of any kind I've ever seen."
—Joe Orr (Brooklyn, NY)

Credits

Project Editor
Maureen Spears

Acquisitions Editor
Jody Lefevere

Product Development Manager
Lindsay Sandman

Copy Editor
Marylouise Wiack

Technical Editor
Dennis R. Cohen

Editorial Manager
Robyn Siesky

Manufacturing
Allan Conley
Linda Cook
Paul Gilchrist
Jennifer Guynn

Book Design
Kathie Rickard

Screen Artist
Jill A. Proll

Illustrator
Ronda David-Burroughs

Project Coordinator
Nancee Reeves

Layout
Amanda Carter
Carrie Foster
Denny Hager
Jennifer Heleine
Heather Pope

Proofreaders
Susan Sims

Quality Control
John Greenough
Susan Moritz
Carl William Pierce

Indexer
Steve Rath

Special Help
Adrienne Porter

Vice President and Executive Group Publisher
Richard Swadley

Vice President and Publisher
Barry Pruett

Composition Director
Debbie Stailey

About the Author

Joe Kraynak Joe Kraynak has been writing and editing training manuals and computer books for over fifteen years. His long list of computer books include *Internet: Top 100 Simplified Tips and Tricks, Google: Top 100 Simplified Tips and Tricks,* and *The Complete Idiot's Guide to Computer Basics.* Joe has a Master's degree in English and a Bachelor's degree in Philosophy and Creative Writing from Purdue University.

Author's Acknowledgments

Every book is a team project that demands the expertise and contributions of many individuals. I would like to thank several people who played a key role in perfecting and producing this book. Special thanks to Jody Lefevere, acquisitions editor, for choosing me to write the book, and to Maureen Spears, project editor, who carefully guided the manuscript and artwork through the many stages of production. Special thanks also goes to Dennis Cohen, technical editor, for eliminating technical errors, and to Marylouise Wiack, copy editor, for tightening up the language, clarifying key concepts, and ensuring consistency throughout the book.

Thanks to Lindsay Sandman, Product Development Manager, and Robyn Siesky, editorial manager, for working behind the scenes to make everything run smoothly. Thanks also to screen artist Jill A. Proll and Illustrator Ronda David-Burroughs for creating the screens and illustrations that are so critical in showing readers how to perform specific tasks. The manufacturing team of Allan Conley, Linda Cook, Paul Gilchrist, and Jennifer Guynn, merit great appreciation for transforming a loose collection of pages and pictures into an attractive, bound book. Thanks also to Adrienne Porter for handling all of the assorted details and to the rest of the crew at Wiley Publishing for their contributions to creating, editing, designing, and producing this book

PART I — Understanding Web Page Coding

1) Introducing Web Page Languages

2) Viewing and Editing HTML

PART II — Creating and Formatting Web Pages

3) Creating a Basic Web Page

4) Formatting with Cascading Style Sheets

5) Enhancing a Web Page with Images

6) Building Image Maps

7) Improving Navigation with Frames

PART III — Adding Interactivity with JavaScript

8) Mastering JavaScript Basics

9) Implementing JavaScript in HTML Documents

PART IV — Collecting Data with Forms

10) Building Forms to Collect Data

11) Capturing Form Data

WHAT'S INSIDE

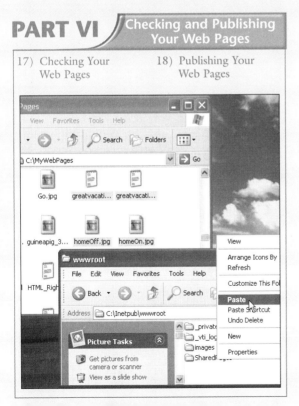

HTML Name	Octal Number	Symbol	Description
	40		Space
	41	!	Exclamation
&quot;	42	"	Quotation
	43	#	Hash mark
	44	$	Dollar sign
	45	%	Percent sign
&amp;	46	&	Ampersand
	47	'	Apostrophe
	50	(	Left parenth
	51	)	Right parent
	52	*	Asterisk
	53	+	Plus sign
	54	,	Comma
	55	-	Hyphen
	56	.	Period
	57	/	Forward slas
	60–67, 70, 71		
	72	:	Colon
	73	;	Semicolon
&lt;	74	<	Less-than si
	75	=	Equals sign
&gt;	76	>	Greater-tha
	77	?	Question m

PART I

Understanding Web Page Coding

PART II

Creating and Formatting Web Pages

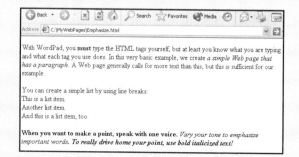

TABLE OF CONTENTS

4 Formatting with Cascading Style Sheets

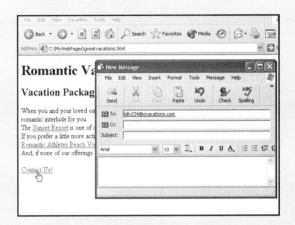

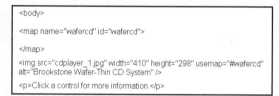

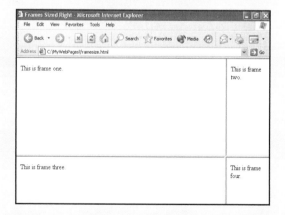

TABLE OF CONTENTS

PART III — Adding Interactivity with JavaScript

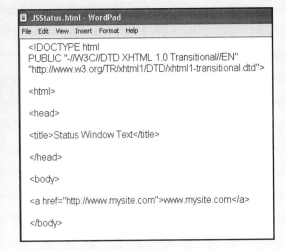

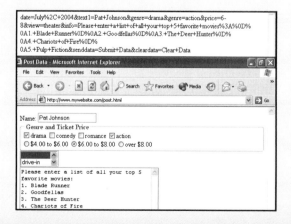

PART IV — Collecting Data with Forms

⑩ Building Forms to Collect Data

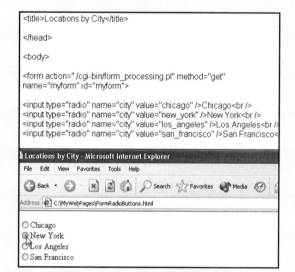

⑪ Capturing Form Data

TABLE OF CONTENTS

PART V — Adding Embedded Objects

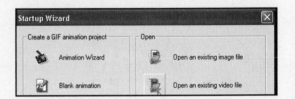

```
test.html - WordPad
File  Edit  View  Insert  Format  Help
<html>
<head>
</head>
<body>
 <object classid="java:test4.class" codetype="application/octet-stream">
   This page loads a java applet.
 </object>
</body>
</html>
```

The Social Registry

Welcome to the *Social Registry*, your key to a better tomorrow! Our editors are dedicated to pointing out the most significant social problems we, as a nation, face. We are also dedicated to highlighting the efforts of those who seek to strengthen out social values.

RSS You can subscribe to our site to keep abreast of the latest news and information.

Good Kids Gone Bad

PART VI Checking and Publishing Your Web Pages

Welcome to Animal House

Your One-Stop Pet Emporium

☒ Another satisfied customer! When you and your pet enter Animal House, you not only step into the largest

TABLE OF CONTENTS

PART VII   Appendixes

! Exclamation · " Quotation · <
Hash mark · $ Dollar sign · % Per
& Ampersand · ' Apostrophe · (
Asterisk · + Plus sign · , Comma

How to Use this Master VISUALLY Book

Master VISUALLY Creating Web Pages contains straightforward examples to teach you how to create, test, and publish your own Web pages; accent them with illustrations; add sound, video, and animation; and make them more dynamic and interactive with programming scripts and forms.

This book is designed to help a reader receive quick access to any area of question. You can simply look up a subject within the Table of Contents or Index and go immediately to the task of concern. A *section* is a set of is self-contained unit that walks you through a computer operation step-by-step. That is, with rare exception, all the information you need regarding an area of interest is contained within a section.

The Organization of Each Chapter

Each section contains an introduction, a set of screen shots with steps, and, if the steps goes beyond 1 page, a set of tips. The introduction tells why you want to perform the steps, the advantages and disadvantages of performing the steps, a general explanation of any procedures, and references to other related tasks in the book. The screens, located on the bottom half of each page, show a series of steps that you must complete to perform a given task. The tip section gives you an opportunity to further understand the task at hand, to learn about other related tasks in other areas of the book, or to apply more complicated or alternative methods.

A chapter may also contain an illustrated group of pages that gives you background information that you need to understand the tasks in a chapter.

The General Organization of This Book

Master VISUALLY Creating Web Pages has 18 Chapters and 2 Appendixes and is divided into 6 Parts.

Part 1, "Understanding Web Page Coding," introduces you to the various languages used on the Web to create Web pages. Here, you learn the basics of using HTML tags to mark up the elements that comprise your Web pages. You learn the differences between HTML and XHTML and why they are significant. You also learn the various types of HTML editors you can use to create and design your pages.

Part 2, "Getting Started," provides everything you need to know to create a Web page, format it, and illustrate it. In a single chapter, you learn how to create a Web page that is ready for publication, simply by typing your text and adding the required HTML tags. In another chapter, you learn how to modify the appearance of a Web page by adjusting margins, specifying font sizes and styles, adding background and text colors, and positioning various elements in precise locations. You learn how to enhance your Web pages with illustrations, photographs, and other images and use images as clickable

site maps. You also learn how to how to insert special tags on a Web page that instruct a browser to display two or more frames in a single window, so you can display multiple pages in a single Web browser window.

Part 3, "Adding Interactivity with JavaScript," shows you how to write and implement JavaScript inside a Web page to have the page respond to user actions in some way. You learn how to use JavaScript to prompt a user for a response, verify form data, count the number of times your page has been opened, and open and close Web browser windows.

Part 4, "Collecting Data with Forms," provides instructions on how to create online forms, complete with text boxes, check box options, radio button options, and command buttons for canceling the form or submitting the data. Once you have created a form, you need some way to pass the form data to a database have it sent via e-mail back to you. This chapter provides instructions on setting up your form so that you can receive the data a user enters.

Part 5, "Adding Embedded Objects," shows you how to add objects to your page that are saved in formats that a Web browser alone cannot display or play. Here, you learn how to add sounds and video; create and publish animated, interactive Flash presentations; and create and insert Java applets, which are small programs that run right on a Web page in the Web browser window. You also learn how to syndicate your page by creating an RSS feed; this enables other sites to use content from your site, which can increase traffic at your site.

Part 6, "Checking and Publishing Your Web Pages," explains the process of publishing your pages—placing them on a Web server so that other users can open your pages in their Web browsers. This part begins by teaching you various ways to test your page for source code errors, broken links, and spelling errors and showing you how to validate your source code to ensure that it meets the latest standards. The part then shows you various ways to publish your pages on a Web server, so you know your options and what to expect from your Internet service provider or a Web hosting service.

Two appendixes provide additional reference material. Appendix A provides a list of codes you can type to insert special characters into your HTML pages. Appendix B provides a list of CSS—Cascading Style Sheet—properties and values that you can use along with Chapter 4 to format your Web pages. This book also includes a color chart you can use to select colors for various Web page elements, including the page background, text, and image borders.

Who This Book is For

This book is for the beginner, who is unfamiliar with the various Web technologies, programs, and techniques required to design, create, and publish Web pages. This book shows the beginner how to create, code, format, and illustrate Web pages using a simple text editor, such as Windows WordPad. It also goes beyond the basics by introducing beginners to dynamic, interactive Web development tools, including Flash, Java, and JavaScript. This book is also for more computer literate individuals who want to expand their knowledge of the different features that Web publishing has to offer.

What You Need to Use This Book

To perform the tasks in this book, you must have a computer equipped with the following hardware, software, and services:

- A PC with a Pentium 133 MHz or faster processor or a Macintosh with a 68040 or faster processor. A 600 MHz Intel Pentium III processor or equivalent is required for creating Flash movies.
- Microsoft Windows 98, ME, 2000, XP, NT 4 or later, or Mac OS 7.5.5 of later.
- At least 32MB RAM. 128MB is required for creating Flash movies.
- A sound card for PCs, if you want to add audio clips to your Web pages.
- A monitor capable of displaying at least 800 x 600 resolution in 256 colors.
- A modem with a speed of at least 28.8 Kbps. To host your own Web site, you need a broadband connection, such as DSL or cable.

Conventions When Using the Mouse

This book uses the following conventions to describe the actions you perform when using the mouse:

Click

Press and release the left mouse button. You use a click to select an item on the screen.

Double-click

Quickly press and release the left mouse button twice. You use a double-click to open a document or start a program.

Right-click

Press and release the right mouse button. You use a right-click to display a shortcut menu, a list of commands specifically related to the selected item.

Click and Drag, and Release the Mouse

Position the mouse pointer over an item on the screen and then press and hold down the left mouse button. Still holding down the button, move the mouse to where you want to

place the item and then release the button. Dragging and dropping makes it easy to move an item to a new location.

The Conventions in This Book

A number of typographic and layout styles have been used throughout this book to distinguish different types of information.

Bold

Indicates any information that you must type.

Italics

Indicates a new term being introduced or any variable in an entry. For example, a step may instruct you to type ***filename*.html** in which you can type a unique entry in place of *filename*.

Numbered Steps

Indicate that you must perform these steps in order to successful perform the task.

Bulleted Steps

Give you alternative methods, explain various options, or present what a program does in response to the numbered steps.

Notes

Give you additional information to help you complete a task. The purpose of a note is three-fold: It can explain special conditions that may occur during the course of the task, warn you of potentially dangerous situations, or refer you to tasks in the same, or a different chapter. References to tasks within the chapter are indicated by the phrase "See the section..." followed by the name of the task. References to sections in other chapters are indicated by "See Chapter..." followed by the chapter number.

Icons

Icons in the steps indicate a button that you must press.

 Most of the sections in this book are supplemented with a section called Master It. These are tips, hints, and tricks that extend your use of the section beyond what you learned by performing the steps in the section.

Conventions that are Assumed with this Book

This book uses WordPad in all of its examples, but you can use any text-based HTML editor.

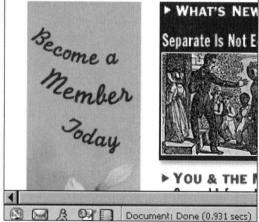

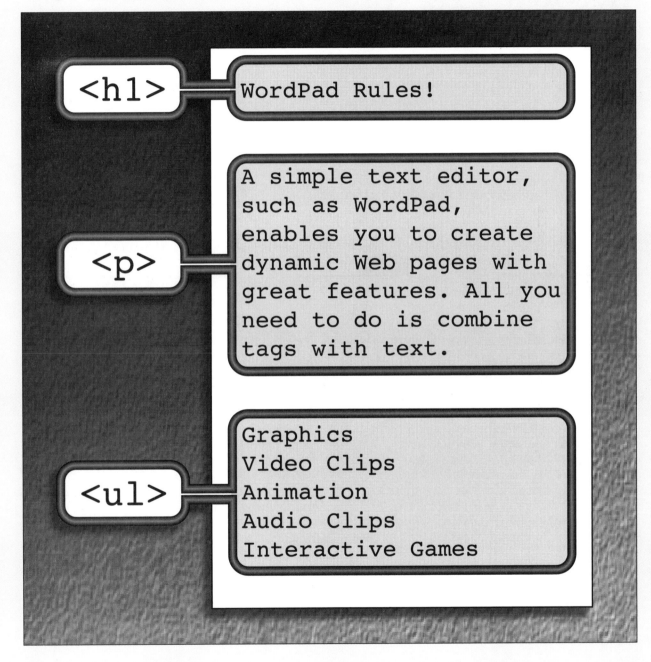

Introducing Web Page Publishing

Before the advent of the Web, whenever you wanted to publish anything for distribution to a large audience, you needed access to a printing press and a distributor. The Web simplifies publishing. It empowers anyone who has a computer and an Internet connection to publish professional-looking documents and to make them instantly available worldwide. Using a basic text editor, such as Windows Notepad, you can create and format dazzling Web pages, complete with graphics, colorful backgrounds, fancy text, and links to other pages.

You can collect input and take orders online with forms. You can even add multimedia elements, including audio and video clips and animations.

The Web makes all of this possible through a clever design in which a text-only document uses *tags*, or codes, to instruct a Web browser on how to display the page. Collectively, a document's *source code* influences everything: the page layout, text size and color, image size and dimensions, any music that plays in the background, and all other facets of the appearance and performance of the Web page.

Creating a Web Page

As a Web page author, you create a page by typing text and inserting tags. You can type the tags manually or, if you use a Web page editing program, you can select the tags from a list or menu to have the program insert them. Tags identify the types of objects that make up a page, but they provide few details on how to display those items. For example, a tag may label a block of text as a paragraph with no specifications to set margins, indents, text size, or color. Another tag may insert an image without indicating where the image should appear or how text should wrap around it. A Web page that uses only these basic tags relies heavily on the Web browser to determine its appearance. In Chapter 3, you discover how to insert the tags required to create a Web page.

Formatting a Web Page

Although Web browsers are designed to interpret basic tags and determine how to properly display Web pages, leaving final decisions about formatting up to the Web browser often results in undesirable effects. As a Web page author, you can assign *properties* to the various objects that make up a Web page. These properties provide formatting instructions that specify how you want the Web browser to present the objects onscreen. For example, you can assign a property to a block of text that presents it as red, 12-point Arial text. You can also assign a property to an image that makes any neighboring text wrap around the right side of the image. Chapter 4 shows you how to enhance the appearance of your Web page with formatting.

Enhancing a Web Page with Multimedia

Paper publications limit themselves to two types of content: text and pictures. Except for some children's books, few printed publications can play background music or display video clips or animations. Web publications can include a wide variety of media, including audio and video clips, animations, games, and slide shows.

To enhance your Web page with various multimedia elements, you usually create the element in a special program and then insert a tag or script that pulls the multimedia content into your Web page. You can also embed scripts in your Web page that make various elements on the page more dynamic. The chapters in Part 5, along with other chapters in this book, show you various techniques for incorporating multimedia.

Making a Web Page Interactive

By its nature, the Web is an interactive publication that encourages visitors to take a self-directed tour of what it has to offer. However, you can make your Web site even more interactive by programming interactivity into your Web pages. One of the most basic ways to add interactivity is to use a form — as explained in Part 4 — that enables the user to provide you with feedback or to order products at your Web site. You can also use authoring programs, such as Flash and Shockwave, to create interactive presentations and games, which can attract more visitors to your site.

Testing Your Web Pages

A completed Web page typically contains a lot of text and source code. If you created the Web page in a text-based editor, as this book recommends, then you have a page filled with text and codes, or source code that gives you no indication as to how the Web page may look in a Web browser. Before publishing the page on the Web, you should test it to make sure that the Web page looks as you expect it to look.

Every Web browser interprets the source code differently, and not all Web browsers support the same source codes, so testing the page in several different Web browsers is prudent. Thorough testing ensures that a wide selection of Web browsers can open and display your page properly. Chapter 17 guides you through the process of performing the recommended tests.

Publishing Your Pages on the Web

After composing, formatting, and testing your Web pages thoroughly, you are ready to publish them on the Web. Publishing consists of copying, or *uploading*, the pages along with any related files, such as images and linked pages, to the Web server, where visitors can go to open and view the pages. You can find out how to upload pages in Chapter 18.

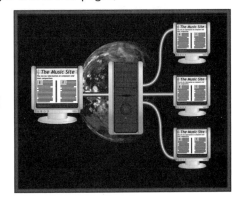

Understanding HTML Basics

When you surf the Web, you may notice a variety of Web pages containing plain text, images or illustrations, audio, video, and animation. Although content may differ, almost all Web pages have one thing in common: They use the same coding system or language to control appearance and functionality in a Web browser. This language is called *HyperText Markup Language*, or *HTML*.

By inserting HTML codes, or *tags*, into a plain text document, you can mark a block of text to appear as a plain paragraph, a heading, a list, or a table. You can specify where an image appears and the location and name of the image file that displays. You can designate which words or phrases appear boldface or italicized. You can also transform text and images into links that visitors can click to view other pages.

HTML Versions and Variations

W3C, the organization that maintains HTML specifications, has released several versions of the HTML specifications over the course of its development. Each version introduces new tags and *deprecates* — marks as archaic — tags that W3C no longer recommends. In addition, Web browser developers introduce their own *extensions* to HTML, enabling browsers to perform tasks that the HTML specification does not support. When writing HTML source code, addressing these differences in Web browsers and version numbers helps you create more universally accessible Web pages.

Text and Lists

The most basic content on a Web page is text. HTML offers several tags that work in tandem with Web browsers to control text appearance. Using these tags, you can mark six different heading levels, specify paragraph divisions, transform two or more paragraphs into a numbered or bulleted list, and display text as bold or italic.

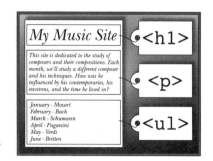

Although HTML tags control the layout and appearance of text, the Web browser does most of the formatting. HTML tags instruct the Web browser to display several blocks of text as a bulleted list, but provide little control over the bullet's appearance including size, shape, or color. For more detailed formatting, you can use Cascading Style Sheets (CSS), as shown in the section "Understanding CSS Formatting."

Hyperlinks

Hyperlinks tie different Web pages together. When you browse the Web, you can click a hyperlink, which typically appears as blue, underlined text and opens the page to which the hyperlink points. The hyperlink usually changes color to show that you have visited the page. Hyperlinks can point to different areas of the same page, different pages on the same Web site, or pages on Web sites anywhere in the world. Users can quickly skip from one page to another with a single mouse click.

HTML can convert standard text or images into hyperlinks, as well. You can even use HTML to create clickable image maps, linking different pages to specific areas, or *hot spots*, on the image. Chapter 3 introduces hyperlinks, and Chapter 6 shows you how to create your own image map.

Images

Most Web pages include graphic elements for visual appeal or to relate information that the author can more effectively show than tell. With HTML, you can use tags to have a Web browser pull digital images, called *inline images*, into the page. HTML refers to images as inline images because they generally appear in line with the text; if you insert an HTML image tag at the beginning of a paragraph, the image appears at that point, and the paragraph begins at the lower-right corner of the image. Chapter 5 shows the types of images you can display on Web pages and provides steps on how to insert and manipulate images on a Web page.

Tables

Tables provide structures that align data in rows and columns. HTML includes a variety of codes for controlling table structure and controlling the alignment of entries within the individual cells. You can also use style sheets to control the table's appearance and the alignment of text entries.

You can even use a table to structure an entire Web page by placing each image and each block of text in its own cell. Chapter 3 tells you how to create basic tables, and Chapter 4 includes instructions for formatting tables.

Frames

HTML frames divide a Web browser window into two or more panes, each of which can display a different Web page. Typically, a Web site displays a narrow pane on the left or near the top of the Web page viewing area that contains a table of contents of the Web site. When a visitor clicks a heading in the table of contents, the larger pane to the right of or below the table of contents displays the information for that heading. Chapter 7 shows you how to create and manipulate frames.

Continued

Understanding
HTML Basics *(Continued)*

U nlike traditional media such as television, film, and print, the Web is fundamentally interactive. The Web is a two-way communication system where the user's action dictates the response.

When you browse the Web, think about the ways in which a Web site responds to your actions, whether they are mouse clicks, keystrokes, or even voice commands. Interactivity can be something as simple

as clicking a link to load a new Web page, or having an image change in response to a mouse event. On some Web sites, interactive elements are highly complex, allowing visitors to decide exactly what content they want and how they want to format them. As you design and implement your Web site, you can take advantage of the medium's capabilities by incorporating interactive elements that allow visitors to take an active role in their online experience.

Using Links for Interaction

The ways in which you navigate the Web are interactive. For example, hypertext links, which form the backbone of the HTML language, allow you to jump to different pages or to specific locations on the current page with a mouse click. You can add an element of basic interactivity to your Web site by including links to both internal pages and external Web sites. You can use hypertext links as navigation aids to help users find what they are looking for, or embed links within Web page content as a way of presenting supplemental information. Some Web sites use embedded links to take visitors to unexpected destinations. You can learn how to add hypertext links to Web pages in Chapter 3, which shows you how to transform both text and images into live, clickable links. In Chapter 6 you learn how to transform different areas of a single image into clickable *hotspots*.

React to User Events

A simple yet effective way of responding to user events is to have an image or link change when the user moves the mouse over it. *Mouseover*, or *rollover*, events that swap one image for another are often used in Web site navigation components. You can add this interactive element to Web pages by using JavaScript. JavaScript is a simple programming language that you can embed within the HTML source code. You can use JavaScript functionality to validate forms and generate messages, or create interactive quizzes, polls, and games. You can explore these and other applications of JavaScript in Part 3. With a little more programming experience, you can create and embed your own Java applets, as well. Chapter 15 shows you how.

Respond to Input

Forms enable users to enter information such as their names, addresses, or comments. Form elements can include text fields, buttons, drop-down lists, and radio and check-box options that make the form appear very similar to a dialog box. Visitors to your Web site can type in the text boxes, click check boxes or radio buttons to select options, and click command buttons to submit the data that they typed or to cancel the form. You can use forms to collect data for many uses: to take a survey, to prompt users to log in, or to enable users to order products or services.

When a visitor clicks the button on your form to submit the data, you can include instructions on where you want to send the data. For example, you can have the data e-mailed to you, or you can have it sent to a database for processing, which is more common. Chapter 10 shows you how to create your own forms, complete with text boxes, check box and radio button options, clickable option lists, and command buttons. Chapter 11 shows you how to collect the data that a user submits. You can also add JavaScript functionality to validate form data before accepting it.

Interactivity and Multimedia

When implementing interactive elements on your Web site, remember that multimedia components such as audio, video, or Flash movies are not necessarily interactive. They are truly interactive only if they invite input and respond to user actions. Most multimedia that you encounter on the Web is passive; the user can sit back and enjoy the show without having to respond. However, online slide shows, Shockwave presentations, and other multimedia elements can include interactive features. Part 5 shows you how to enhance your Web pages with multimedia and how to add interactivity to some degree.

Human Interaction

When people discuss Web interactivity, the discussion usually centers on how users interact with the content of the Web site or with the interface. However, one of the most powerful aspects of interactivity on the Web is the ability to communicate with other visitors and with the Web site author. You can provide visitors with the means to communicate with each other by implementing a message board, discussion forum, or chat component. At the very least, you should always give visitors the ability to interact with you. Chapter 3 shows you how to add a link that visitors can click to contact you through e-mail.

Understanding XML and XHTML

HTML offers a relatively fast and easy way to publish Web pages. It labels objects on a page, such as titles, headings, paragraphs, and lists, but provides little or no formatting instructions. HTML also does not distinguish between different types of data; HTML treats all text entries in the same way, regardless of whether the text represents a name, address, or dollar amount. If you are using a Web page simply to display data, then HTML is fine, but if you need to do something with that data, such as automate its entry into a database, then HTML proves inadequate. For this and other reasons, serious Web page developers need a more robust language that overcomes the limitations of HTML.

Enter XML, which stands for *eXtensible Markup Language*. Web page authors can use XML to extend the functionality of HTML in order to meet specific needs. With XML you can extend HTML by creating `<fname>`, `<lname>`, `<street>`, `<city>`, `<state>`, and `<zipcode>` tags to identify each data entry, making the data easier to manage and parse to other applications.

Even if you prefer to create Web pages using straight HTML, you should be aware of the potential of XML. This brief overview, and the sections that follow, offer a basic introduction to XML.

XML Traits

XML is a very simple, and very strict, language that does little more than label data, so that Web authors can manage the data separately from their HTML documents. XML documents share the following traits:

- They define data in a precise, structured format that follows a simple, repeating pattern: `<tag>somedata</tag>`. Unlike HTML, which defines the tags that you insert in the document, XML requires you to create the tags.

- They can include arbitrary amounts of white space for readability, as long as the white space does not appear between tags. White space enables you to break up the coding so that you can follow it more easily.

- You save them as simple text files with the .xml extension.

- You can create them with a text editor or an XML-supporting editor.

- You transfer them from Web server to Web client through HyperText Transfer Protocol (HTTP), just like HTML files.

- They are an essential component of an XML-based application.

- They require a Document Type Definition (DTD) or XML schema to describe the data.

How XML Works

XML separates content and presentation by eliminating presentation-related tags from the document. Instead, tags in an XML document describe the actual data — what is commonly referred to as *metadata*, or "data about data."

Below is an example of XML code. Suppose you want to have a document that supplies weather information. An XML fragment within that document may look like this:

```
<weather>
      <city>Seattle</city>
      <state>Washington</state>
      <temp>65</temp>
      <wind>
            <speed>5</speed>
            <dir>SSW</dir>
      </wind>
      <sky>Partly Cloudy</sky>
</weather>
```

You can see that the tags are human-readable and define what the data is. You do not have to guess to understand what the particular elements are. In addition, no presentation or formatting information is included anywhere in the fragment.

XML as an Exchange Agent

XML can also help with information interchange. If you are building a commerce site that moves information between databases, then you have probably experienced problems with data being in different formats in the different databases. Using the weather example above, one database may have the location in two fields: one for city and one for state. Another database may have the location in a single field: city, state. With XSLT (eXtensible Stylesheet Language Transformation) you can write a simple routine to concatenate the two fields into one and place the single field into the second database. For more information about XSLT, see the section "Understanding XSLT."

XML, DTDs, and Schemas

With XML, you define the tags, attributes, and their meanings in a separate document called a Document Type Definition, or DTD. By default, current Web browsers compare HTML documents against the HTML 4.01 or XHTML 1.0 DTD. Using the <!doctype> tag, you can specify that the Web browser use a different DTD, an XML DTD that you create. The Web browser can then use the additional tags and attributes that are defined in that DTD to display the page.

HTML, XML, and XHTML

HTML is an element-driven language that focuses on enabling a Web browser to display data. XML is a stricter coding system that focuses on data management. XHTML is the bridge between the two languages, enabling you to mix HTML and XML content in such a way that Web browsers can display *and* manage the data more efficiently and precisely. XHTML places restrictions on HTML syntax; with XHTML, for example, all tag sets require a closing tag.

Explore Differences between HTML and XHTML

In the Web's early days, HTML provided very basic codes to identify page elements, so that the Web browser could display the page properly. Because HTML tags were so basic, the rules for composing HTML source code were relatively lax, and they remain so today. HTML, for example, makes no distinction between the paragraph tags <p> and <P>. In HTML, you can type a closing </p> tag at the end of a paragraph or omit it — it really does not matter. In fact, you can compose fairly sloppy code, and most Web browsers still display your page as you intend it to appear.

Today, the Web is much more sophisticated. You can still find plenty of Web pages that follow the older HTML guidelines, but the more attractive pages require precise positioning and formatting of the objects that comprise the page. This sophistication requires cleaner source code that follows stricter guidelines. XHTML provides these stricter guidelines and is intended to replace HTML as the Web evolves. In the following text you can learn what separates HTML from XHTML, and become more aware of the XHTML rules for composing Web pages.

Lowercase Tags

HTML is not case sensitive. That is, you can type HTML tags in all uppercase, all lowercase, or a mix of upper- and lowercase. Web authors who follow the older standards often choose to type their tags in all uppercase to help them distinguish tags from the rest of the text on the page. To compose a page that conforms to the strict XHTML guidelines, you must lowercase all tag names.

Close All HTML Elements

HTML contains two types of tags: paired and unpaired. A paired tag set includes an opening and closing tag. For example, the tag set for boldface type consists of <b> and </b>: <b> turns boldface on and </b> turns it off. An unpaired tag, such as the <img>

tag that inserts an image on a page, has no closing tag. In HTML, this is perfectly acceptable. Moreover, HTML allows you to omit some closing tags when entering paired tag sets. For example, the tag set for marking paragraphs includes the <p> tag at the beginning of the paragraph and the </p> tag at the end, but HTML allows you to omit the closing </p> tag.

XHTML requires you to close *all* tags, including unpaired tags. In other words, for all paired tags, you must enter an opening and a closing tag. In addition, you must close all unpaired tags by typing a forward slash before the ending angle bracket. The tag for inserting an image therefore appears as <img />. This book recommends inserting a space between the tag name and the forward slash to retain compatibility with older Web browsers.

Nest Elements Properly

Web browsers are very forgiving when you choose to embed one tag set within another. You can insert the opening tag of one set followed by the opening tag of another set, close the first tag set, and then close the second tag set, and most browsers would have no difficulty displaying your Web page. However, this technique, often referred to as *overlapping tags,* is definitely unacceptable in XHTML. Below is an example of overlapping tags:

```
<b>This is boldface and <i>this is
boldface italic.</b></i>
```

Notice that the <b> tag opens before the <i> tag and closes before the </i> tag, as well. You must completely embed or *nest* one tag set within the other tag set. Below is an example of the same line that shows proper nesting:

```
<b>This is boldface and <i>this is
boldface italic.</i></b>
```

Notice that the opening and closing <i> tags are inside the opening and closing <b> tags.

If you wonder about the logic behind this rule, just think of how confusing it is when humans do not follow a similar rule in written communication. Imagine reading the sentence: Mary said, "I am now going to read the poem 'The Road Not Taken," by Robert Frost.' This sentence may leave you a little confused. Proper nesting ensures that the tags adhere to a predictable pattern that any Web browser can interpret correctly.

Form Documents Properly

The nesting rule also applies to the overall structure of your Web page. All pages must have an opening and closing <html> tag, which forms the root element of the page. Sub-elements, including the <head> and <body> tags, must nest properly

within the root element to provide an overall page structure that looks like this:

```
<html>
     <head>
     <title></title>
     </head>
     <body>
     </body>
</html>
```

Include Values in Quotes for All Attributes

HTML tags often include attributes that provide additional information concerning a particular element. The <img /> tag, for example, includes the src attribute, which is set to equal the location and filename of the image. In HTML, some attributes can function perfectly well without a value because they have only one value. One such attribute is nowrap, which instructs a Web browser not to wrap a line of text that is wider than the Web browser window.

In XHTML documents, all attributes must be set equal to a value. For example, the XHTML entry for disabling word wrap is nowrap="nowrap". This brings up another difference between HTML and XHTML. In HTML, you must enclose attribute values in quotes only if the value has more than one word. In XHTML, you must enclose all attribute values in quotes.

Comment Out All Sections to Ignore

You can mark sections of an XHTML document that you want the Web browser to ignore when displaying the page. These sections contain the CDATA keyword. This keyword needs to include comments and brackets on either end, beginning with <![CDATA[and ending with]]>. These markings should surround all <script> and <style> tags included in the document.

Understanding CSS Formatting

HTML tags mark text to indicate how pages elements should appear and the Web browser interprets the tags to layout the page. This system limits a Web author's options. Displaying a heading in a specific color, for example, is impossible with HTML. Specifying the way that text wraps around an image, though not impossible, can lead to undesirable results. To overcome such limitations, Web browser developers created their own tags and attributes, such as `<font color=>`, but this introduced compatibility issues.

To address these issues and to keep HTML documents as uncluttered as possible, W3C developed *Cascading*

Style Sheets (CSS). Cascading style sheets separate content from appearance, and give Web authors more control over layout and page format. The HTML page contains the content, and CSS codes instruct the Web browser how to format each content item. For example, the CSS code `h1 {color: blue}` makes all h1 headings blue.

An added bonus of CSS is that a single style sheet can control the formatting for multiple Web pages. You change the formatting on all your pages by making a single change in your style sheet. CSS allows you to apply fonts, margins, borders, and other formatting to every element on a Web page.

Understanding How Stylesheets Cascade

You can implement styles at three levels: through external style sheets, internal style sheets, or inline styles by using the HTML `style` attribute. You can use all three methods to apply styles to the elements in a single document. Using an external style sheet, you can enter the most common formatting settings for all of the Web pages that you create. The style definitions in the external style sheet control the appearance of your Web pages unless you override those styles in an internal style sheet or by using the HTML `style` attribute.

You can define styles within the head of a Web page document to apply styles to elements within the document, such as all paragraphs or to only those paragraphs that you tag as being in a specific class. Any styles that you define at the document level override style definitions in external style sheets.

To apply a style to a specific element on a Web page, such as a heading or a paragraph, you can use the HTML `style` attribute. For example, you can color the text in a paragraph by setting the `style` attribute in the opening `<p>` code to color the text red: `<p style="color:red">`. When you apply a style to a specific element, the style overrides any definitions set in the external or internal style sheets.

Create Selector Rules

To apply a style to an element, you create a selector rule and include appropriate style properties and values. These rules take the form of `selector {property: value}`. The selector, or *tag selector*, specifies the HTML element to which you want to apply the format; for example, `p` for paragraphs or `h1` for level-1 headings. The *property* specifies the aspect of the element that you want to format, such as its text alignment or color. The *value* defines the specific format that you want to apply. For example, `p {text-align: center}` sets paragraph text alignment to center.

Within the curly braces of a style rule, you can add multiple properties as long as you separate them with semicolons. For example, you can center paragraphs and make their text red by creating the following rule: `p {color: red; text-align: center}`. If a particular value consists of more than one word, you must enclose the value in quotes or connect the words with hyphens, for example, `p {font-family: sans-serif}`.

Create Classes

Instead of creating a style rule that applies the same format to every occurrence of a given element, you can create several classes for an element and apply a different set of formatting properties to each class. For example, you can create two classes for the `<img />` element, one called `img.left` and the other called `img.right`. You can then define a different style rule for each class. The `img.left` class positions the image on the left side of the page and wraps text around its right side. The `img.right` class positions the image on the right side of the page and wraps text around its left side. You can then apply a style definition to an individual element by adding the HTML `class` attribute and setting it equal to the desired class, such as `<img class="left">`.

The CSS Box Model

Cascading style sheets use a simple box model to format elements on a Web page. When you apply style sheets to HTML pages, think of every piece of content, from a paragraph of text to a list, as a box with padding, borders, margins, and dimensions that you can control through style rules. The box model enables you to paste various objects on a page, as you would do in a desktop-publishing program. Chapter 4 shows you how to do this.

Understanding XSLT

Extensible Stylesheet Language Transformations, or XSLT, is a part of XSL that converts XML documents into different types of XML documents, into HTML documents, into database documents, or into other many other types of documents. For example, you may use an XML document as a database to store information about various products, including an ID number, product name, product description, price, and quantity in stock. You can use XSLT to convert the database into an HTML catalogue that customers can use to shop online. You can also use XSLT to extract information from the database to create an inventory report. In short, XSLT enables you to use and present data stored in an XML document in numerous ways.

For those who are unfamiliar with XML and XSL, the role that XSLT plays may seem insignificant. To gain a better understanding of XSLT, you can explore its background and history.

XML's Shortcomings

As explained in the section, "Understanding XML and XHTML," the role of XML is to identify data types to facilitate data processing. With XML, developers can create tags to serve their unique needs. For example, a developer may create the `<name>` tag to identify specific data entries as names.

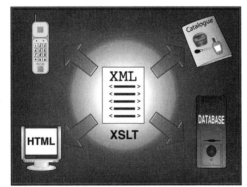

The ability to create tags makes XML very flexible, but it makes the source code much less uniform and predictable than XHTML. It enables the same tag to have a different meaning, depending on how a developer decides to use it. One company may use the `<name>` tag to identify people, whereas another may use it to identify parts. Neither use is right or wrong, but the difference in usage makes it difficult to develop any uniform system for handling data marked with XML tags.

This also complicates any attempts to format XML pages. With HTML, you can use the `<h1>` tag to mark a level-1 heading and be sure that the Web browser knows how to display it. You can apply additional formatting to HTML elements by using CSS styles to specify formatting for elements identified by their HTML tags. Because XML has no fixed tags, Web browsers have no set way to identify distinct elements. In addition, you cannot add any consistent formatting with a system like CSS, because you cannot target specific tags.

XSL

To overcome the limitations of XML, developers invented XSL — style sheets for XML documents. XSL actually consists of a collection of languages: XPath, XSLT, and XSL-FO (XSL-Formatting Objects). XPath defines the parts of an XML document, XSLT converts documents into XML and XHTML, and XSL-FO formats XML documents. Collectively, XSL can filter and sort data, parse it to different locations and applications, output the data to various media, and transform XML documents into different types of XML documents or into HTML or XHTML documents.

From Source Tree to Result Tree

XSLT transforms a *source tree* into a *result tree*. The source tree is the original XML document. The result tree is the document created by the transformation.

XSLT accomplishes the transformation by retagging the data in the original document. For example, if a document contains product names coded with opening and closing `<name>` tags and you want the product names to appear as level-3 headings in a new HTML document, you can use XSLT to convert the opening and closing `<name>` tags into opening and closing `<h3>` tags.

For XSLT, each tag and attribute in an XML document is an identifiable *node*. You use the `match` command in an XSLT style sheet to have the style sheet identify a node, and then you add tags that specify the transformations to apply to that particular node. For example, to convert <name> tags into <h3> tags, you can use the following code:

```
<xsl:template match="name">
        <h3>
        <xsl:value-of/>
        </h3>
</xsl:template>
```

In this simple example, the style sheet searches for occurrences of the <name> tag, replaces them with <h3> tags, and uses <xsl:value-of/> to fetch the text that appears between the <name> tags.

To execute a transformation, you can start with an XML document, create an XSLT style sheet to perform the transformations, and then link the original XML document to the style sheet, as explained in the following sections. A server equipped with an XSLT processor can then perform the transformations automatically. Office XP uses XML and XSLT to perform many of its import and export operations.

Start with an XML Document

Before you can transform a document, you need a document to transform — an XML document, with a filename with the .xml extension, which contains the XML tags that you want to convert, and data that you want to process. The following is a very basic XML document that functions as a video database:

```
<?xml version="1.0"?>
<videolist>
        <title>Goodfellas</title>
        <director>Martin Scorsese</director>
        <lead>Robert De Niro</lead>
        <year>1990</year>
        <price>24.99</price>
        <title>Mystic River</title>
        <director>Clint Eastwood</director>
        <lead>Sean Penn</lead>
        <year>2003</year>
        <price>21.99</price>
</videolist>
```

Create an XSLT Style Sheet

You can now create an XSLT style sheet and name the file using the .xsl filename extension. This style sheet functions as a template to instruct the XSL processor on how to perform the transformations. Below is a sample XSLT style that transforms the XML example in the previous section into an HTML document, and extracts the movie title and price to create a price list:

```
<?xml version="1.0"?>
<xsl:stylesheet
xmlns:xsl="http://www.w3.org/TR/WD-xsl">

<xsl:template match="/">
<xsl:apply-templates />
</xsl:template>

<xsl:template match="videolist">
        <html>
        <head>
        <title>Video Library</title>
        </head>
        <body>
        <h1>Video Library</h1>
        </body>
        </html>
<xsl:apply-templates />

</xsl:template>

<xsl:template match="title">
<h2>Movie Title: <xsl:value-of /></h2>
</xsl:template>

<xsl:template match="price">
<p><i>Price: <xsl:value-of/></i></p>
</xsl:template>

</xsl:stylesheet>
```

Link the XML Document to the Style Sheet

When you have a style sheet in place, you can add a style-sheet reference to the top of the XML document to reference the style sheet. If you name your style sheet pricelist.xsl, the reference looks something like this:

```
<?xml-stylesheet type="text/xsl"
href="pricelist.xsl"?>
```

When you open the XML file in your Web browser, the XSLT processor automatically performs the transformation and displays the resulting page.

Using HTML Tag Sets

You can mark headings and paragraphs, insert images, and transform text and images into links using HTML *tags*. These tags are text-based codes surrounded by angle brackets, such as <b> for turning on boldface, and </b> for turning it off. Tags typically do not include space between the angle brackets and the text they enclose. A forward slash (/) always marks the closing tag.

HTML tags can be *paired* or *unpaired*. Paired tags, such as <b> and </b>, turn an option on and off. Any text between the two codes appears in the specified format when a Web browser displays the page. For example, if you type <b>Attention!</b> in an HTML Web page, it

appears as **Attention!** when a browser opens and displays the page.

Unpaired tags, discussed in the next section "Using Unpaired HTML Tags," typically insert an object, such as an image or a hyperlink, on a page. Although they require no closing tag in HTML, XHTML requires some indication of closure. To conform to XHTML guidelines, you must type a forward slash at the end of the tag, just before the closing angle bracket.

Using HTML Tag Sets

① Create a new file in your HTML editor.

② Type a line of text.

③ Save the document as a text-only file with the .htm or .html extension.

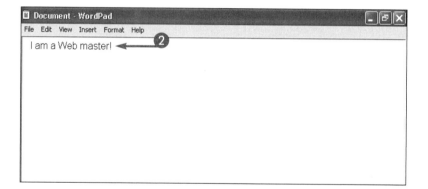

④ Open the document that you just created in a Web browser.

● The browser displays the line of text.

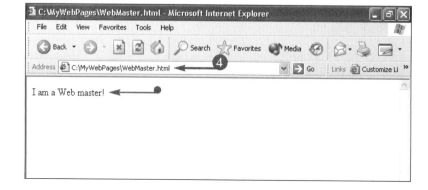

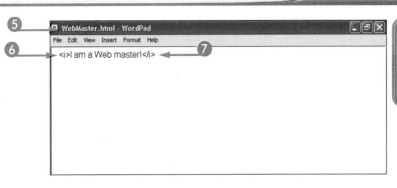

⑤ Open the document in your HTML editor.

⑥ Add an opening formatting tag to the front of the line of text.

⑦ Add a closing formatting tag to the end of the line of text.

⑧ Save the document.

⑨ Open the document that you just edited in a Web browser.

● The line of text appears as formatted.

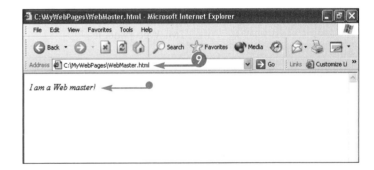

What if I forget to type a closing tag?

▼ An opening tag turns on formatting from the point of the tag up to its paired closing tag or to the end of the document, whichever comes first. If you insert an opening tag at the beginning of a page and forget to type a closing tag, the entire page appears in the format specified by the opening tag. Fortunately, this error is easy to fix. Simply open the document in your HTML editor and type the closing tag. You can avoid making this common error by using a dedicated HTML editor, such as Netscape Composer or HandyHTML Studio, as shown in Chapter 2.

Can you apply several sets of tags to the same line of text?

▼ Bracketing a line of text with both <b> and <i> tags makes the text appear bold and italic. When applying two or more sets of tags, nest the tags properly to avoid *overlapping*; the first tag set should bracket the entire line, including the second tag set. For example, type **<b><i>Bold Italics</i></b>** rather than **<b><i>Bold Italics</b></i>**. Some Web browsers correctly display text that is formatted with overlapping codes, but others may recognize only the first tag set. If you check your source code with a validator, as shown in Chapter 17, and it contains overlapping codes, the validator highlights the errors, so you can correct them.

Using Unpaired HTML Tags

You can use unpaired tags to insert line breaks and horizontal rules, place images inside a document, and create frames. You can use the unpaired `<meta />` tag to insert text that does not appear in the Web browser but that search engines can use to index your site. Unpaired HTML tags work alone, acting as both an opening and closing tag. Instead of turning an option on and then off, they perform a single act, such as inserting a hyperlink on a page. To conform to XHTML standards, unpaired tags include the forward slash symbol (/) after the tag name and before the closing bracket (>).

An example of an unpaired tag is the image tag, which is represented as `<img />`. The image tag specifies the location and name of the image file and requires no additional text, and so a closing tag is unnecessary.

Other single-tag elements include the line break tag (`<br />`), the horizontal rule tag (`<hr />`), the frame tag (`<frame />`), the metadata tag (`<meta />`), and the form element tag (`<input />`).

Note the space between the tag name and the forward slash. Without this space, some Web browsers may have trouble identifying the tag.

Using Unpaired HTML Tags

① Open a file in your HTML editor.

② Add an unpaired tag below a line of text.

● This example uses the `<hr />` tag for inserting a horizontal rule.

③ Save the document as a text-only file with the .htm or .html extension.

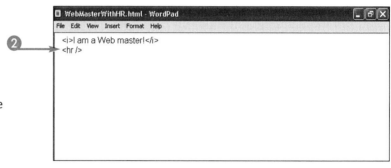

④ Open the document in a Web browser.

● The Web browser displays the Web page. In this example, a horizontal rule appears.

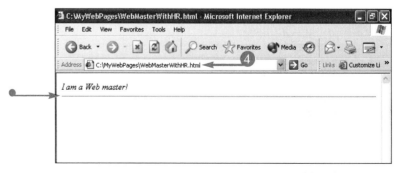

PART I

5 Open the document in your HTML editor.

6 Move the unpaired tag inside the line of text.

7 Save the document, giving it a different name.

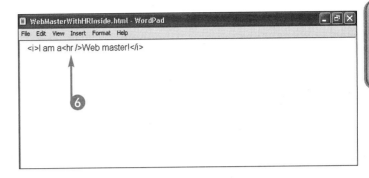

8 Open the document in a Web browser.

- The Web browser displays the document.

- In this example, the horizontal rule divides the line of text.

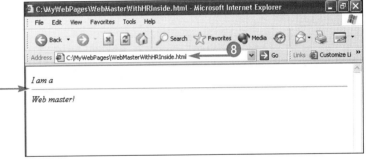

Do some tags have optional closing tags?

▼ Yes. These include tags for defining table rows and cells, `<tr>` and `<td>`, and for ending a paragraph `</p>`. For these tags, the Web browser knows that one line ends where the next line begins. However, to conform to the newer XHTML standard, you should always include a closing tag. Most dedicated HTML editors, including those mentioned in Chapter 2, can insert both tags of a paired tag set for you when you enter a single command.

Do I need to use paired or unpaired tags to insert a link?

▼ Although you would expect an unpaired tag to insert a link, a paired tag set is required: `<a>` and `</a>`. The opening and closing tags bracket the text or image that acts as a link on the page. The opening `<a>` tag contains most of the pertinent information that provides the link's functionality, including the location and name of the linked file. For instructions on how to create links, see Chapter 3.

Besides table rows and cells, what other tags have an optional closing tag?

▼ In HTML, several closing tags are optional, including the closing tags for individual list elements — `</dt>`, `</dd>`, and `</li>` — and the closing tags for tables (`</th>`), (`</thead>`, `</tbody>`, and `</tfoot>`). However, including a closing tag is good form and helps you to become accustomed to coding in a stricter language, such as XHTML.

Using HTML Attributes

Y ou can specify additional preferences for a tag by including attributes and setting them to specific values. The general structure of an opening tag that contains attributes is:

`<tagname attribute="value">`.

For example, you can add the `href` attribute to a hyperlink tag to specify the address of the Web page to open:

`<a href="http://www.wiley.com/index.html">`.

For single HTML tags, the attributes appear between the end of the tag name and the slash symbol:

`<img src="image.gif" />`.

Some tags have multiple attributes. You can include multiple attributes within a tag by separating them with a

single space:

`<img src="image.gif" alt="smiley face image" />`. Other tags have no attributes. Some attributes, such as `nowrap`, have no optional values, in which case you can set the attribute to equal itself: `nowrap="nowrap"`. Each tag has a default attribute value that the Web browser uses if the tag specifies no attribute value. For example, paragraphs default to left alignment unless you use a CSS style to align the paragraph differently.

HTML includes dozens of attributes, some of which apply to multiple elements, and some of which are unique to specific tags. Chapter 3 shows you how to use the most common HTML attributes.

Using HTML Attributes

① Open or create a new HTML document in your HTML editor.

② Type a tag for which you can specify an attribute.

- This example uses the `<img />` tag. To follow the example, you do not need an image.

Note: *If inserting a paired tag set, type the closing tag for the set and any additional text that is required.*

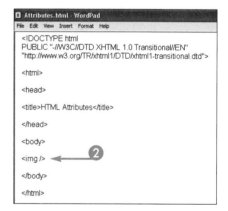

③ Type an attribute for the tag setting the attribute equal to a valid value.

Note: *Enclose the value in quotation marks.*

- This example uses two attributes: `src` specifies the location and name of the image to load, and `alt` attribute specifies text to display when a browser cannot load the image.

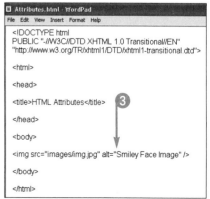

④ Save the document as a text-only file with the .htm or .html extension.

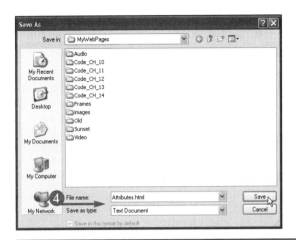

⑤ Open the document in a Web browser.

● The Web browser displays the document, including any visible effects created by the attribute you added.

Can I set attribute values to anything, or are there specific values that they accept?

▼ You can set some attributes to only predefined values. For example, you can set the align attribute only to left, right, center, or justify. Other attributes, such as width, can accept any numerical value that represents the number of pixels that you want to use for the width of the element. In addition, many tags require specific attributes; for example, the opening <a> tag requires the href attribute set equal to the location and name of the linked file. For a more comprehensive list of HTML 4.01 tags and attributes, go to www.w3schools.com/html/html_reference.asp.

I saw a tag marked as "deprecated." What does that mean?

▼ As the HTML language evolves, newer standards supplant some of the older, obsolete standards, making some tags and attributes no longer useful. W3C designates these tags and attributes as *deprecated* to indicate that they are being phased out. Most presentation attributes, which control the appearance of elements on a page, have been deprecated. However, Cascading Style Sheets, or CSS, give you much more control over formatting. For more on how to apply CSS formatting, see Chapter 4. The Library of Congress Web site has a list of codes being deprecated in HTML 4.01: www.loc.gov/iug/html40/40tags.html.

View HTML Source Code

You can understand a great deal about HTML tags, XHTML, and other Web page languages and scripts by viewing the source code of Web pages. As you browse the Web, your Web browser automatically interprets the HTML tags included in Web page files, and displays the pages, complete with formatting, graphics, and other enhancements. HTML tags do not appear in the Web browser window, but they affect the appearance of other objects on the page. However, your Web browser does include a feature that enables you to look at the HTML source code.

Most Web browsers, including Internet Explorer and Netscape Navigator, include a View menu with several options for configuring the Web browser window and controlling the overall appearance of Web pages. The View menu also contains the command for viewing the source document.

When you notice interesting Web page formatting or features, you can study the source code to discover how the author created the Web page. You may even copy and modify the code for your own use, assuming the original author gives you permission.

View HTML Source Code

View Source Code with Internet Explorer

① Open a Web page in Microsoft Internet Explorer.

② Click View.

③ Click Source.

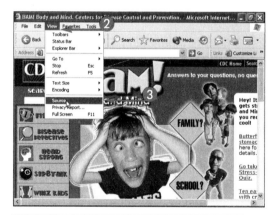

● Internet Explorer launches the text editor that Windows associates with HTML files and displays the source code.

Note: Internet Explorer typically runs Notepad, as in this example, or FrontPage, if it is installed.

View Source Code with Netscape Navigator

① Open a Web page in Netscape Navigator.

② Click View.

③ Click Page Source.

● A new window appears, displaying the HTML source code.

Note: Netscape Navigator uses an internal text viewer to display the source code.

Why does the source code sometimes look like it is writing over itself?

▼ Depending on the operating system that you use to generate the HTML code, the line returns can cause the two lines of code to appear on top of each other in Notepad. To fix this problem, click Format, and then Word Wrap. More commonly, a line runs past the right edge of the window, so you need to use the scroll bar to bring it into view. This can be annoying when you are trying to edit your source code. By turning on Word Wrap, you ensure that all text appears within the left and right edges of the window.

Can I copy source code into my Web pages?

▼ When you view the source code of a Web page, you can press Ctrl+A to select all of it, press Ctrl+C to copy it and then press Ctrl+V to paste it into your own document. Many Web authors learn various techniques from studying and using existing source code. By copying and pasting the source code and then modifying it, you can discover how source code functions and how to tweak it to produce the desired effects. Remember, however, that pages on the Web are copyrighted and that you must ask the Webmaster for permission.

Edit Web Pages from Internet Explorer

U sing Microsoft Internet Explorer, you can edit the cached version of a Web page. This provides a great opportunity to experiment with pages you download from the Web.

When you open a Web page, your Web browser downloads a copy of the page to your computer and stores it in a *disk cache.* This copy is saved to your hard drive, so that if you visit the page again, your Web browser can quickly load the page from your hard drive and then update anything on it that has changed.

You can open this cached copy to view or edit its source code. You can then save the edited Web page to your hard drive and open it in your Web browser to view the effects of your changes. However, you cannot save the edited page back to the Web server, because this would enable anyone to modify other Web sites.

Using the File menu in Internet Explorer, you can edit cached Web pages with Notepad, Microsoft Word, or FrontPage, depending on the software that is installed on your computer. You can specify the HTML editor that Internet Explorer uses in the Internet Options dialog box.

Edit Web Pages from Internet Explorer

① Open a Web page in Internet Explorer.

② Click Tools.

③ Click Internet Options.

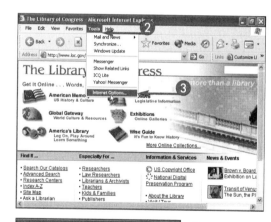

● The Internet Options dialog box appears.

④ Click the Programs tab.

⑤ Click here and click the HTML editor you want.

⑥ Click OK.

● Internet Explorer saves your selection, and the dialog box closes.

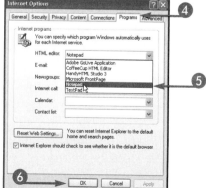

⑦ Click File.

⑧ Click Edit with *?*, where *?* is the name of the editor you selected in step 5.

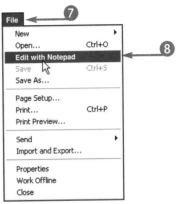

● The HTML editor opens and displays the HTML source code for this page.

● You can now edit the content and tags.

● You can save the file to your hard drive.

Can I instruct Internet Explorer to run a different HTML editor?

▼ Yes. You can instruct Internet Explorer to run any HTML editor that is currently installed on your computer. When you install an HTML editor, Internet Explorer adds it to the list of available editors. In some cases, the editor's installation routine automatically makes it the default editor in Internet Explorer.

Why does the HTML source code for some very basic Web pages seem so complex?

▼ Typing HTML tags in Notepad or another text editor typically results in the most efficient code. Some Web-page editing programs, including Microsoft Word, insert additional codes that complicate the source code and challenge even an experienced Web developer's ability to determine the purpose of specific codes.

Are Web pages copyrighted?

▼ Yes. Web pages are automatically copyrighted. You can include a copyright statement in the head of your Web pages using a `<meta />` tag. If a Web page does not include a copyright statement, you still cannot freely copy and use the code. Send an e-mail message to the Web author or Webmaster first, asking permission to use the code. Many Web authors are more than willing to give permission.

Edit Web Pages with Netscape Composer

When you install Netscape Navigator, you install a suite of Internet programs, including the Netscape Navigator browser as well as Netscape Composer. Netscape Composer is an *HTML authoring program* that is commonly called a WYSIWYG (pronounced "wizzy-wig"), or *What You See Is What You Get* editor. Netscape Composer acts like a word-processing or desktop publishing program for the Web, displaying a Web page as it will appear in a Web browser and hiding the HTML code that modifies the appearance of the Web page.

Because Netscape Composer is a WYSIWYG visual editor, it makes the process of creating a Web page much more intuitive. You can insert and format text as you do in a word-processing or desktop publishing program by dragging and dropping it on a Web page or selecting menu commands.

Netscape Composer also provides several tabs that you can click to view and edit the source code directly, preview a Web page as it will appear in a Web browser, and display the tags graphically to see your code. And, best of all, you can run Netscape Composer directly from Netscape Navigator.

Edit Web Pages with Netscape Composer

① Open a Web page in Netscape Navigator.

② Click File.

③ Click Edit Page.

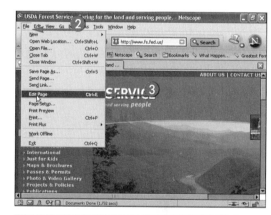

● The Web page appears in the Netscape Composer window.

④ Click the <HTML> Source tab.

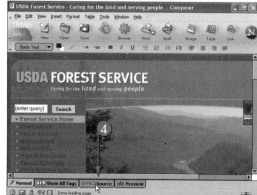

- The HTML source code appears for the Web page.

⑤ Click the Preview tab.

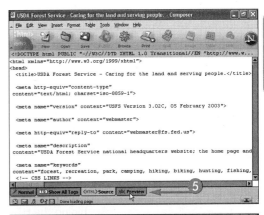

- Composer displays the page as it appears in a Web browser.

- The Show All Tags tab displays the tags graphically, like screen tips.

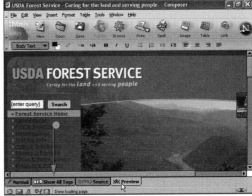

What are the advantages and disadvantages of using a visual editing tool like Netscape Composer?

▼ Visual editors are more like desktop publishing packages, which makes them easier to use when laying out an HTML page. For example, visual editors make it very easy to create tables. However, visual editors determine which codes to use for formatting and laying out the text, which may not be the most efficient or easily identifiable codes to use. Also, when you select text and increase its size, the editor may insert a `<font>` tag or change the heading level. If you need to edit the source code later, you may have trouble identifying the purpose of each tag.

Can I create a completely new Web page in Netscape Composer?

▼ Yes. To create a new Web page, click File, New, and then Composer Page. A blank page appears, with the HTML tags that define the overall structure of your Web page. You can then begin to enter and format text.

How can I publish my finished Web page to the Web?

▼ Once you save a local copy of the Web page, you can publish it to the Web by following any of the procedures in Chapter 18. Publishing typically requires that you *upload* your Web page and any files it uses, such as graphics and other related Web pages, to a publically accessible Web server. Uploading consists of copying the files from your computer to the Web server. The process varies depending on how the Web server is configured.

Write and Save HTML with WordPad

An HTML document consists of plain text. As a result, you do not need a special authoring or page-layout application to create and format your Web pages. If you know how to compose source code, you can create an HTML document using a basic text editor such as Windows WordPad.

You can create HTML source code by typing your text and HTML tags into the text editor and then saving the document as a text-only file. A text-only file does not contain the word-processing or desktop publishing codes

that determine the formatting of a page. These codes can interfere with the appearance of the page. When naming an HTML document file, you should always add the .htm or .html filename extension. If you use a different filename extension, a Web browser may not be able to open the file.

After you enter the HTML source code into a text editor and save it as a text-only file, you can open the file in a Web browser to view the results. See Chapter 3 for more information about creating source code.

Write and Save HTML with WordPad

① Click Start.

② Click All Programs.

③ Click Accessories.

④ Click WordPad.

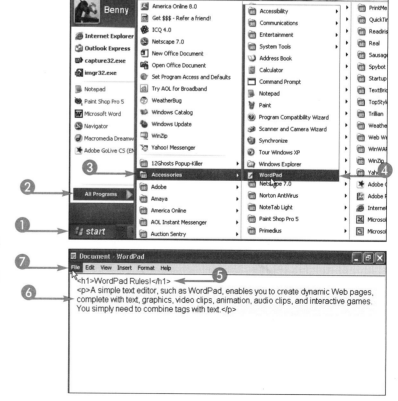

- The WordPad window appears with a blank document.

⑤ Type **<h1>**, followed by a heading name, and then type **</h1>**.

⑥ Type **<p>**, followed by a paragraph of text and then type **</p>**.

⑦ Click File.

⑧ Click Save.

● The Save As dialog box appears.

⑨ Navigate to the folder in which you want to store the file.

⑩ Type a filename for the document, followed by the .htm or .html extension.

⑪ Click the Save as type area and click Text Document.

⑫ Click Save.

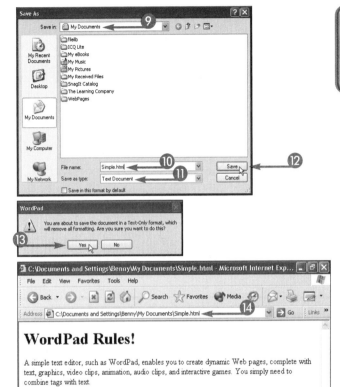

⑬ When the confirmation dialog box appears, click Yes.

● WordPad saves the HTML document.

⑭ Launch your Web browser, and type the location and name of the file in the address bar.

⑮ Press Enter.

● Your Web browser displays the Web page.

WordPad Rules!

A simple text editor, such as WordPad, enables you to create dynamic Web pages, complete with text, graphics, video clips, animation, audio clips, and interactive games. You simply need to combine tags with text.

Can I format my text in WordPad?

▼ WordPad features a Format menu that includes options for changing fonts, selecting a bullet style, formatting paragraphs, and adjusting tab settings. You can use these options to format an HTML document in WordPad, but when you save the document as a text-only file, WordPad strips out all of the formatting. If you close the file and reopen it, any formatting changes you made are lost. In addition, none of the formats you apply appear when you open the HTML document in a Web browser. To format the document for a Web browser, use HTML tags and attributes and CSS styles, as explained in Chapters 3 and 4.

How do I type an address in my Web browser to a Web page on my computer?

▼ If you know the complete path and filename, type it in the Address box as follows: **c:\directory\subdirectory\filename.html**. If you do not know the location and filename, click File, click Open, click the Browse button, and navigate to the file.

Does a Web page need any other files for you to view it in a Web browser?

▼ If the Web page references external files, such as images, place those files on the Web server. When you have only a few related files, consider placing all of the files in the same directory, so you can refer to the files by name without specifying a location.

Introducing HTML Text Editors

Manually typing and editing HTML tags can become tedious. To simplify the process, you can compose your Web pages in an HTML text editor. An HTML text editor enables you to enter tags by selecting them from menus, toolbars, or palettes rather than by typing them. The editor enters both opening and closing tags in a tag set for you, so you can avoid the common mistake of forgetting to enter a closing tag.

Most experienced Web page authors recommend that beginning programmers type the tags to better understand how the language works. This may seem complicated and time consuming at first, but it helps you when you need to adjust the page layout or text formatting or to troubleshoot problems. Manual input of HTML code trains you to identify common errors. Source code that you enter manually is also usually less cluttered than the source code that many visual editors generate. This clean code also results in Web pages that are compatible with a wider range of Web browsers. For information on visual editors, see the next section, "Introducing HTML Visual Editors."

A variety of commercial and shareware HTML text editors are available. The more popular text editors are described below.

Macromedia HomeSite

Macromedia HomeSite is a full-featured HTML text editor with support for HTML, XHTML, and CSS. It provides an integrated CSS editor, which enables you to use the same program to create a basic HTML page and then format it. HomeSite also includes tools to help you manage your entire Web site, including a tag inspector, productivity wizards, a find-and-replace feature, and FTP file uploading which enabled you to publish your pages to the Web after you create them.

HomeSite requires Windows 98 SE, Windows 2000, Windows XP, or Windows Server 2003. You can find more information and download a trial version of this program at www.macromedia.com/software/homesite/. Macromedia also features an excellent collection of additional tools that allow you to add

CoffeeCup HTML Editor

CoffeeCup HTML Editor is probably the most popular HTML text editor. Like Macromedia HomeSite, CoffeeCup allows you to select HTML tags from menus rather than having to type them, and it inserts the opening and closing tags of a tag set for you. In addition, CoffeeCup HTML Editor includes 125 JavaScripts, 25,000 graphics, 175 animated GIFs, table and frame designers, and an integrated spell checker. Also, with a single mouse click, you can change to preview mode and see how your page will appear in a Web browser. You can find more information and download a trial version of this powerful HTML text editor at www.coffeecup.com/html-editor/.

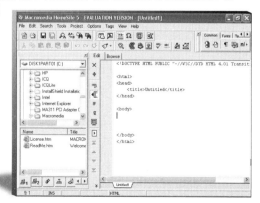

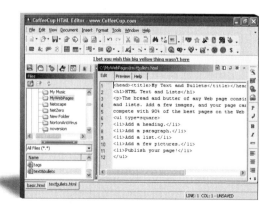

Hot Dog Professional

Hot Dog Professional by Sausage Software is another popular HTML editor. This program automates the tasks of inserting and editing source code, includes a built-in Web page preview feature that allows you to quickly see the results of your edits, and provides additional powerful tools, including a GIF image animation wizard and a Flash wizard for inserting dynamic Flash presentations.

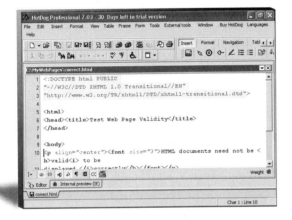

Sausage Software also offers HTML editors for novice authors, including HotDog PageWiz, which allows you to select from ten Web page templates and HotDog Junior for children six years old and up. You can find more information about Hot Dog Professional, PageWiz, and other Internet programs at www.sausage.com.

HandyHTML Studio

HandyHTML Studio is a powerful HTML text editor with an interface that includes several convenient toolbars. These toolbars can simplify greatly the process of creating tables and forms, formatting text, previewing the document you are currently editing, and uploading pages when they are complete. Best of all, as you become more experienced with HTML, you can hide the toolbars to provide yourself with the maximum amount of screen space for composing your source code. You can learn more about Handy HTML Studio and download a trial version of the program at www.silversoftware.com.

BBEdit

BBEdit by Bare Bones Software is the most popular HTML text editor available for the Macintosh platform. It works directly with HTML text and offers many different features for controlling and manipulating the source code. Like most HTML text editors, BBEdit uses colored text to visually indicate the different types of source code that you enter. It also automates the process of entering tags, to help you code your document correctly every time.

BBEdit is available only for the Macintosh platform. You can find more information at www.barebones.com.

Web Weaver

Web Weaver is an HTML text editor that includes wizards that can help you create a basic Web page, forms, frames, and tables. You can then modify the Web page by inserting additional text and codes. Web Weaver includes tools that allow you to create clickable image maps and special effects, validate HTML code, and check for broken links.

You can learn more about Web Weaver and download a 30-day version at www.mcwebsoftware.com/webweav.asp.

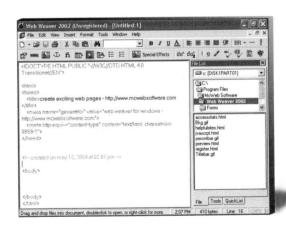

Introducing HTML Visual Editors

Learning to edit HTML source code is essential for troubleshooting and fixing Web page errors, so every Web page author should be familiar with HTML tags and what they do. However, controlling the appearance and layout of a page may be difficult when you cannot immediately see the effects of your changes. For example, if you type source code to tell a Web browser to wrap text around an image, you may be surprised to find the text immediately next to the image when you view your page in a Web browser. To avoid this problem,

you can use a visual Web-page authoring program, commonly called a visual editor.

In addition to allowing you to format and enhance Web pages by clicking buttons and selecting menu commands, most visual editors enable you to view the source code and edit it directly. By examining the source code in a completed HTML document, you can learn a great deal about the purpose and effects of the various HTML tags that comprise the source code.

Formatting with Visual editors

With a visual editor, you can format text as you would in a word processing program. For example, you can highlight text to select it and then click a button in the formatting toolbar to apply bold or italic formatting. The program inserts the necessary HTML tags for you and displays the text as it will appear in a Web browser. You can drag and drop many elements, such as images, exactly where you want them. To create a table, you simply specify the number of columns and rows you want. To create a form, you can point and click to create the form objects you want, such as check boxes, text boxes, and command buttons.

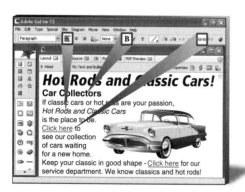

Microsoft FrontPage

Microsoft FrontPage is a powerful visual editor and Web site management tool for Windows. Microsoft FrontPage can display a schematic diagram of your Web site structure, showing you how the Web pages link together and helping you to track down any broken links. To edit a Web page, you can double-click its icon and edit or format the Web page as you would in Microsoft Word. FrontPage also enables you to view and edit the source code, and includes powerful tools to help you 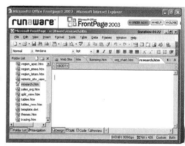 remove extraneous code from HTML documents created in Microsoft Word. Microsoft FrontPage features pre-existing scripts and design codes that can help you enhance your Web site and extend your knowledge of HTML.

FrontPage is primarily for Windows users, although an older version of it is available for Macintosh computers. Most of FrontPage's high-end features require non-standard, proprietary extensions, or server add-ons, that work only on a Microsoft Web server.

To learn more about Microsoft FrontPage and its latest features, and to download a trial version, visit www.microsoft.com/frontpage.

Yahoo! PageWizards

Yahoo! PageWizards are online forms that lead you through a four-step process to create a personal Web page. You first select a Web page design template, type a page title and introductory text, select or upload an image, and then enter your personal information and links to your favorite sites. Because you build the page directly online, you do not need to upload files to a Web server when your page is complete. Visit geocities.yahoo.com for more information about PageWizards and about PageBuilder, which allows you to design more sophisticated Web pages.

Adobe GoLive

Adobe GoLive is a Web site design and management tool that is especially useful for companies that have invested in other Adobe products, including Photoshop and Illustrator. GoLive smoothly integrates graphics and other objects created in Adobe applications into its Web pages. It also offers a Co-Author feature to enable team design and management of Web sites.

Adobe GoLive is available for Windows and Macintosh platforms. For more information, go to www.adobe.com/products/golive.

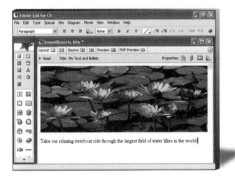

Macromedia Dreamweaver

Macromedia Dreamweaver is a program that enables you to create Web pages that feature text, images, and multimedia. It also helps you to link your pages together and to publish them on the Web.

Unlike other WYSIWYG editors, Dreamweaver focuses on producing Web-enabled applications, of which Web pages are only the beginning. Dreamweaver can build multimedia pages that contain Flash and Shockwave animations and other dynamic, interactive media.

Dreamweaver is available for Windows and Macintosh platforms. You can find more information at www.macromedia. com/software/ dreamweaver.

NetObjects Fusion

NetObjects Fusion combines power with simplicity to enable both beginners and advanced users to create sophisticated Web sites. Its Site Wizard can help you to quickly structure your site, and its formatting tools enable you to adjust the design even if you have no knowledge of HTML. Fusion also features several powerful components, including ad banners, form handlers, and picture rollovers that allow you to add dynamic elements to your pages with a single mouse click. Perhaps best of all, NetObjects Fusion can help you to create an e-commerce-enabled Web site by managing some of the more complex source code for you.

Fusion is available for Windows and Macintosh platforms. You can find more information at www.netobjects.com.

```
Skeleton.html - WordPad

File   Edit   View   Insert   Format   Help

<!DOCTYPE html
PUBLIC "-//W3C//DTD XHTML 1.0 Transit
"http://www.w3.org/TR/xhtml1/DTD/xhtml1-

<html>
<head>
<title>HTML Web Page Skeleton</title>
</head>
<body>
</body>
</html>
```

PART II

CREATING AND FORMATTING WEB PAGES

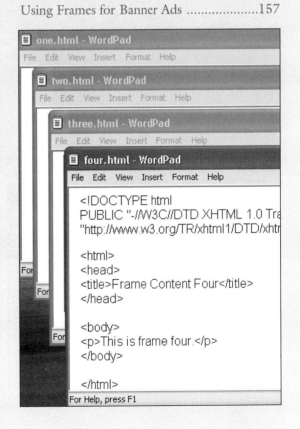

Specify an XHTML DTD

E very Web page should start with a *document type declaration* (DTD). The DTD designates the HTML or XHTML standard that the document follows and instructs the browser which set of rules to follow in order to interpret the source code.

XHTML has three different DTDs: *strict, transitional,* and *frameset.* The strict DTD is very particular, requiring clean tag markup and the use of the latest tags throughout the document. The transitional DTD is the most widely used DTD, because it includes support for many older tags and attributes that are being phased out (*deprecated*). If you plan on incorporating frames, you can use the frameset DTD as shown in Chapter 7.

Within each of these DTD documents is a public line of text that shows the correct syntax for including the DTD in the `<!DOCTYPE>` tag. For example, the public line for the

transitional DTD is:

```
PUBLIC "-//W3C//DTD XHTML 1.0
Transitional//EN"
SYSTEM
"http://www.w3.org/TR/xhtml1/DTD/xhtml1-
transitional.dtd".
```

You can copy this text from the W3C Web site, paste it at the top of a Web page you are creating, and edit it to place it in the proper syntax:

```
<!DOCTYPE html PUBLIC "-//W3C//DTD XHTML 1.0
Transitional//EN"
"http://www.w3.org/TR/xhtml1/DTD/xhtml1-
transitional.dtd"
```

You can view all of these DTDs along with much more XHTML information online at www.w3.org/TR/xhtml1/#dtds.

Specify an XHTML DTD

① Open the Web page that lists the various XHTML DTDs at www.w3.org/TR/xhtml1/#dtds.

② Click the link for the DTD you want to use.

● This example uses the XHTML-1.0-Transitional DTD.

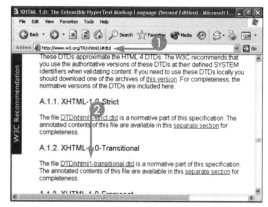

● The `PUBLIC` line of text allows the DTD to be specified within a `<!DOCTYPE>` tag.

③ Click and drag over the DTD to highlight it.

④ Click Edit.

⑤ Click Copy.

● The DTD copies to the clipboard.

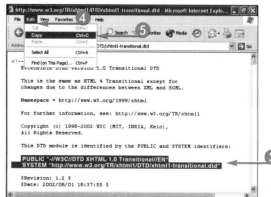

⑥ Open a document in your HTML editor.

⑦ Click to place the cursor at the very top of the document.

⑧ Click Edit.

⑨ Click Paste.

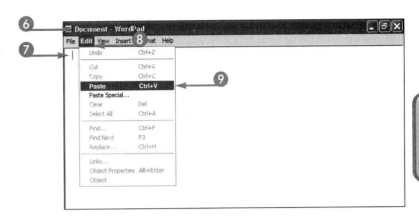

● The HTML editor pastes the DTD at the top of the document.

⑩ Delete the word "SYSTEM."

⑪ Type <**!DOCTYPE html** before the DTD.

⑫ Add a closing bracket.

⑬ Save the file as *?*.html, where *?* is the name of the file.

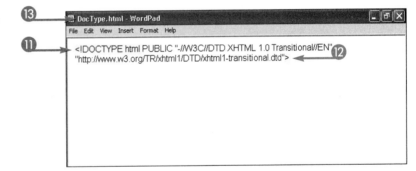

```
<!DOCTYPE html PUBLIC "-//W3C//DTD XHTML 1.0 Transitional//EN"
"http://www.w3.org/TR/xhtml1/DTD/xhtml1-transitional.dtd">
```

What happens if I omit the DTD specification?

▼ Web browsers are very forgiving if you omit the DTD specification. Most Web browsers default to the HTML 4 transitional DTD when a Web page does not specify a DTD. However, to adhere to XHTML standards, you should insert one of the three XHTML DTDs at the top of every Web page. Three XHTML DTDs are available: transitional, strict, and frameset. Always use the frameset DTD for any frameset documents you create, as discussed in Chapter 7. Strict DTD is difficult to achieve. This book recommends you use transitional DTD for any documents that do not include <frameset> tags. You can find links to these DTDs at www.w3.org/TR/html4/.

Why would I want to use the XHTML specification instead of the HTML specification?

▼ XHTML 1.0 is almost identical to HTML 4.01, but follows a stricter set of rules. Because XHTML will eventually supplant HTML, you should follow the XHTML rules. However, most Web browsers are capable of displaying pages that adhere to HTML 4.01 and earlier standards.

Does my Web browser support XHTML?

▼ Because the XHTML specification is a streamlined version of HTML that follows a stricter set of rules, most browsers have no trouble interpreting source code that adheres to the XHTML specification. A more significant concern is whether your browser provides full support of CSS, because CSS fills in the gaps created by deprecating most presentation attributes. Most current Web browsers do support CSS to varying degrees.

Create a Web Page Skeleton

To create a Web page from scratch, you can open a blank document, insert the XHTML DTD, and then insert tags that define the content of the Web page. The tags mark the beginning and end of the source code you will enter. They also create a header for the document, which contains text that does not appear on the page, and they define the body of the document, where you eventually enter the text and tags that make up your Web page. The header typically contains the page title, which appears not on the Web page itself, but in the browser's title bar. The overall structure of the Web page skeleton, including the XHTML transitional DTD, looks like this:

```
<!DOCTYPE html
PUBLIC "-//W3C//DTD XHTML 1.0
Transitional//EN"
```

```
"http://www.w3.org/TR/xhtml1/DTD/xhtml1-
transitional.dtd">

<html>
<head>
<title>Sample Document Title</title>
</head>
<body>
</body>
</html>
```

This Web page skeleton forms the framework for your Web page. The document body houses all of the page's contents, including text and tags for inserting images and media files. Within the <body> tags, you can add tags and attributes that format the contents, but you should specify most of your formatting with Cascading Style Sheets.

Create a Web Page Skeleton

① Open a new document in your HTML editor.

② Save the document as a text-only file with the .htm or .html extension.

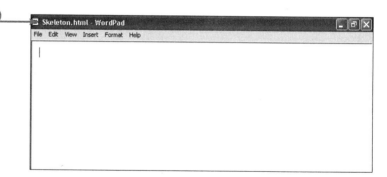

③ Add the DOCTYPE declaration.

Note: To add a DOCTYPE-declaration, see the section "Specify an XHTML DTD".

④ Add the opening and closing <html> tags, remembering to include a slash (/) before the tag name in the closing tag.

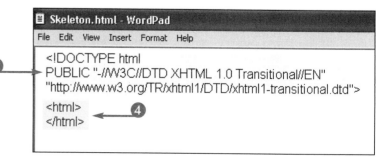

⑤ After the opening `<html>` tag, add opening and closing `<head>` tags.

⑥ Within the `<head>` tags, add a descriptive page title bracketed by `<title>` tags.

⑦ Add opening and closing `<body>` tags.

⑧ Save the document.

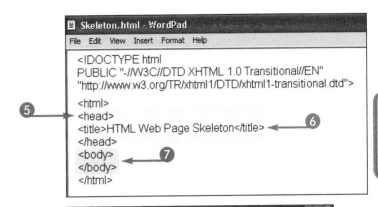

⑨ Open the document in a Web browser.

● Your Web browser displays your document as a Web page, which is blank except for the title appearing in the Web browser title bar.

If I have an HTML file on my computer, how do I open it in my Web browser?

▼ You can select File ➜ Open or File ➜ Open File to display a dialog box that helps you browse for the file. You can also type a complete path to the file, including its filename, in the address bar of your Web browser window where you normally type the URL. The URL is an address that indicates the location and name of a file on the Internet or on your computer.

Do I have to be online to view my HTML document in a Web browser?

▼ No. You can load and view HTML pages on your local disk drive while you work offline. You can open a page by clicking File ➜ Open and selecting the file you want to open or by typing a complete path and filename in your Web browser's address bar and pressing Enter. If your page contains hyperlinks to pages stored on other Web servers, however, you must be online to test those hyperlinks.

Can I use special characters or other HTML elements within the `<title>` tags?

▼ Yes, you can add special characters to the title content. To add special characters see the section "Insert Special Characters." However, Web browsers do not display any HTML formatting styles, such as bold or italic, that you type within the opening and closing `<title>` tags. Your Web page title appears in the Web browser's title bar in whichever format the browser is set up to display it.

Create Paragraphs and Line Breaks

You can break up text within the body of an HTML page using the paragraph <p> tag and the line-break <br /> tag. Unlike word-processing documents, HTML documents ignore returns you insert when you press Enter, so you need to indicate paragraph divisions and line breaks with tags.

Although the closing </p> tag is optional in HTML, XHTML requires it, so always insert the closing </p> tag at the end of a paragraph. You can also press Enter at the end of a paragraph to show that you are beginning a new paragraph. You can press Enter to insert as many blank lines

as you want; this method breaks up the source code so that you can better see what you are doing. The Web browser ignores these blank lines when rendering the page.

When a Web browser encounters a new <p> tag, it breaks the line and adds white space. If you just want a line of text to break and resume directly on the next line, you can use a line-break <br /> tag. This tag simply tells the Web browser where a new line should begin and does not have a corresponding end tag.

Insert a paragraph

① Open a document in your HTML editor.

② Add an opening <p> tag between the <body> tags.

③ Type a paragraph of text.

④ Add a closing </p> tag.

⑤ Save the document as a text-only file with the .htm or .html extension.

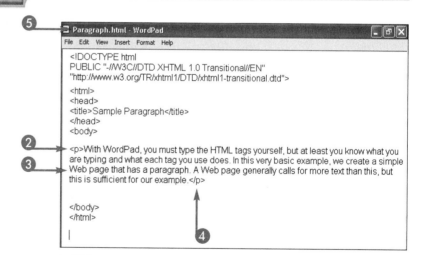

⑥ Open the document in a Web browser.

● The Web browser displays your paragraph.

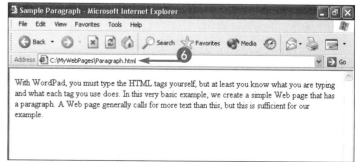

Insert a Line Break

1. Open a document in your HTML editor.

2. Type two or more short lines of text.

3. Add a line break (<br />) at the end of each line of text.

4. Save the document as a text-only file with the .htm or .html extension.

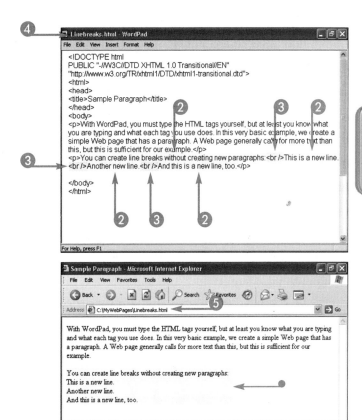

5. Open the document in a Web browser.

   - The Web browser displays the text with the line breaks that you inserted.

PART II

Can I control right text margins with line breaks?

▼ In a way. Normally a Web browser continues a line of text until it fills the width of the Web browser window, and then wraps the text to the next line. If you want your text to break at a specific width, you can insert explicit line breaks. However, the recommended way to control margins is to create styles that define the margins for HTML elements, as shown in Chapter 4. To create a paragraph that the Web browser indents from both the left and right margins, insert a quote, as shown in the section "Add a Quote."

How do I control the amount of space between paragraphs?

▼ The most efficient way to control space between paragraphs is to use Cascading Style Sheets, as shown in Chapter 4. With Cascading Style Sheets, you can create a rule that specifies the top or bottom margins for specified paragraphs. You can use one or more line-break <br /> tags, but this can result in cluttered source code.

What happens if I press Enter to insert Return characters in my HTML document?

▼ Under most circumstances, Web browsers do not render Return characters, so they are visible only when you edit your source code. However, if you try to seamlessly stack adjacent images, you may find that Return characters in between the images produce a slight gap.

Emphasize Text

Emphasizing text typically calls for you to display it in boldface, italics, or both. You can emphasize text by using either physical style tags or content-based style tags. Physical style tags tell the Web browser exactly how the text should appear. Content-based style tags simply indicate that the enclosed text should be emphasized, allowing the Web browser to determine which text enhancements to apply.

Physical tags include <b> </b> for boldface and <i> </i> for italics. The content-based equivalents of the physical <b> and <i> tags are the <strong> and <em> tags. Although these tags do not explicitly dictate how the

text should be formatted, most Web browsers apply bold formatting to any text within <strong> tags and italic formatting to any text within <em> tags.

The advantage of content-based tags is that they transmit contextual meaning to the Web browser rather than specific directions for appearance. For some browsing clients, such as those used by blind or otherwise disabled visitors, physical styles may have little meaning. Instead, these Web browsers look for contextual markers provided by content-based tags to render the text in an appropriate way.

Emphasize Text

① In your HTML editor, open a document that contains plain text.

② Enclose a portion of the text within opening and closing <b> tags.

③ Enclose another portion of the text within opening and closing <i> tags.

④ Add opening and closing <strong> tags to one sentence.

⑤ Add opening and closing <em> tags to another sentence.

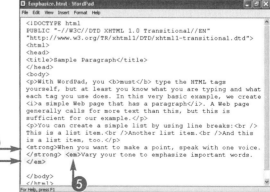

PART II

6 Add an opening `<b>` and `<i>` tag.

7 Add a line of text.

8 Add a closing `</i>` tag and a closing `</b>` tag.

9 Save the document as a text-only file with the .htm or .html extension.

10 Open the document in a Web browser.

● Text with the `<strong>` tag is bold in most Web browsers.

● Text with the `<em>` tag is italicized in most Web browsers.

● Text with the `<b>` tag is bold.

● Text with the `<i>` tag is italicized.

● Text with both the `<b>` and `<i>` tags is bold and italicized.

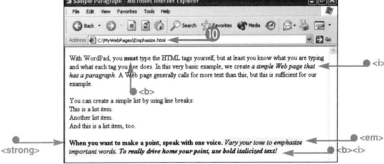

What other HTML tags can I use to control the appearance of text?

▼ The HTML codes for setting text size and adding enhancements are listed below. For additional text formatting, use CSS, as shown in Chapter 4.

Code	Purpose
`<big>`, `<small>`, `<code>`	Computer code
`<kbd>`	Keyboard code
`<tt>`	Teletype code
`<sub>`,`<sup>`	subscript and superscript
`<bdo dir="rtl" />`	Displays text that reads from right to left
`<pre>`	Makes text appear exactly as you type it in a fixed-width font that preserves line breaks and spacing. This is often useful for displaying computer code on a page.

How do I create a strikethrough effect?

▼ Although HTML offers two physical style tags, `<s>` and `<strike>`, that place a line through the enclosed text, both tags are deprecated. To mark revisions in a document, use the `<del>` tag to display deleted text with strikethrough and `<ins>` to display inserted text as underlined. These tags are especially useful if you are team-editing a document.

Is there a way to make text blink?

▼ Netscape Navigator supports the `<blink>` tag, which toggles the text on and off. CSS features a `text-discoloration` property whose value you can set to `blink`. Because blinking objects may annoy your visitors, use this effect only when no other option is available. Appendix B lists additional values for the `discoloration` property.

Add
Headings

You can add headings to your Web page with the six available heading tags, <h1> being the largest, top-level heading and <h6> being the smallest. Although the rendering of the heading text may vary from browser to browser, the text enclosed within a set of heading tags usually appears bold.

The advantage to using heading tags rather than formatting headings with enhancements, such as boldface and italics, is that the heading tags provide the Web browser with specific information about the content of the tag rather than just telling the Web browser how to format the text.

Can I include any attributes in heading tags?

▼ No. The `align` attribute for aligning headings left, right, center, or justified has been deprecated in favor of CSS styles. However, you can use the `class` or `style` attribute to assign a CSS style to a heading, as shown in Chapter 4. You can add the `title="tooltip text"` attribute to have text pop up in a tooltip when the mouse is over the heading. To do this, replace *tooltip_text* with the text you want. Chapters 8 and 9 show various attributes that you can add to trigger scripted events.

Add Headings

1 Open a document in your HTML editor.

2 Insert the opening tag for the desired heading level.

3 Type the text you want the heading to contain.

4 Insert the closing tag for the heading level specified in step 2.

5 Save the document as a text-only file with the .htm or .html extension.

```
Mississippi.html - WordPad
File  Edit  View  Insert  Format  Help
<!DOCTYPE html
PUBLIC "-//W3C//DTD XHTML 1.0 Transitional//EN"
"http://www.w3.org/TR/xhtml1/DTD/xhtml1-transitional.dtd">
<html>
<head>
<title>Historical Perspectives</title>
</head>
<body>
<h1>Mississippi River Commerce</h1>
</body>
</html>
```

6 Open the document in a Web browser.

● The Web browser displays the heading, which is usually bold and larger than standard paragraph text.

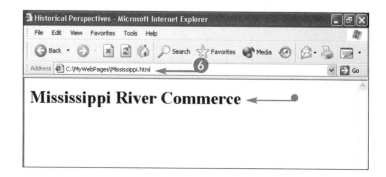

```
Historical Perspectives - Microsoft Internet Explorer
File  Edit  View  Favorites  Tools  Help
Back ·  ·  ·  ·  ·  Search  Favorites  Media  ·  ·  ·  ·
Address  C:\MyWebPages\Mississippi.html                      Go
```

Mississippi River Commerce

Add Horizontal Rules

PART II

Y ou can visually separate content sections on a Web page using the standalone horizontal rule `<hr />` tag. The `<hr />` tag has no corresponding end tag and simply tells the Web browser to break to a new line and insert a horizontal rule across the width of the page.

By default, the horizontal rule on most Web browsers is three pixels thick and appears with a slight 3D effect. HTML does provide attributes for controlling the width, thickness, and shading of the line. However, W3C has deprecated these *presentation attributes* and now recommends using style sheets to control the appearance

and positioning of horizontal rules. For example, shortening the horizontal line and centering it often produces a nice effect.

Horizontal rules are helpful formatting tools that serve to break text into discrete, readable blocks. However, like any formatting element, excessive use of the horizontal rule clutters a page and distracts the visitor, so you should use it sparingly.

For more information about applying CSS styles, see Chapter 4. You can also refer to Appendix B for a list of common CSS styles.

Add Horizontal Rules

1 Open a document in your HTML editor.

2 Insert the `<hr />` tag where you want the horizontal rules to appear.

3 Save the document as a text-only file with the .htm or .html extension.

4 Open the document in a Web browser.

● The horizontal rules appear.

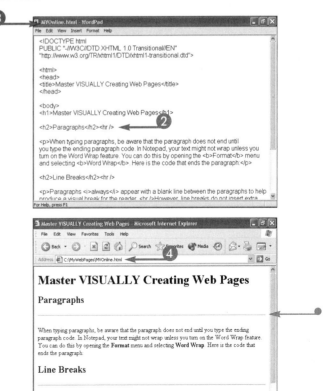

Add Hyperlinks and Mailtos

You can add hyperlinks and mailtos to your Web page to visit other Web pages and to send e-mail messages. To add a hyperlink, you can use the `<a>` tag and the `href` attribute. The syntax for the hyperlink tag is as follows:

```
<a href="http://www.site.com/directory/
subdirectory/filename.html">Link Name</a>
```

where *Link Name* is the text that appears blue and underlined on a Web page. The visitor clicks this text to open the linked page. In place of text, you can also use an image to represent the link. The value for the `href` attribute can be an HTTP or FTP URL that points to a file on another server or to a file on your own server.

To enable users to send you feedback, you can use a `mailto` URL with the `href` attribute. When the user clicks the link, the Web browser opens the default e-mail client and automatically adds the e-mail address in the To field.

For links to other documents on your own server, you can use either *absolute* or *relative* URLs. Absolute URLs include the protocol, such as `http://`, and the server name, in addition to the specific file location. With relative URLs, you can indicate the file location in relation to the current document.

Add Hyperlinks and Mailtos

① Open a document in your HTML editor.

② Add a link to an external Web site.

③ Add a relative link to another page stored in the same directory as you store this document.

Note: *To link to a page stored in the same directory, you only need to enter the filename of the page.*

④ Add a mailto link with your e-mail address, complete with text that the user can click to activate the link.

⑤ Save the document as a text-only file with the .htm or .html extension.

⑥ Open the document in a Web browser.

⑦ Click one of the links to a Web page.

● The Web page or external site appears in the Web browser window.

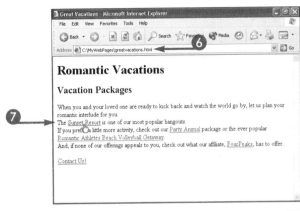

⑧ Click your Web browser's Back button to reload the document from step 5 in your Web browser.

⑨ Click the mailto link you added in step 4.

● Your default e-mail program runs, and displays a new blank message addressed to the mailto addressee.

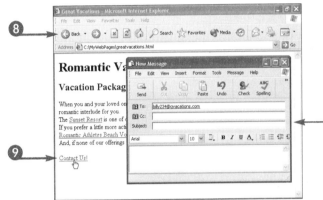

Can I hide my e-mail address from spammers?

▼ Yes, you can deter e-mail search bots by typing `&#64;` instead of the @ sign in your e-mail address. For example, type `<a href="mailto:myname&#64; mailserver.com">Email Me! </a>`. The code `&#64;` functions as an @ sign but cloaks your e-mail address. This trick is not foolproof, however; many search bots includ `&#64;` in their searches. Contact your Web hosting service for additional options.

How can I get a link to load into a separate Web browser window?

▼ If you want the linked page to load into a new Web browser window, add the `target="_blank"` attribute to the `<a>` tag. For example, type `<a href="http://www.wiley.com/" target="_blank">`. This causes the browser to launch a new window, which then displays the linked page. You can also use the target attribute to load a linked page into a frame, as discussed in Chapter 7.

Do I need to type the complete path to every linked page and object?

▼ No. If the linked page is in the same directory as the current page, you can define the URL by simply entering the filename of the linked document. If the file you link to is stored on the same server, but in a different directory, you can omit the domain name; type a path to the directory followed by the filename. You can also define a base URL, as explained in the next section, to indicate the location of most of the links in your document.

Define a
Base URL

To insert a file or link into your Web page, you typically type the file's URL to specify its location. However, when you insert a link to a file or Web page in the same directory as your Web page, you can simply type the file's name; the browser looks in the current directory for the file. If you store files that your Web page links to in another directory, you can add a `<base/>` tag between your Web page's opening and closing `<head>` tags to specify the location. The syntax for using the `<base/>` tag is as follows:

`<base="http://www.site.com/directory/subdirectory/" />`

where *www.site.com* is the domain name of the Web server on which the files are stored, and *directory/subdirectory/* is

the path to the directory in which the files are stored. If the files are stored on an FTP server, you must replace `http:` with `ftp:`.

The `<base/>` tag applies to other files, as well, including any images, audio clips, and video clips to which you might want to link later. For example, if you insert the `<img />` tag to add a graphic stored in the base URL, you can use the image filename as its source, for example, `<img src="image.gif" />`.

Define a Base URL

① Open a Web document in your HTML editor.

② Place the cursor between the opening and closing `<head>` tags.

③ Add the `<base/>` tag, complete with a URL that specifies the location of files to which this document links.

Note: *When specifying a path to a folder on your computer, type it in the form* `href="file://c|/folder/subfolder"`. *With Windows operating systems, the drive designation, c|, may not be necessary.*

④ Add a hyperlink that points to files stored in the directory whose location the `<base/>` tag specifies.

Note: *See the section "Add Hyperlinks and Mailtos" for instructions on creating hyperlinks.*

⑤ Save the newly edited Web page.

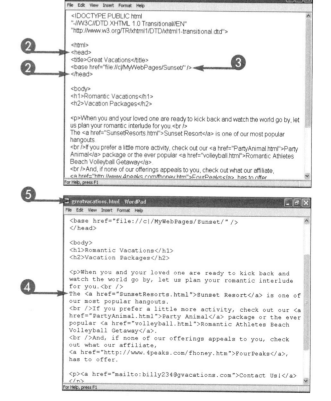

⑥ Open the Web page in your Web browser.

⑦ Click a link for one of the files stored in the directory whose location the <base/> tag specifies.

● Your browser displays the contents of the selected file.

Can I use the `target` attribute with the `<base>` tag?

▼ Yes, you can use the `target` attribute with the `<base>` tag to specify the window or frame in which you want the linked content to display. For example, `<base href="http://www.wiley.com/files/myfiles/html" target=_blank />` directs the Web browser to open all links in a new window unless otherwise specified. You can override this setting for a specific link by typing the desired target value for that link. For example, setting `target` equal to `"_top"` opens the link in the current window. You can also use the `"_self"` and `"_parent"` values with frames, as shown in Chapter 7.

How can I link to files not stored in the base URL directory?

▼ A Web browser refers to the base URL only when an `<a href=>` tag does not specify a URL. If you have a link that points to a location other than the base URL, type the entire URL, starting with `http://` or `ftp://` to link to the page or file.

How can I link to files stored in a subdirectory of the base URL?

▼ If your base URL is http://www.site.com/images/ and a file is stored in http://www.site.com/images/kites/ you can specify the file location by typing **<img src="kites/kite.jpg"/>**. If you specify your base URL as http://www.site.com/, then you would specify the relative file location by typing **<img src="images/kites/kite.jpg"/>**.

Create Internal Page Links

Y ou can create a link to specific sections of a Web page by using the name attribute with the <a> tag. You can use the name attribute to identify sections of your page and then create links to these sections using regular <a href=> tags. These internal links do not lead to other pages, but instead direct the user to sections of the current page.

When you use the <a> tag with the name attribute, the text contained within the tag does not display as a link but

as regular text. When you want to link to a section with a name value, you can use another <a> tag with the href attribute set to the section name preceded by a pound sign (#). When visitors click the link, they go directly to the section with that name value.

By using internal page links, you can lead your visitors directly to the section of content they are looking for or provide a clickable table of contents at the top of a page.

Create Internal Page Links

① Create or open a document that contains more than one screen full of text.

Note: A document with two or more headings is best.

② Place the cursor at the beginning of a block of text to which you want to link.

③ Add an opening <a> tag with the name attribute set equal to the name you want to assign to this text.

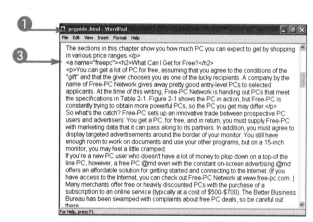

④ Place the cursor at the end of the block of text to which you want to link.

⑤ Add a closing </a> tag.

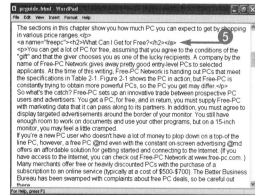

6 Near the top of the page body, add an `<a>` tag with the `href` attribute followed by # and the name you typed in step 3.

7 Type a closing `</a>` tag.

8 Save the document as a text-only file with the .htm or .html extension.

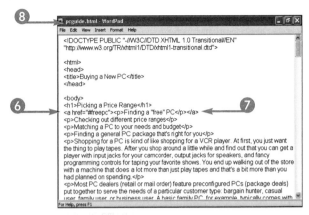

9 Open the document in your Web browser.

10 Click the link that points to the named block of text.

- The Web browser takes you to the block of text you tagged with the `name` attribute.

Can I provide a link to return visitors to the top of the page?

▼ Yes. Simply tag some text near the top of the page using the `<a name="top"> </a>` tags. To insert a link that goes to the top of the page, move the insertion point where you want the link and type `<a href="top">Return to Top</a>`. Consider including a clickable table of contents at the top of the page that links to each section of your page, especially if your page is longer than three screens. At the end of each section, insert a link to the table of contents.

Can I link to a named section on a different page?

▼ Yes. If the linked page has a named anchor on it, you can link directly to that anchor. Follow the URL of the linked page with the number sign (#) and the named anchor enclosed in quotation marks. For example, type `<a href="www.url.com/thispage/index.html#`*anchorname*`">Skip ahead to the tips page.</a>`.

I added the `name` attribute to some text, but the text looks the same in my Web browser. Did I do something wrong?

▼ No. Marking an anchor with the `<a name="anchorname"> </a>` tags does not change the appearance of the text. Marking an achor simply inserts a marker in the document to which another `<a>` tag can link. Of course, you can format any text between the opening and closing `<a>` tags by using style rules, as discussed in Chapter 4.

Create a List

You can create an indented list of items by using the `<ul>` and `<ol>` tags. The `<ul>` tag creates unordered, or bulleted, lists, while the `<ol>` tag creates numbered, or ordered, lists. Lists are useful when you have groups of related items or step-by-step instructions. They also allow users to scan documents quickly to find the information they need.

A list consists of list items, each enclosed within `<li>` tags. Most Web browsers allow you to omit the closing `</li>` tag, but XHTML prohibits the omission, so you must include the closing list tag.

You can also nest lists within other lists to create an outline displaying two or more heading levels. For bulleted lists, each time you nest an additional list, the bullet type reflects the nesting relationship by alternating between solid disks, hollow circles, and squares. You can explicitly change the type of bullet for both nested and single lists by including the `type` attribute with `<ul>`, `<ol>`, and `<li>` elements. However, this attribute is deprecated in favor of style sheet properties. For more information about CSS properties, see Chapter 4.

Create a List

Create an Unordered List

1. Open a document in your HTML editor.

2. Add a set of opening and closing `<ul>` tags.

Note: *The list must be somewhere between the opening and closing `<body>` tags.*

3. Add two or more unordered list items, each marked with an opening and closing `<li>` tag.

Create an Ordered List

4. Add a set of opening and closing `<ol>` tags.

5. Add two or more unordered list items, each marked with an opening and closing `<li>` tag.

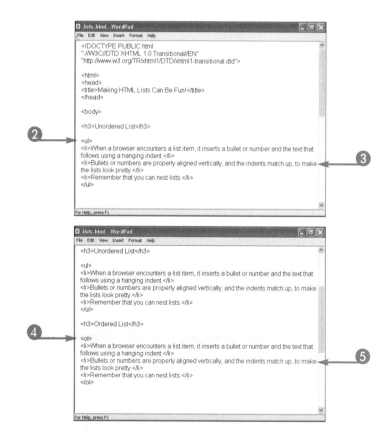

Nest Lists

6 Add a set of opening and closing `<ul>` tags.

7 Add two or more unordered list items, each marked with an opening and closing `<li>` tag.

8 After the first list item, add a second unordered list.

9 Save the document as a text-only file with the .htm or .html extension.

View Lists in a Web Browser

10 Open the document in your Web browser.

● The Web browser displays the lists.

● The disk is the default bullet type for unordered lists.

● For nested unordered lists, the bullet type changes for each consecutive list.

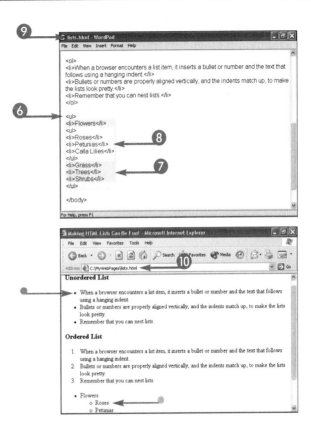

Can I set ordered lists to begin numbering items at a particular number?

▼ Yes. You can add the `start=?` attribute to the opening `<ol>` tag, where `?` specifies the first number, or letter, in the list. You can also add the `value=?` to an opening `<li>` tag to specify a number for a single list item. Unfortunately, the `start` and `value` attributes are deprecated, and CSS does not provide substitutes.

What bullet types are available for lists?

▼ The `type` attribute lets you choose from three types of bullets for unordered lists: the disk, which is the standard bullet; the circle, which is a hollow bullet; or the square. However, CSS features a `list-style-type` property that you can set to `circle`, `disc`, `square`, `decimal`, `lower-alpha`, `lower-roman`, `upper-alpha`, or `upper-roman`. See Chapter 4 to learn how to format lists with CSS styles and refer to Appendix B for a list of options.

How do I add space between list items?

▼ When a Web browser displays a list, it automatically inserts space above and below the list. You can add white space between list items by inserting paragraph tags or line-break tags between the list items. However, this method gives control of the spacing to the Web browser. To set spacing more precisely, use CSS styles, as shown in Chapter 4.

Add a Mailing Address

If you are constructing a Web site for your business, or want to include your personal address on a Web page, you can type the address where you want it to appear and use the <address> tag to format it. Most Web browsers display the address in italics. The source code typically uses the following syntax:

```
<address>
Business Name<br />
Street Address<br />
City, State ZIP<br />
</address>
```

You can use other text formatting to make the address appear the same way, but regular text formatting does not identify the content type, it only affects the appearance of the content. Using the <address> tag enables catalogue

and indexing software to identify and extract the data from your Web page. You can also use the <address> tag for telephone numbers.

MASTER IT

Does the <address> tag make an address appear on a new line?

▼ Yes. The <address> tag is similar to the <p> tag in that it starts the address on a new line and inserts space before the address entry. Likewise, the Web browser starts a new line and inserts space after the closing </address> tag. However, to display each entry in the address on its own line, you must type a <br /> tag at the end of each line.

Add a Mailing Address

① Open a document in your HTML editor.

② Add an opening <address> tag.

③ Type your address, including a line break code at the end of each line.

④ Type a closing </address> tag.

⑤ Save the document as a text-only file with the .htm or .html extension.

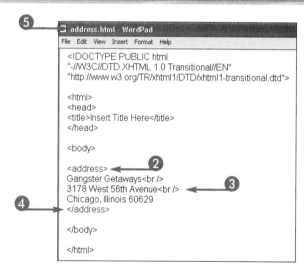

⑥ Open the document in your Web browser.

● The Web browser displays the address.

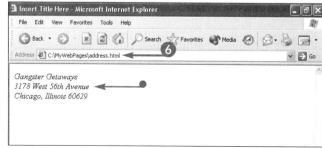

Add a Quote

I f your Web page contains a lengthy quotation, you can set off the quotation as a blockquote, using <blockquote> tags. When you enclose a section of text within <blockquote> tags, the text indents from the left and right edge of the Web browser window.

For smaller quotations, such as a single line, you can use <q> tags. These tags mark quotes like the <blockquote> but are reserved for inline use and do not indent the text.

Both the <blockquote> and <q> tags have a cite attribute that you can use to reference the URL of your source. The cite attribute has no interactive function. It does not pop up on mouseovers or perform any other action unless you program it to by using an *event attribute* — an attribute that triggers an event to occur when the user performs a specific action.

Can I give special treatment to the names of authors whom I quote?

▼ Yes. You can display an author's name in italics by placing the name between <cite> tags. These tags offer the added benefit of marking the author's name as a citation. However, style sheets provide you with a greater variety of formatting options.

Add a Quote

1 Open a document in your HTML editor.

2 Type a standard paragraph to introduce the block quote.

3 Type the opening <blockquote> tag.

4 Type your quotation.

5 Type the closing </blockquote> tag.

6 Save the document as a text-only file with the .htm or .html extension.

7 Open the document in your Web browser.

● The quote appears as indented text.

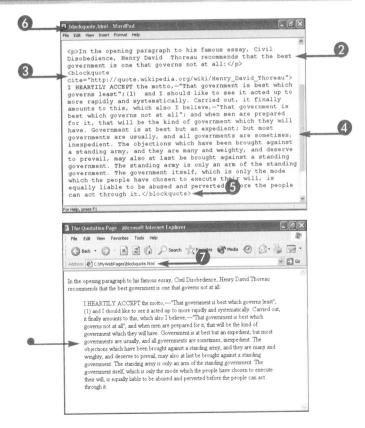

57

Create a Definition List

I f you create an educational site that introduces unfamiliar terms or acronyms, you can include a glossary that can help visitors to understand these terms. Although you can define terms in an unordered list, search indexes such as Google, which collect and index definitions, may exclude your definitions.

To create a list of terms and their definitions that a search index can recognize, you can use the definition list tags: <dl> and </dl> to open and close the list; <dt> and </dt> to mark each term; and <dd> and </dd> to mark each definition. When you display them in a Web browser, each term appears on a separate line, left justified, with its definition indented and on the next line down.

If I have only one term to define, do I still need to add the <dl> and </dl> tags?

▼ No. If you have only one term, type the term followed by its definition, and place the entire line between <dfn> </dfn> tags. For example, when you type **<dfn>Otolaryngology: n. A branch of medicine that deals with the ear and throat.</dfn>**, a Web browser displays the term and its definition in italics.

Create a Definition List

① Open a document in your HTML editor.

② Add opening and closing <dl> tags.

③ Type your list of terms and definitions between the <dt> tags.

④ Enclose each term with <dt> tags.

⑤ Enclose each definition with <dd> tags.

⑥ Save the document as a text-only file with the .htm or .html extension.

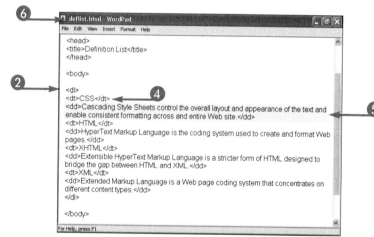

⑦ Open the document in your Web browser.

● The Web browser displays the definitions in definition list format.

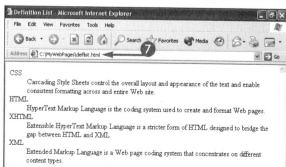

Define an Acronym

In HTML, acronyms, such as WWW and CIA, get special treatment. You can place acronyms within opening and closing <acronym> tags to pass valuable information to Web browsers, spell checkers, translation programs, and search bots. Search indexes, including Google, often look specifically for definitions and acronyms to add them to their indexes.

You can also add the title attribute to the <acronym> tag to include the full spelling for which the acronym stands. When a visitor rests his or her mouse cursor on the acronym, a small box pops up, displaying the full spelling. Most Web browsers support the title attribute. If you include the title attribute, you should set it equal to the acronym's meaning, as follows:

```
<acronym title="American Civil Liberties
Union">ACLU</acronym>
```

What should I do if I have an abbreviation rather than an acronym?

▼ Type **<abbr>** then type the abbreviation followed by **</abbr>**. The <abbr> tags serve the same purpose as the <acronym> tags, providing Web browsers, spell checkers, and search bots with information on how to display and identify the abbreviation.

Define an Acronym

1. Open a document in your HTML editor.

2. Type an opening <acronym> tag with the title attribute set equal to the spelled out version of the acronym.

3. Type your acronym.

4. Type a closing </acronym> tag at the end of the acronym.

5. Save the document as a plain-text file with the .htm or .html extension.

6. Open the document in your Web browser.

7. Position the cursor over the acronym.

   ● The full spelling appears.

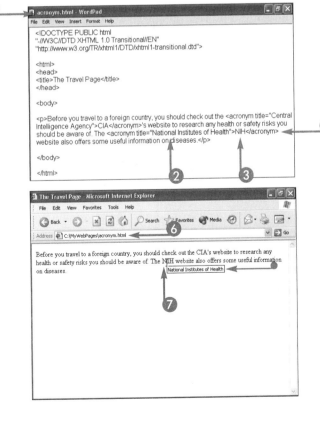

Create
a Table

Y ou can arrange data on your Web pages in rows and columns using the HTML table tags, <table>, <tr>, and <td>. Every table that you create is composed of opening and closing <table> tags and one or more sets of table row <tr> tags. Within each table row, <td> tags define table data cells — the boxes in which you type data.

When you use the <table> tag without any optional attributes, the Web browser creates a borderless table with a small amount of space between the table data cells and a small amount of padding within each cell. You can change these values by adding the optional border,

cellspacing, and cellpadding attributes to the opening <table> tag. In addition, you can specify the width of the table using the width attribute, which you can set to a specific pixel value or a percentage of the Web browser window.

Although not intended for layout purposes, HTML tables offer a way to create stable, structured pages and more visually pleasing designs. However, CSS styles, covered in Chapter 4, provide much more precise control of the various Web page components.

Create a Table

Create a Table

1 Open a document in your HTML editor.

2 Type opening and closing <table> tags.

3 Add a set of table row tags for each row.

4 Within each table row, insert <td> tags with text entries for those cells.

Note: Each row should contain the same number of table cells.

5 Save the document as a text-only file with the .htm or .html extension.

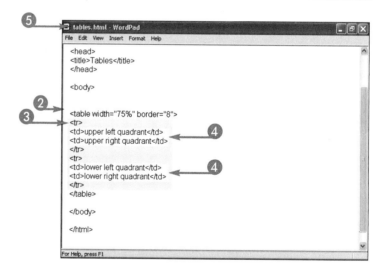

6 Open the document in your Web browser.

● Your Web browser displays the table with its default settings for cellspacing and cellpadding.

● By default, the cellspacing attribute on the table is two pixels.

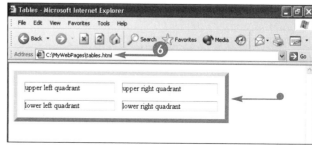

Specify Spacing in the Table

⑦ Open the HTML document in your HTML editor.

⑧ Add `cellpadding` and `cellspacing` attributes to the `<table>` tag and set their values.

⑨ Set the `border` to the desired number of pixels

⑩ Save the document.

⑪ Open the document in your Web browser.

● Your Web browser displays the table, reflecting your changes.

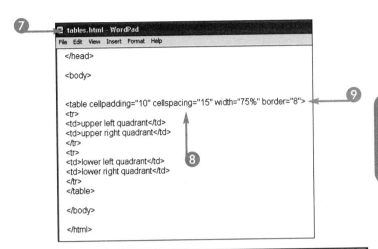

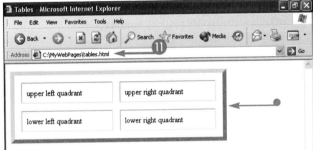

Is possible to to add a caption to my table?

▼ Yes. You can use the `<caption>` tag to add a caption that appears above the table. For example, `<caption>Table 3.2 Ingredients</caption>` displays the text "Table 3.2 Ingredients" above the table. HTML also offers a `<tbody>` tag to collectively tag the table body elements, as opposed to the table head or heads, and a `<tfoot>` tag to add a table footer.

Can I place one table inside another?

▼ Yes. You can nest tables within other tables. To nest tables, insert the additional table inside an existing table data cell, just as you would insert text or an image into the table. Nested tables can be somewhat difficult to control in the limited amount of space available in most Web browser windows.

Do I have to include content in every table data cell?

▼ Yes. A table with empty data cells is unstable and tends to lose the cell borders, which makes the table appear broken. If you do not want any visible content in the table cell, use a non-breaking space entity, ` ` as a filler. With a non-breaking space, the cell borders remain intact.

Adjust Rows and Columns

HTML provides some control over the structure of a table. However, many of the presentation attributes for tables have been deprecated, including the `align` attribute for aligning the table left, right, or center, and the `bgcolor` attribute for setting the background color. Most of the attributes for controlling the overall structure of the table and position entries inside cells are still available. You can add these attributes to both the `<tr>` and `<td>` tags to specify the table height and width, to extend cells across multiple rows and columns, and to make other structural changes.

You can stretch the content of a cell across multiple columns or rows by including the `colspan` or `rowspan`

attribute within the opening `<td>` tag. For example, if you want one cell to stretch across four columns, you can add a `colspan=4` attribute to that `<td>` tag.

You can add the `align` and `valign` attributes in the `<td>` or `<tr>` tags to control the alignment of text within cells. The `align` attribute supports the values `"left"`, `"right"`, `"center"`, and `"justify"` as well as `"char"`, which aligns text on a specific character. The `valign` attribute supports the values `"top"`, `"bottom"`, `"middle"`, and `"baseline"`. For example, `<tr align="center" valign="middle">` centers text in the middle of each cell in the row.

Adjust Rows and Columns

1. Open or create an HTML document that contains a table.

2. Set the `cellpadding`, `cellspacing`, and `width` attributes to the desired values.

3. Set the `border` attribute to specify the border width in pixels.

   ● You can set the `border` attribute to `"0"` to display a table without borders.

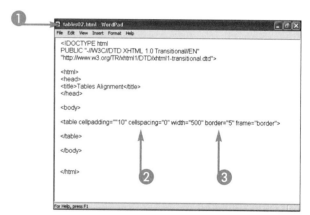

4. Add the `height`, `align`, or `valign` attributes to the table row tags.

5. For the first table data cell, set the `rowspan` attribute to the number of rows the cell should span and set the `width` attribute to equal `"100"`.

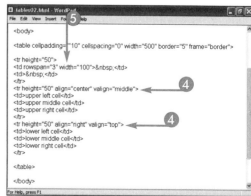

62

6 Set the `colspan` attribute to the number of columns the cells should span.

7 Save the document as a text-only file with the .htm or .html extension.

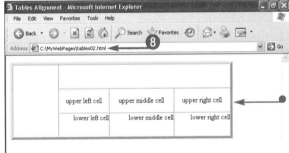

8 Open the document in a Web browser.

● The table reflects your changes.

Can I apply CSS properties to table rows and cells?

▼ Yes. You can create style rules or use the `id` and `class` attributes with both `<tr>` and `<td>` tags in order to reference style properties. CSS provides properties for changing the background color, text color, padding within the cells, border thickness and style, and other qualities of a table. For more information on using CSS, see Chapter 4.

How do I define column headings within a table?

▼ Use `<th>` tags in the top cells to mark column headings and in the leftmost cells to mark row headings. These tags are similar to `<td>` tags, except that the Web browser displays the text within these cells as bold and may align the content differently. For additional formatting options, you can define a CSS style rule for the `<th>` tag.

Can I change the border that surrounds the entire table?

▼ Yes. Add the `frame` attribute to the table and set its value to equal the sides on which you want the frame to appear: `"void"` (no frame), `"above"` (top), `"below"` (bottom), `"hsides"` (top and bottom), `"lhs"` (left side), `"rhs"` (right side), `"vsides"` (left and right sides), `"box"` or `"border"` (around the table). The `border` attribute must accompany the `frame` attribute to specify the border width.

Add Comments

HTML provides a way to insert text that does not appear when a Web browser opens and displays your page. By marking text as a comment, you can include notes to yourself or, if you collaborate on creating the page, you can add notes to other members of your team. Comments are also useful for preventing older Web browsers from displaying script or style elements. Some older Web browsers that do not support the <script> and <style> tags may display the text inside those tags. Commenting out the <script> and <style> tags prevents the Web browser from displaying the text, but the Web browser can still read and use the tags.

To mark text as a comment, you simply place the text that you want to hide within comment tags, <!– and –> . You must include a space after the initial comment tag and another space before the end tag.

Although Web browsers do not display any code that you place within comment tags, the comments and enclosed elements are still part of the source code and remain accessible to any visitor who views your source code.

Add Comments

1. Open a document in your HTML editor.

2. Insert the opening comment indicator <!– followed by a space.

3. Type your comment.

4. At the end of the comment, insert a space followed by a closing comment indicator –>.

5. Save the document as a text-only file with the .htm or .html extension.

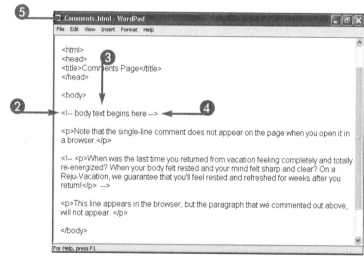

6. Open the document in your Web browser.

- The Web browser does not display the text that you typed between the comment indicators.

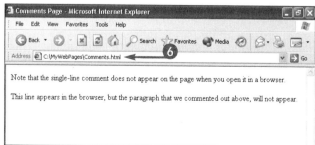

Insert Special Characters

Y ou can type most characters, including special characters, such as dollar signs ($), pound signs (#), and "at" signs (@). However, keyboards do not contain keys for inserting some common symbols, such as the copyright symbol (©) or the cents (¢) sign. HTML refers to these symbols as *character entities*. Character entities also include language diacritical marks, mathematical symbols, and brackets that identify HTML tags (< >).

You can include special symbols, signs, characters, and diacritical marks by typing HTML character entity codes into your document. The code typically starts with an ampersand symbol (&) followed by a number and then a

semicolon. For more common symbols and diacritical marks, HTML provides an optional keyword code in place of the number. When the Web browser sees the code for a character entity, it replaces the code with the appropriate symbol.

For example, to have a Web browser display the copyright symbol (©), you can type **©** or **©** in your HTML file. If you want to display an angle bracket on your page, you can type **&#lt;** or **<** for a less-than sign, and **&#gt;** or **>** for a greater-than sign. See Appendix A for a list of character entities.

Insert Special Characters

① Open a document in your HTML editor.

② Type an HTML name or number entry for the desired character entity.

Note: *Refer to Appendix A for a list of character entities that have name codes.*

③ Save the document as a text-only file with the .htm or .html extension.

④ Open the document in your Web browser.

● The Web browser replaces the character entity code with the character entity it represents.

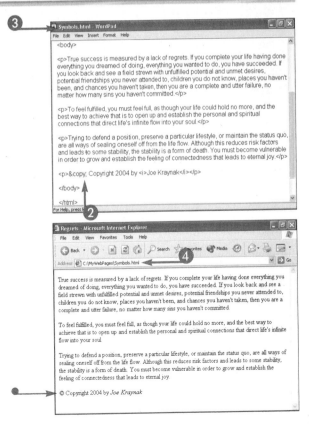

Add \<meta\> Tags

You can add important supplementary information to the head of an HTML document by using a \<meta /> tag. Web browsers do not display any text inside the \<meta /> tag, but the information is still available to visitors who view the source code and to Web browsers and search bots. The tag's name, \<meta />, describes the type of information that the tag contains: meta-information or information about information.

The two most common attributes for the \<meta /> tag are name and content. No predefined name values accompany the name attribute, but two commonly used \<meta /> names are "keywords" and "description". When you use a \<meta /> tag with the keywords name,

you can add a list of descriptive keywords, separated by commas, with the content attribute. When using the description \<meta /> name, you can provide a brief sentence that describes the Web site. You can make this description up to 200 characters long, or approximately 25 words.

Several years ago, search bots used \<meta /> tag keywords and descriptions to index sites and determine their rankings in a search. Now search bots commonly ignore the content of the \<meta /> tags and rely on other data to determine Web page rankings, such as the number of sites that link to your Web pages.

Add \<meta\> Tags

① Open a document in your HTML editor.

② Add a \<meta /> tag with the name attribute set equal to "keywords" and content attribute set equal to a series of keywords.

Note: The \<meta /> tag must appear between the opening and closing \<head\> tags.

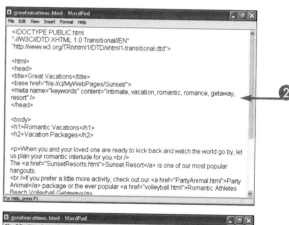

③ Add a second \<meta /> tag with the name attribute set equal to "description" and the content attribute set equal to a brief description of your site.

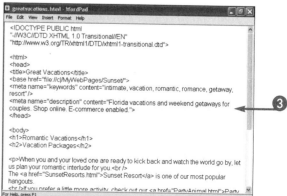

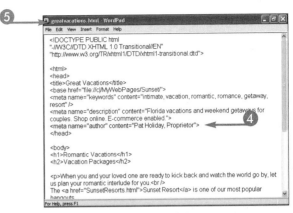

④ Add a third `<meta />` tag with the `name` attribute set equal to `"author"` and the `content` attribute set equal to information about you.

⑤ Save the document as a text-only file with the .htm or .html extension.

⑥ Open the document in your Web browser.

● The Web browser displays the page, although anything inside `<meta />` tags remains hidden.

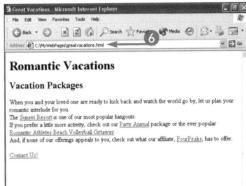

What are some other `<meta />` attributes?

▼ A `<meta />` tag can also accept the `http-equiv` attribute, which sends additional information to the Web browser through the document header. If you set the `http equiv` attribute to equal `"refresh"` and add the `content` attribute, settting it equal to a number of seconds, the Web browser refreshes the page after the specified time period. You can add a URL to the tag to redirect the Web browser to another page after a set period of time. For example `<meta http-equiv="refresh" content="5; URL=http://www.wiley.com">` sends the Web browser to Wiley's home page after five seconds elapse.

Do all search engines use the information in `<meta />` tags?

▼ No. Some indexing search engines index only the keywords or the description content, while others bypass the `<meta />` tags entirely and index words within the actual body content of the page. This is because some people try to trick a search index into giving their pages higher rankings by filling `<meta />` tags with words that Web users often search.

Can I prevent search engines from indexing certain pages?

▼ Yes. You can prevent some search engines from indexing pages by including `<meta name="robots" content="noindex">`. However, this does not work for all search engines.

Understanding CSS Basics

The Cascading Style Sheets (CSS) standard applies a hierarchical layering model to the formatting of text and other Web page elements. Formatting with CSS follows a two-step process. You first create style sheets, which define the style rules that govern the formatting, and then you apply the style rules to text and other elements within the document. This sounds easy enough, but by examining the steps and understanding your options, you can format your Web pages more successfully.

Creating Style Rules

In CSS, you can specify formatting by creating style rules. A *style rule* consists of a *selector,* followed by a *declaration*; for example, in the style rule `p {font-family: arial; color: red; text-align: center}`, p is the selector and `{font-family: arial; color: red; text-align: center}` is the declaration. The *declaration* contains at least one *property,* set to a particular *value,* in the form `{property: value}`. In this example, the declaration sets the value for three properties: `font-family: arial`, `color: red`, and `text-align: center`.

You can include this style in an external style sheet and link one or more Web pages to that style sheet to apply the style to *all* paragraphs in *all* of those pages. You can insert the style rule in an internal style sheet of a page to apply the formatting to *all* paragraphs in this page *only*.

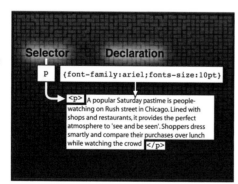

Using Class and ID Selectors

In both external and internal style sheets, you can compose style rules that apply to a class or ID rather than to all HTML elements of a particular type. The class selector enables you to create multiple style rules for a given HTML element. For example, you can create three paragraph classes — `p.left {text-align: left}`, `p.center {text-align: center}`, and `p.right {text-align: right}`. You can then add the `class` attribute to a paragraph's opening tag to specify which class you want to apply, for example `<p class="center">`.

You can also create a class that is not associated with any given HTML element by omitting the HTML element designation from the selector. For example, you can create a `.center {text-align: center}` class, which you can then apply to any text element, such as paragraphs, headings, addresses, and definitions.

The ID selector is similar to the class selector, but it uses a pound sign (#) instead of a period, and it applies formatting to only a single occurrence of a specific HTML element. For example, you can apply `p#footer {font-size: small; font-style: italic}` to a paragraph at the bottom of a page to display the paragraph as a footer in small, italicized text.

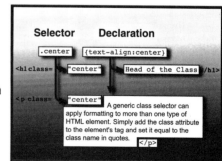

Linking to External Style Sheets

In order for a Web browser to apply the style rules defined in an external style sheet to your Web pages, you must add a link near the top of each Web page that specifies the location and name of the style sheet. To link to a style sheet, you insert a `<link />` tag between the opening and closing `<head>` tags near the top of the page. The resulting code looks like this:

```
<head>
<link rel="style sheet" type="text/css"
href="formats.css" />
</head>
```

If you store the style-sheet file in the same directory as the Web pages that link to it or in a directory you specified using the `<base>` tag, you can set the `href` attribute equal to the style sheet's filename. Otherwise, you must specify its location, in addition to its filename, for example `href="formatting/styles/formats.css"`.

Adding Internal Style Sheets

You can add internal style sheets to a Web page by typing your style rules near the top of the page, rather than in a separate file. The style rules use the same syntax as if you were to include them in an external style sheet: `selector {property: value}`. The selector can be the name of an HTML element, a class selector, or an ID selector. An opening `<style>` tag precedes the style rules, and a closing `</style>` tag marks the end of the style sheet.

Applying Formatting with Styles

Style rules that use the names of HTML elements as their selectors automatically apply formatting to the specified elements. For example, `body {color: yellow}` automatically makes the Web page background yellow. However, Web browsers do not automatically apply style rules that define a class or ID selector.

HTML includes two attributes, `class` and `id`, that you can use to apply styles to individual HTML elements. To apply formatting associated with a class selector, you can add the `class` attribute to the HTML element's opening tag and set it equal to the desired class, for example `<p class="center">`. You can use the `id` attribute in exactly the same way: `<p id="footer">`. Remember to use `id` only to format a single instance of an element on a page.

HTML also provides two tags, `<div>` and `<span>`, for applying styles to selected text within an HTML element. You can use opening and closing `<div>` tags to mark the beginning and end of a section that you want to format. Include the `class` or `id` attribute in the opening `<div>` tag to specify the styles that you want to apply to the division. Use `<span>` tags in the same way to format selected text within a paragraph.

HTML also supports the `style` attribute, which you can use to apply inline styles. You can set the `style` attribute equal to one or more style declarations in the form `property: value`, for example `<p style="text-align: center; font-size: large">`. Because inline styles mix formatting with content, which CSS is designed to avoid, you should use inline styles sparingly, if at all.

Create and Link to an External Style Sheet

You can define style rules and apply them to multiple Web pages by creating an external style sheet and linking HTML documents to it. External style sheets are text-only documents with a .css filename extension. They contain the style rules that you want to apply to one or more HTML documents.

This section shows how to create a CSS file and link HTML documents to it, but it does not show you how to structure your style-rule definitions. You can refer to the sections, "Define Tag-Selector Style Rules," "Define Class-Selector Style Rules," and "Define ID-Selector Style Rules," for details. Also, you can refer to Appendix B for a list of CSS properties and values.

You can use the `<link />` tag to attach a style sheet to an HTML document. Within the `<link />` tag, you must include the `href` attribute and indicate the location of the style sheet on the Web server. In addition, you must include the `type="text/css"` attribute and the `rel="stylesheet"` attribute with the `<link>` tag. The `rel` attribute indicates the relationship of the linked document to the HTML document.

Create a Style Sheet

① Open a new document in your HTML editor.

② Define style rules for one or more HTML elements.

Note: *Refer to other sections in this chapter and to Appendix B for instructions on defining style rules.*

③ Save the document as a text-only file, adding the .css filename extension.

● Your document is saved.

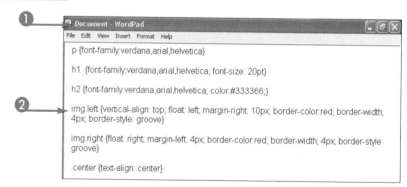

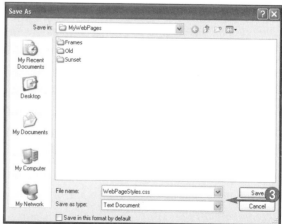

Link to a Style Sheet

1 Open an HTML document in your HTML editor.

2 Add a `<link />` tag between the opening and closing `<head>` tags with an `href` tag that indicates the location and name of the style sheet.

Note: *If you store the style sheet in the same directory as your Web page or in a directory specified by the `<base/>` tag, you need not specify its location, only its name.*

3 Save the HTML document.

4 Open the document in your Web browser.

● The Web browser applies the style rules defined in the linked external style sheet.

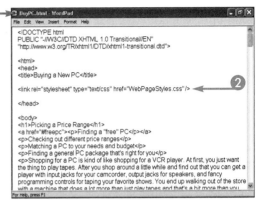

Can I use HTML comments within external style sheets?

▼ No. To add comments, you must use special style comment indicators, which are commonly used in programming. If your style sheet is complex, comments can help remind you which element each style applies to and the way you intended the style to be used. This is especially useful if you collaborate on Web page creation. For more information see the section, "Comment within Style Sheets."

Can I link to more than one external style sheet?

▼ Yes, according to the CSS standard, you can link to more than one style sheet. When a Web browser displays the page, it applies styles from all linked style sheets. If two style sheets contain conflicting style rules, the Web browser follows the last defined rule.

What happens if a style rule in my external style sheet conflicts with a rule in my internal style sheet?

▼ Internal style rules take precedence over rules defined in external style sheets. However, if a style rule in an external style sheet specifies a format that the internal style sheet does not specify, the Web browser applies that format. For example, if the external style sheet contains a style rule `p {color: red; font-size: large; text-align: center}` and the internal style sheet contains `p {color: blue; text-align: right}`, then paragraphs appear blue and right-aligned, but the text size is large.

Create an Internal Style Sheet

You can set style properties for an entire HTML document by using an internal style sheet. You define an internal style sheet within the head of the document. Any styles that have an HTML element name as the selector automatically apply their formatting to every occurrence of the element in the document.

You can apply style rules for class or ID selectors to any HTML elements by adding the `class` or `id` attribute to the element's opening tag and setting the attribute equal to the class or ID name. For more information, see the sections "Define Class-Selector Style Rules" and "Define ID-Selector Style Rules." To apply styles to selected text, see the section "Set Style Properties with `<div>` and `<span>` Tags."

An internal style sheet can include the same type of style rules that you define in an external style sheet. The only difference is that in an internal style sheet, you must precede the style-rule definitions with an opening `<style>` tag and follow the last definition with a closing `</style>` tag to instruct Web browsers that this section of the source code is a style sheet. You should also enclose your style rules with HTML comment indicators so that older Web browsers do not display the text. See the section "Comment within Style Sheets."

Create an Internal Style Sheet

① Open an HTML document in your HTML editor.

② Between the opening and closing `<head>` tags, add an opening `<style>` tag with `type="text/css"`.

③ Add HTML comment tags to hide style rules from older browsers.

④ Add the closing `</style>` tag.

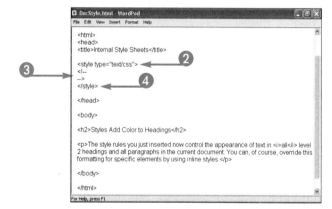

⑤ Define style rules for one or more HTML elements in the document.

Note: *Refer to other sections in this chapter and to Appendix B for instructions on defining style rules.*

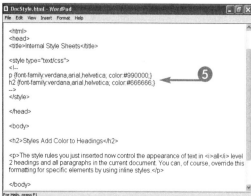

⑥ Save the document as a text-only file with the .htm or .html filename extension.

Note: Even though the document contains CSS styles, it is an HTML document, not a CSS document.

⑦ Open the document in a CSS-compliant Web browser.

Note: Most new Web browsers support most CSS styles, but some styles may not function in all Web browsers.

● Your Web browser opens and displays the page, applying the formatting as specified in the internal style sheet.

Styles Add Color to Headings

The style rules you just inserted now control the appearance of text in *all* level 2 headings and all paragraphs in the current document. You can, of course, override this formatting for specific elements by using inline styles.

Can I override the style rules that the internal style sheet defines?

▼ Yes, you do so by using an inline style, as shown in the section "Apply Inline Styles." However, you should do this sparingly, because keeping format and content separate is usually more efficient. A better way to selectively apply styles is to use the class or ID selector, as shown in the sections "Define Class-Selector Style Rules" and "Define ID-Selector Style Rules."

Besides `text/css`, what other values can I use for the `type` attribute?

▼ Currently the only other value that you can use with the `type` attribute is `"text/javascript"`. However, you typically use this value only in `<script>` tags. When you use it in the `<style>` tag, set the type attribute to `"text/css"`.

What attributes can I add to the opening `<style>` tag?

▼ Optional attributes for the `<style>` tag include `title`, `media`, `dir`, and `lang`. Use the `media` attribute to indicate the type of display for which the style sheet is intended. Possible media values include `screen`, `tty` (teletype), `tv`, `projection`, `handheld`, `print`, `braille`, and `speech`. You use the `dir` attribute to indicate the direction of any text set with the `title` attribute, and you can set it to either `ltr` (left-to-right) or `rtl` (right-to-left). The `lang` attribute specifies the language for the `<style>` tag title and accepts two-character ISO language names, such as "en" for English.

Apply Inline Styles

HTML 3.02 introduced many presentation tags and attributes that format HTML elements. For example, using the `<basefont>` tag, you set the font color, typeface, and size for all of the body text — any text bracketed by `<p>` tags. You can also add the `bgcolor` attribute to the opening `<body>` tag to specify a background color for your document.

HTML 4.01 deprecates almost all presentation tags and attributes, but CSS offers the same capability through *inline styles*. In the opening element tag, you can add the `style` attribute set equal to one or more style properties, each with a corresponding value. For example, you can make a

single paragraph appear italicized, red, and indented from both the left and right margins. The resulting source code looks like this:

```
<p style="font-style: italic; color: red;
margin-left: 10; margin-right: 10">
</p>
```

Using inline style attributes delivers few advantages. Unlike style rules defined in internal and external style sheets, inline styles apply to only one element. In addition, to change the style attributes, you must edit each individual tag rather than alter a single global style rule. For these reasons, you should use inline styles sparingly, if at all.

Apply Inline Styles

1 Open an HTML document in your HTML editor.

Note: For more information about creating HTML documents, see Chapter 3.

2 Type an opening tag for an HTML element that you want to format with an inline style.

Note: This example uses an inline style to format a paragraph.

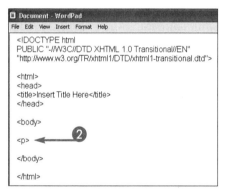

3 Type a space followed by the `style` attribute set equal to the style properties and values that you want to apply.

- This example uses `<p style="color: #cc0000">` to set the text color to red.

4 Type a paragraph and a closing `</p>` tag.

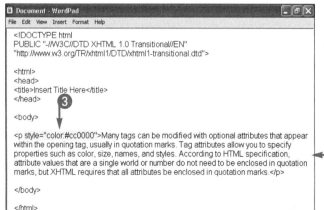

⑤ Save the document as a text-only document, adding an .htm or .html filename extension.

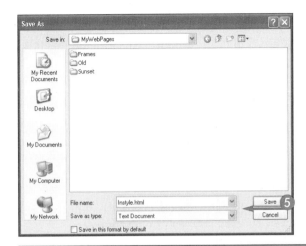

⑥ Open the document in your Web browser.

● The HTML element appears formatted with the inline style.

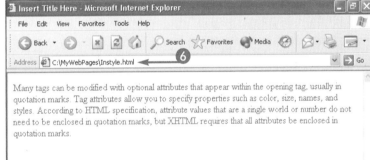

Where can I find color codes for the CSS color property?

▼ You can use a wide variety of colors in your Web pages to control the appearance of text, links, and backgrounds. CSS supports several named colors, including aqua, black, blue, fuchsia, gray, green, lime, maroon, navy, olive, purple, red, silver, teal, orange, white, and yellow. You can also use hexadecimal codes, such as #0000FF for blue. Refer to the color chart at the back of this book for additional color codes. Refer to the sections "Define Font Properties" and "Define Hyperlink Properties" for more on changing colors of other elements.

Can I use both inline style attributes and standard HTML tags to control appearance?

▼ Yes, but this further complicates your source code and defeats the purpose of CSS. Some Web authors use HTML presentation tags and attributes, and CSS styles to apply redundant formatting to their documents so that the pages appear as the authors intended in both old and new Web browsers. However, with so many presentation tags and attributes being deprecated, and the latest generation of Web browsers supporting CSS, you have little reason to continue using HTML formatting tags and styles. Use HTML to tag elements, such as headings and paragraphs and CSS to apply the formatting.

Define Tag-Selector Style Rules

You can apply styles to a particular HTML tag by creating a *style rule*. The style rule consists of a *tag selector* and a *style declaration*. The tag selector corresponds to the HTML element's name; for example, the tag selector for the <body> tag is body. The style declaration appears in curly brackets, and includes one or more of the element's properties, each set to a specific value. A tag-selector style rule follows this syntax:

```
selector {property: value; property: value;
property: value}
```

You can apply styles to multiple HTML tags by defining a list of selectors. For example, to apply the same style to multiple levels of headings, you can list the heading tags to which you want the style to apply, including a comma between each tag. This technique, called *grouping*, follows this syntax:

```
selector1,selector2,selector3 {property:
value; property: value; property: value}
```

You can include tag-selector style rules in internal or external style sheets. Refer to the sections "Create and Link to an External Style Sheet" and "Create an Internal Style Sheet." When defining tag-selector style rules in an internal style sheet, you must ensure that you insert the rules between the opening and closing <style> tags.

Define Tag-Selector Style Rules

① Display an internal or external style sheet in your HTML editor.

● This example shows style rules defined in an internal style sheet.

② Add a tag selector.

③ Add a style declaration that sets the value of at least one of the element's properties.

④ Save the style sheet or HTML document.

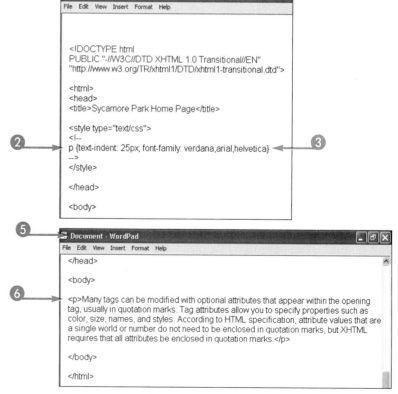

⑤ In your HTML editor, create or open an HTML document that you want to format with styles.

Note: *If you added the tag-selector style rule to an external style sheet, the HTML document must link to that style sheet.*

⑥ Make sure the HTML document has an element that corresponds to the tag-selector style rule that you defined.

7 Save the HTML document as a text-only file, adding the .htm or .html filename extension.

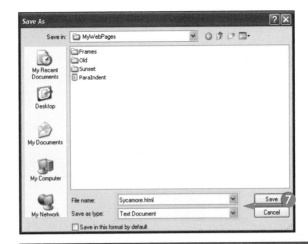

8 Open the HTML document in your Web browser.

- The Web browser displays the document, reflecting the formatting defined by the tag-selector style rule.

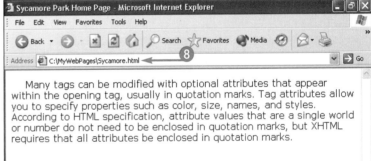

Are style rules case-sensitive?

▼ No, Web browsers that support style sheets ignore whether style rules are uppercase or lowercase. However, when using the style attribute to apply an inline style, type the attribute in all lowercase characters. For consistency, this book recommends that you type style rule definitions in lowercase characters, as well.

I have a style rule that defines several properties. Can I place each property on a separate line?

▼ Yes. Many Web authors like to place each property on its own line to make the style-rule definitions more readable. The syntax remains the same, but you press the Enter key after each value:

```
p
{
property: value;
property: value;
property: value;
}
```

Does CSS offer any way to apply a different style rule to a tag set that is nested in another tag set?

▼ Yes, with CSS, you can use a *contextual tag selector* to apply a different style rule to an HTML element when you embed the element in another element. For example, if you have `<h2>` headings that include emphasized `<em>` text, you can define a style rule such as `h2 em {color:blue; background-color: yellow}` to display blue text on a yellow background. In this case, the style applies only to `<em>` tagged text that is nested inside an `<h2>` tagged heading.

Define Class-Selector Style Rules

C lasses enable you to set two or more styles for a particular element and then apply whichever style you choose to each occurrence of the element. For example, you can create two classes of paragraphs, `p.right {text-align: right}` and `p.center {text-align: center}`, and then quickly format a paragraph by typing the desired class in the opening `<p>` tag, for example `<p class="center">`.

Unlike style rules associated with tag selectors, style classes do not automatically apply formatting to every instance of an HTML tag. Instead, you reference classes explicitly by

adding the `class` attribute to the opening tag of each HTML element that you want to format.

To define class-selector style rules, you indicate the tag selector and then add a period and a class name, such as `p.center` or `h2.green`. You must omit the tag name if you want to apply the style rule to different HTML elements. For example, you can create a class named `.center` for centering headings, paragraphs, and other elements. Class names can contain letters, numbers, and hyphens, but they must always begin with a letter.

Define Class-Selector Style Rules

1. Display an internal or external style sheet in your HTML editor.

Note: *This example shows style rules defined in an internal style sheet.*

2. Type a class name.

3. Add a style declaration that sets the value of at least one of the class properties.

4. Save the style sheet or HTML document.

5. In your HTML editor, open an HTML document that you want to format with the new class.

6. Add the `class` attribute to the opening tag of an element that you want the class style rule to format.

Note: *If you added the class-selector style rule to an external style sheet, make sure the HTML document links to that style sheet. See the section "Create and Link to an External Style Sheet" for more information.*

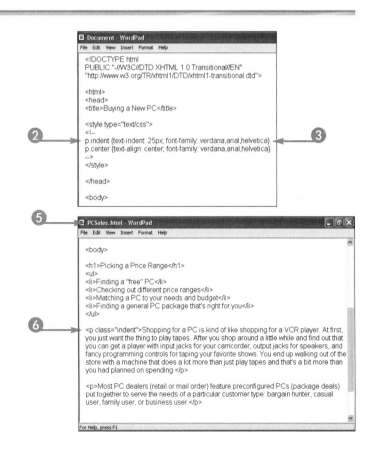

7 Save the HTML document as a text-only file, adding the .htm or .html filename extension.

8 Open the HTML document in your Web browser.

● The Web browser displays the document, reflecting the formatting defined by the class-selector style rule.

Can I use contextual style rules with class names?

▼ Yes, you can include classes to define a contextual selector. Using contextual selectors, you can apply different formatting to a specific element when that element is nested inside another element. For example, you can create a `.caution` style rule like this: `.caution {color: red; font-size: xx-large}` to display warnings in large, red type by adding the `class="caution"` attribute to an element's opening tag. You can create a contextual style rule to display warnings in tables in small type: `td .caution {font-size: small}` This affects only table data entries marked with a `<td class="caution">` tag.

If I create a style rule for an HTML tag and then create classes for the tag, do the style rules for the tag apply to the classes?

▼ Yes. Classes *inherit* the style rules defined in the main tag rule. For example, if you define the `color` property for the `p` element, this color carries over to any `p` classes that you create. However, you can override this inheritance by specifying different values for the same property within the class-selector style declaration. For example, you can add a `color` property to a class-selector style declaration that overrides the `color` property set in a tag-selector style declaration.

Define ID-Selector Style Rules

You can define ID-selector style rules to apply formatting to a specific HTML element that appears only once in a document. The ID-selector style rule is useful for formatting unique elements in a document, such as a header or footer, but in most cases, you can use a class-selector style rule to apply the same style.

The ID-selector style rule follows the same syntax as the class-selector style rule, except that, instead of using a period to designate an ID name, you use a pound sign (#). For example, you can define a body ID such as

`body#fancy {background-color: #cc9900}`. You then include the `id` attribute within the `<body>` tag and set the value to "fancy" to apply the style rule to the document.

An ID-selector style rule within a document is supposed to be unique to a specific tag, so in theory you cannot apply an ID-selector style rule to multiple tags. In practice, some Web browsers allow you to apply the same ID-selector style rule to multiple tags, while others do not. In most cases, period-defined class-selector style rules are a better solution.

---

① Display an internal or external style sheet in your HTML editor.

Note: This example shows style rules defined in an internal style sheet.

② Type an ID name.

③ Add a style declaration that sets the value of at least one of the element's properties.

④ If you edited an external style sheet, save the file.

⑤ If you edited an external style sheet, open the HTML document that contains the element you want to format.

⑥ Add the `id` attribute to an HTML tag for an element that you want the ID-selector style rule to format, and set `id` equal to the ID selector.

⑦ Save the HTML document as a text-only file, adding the .htm or .html filename extension.

● When you view the page in a Web browser, the ID-selector style is applied to the tag that references it.

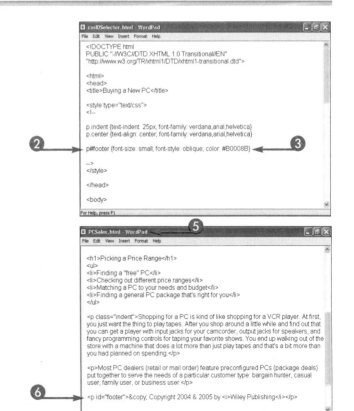

Set Style Properties with <div> and <span> Tags

You can apply styles to divisions of text, rather than specific HTML elements, by using the HTML <div> and <span> tag sets along with class-selector style rules. The opening <div> or <span> tag must contain a class attribute set equal to a class name that is defined in an external or internal style sheet.

The <div> element divides an HTML page into organizational pieces in the same way that you divide an article into a headline, byline, lead paragraph, and body sections. You can use <div> tags to organize a Web page

in a similar fashion and then apply styles to each division by adding the class attribute to the opening <div> tag.

You can use <span> tags to format a specific portion of text rather than an entire element. For example, you may want to apply a different style to one sentence or a few words, rather than an entire paragraph. You can do this by bracketing the text with an opening and closing <span> tag and then referencing a style class through the class attribute. You can even nest <span> tags within other <span> tags.

Set Style Properties with <div> and <span> Tags

① At the beginning of a section or a portion of text, add an opening <div> or <span> tag with a class attribute set equal to a class selector that you defined.

② Type a closing </div> or </span> tag at the end of the section or portion of text.

③ Save the document as a text-only file with the .htm or .html filename extension.

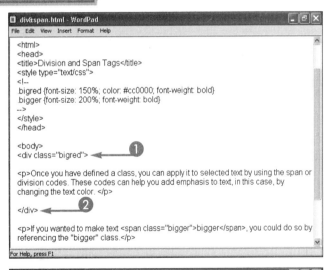

④ Open the document in your Web browser.

● The style applies only to the text contained within in the <div> or <span> tags.

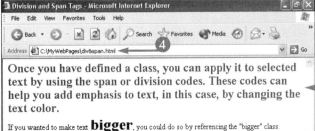

Comment within Style Sheets

Style sheets can become quite complex when you attempt to execute a sophisticated design. To help you keep track of the effects of particular style rules and details about your design strategy, you can add comments to your style sheets. Comments are especially useful when you collaborate on a design with other authors.

Chapter 3 shows you how to use HTML comment indicators <!- -> to mark comments in an HTML document. You can use these same comment indicators to hide comments in your internal style sheets, but they do not work in external style sheets. For external style sheets, you must bracket your comments with CSS comment indicators.

Style comments, like those in C programming, begin with a forward slash and an asterisk (/*), and end with another asterisk and forward slash (*/). Web browsers do not process any text within style comment, treating it as white space.

You can use comments to organize your style rules and provide additional annotation to explain how you are implementing individual styles. If you define several classes, note the proper application of each class within the HTML document.

Comment within Style Sheets

① Display an internal or external style sheet in your HTML editor.

② In an internal style sheet, add HTML comment indicators to hide the style rules from old browsers.

③ Add an opening CSS comment indicator.

④ Type your comment.

⑤ Type a closing CSS comment indicator.

⑥ Save the file.

⑦ Open an HTML document in your Web browser that contains the internal style sheet or that links to the external style sheet that contains the comment.

● The Web browser displays the page but does not display any comments.

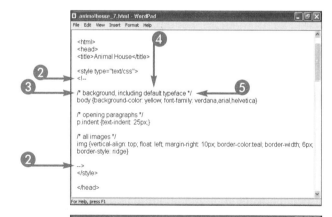

Assign CSS Color Values

With CSS, you can add color to most HTML elements, including headings, paragraphs, backgrounds, and borders. Some properties, such as `background-color` and `border-color`, specifically call for a color value. For other elements, such as heading or paragraph text, you can add the `color` property to the style declaration and set its value to the desired color.

You specify a color using a color name, a hexadecimal value, or a mix of the primary colors red, green, and blue. W3C CSS standards support 17 named colors: aqua, black, blue, fuchsia, gray, green, lime, maroon, navy, olive, orange, purple, red, silver, teal, white, and yellow. Simply type the color name as the property value, for example `p {color: purple}`. Hex values are six-character codes that represent colors, for example, #0000FF for blue. Refer to the color chart included with this book for additional hex-value color codes.

To mix colors, type the amount of each primary color expressed as a number from 0 to 255; for example, `p {color: rgb(192,192,192)}` produces a medium shade of gray. Because accurately guessing how a color will display based on a combination of three numbers is difficult, most Web authors commonly use color names and pre-defined codes to add color.

Assign CSS Color Values

① Display an internal or external style sheet in your HTML editor.

② Add a style rule that includes a color property and a color value.

Note: *Refer to the color chart included with this book for hexadecimal color values.*

③ Save the style sheet or html document.

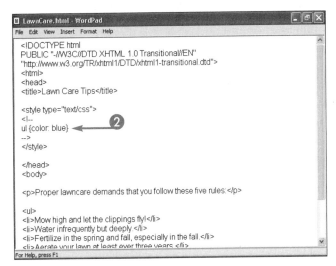

④ Open an HTML document that the color property applies to in your Web browser.

Note: *This document must contain the style rule or link to the external style sheet that contains the style rule.*

● The element appears in the specified color.

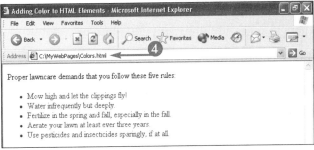

Assign CSS Measurement Values

CSS measurement values, commonly called *lengths*, specify size or distance. You can use measurement values to specify the size of a wide range of elements, including font sizes and border length and width. You can also use measurement values to specify distances, such as margins, object positions, word spacing, padding, and line spacing.

When entering measurement values, you must enter a numerical value followed by a unit. Unit identifiers include: em (width of an M in the active font), ex (height of an x in the active font), px (pixels), in (inches), cm (centimeters), mm (millimeters), pt (points), pc (picas), and % (percentage of an element's size).

Using measurement values, you can create style rules that specify font sizes for various text elements, for example, h1 {font-size: 20pt} or body {font-size: 10pt}. You can also create a style rule that sets paragraphs to indent three "em spaces" by entering p {text-indent: 3em}. Other sections in this chapter show specific applications of these measurement values.

You can also enter negative values to subtract lengths and distances. For example, you can enter a negative margin-bottom setting for a heading, in order to provide less space between the heading and the paragraph that follows it.

Assign CSS Measurement Values

1 Display an internal or external style sheet in your HTML editor.

2 Add a style rule that includes a property that calls for a measurement value.

3 Save the style sheet or HTML document.

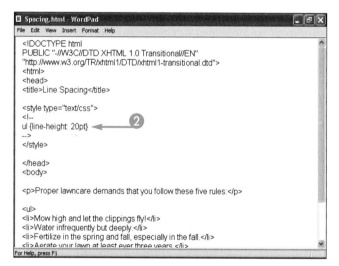

4 Open an HTML document that the measurement property applies to in your Web browser.

Note: This document must contain the style rule or link to the external style sheet that contains the style rule.

● The Web browser displays the element, reflecting the change affected by the measurement property.

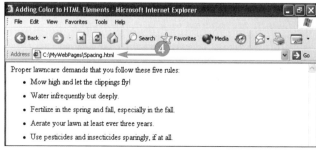

Set Margins

CSS supports five margin properties: `margin`, `margin-bottom`, `margin-left`, `margin-right`, and `margin-top`. You can set individual margins for each edge of an element separately, or you can use the shorthand `margin` property to set margins for multiple sides of an element. To set all four margins at once, use the `margin` property with a single value, for example `margin: 0px`. If you include two values, such as `margin: 10px 20px`, the first value controls the top and bottom margins, while the second value controls the left and right margins. A `margin` property with three values sets the top, side, and bottom margins in that order. You must include four values to set the top, right, bottom, and left margins.

You can enter `margin` property values as percentages or as measurement units. Percentages specify the margins as a percentage of the element's size. Measurement units can be in: `in` (inches), `cm` (centimeters), `mm` (millimeters), `px` (pixels), `pt` (points), `pc` (picas), `em` (width based on font size), or `ex` (height based on font size).

Can I indent the first line of a paragraph?

▼ Yes. Add the `text-indent` property to the style declaration and set it equal to the amount of space that you want to indent the first line.

Set Margins

① Display an internal or external style sheet in your HTML editor.

② Add a selector to specify the element, class, or ID whose margins you want to set.

③ Add the `margin` properties and assign the desired values to the properties.

④ Save the external style sheet or HTML document.

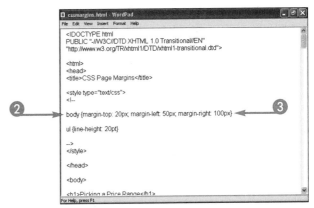

⑤ In your Web browser, open an HTML document to which the `margin` properties apply.

Note: *This document must contain the style rule or link to the external style sheet that contains the style rule.*

● The Web browser displays the margins according to the values set in the style rule.

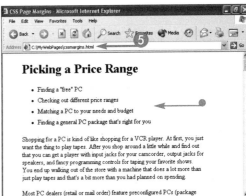

Define Font Properties

You can define font properties in style sheets to control text appearance. The `font-family` property specifies the desired typeface, for example `p {font-family: times-new-roman}`. You include multiple font families, separated by commas, to specify optional fonts, if fonts earlier in the list are unavailable. You can set the size of the font using the `font-size` property, which accepts sizes expressed as points, pixels, percentages, or keywords such as `x-small`, `small`, `medium`, `large`, and `x-large`.

The `font-weight` property is the style-equivalent of the `<b>` tag, and controls the boldness of a font. You can set the value to `normal` or `bold`, or indicate a degree of lightness or boldness by setting the value to a multiple of `100`, with `100` being the lightest and `900` being the boldest.

You can set all font properties using the single `font` property, followed by the value of each font property. You separate the font properties with a space in the following order: `{font: font-style font-variant font-weight font-size line-height font-family}`

For example, you can type **{font: italic small-caps bold 14pt 16pt arial}** to specify the font-style, font-variant, font-weight, font-size, line-height, and font-family, using a single property. If you use multiple `property: value` combinations, separate them with semicolons: `{font-family: arial, tahoma, verdana; font-size: 14pt; line-height: 16pt}`

Define Font Properties

① Display an internal or external style sheet in your HTML editor.

② Add a selector to specify the element, class, or ID whose font you want to define.

③ Add the font properties and assign them the desired values.

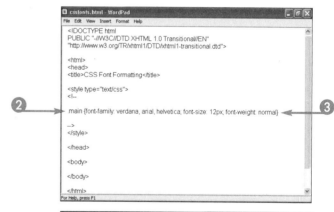

- You can create additional style rules in order to assign different font properties to other elements, classes, or IDs.

- This example shows the `font` property being used to define all font property values.

④ Save the style sheet or HTML document.

⑤ Open an HTML document that the font properties apply to in your HTML editor.

Note: *This document must contain the style rule or link to the external style sheet that contains the style rule.*

⑥ Make sure that the document has HTML tags, classes, or IDs to which the font properties apply.

⑦ Save the HTML document.

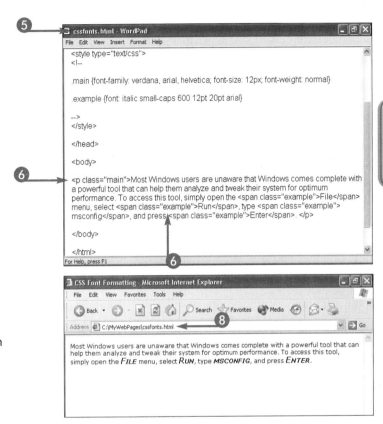

⑧ Open the HTML document in your Web browser.

● The Web browser displays the document, reflecting any formatting changes to which the font properties apply.

Can I include any font name within the `font-family` property?

▼ Yes. You can specify any font and even list several alternative font families by separating their names with commas. If the user does not have the first font installed, the Web browser attempts to use the next font in the font-family list. If a font name has multiple words, such as "Times New Roman," you must enclose that name in quotation marks or use hyphens, for example `times-new-roman`.

Can I indicate generic font types rather than specific fonts?

▼ Yes. The CSS standard supports five generic font types: `serif`, `sans-serif`, `cursive`, `fantasy`, and `monospace`. You can use these font types alone or combine them with font names in your font-family list. By using generic fonts, you give the Web browser more flexibility in choosing a font.

How do I change the color of a font?

▼ Add the `color` property and the value for the desired color to the style declaration for the tag, class, or ID selector. The `color` attribute is not technically associated with font properties, but rather controls the foreground color of an element. You can also set a background color by adding the `background-color` property and setting it to the value for the desired color.

Define Hyperlink Properties

Y ou can control the appearance of links using *pseudo classes*. Unlike class selectors, which separate the tag name and class with a period, pseudo classes use a colon, for example `selector:pseudoclass`. Pseudo classes also have predefined names; you do not make up your own names as you do with classes.

Four pseudo classes control the appearance of hyperlinks: `a:link` defines the general appearance of links on a page, `a:visited` defines the appearance of links that a user has already visited, `a:hover` controls the appearance of a link when the mouse cursor rests on it, `a:active` specifies the link's appearance when a visitor first clicks it. You must

define `a:hover` after `a:link` and `a:visited` to ensure that it functions properly. You must also define `a:active` after `a:hover`.

The style declaration for these pseudo classes typically consists of various font properties combined with the color property. Below is an example of source code that defines styles for all four hyperlink pseudo classes:

```
a:link {color: 000066 }
a:visited {font-weight: lighter; color:
  FF00CC }
a:hover {font-weight: bolder; color:
  9900CC }
a:active {font-weight: bold; color: FF0000 }
```

Define Hyperlink Properties

① Display an internal or external style sheet in your HTML editor.

② Add an `a:link` style rule that defines the desired font or color properties.

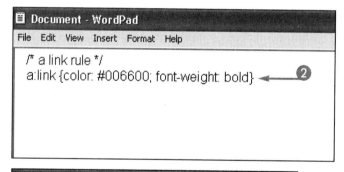

③ Add an `a:visited` style rule that defines the desired font or color properties.

④ Add an `a:hover` style rule that defines the desired font or color properties.

⑤ Add an `a:active` style rule that defines the desired font or color properties.

⑥ Save the HTML document or CSS style sheet.

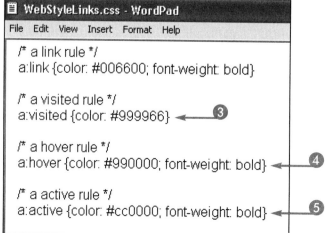

⑦ Open the HTML document that you want the hyperlink pseudo classes to affect in your HTML editor.

Note: This document must contain the style rules or link to the external style sheet that contains the style rules.

⑧ Make sure that the document has at least one hyperlink that you can test.

Note: Chapter 3 shows you how to create hyperlinks.

⑨ Save the HTML document.

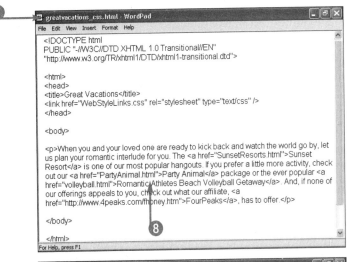

⑩ Open the HTML document in your Web browser.

● Your Web browser displays the document, reflecting any changes in formatting that you applied to the links.

⑪ Position your mouse cursor on a link.

● The link's appearance changes, based on the style declaration that you specified for `a:hover`.

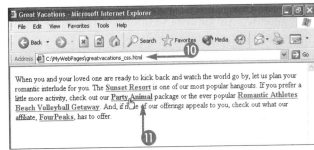

MASTER IT

What if I use a font size or font weight for the `hover` pseudo class that differs from the properties that I set for the other link classes?

▼ If you change the size or weight of the font for one of the dynamic pseudo classes (`active` or `hover`), any text surrounding the link shifts accordingly when the user mouses over or clicks the link. This effect is jarring on slower dial-up connections.

What colors should I not use for hyperlinks?

▼ If you are coding for accessibility, avoid red, green, and blue for hyperlinks, as color-blind visitors may have trouble distinguishing these hues. You can use the `text-decolorization` property to add other types of formatting to links that do not specify a particular color. For example, `text-decolorization=overline` displays a line above the hyperlink text. Setting the `text-decoration` value to `none` removes underlining.

Can I use any other pseudo classes?

▼ Yes. Three additional pseudo classes are available but are rarely used: `:first-child`, `:lang`, and `:focus`. `:first-child` applies formatting to the first child of an element. For example, `div > p:first-child {font-size: x-large}` makes paragraph text inside a division extra large. `:lang` specifies different formatting for a specific language. `:focus` changes the formatting of a selected element that you click on, tab to, or highlight. Support for these psuedo classes varies.

Format Lists

HTML presentation attributes for lists have been deprecated, but you can define CSS style rules to control the appearance of lists. In fact, CSS provides much more precise control over lists than the old HTML attributes. You can use styles to define the appearance of both ordered and unordered lists. Styles can control the type of bullet or number used to mark list items, insert an image in place of a bullet, and change the way that list items indent.

CSS features three list properties: `list-style-image`, `list-style-position`, and `list-style-type`. `list-style-image` specifies an image file to use in place of a bullet or number; for example, `ul {list-style-image:`

`url(teacup.gif)}` tells the Web browser to use the image teacup.gif as the bullet character. `list-style-position` controls the way that text indents from the bullet or number and can be set to `inside` or `outside`. For example, `list-style-position: outside` creates a hanging indent with the bullet or number to the left of the list item, and `list-style-position: inside` indents the bullet or number with the text. `list-style-type` defines the bullet or number type: `circle`, `disc`, `square`, `decimal` (for numbers), `lower-alpha`, `upper-alphadecimal-leading-zero`, `lower-greek`, `lower-latin`, `upper-latin`, `armenian`, `georgian`, `non`, `inherit`, `lower-roman`, and `upper-roman`.

Format Lists

① Display an internal or external style sheet in your HTML editor.

② Add a tag or class selector for ordered lists.

③ Add the desired `list-style` properties and values.

Note: *You can use the `list-style` property as shorthand to define all three values — image, position, and type — in no specific order.*

④ Add a tag or class selector for ordered lists.

⑤ Add the desired `list-style` properties and values.

⑥ Save the style sheet or HTML document.

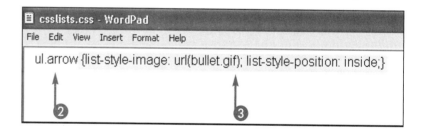

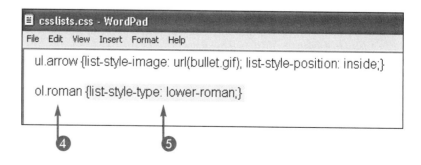

⑦ Open the HTML document that you want the `list-style` rules to affect in your HTML editor.

Note: *This document must contain the style rule or link to the external style sheet that contains the style rule.*

⑧ Make sure the document contains at least one list that the new `list-style` properties can format.

Note: *Chapter 3 shows you how to create lists.*

⑨ Save the HTML document.

⑩ Open the HTML document in your Web browser.

● The Web browser displays the document, reflecting the formatting changes you made using the `list-style` properties.

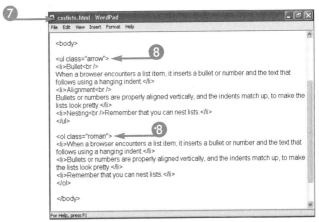

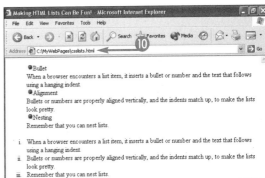

What are the possible values for the `list-style-type` property?

▼ For unordered lists, you can set the `list-style-type` property to `disc`, `circle`, `square`, or `none`. These values replace the HTML `type` attribute values that have been deprecated. For ordered lists, common values are `decimal`, `lower-roman`, `upper-roman`, `lower-alpha`, `upper-alpha`, or `none`. The `decimal` value is the most common, because it enables you to create a numbered list. The other values for ordered lists are more commonly used for creating outlines.

How do Web browsers display lists if they do not support style sheets?

▼ Web browsers that are not CSS-compliant simply ignore style properties and display default HTML lists. Web browsers display unordered lists with the default disk bullet, and ordered lists with the decimal numbering scheme. Most Web browsers, however, are CSS-compliant and should have no trouble displaying your lists as you intend.

Can I use any image as my bullet character?

▼ You typically use very small images as bullet characters to prevent your bullets from taking too long to download and to prevent the bullets from taking up so much space that your list no longer looks like a list. Many clip-art collections contain images specifically designed for use in HTML lists, but you can easily design your own in most graphics programs.

Format Tables

Most of the HTML presentation attributes for tables have been deprecated, but CSS fills the gap, featuring several properties that you can apply to control background colors, borders, alignment of table-data entries, and other elements that make up a table. Most of the properties are not specific to tables, but you can use general properties, such as `border`, `background-color`, `padding`, and `text-align`, to apply all of the desired formatting.

Borders and shading are the two main properties that you can add to a table. You can add them to the entire table by creating a class for the `table` and `td` (table data) elements that set the desired `background-color` property and `border` property values. You can format individual table

data cells, table rows, and table headings. For example, you can create a simple style sheet that contains the following style rules:

```
table {border: 3px groove ridge}
th {background-color: #C0C0C0; font-weight:
  bolder; padding: 4px}
th.ital {background-color: cyan; font-style:
  italic}
td {padding: 4px}
```

This style sheet contains three tag selectors, `table`, `th`, and `td`, that automatically apply their formatting to those three table elements. `th.row` is a class selector that you can apply to individual table data cells by adding the `class="row"` attribute to their `<th>` tags.

Format Tables

① Open or create a Web page that contains a table.

② Add opening and closing `<style>` tags to define an internal style sheet.

③ Add a `table` selector with properties and values to control the overall appearance of the table.

④ Add a `th` selector with properties and values to control the appearance of table headings.

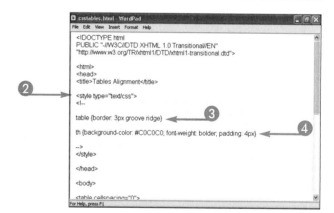

⑤ Add a `th` class selector that defines a background color and font style for row headings.

⑥ Add a `td` selector to specify cell padding for data cells.

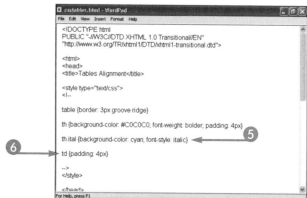

⑦ Save the HTML document you just edited.

⑧ Open the HTML document in your Web browser.

● The Web browser displays the Web page, reflecting the table formatting applied by the CSS styles.

	2003	2004	2005
Gross Income	$500,000	$675,000	$700,000
Expenses	$150,000	$222,000	$275,000
Net Profit	$350,000	$453,000	$425,000

MASTER IT

Can I use the `padding` property to format any other elements?

▼ Yes, you can add padding around any element, including headings, paragraphs, and images, to increase space between the element and neighboring elements. Furthermore, you can apply padding separately to each edge of an object by using the `padding-bottom`, `padding-top`, `padding-left`, and `padding-right` properties.

Can I change the font for the text in my table?

▼ Yes, you can change the font for the entire table or apply fonts to individual elements by adding `font` properties to the style declarations for those selectors. See the section "Define Font Properties" for more details.

Can I wrap text around a table?

▼ When the Web browser encounters a `<table>` tag, it breaks to a new line and displays any surrounding text above or below the table. To wrap text around one side of the table, add the `float` property to the style declaration for the `table` tag selector and set it equal to `left` or `right`. The `left` value moves the table to the left and wraps text around its right side. The `right` value moves the table to the right and wraps text around its left side. Refer to Chapter 5 for more information about wrapping text around objects.

Add Scrolling Elements

ext normally flows freely on a page from one line to the next. The only boundaries it encounters are the edges of the Web browser window. If text extends beyond the edge of the Web browser window, or on the edge of a table cell, the window displays scroll bars so that you can view the rest of the text. With CSS, you can create boxed text elements on Web pages that contain their own scroll bars. These boxes of scrolling text are useful for presenting content such as a user agreement or terms of service.

You can create boxed text by setting width and height limits for a division of text. You can then add the overflow property and set it to scroll to indicate that you want to be able to scroll any additional text into view. Setting the overflow property to scroll adds horizontal and vertical scroll bars to the box so that users can view any content that extends beyond the set dimensions of the element.

Add Scrolling Elements

① Display an internal or external style sheet in your HTML editor.

② Add a new class selector.

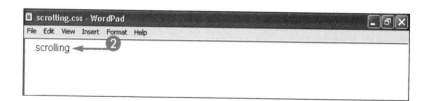

③ Add properties to define the element's dimensions and borders, and set the overflow property to scroll.

Note: Use height and width values to create a box that can display only a limited amount of text.

④ Save the CSS style sheet or HTML document.

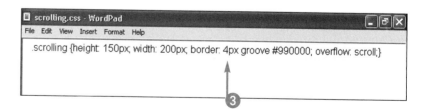

⑤ In your HTML editor, open the HTML document in which you want to add the scrolling element.

⑥ In the body of the document, add an opening `<div>` tag linking to the class selector that you defined.

⑦ Type enough text to exceed what the text box can display.

⑧ Type a closing `<div>` tag.

⑨ Save the HTML document you just edited.

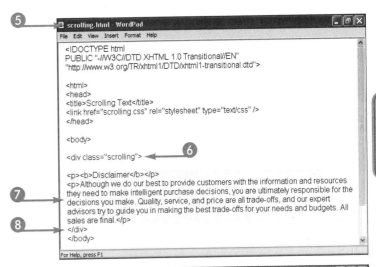

⑩ Open the HTML document in your Web browser.

● The Web browser displays the document, complete with the scrolling text box.

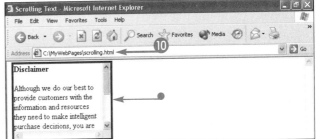

MASTER IT

What are the possible values for the `overflow` property?

▼ The `overflow` property features four values: `visible`, which is the default value, `hidden`, `scroll`, and `auto`. With `overflow` set to `visible`, either the extra content appears outside of the box or the box expands to accommodate the overflow. With the property set to `hidden`, overflow text is clipped and inaccessible to the user. A value of `auto` supplies scroll bars only when necessary. If you do not specify dimensions for the text area, the Web browser creates a box large enough to hold the amount of content present, in which case, setting a scrolling option is unnecessary.

What happens when I set the `overflow` value to `scroll` but the box is large enough to display all of the content?

▼ The Web browser still implements the scroll bars, even with no overflow content to control.

Can I color the border?

▼ Yes, the `border` property can include a color code, border width, and border style (`dashed`, `dotted`, `double`, `groove`, `inset`, `none`, `outset`, `ridge`, `hidden`, or `solid`). The `border` property is actually shorthand for several individual `border` properties: `border-bottom`, `border-bottom-width`, `border-color`, `border-left-width`, `border-right`, `border-right-width`, `border-style`, `border-top`, `border-top-width`, and `border-width`. See Appendix B for available `border` property values.

Position Page Elements

Before style sheets, Web authors had to develop creative ways to control page layout using HTML, a language that was never designed for complex visual layouts. CSS positioning replaces many of the workarounds that HTML authors have resorted to in their efforts to create pleasing visual layouts.

With the `position` property, you can treat every block of text on a page as a separate object, which you can position on the page in a very specific location. This is similar to a desktop publishing program, in which you place various blocks of text on a page, each in its own text box.

You usually set the `position` property to either `relative` or `absolute` and use it in conjunction with offset properties, such as `top`, `right`, `bottom`, and `left`. These offset properties dictate the element's position. Setting the position property to `relative` sets the position of the element relative to its normal location in the document. `absolute` positioning takes the element out of the normal flow and positions it in an exact location measured from the top-left or lower-right corner of the document.

Position Page Elements

① Display an internal or external style sheet in your HTML editor.

② Add a new class selector.

③ Set the `position` property to `absolute` or `relative` and add properties to specify the element's position and dimensions.

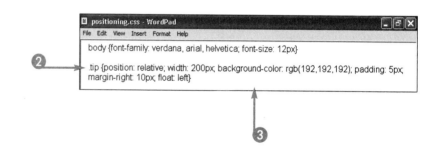

④ Define a second class selector to position another element on the same page.

⑤ Set the `position` property to `absolute` or `relative` and add properties to specify the element's position and dimensions.

⑥ Save the CSS style sheet or HTML document.

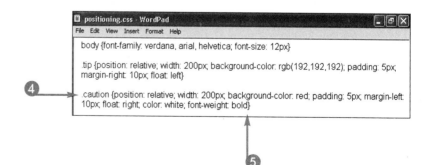

⑦ Open the HTML document that contains the elements that you want to position.

⑧ Add the `class` attribute to the tags of the elements that you want to position.

⑨ Save the HTML document.

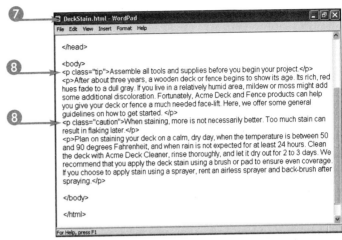

⑩ Open the HTML document in your Web browser.

● The Web browser displays the page, with the elements in the positions that you specified in the style rules.

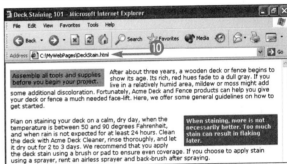

What values does the position property accept?

▼ It accepts `static`, `fixed`, `absolute`, and `relative`. `static`, the default, cannot be used with offset properties. Fixed elements behave much like elements that are set to an absolute position. However, fixed elements are fixed with respect to the screen and should not scroll with the page contents. The `relative` value is especially useful, because it is less likely to result in undesirable overlapping of elements. The element shifts a specified distance from its normal location.

Can I place a box around a division of text?

▼ Yes, you can use the `border` property to have a box appear around the text. Using the border property you can specify a border width, color, and style. See the section "Add Scrolling Elements" for more details and refer to Appendix B for a complete list of border properties and values.

How do I position one element to have other elements flow around it?

▼ The best way to have elements flow around other elements is to use the `float` property. For the element that you want to position, set the `float` property to `left` or `right`. This causes other elements to flow around it, either to the right or the left of the floating element. For any element that you do not want to flow around the floating element, add the `clear` property and set the value to `right`, `left`, or `both`.

Layer Elements with the z-index Property

You can layer and overlap elements by using the z-index property to indicate three-dimensional position. z-index refers to an element's position on the z-axis and is relative to the other elements occupying the same x and y coordinates on the page. Elements with higher z-index values are placed on top of elements with lower z-index values. For example, on a page with two boxes occupying the same x and y positions, the box with a z-index value of 2 is stacked on top of the box with a z-index value of 1.

To make two elements overlap, position the elements and offset them using the top, left, bottom, and right values. Then, use the z-index property to indicate the stacking order. When overlapping two elements, you should set the background color of each element using the background-color property. Otherwise, content within one element spills into the other element.

Using the z-index property, you can build interesting collage effects into your pages. However, when you overlap elements, you must check your pages carefully to ensure that you have not lost any content in the overlap.

Layer Elements with the z-index Property

① Display an internal or external style sheet in your HTML editor.

② Add a new class selector that defines an element's position and dimensions.

③ Add a style declaration that includes a z-index property to display the element on the desired layer.

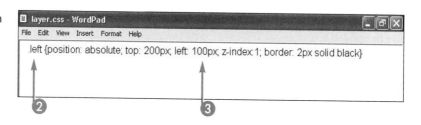

④ Add one or more class-style rules that position elements to overlap.

Note: *Because the amount of overlap depends on the size and dimensions of the elements, you may need to guess at the initial settings and then adjust them later.*

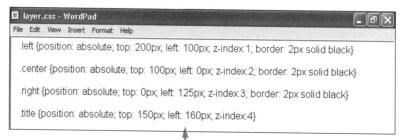

PART II

⑤ Open the HTML document that has elements that you want to overlap in your HTML editor.

⑥ Add the class attribute to the tag for each element that you want to overlap.

⑦ Save the HTML document.

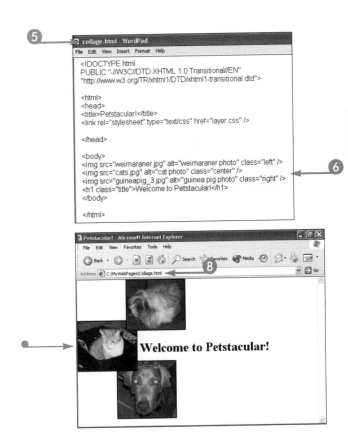

⑧ Open the HTML document in your Web browser.

● The Web browser opens and displays the Web page with the overlapping elements.

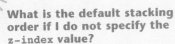

What is the default stacking order if I do not specify the z-index value?

▼ If you do not specify the stacking order, elements stack one on top of the other in the order in which they appear within the HTML code. You can set an element's z-index property to a positive value to move it to a higher layer in the stack. Negative values move elements to lower layers.

What happens when I set the z-index value without adding any position or top-left properties?

▼ The z-index property does not affect the formatting unless the elements are positioned and sharing the same two-dimensional space. Without any explicit positioning, the Web browser simply displays elements according to the normal flow of the page, so they do not overlap and do not require a z-index value.

What happens if two elements share the same z-index value?

▼ In this case, the Web browser reverts back to the default stacking order as if no z-index values are set. This means that the elements are stacked in the order in which they appear in the HTML document. Any element that appears later in a document appears in front of elements that precede it, assuming the objects are positioned to share overlapping x,y coordinates.

Control Visibility

You can use the `visibility` property to control whether elements on a Web page are visible or hidden. Web authors often use this property in conjunction with JavaScript to dynamically control content effects using Dynamic HTML, or DHTML, techniques. The steps in this section demonstrate how you can use a JavaScript script along with the `visibility` property to toggle the display of a boxed note. For more information on JavaScript, see Part 3, "Adding Interactivity with JavaScript."

The `visibility` property accepts three values: `visible`, `hidden`, and `collapse`. The `visible` value, as the name suggests, makes the element display on the page. With a value of `hidden`, the box is not visible, but it still affects layout and occupies space on the page. You can use the `collapse` value with table rows and columns to remove part of the table from the display. For example, you can use this technique to dynamically replace table rows or columns with other content. If you use the `collapse` value with elements other than table rows or cells, it creates the same effect as the `hidden` value.

Control Visibility

① Create an internal style sheet.

② Add an ID selector that defines an element's position and dimensions and sets the `visibility` property to `visible`.

③ Add an ID selector that defines an element's position and dimensions and sets the `visibility` property to `hidden`.

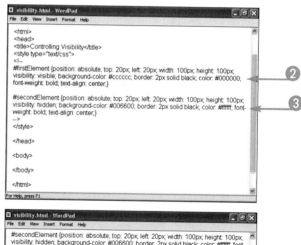

④ Add an opening `<div>` tag that sets the `id` property equal to the ID selector defined in step 2.

⑤ Add a closing `</div>` tag.

Note: The href="#" indicates a link to the top of the current page.

⑥ Add an opening `<div>` tag that sets the `id` property equal to the ID selector defined in step 3.

⑦ Add a closing `</div>` tag.

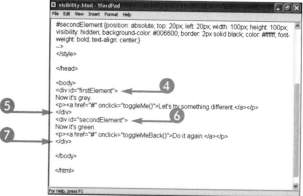

⑧ Add a script to change the `visibility` property.

⑨ Inside each `div` element, add a link to trigger the script event when the user clicks the mouse.

Note: For more information about JavaScript, see Part 3, "Adding Interactivity with JavaScript."

⑩ Save the HTML document.

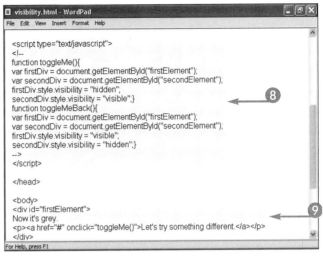

```
visibility.html - WordPad
File  Edit  View  Insert  Format  Help

<script type="text/javascript">
<!--
function toggleMe(){
var firstDiv = document.getElementById("firstElement");
var secondDiv = document.getElementById("secondElement");
firstDiv.style.visibility = "hidden";
secondDiv.style.visibility = "visible";}
function toggleMeBack(){
var firstDiv = document.getElementById("firstElement");
var secondDiv = document.getElementById("secondElement");
firstDiv.style.visibility = "visible";
secondDiv.style.visibility = "hidden";}
-->
</script>

</head>

<body>
<div id="firstElement">
Now it's grey.
<p><a href="#" onclick="toggleMe()">Let's try something different.</a></p>
</div>
For Help, press F1
```

⑪ Open the HTML document in your Web browser.

● When the page loads, the hidden division is transparent.

⑫ Click the link.

● The Web browser hides the initial division, while the second division becomes visible.

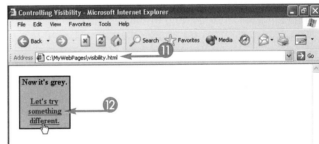

```
Controlling Visibility - Microsoft Internet Explorer
File  Edit  View  Favorites  Tools  Help

Back        Search  Favorites  Media

Address  C:\MyWebPages\visibility.html                    Go

Now it's grey.

Let's try
something
different.
```

What exactly is DHTML?

▼ DHTML stands for *Dynamic HTML* and is a way of combining scripting languages, cascading style sheets, and the Web browser Document Object Model (DOM) to create dynamic changes on a Web page. You can use DHTML to animate elements on a page and to create complex interactive elements such as expandable navigation menus, where clicking a navigation element offers additional buttons or links. To control HTML elements, you must first name the elements you want to control by using the `id` attribute to assign the element a name. Once an object has a name, you can reference it and control it using JavaScript.

Can I control visibility for table rows or columns?

▼ Yes, you can set the `visibility` property to `collapse` to hide a row or column without affecting the actual table structure. The space that the row or column takes up remains available for alternative content if you choose to create a script that makes this content visible. If you apply the `visibility: collapse` value to elements other than table rows or columns, the `collapse` value hides the element, just like the `hidden` value. If your Web page contains layers, you can also control visibility for the overlapping layers. For more on controlling visibility, refer to *JavaScript: A Programmer's Companion from Basic through DHTML, CSS and DOM* by Stefan Koch (John Wiley).

Understanding Web Page Image Basics

The Web was not initially intended to be so visually appealing; Web page authors used the Web to transfer text-based data with a minimum amount of formatting. As the Web developed and Web browsers became more sophisticated, developers added the `<img />` tag to their repertoire to enable Web page authors to insert images on pages.

However, inserting images and displaying them on Web pages was only half of the challenge. Because image files require so much data to display the image properly onscreen, these files can be fairly large and take a long time to transfer over standard modem connections; developers needed to find ways to reduce image file sizes without seriously degrading image quality.

Compressed Image File Formats

You can save images in various file formats, including PCX, TIFF, JPEG, BMP, and GIF. All of these formats provide instructions on how to display the image onscreen and in print. Some image file formats also use compression technology to reduce the size of the image. Because these compressed file formats result in smaller files that travel faster across the Internet, Web browsers require that you use these formats. Most Web browsers support only three image file formats: GIF, JPEG, and PNG. Each of these formats is slightly different, and each has its unique advantages and disadvantages.

GIF Images

GIF, or Graphics Interchange Format, images are the most common images on the Web. This format supports 256 separate colors and includes some additional features such as transparency, interlacing, and animation capabilities.

GIF images are compressed using a *lossless* compression algorithm. This algorithm looks for repeating data strings in the image file. It catalogues these image strings and employs a type of shorthand to reference each

occurrence. The format stores the entire data string only once and then references it using a shorthand representation of it. This dramatically reduces the amount of information needed to display the image without affecting the image quality.

Because of the way in which GIF images are compressed, they provide a suitable format for line drawings such as cartoons and for images with large sections of solid colors, such as company logos.

Because it only supports up to 256 colors, the GIF format is a poor choice for images with more than 256 colors, such as photographs or images that contain gradients. If you convert an image with more than 256 colors, such as a photograph, into the GIF format, the conversion maps any additional colors to one of these 256 colors. This can result in a significant loss of image quality. Web page authors use GIF images primarily for graphic bullets, horizontal and vertical lines, banners, and clip art. For most cartoons and animations, 256 colors are sufficient.

JPEG Images

The JPEG, or Joint Photographic Experts Group, format supports 16.7 million colors and is the preferred format for photographs and images that include a broad range of colors. With this

format, you can specify the amount of compression. The trade-off is between image quality and file size; the more you compress an image, the less detail it contains. JPEG compression is a *lossy* algorithm, meaning that some of the image information is lost during the compression process. However, the compression algorithm accounts for what the human eye can perceive, and leaves out detail that most people cannot detect.

The JPEG format is less useful for line drawings, lettering, or any basic graphic images, because these images have little data that JPEG can "lose" in order to compress the file.

PNG Images

PNG, or Portable Network Graphics, is pronounced "ping," and is a relatively new format that exists in two forms: PNG8 and PNG24. PNG24 is intended to replace GIF images on the Web. GIF uses a patented compression algorithm called LZW, short for Lempel-Ziv-Welch. For 20 years, Unisys owned the patent, and even though the U.S. patent has expired, Unisys still presses developers to license the LZW compression algorithm. The compression algorithm that PNG uses is patent-free and license-free, so anyone can use it.

In many respects, PNG combines the best of both GIF and JPEG formats. The PNG24 format, like the JPEG format, supports 16.7 million colors, but its compression algorithm is *lossless*, like that of the GIF format. This means that graphical information is not removed from the image during the compression calculations. This results in higher-quality graphics that do not take forever to download.

Like GIF, PNG enables you to adjust the opacity or transparency of an object in order to use images as "watermarks" on a page. However, unlike GIF, PNG does not support animation. Currently, the bulk of animation is moving from GIF to Flash.

Using Images on a Web Page

You can add images to a Web page so that they appear as they would in a printed document. You add the image by inserting an <img /> tag where you want the image to appear. The <img /> tag must contain the src attribute set equal to the image file's location and filename and the alt attribute set equal to a text description of the image, which appears when a browser cannot display the image.

You can add background images that act as a wallpaper for a Web page. To add a background image, you can create a style rule for the <body> tag with the background-image property set to the location and name of the image, as shown in the section, "Insert and Position a Background Image." You can also use an image as a link by bracketing the <img /> tag with opening and closing <a> tags, as explained in the section "Create an Image Link."

Add Images to a Web Page

Y ou can bring your Web page text to life with photos, illustrations, clip art, and other images. The images on a Web page are sometimes called *inline images*, because they reside in the text by way of the HTML `<img />` tag.

If you use a visual authoring program, you usually add an image to your Web page by simply dragging and dropping it onto the page or by selecting the command for inserting a picture. For a text-based editor, such as WordPad, you must type the `<img />` tag as part of your page's source code. An `<img />` tag including some common attributes looks like the following:

```
<img src="http://www.mysite.com/directory/
image.jpg" alt="Image description"
width="200" height="200" />
```

This tag instructs the Web browser to insert an image. The `src` attribute indicates where the image is stored and supplies its filename. If you store your images in the same directory as the Web page, you can use the image's filename as the `src` value and omit the rest of the URL. The `alt` attribute, which is required, displays a description of the image if the browser cannot display it. The `width` and `height` attributes specify the dimensions of the image as displayed on the page.

Add Images to a Web Page

① Create or open a document in your HTML editor.

② Between the `<body>` tags, add an `<img />` tag with the `src` attribute set equal to the filename of an image stored on your computer.

③ Save the document in the same directory as the image file.

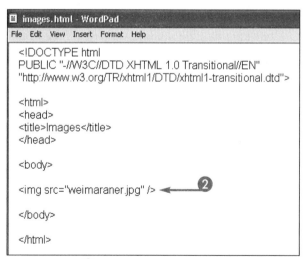

④ Open the document in your Web browser.

● The Web browser displays the page, including the image.

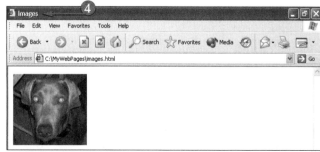

⑤ Open the document in your HTML editor.

⑥ Change the `src` attribute to an absolute URL for an image on the Web.

● This example shows additional text to credit the source of the image.

⑦ Save the document.

⑧ Open the document in your Web browser.

● The Web browser displays the page, including the image.

Where can I find images to use in my Web pages?

▼ You can use digital photos, images that you draw in a graphics program, clip art stored in the JPEG, PNG, or GIF format, or even images from other pages. However, images that other users create are their personal property, so you must obtain permission before using them on your pages. You can subscribe to a clip art service, such as Graphics.com at www.graphics.com, to obtain royalty-free clip art, photos, animations, and other graphics to use on your Web pages. With a digital camera or a scanner, you can create your own online photo album or slide show.

What can I do if I am using an image other than a GIF, JPG, or PNG?

▼ If you create an image and save it in a format other than GIF, JPEG, or PNG, you need to convert the image file to one of the above formats. Most graphics programs let you save images in these formats. Graphics programs also provide tools that enable you to resize images, reduce the number of colors used, decrease the image resolution, and crop out excess background. All of these techniques help to reduce the size of the image file so it takes up less storage space and downloads faster.

Make an Alternative Text Label

The `<img />` tag requires the `alt` attribute to provide a description of the image. This text description appears if the image fails to load in a visitor's Web browser and, while the image downloads, provides the user some idea of the image's content. A browser may not display an image if the Web browser stops loading the page before the images download or because the user enters a setting to browse without graphics. The text description also pops up as a screen tip when the user rests the mouse cursor on the image.

Adding alternative text to your `<img />` tags is required, because it shows your visitors what they are missing if the image fails to load. For example, if visitors decide to browse without graphics and then read an interesting description of an image, they can choose to view it. Without alternative text, an empty box appears on the screen, and the user has little motivation to view it.

Alternative text also provides some context for the image, by allowing you to include a brief description of the image that explains its relevance. Visitors view the description by resting the mouse cursor on the image.

Make an Alternative Text Label

① In your HTML editor, open an HTML document that includes one or more `<img />` tags.

② Add the `alt` attribute to an `<img />` tag and set it equal to a title or description of the image.

③ Save the document.

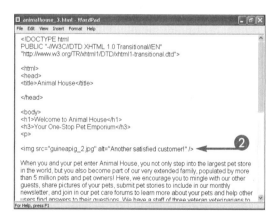

④ Open the document in your Web browser.

⑤ Position the mouse cursor on the image.

● The text that you specified in the `alt` attribute appears.

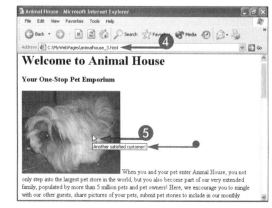

⑥ Disable pictures in your Web browser.

Note: This example shows Internet Explorer's Internet Options dialog box. Refer to your Web browser's help system to learn how to prevent images from loading.

⑦ Click OK.

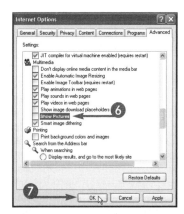

PART II

⑧ Click the Refresh button to reload the page.

● The space for the image appears with the text that you specified in the `alt` attribute.

Do I always need to use the `alt` attribute?

▼ Yes. You should include the `alt` attribute in every `<img />` tag. Your image appears on a page whether you include the `alt` attribute or not, but if you test source code that includes an `<img />` tag in which the `alt` attribute is omitted, the validating utility reports the omission as an error.

Are there any other reasons to use `alt` attributes?

▼ Yes. Another major reason to include the `alt` attribute for most images is that Web browsers that are designed for blind users often read the alternative text to the user. Including a text label for the image gives the Web browser a readable description. For a lengthier description of an image, you can include the `longdesc` tag set equal to the URL of a page that contains the description.

How can I tell if my images will appear when users view my page in other Web browsers?

▼ You must test your page in several Web browsers to ensure that images appear properly, that text formatting appears as you intend it to, and that your links function properly. In addition, use the `href=mailto` attribute to add your e-mail address to the page so that visitors can inform you of any problems. For more information about adding hyperlinks and mailtos, see Chapter 3.

Specify Image Dimensions

When you use an `<img />` tag to insert an image on a Web page, the `<img />` tag automatically instructs the Web browser to display the image in its original dimensions, which is what you may want. However, it places the burden of determining the rest of the page layout on the Web browser, which can add to the time it takes for the Web browser to display the page. This is because the Web browser must wait for the image to download before it can display the rest of the page.

By specifying the image dimensions — the image height and width — in the `<image />` tag, you enable the Web browser to download and display the page immediately and then display any images once they download. This makes the page appear to load more quickly. If the width and height values differ from those of the actual image, the Web browser resizes the image to fit in the space that the `height` and `width` values define. You can find the dimensions of any Web page image by resting your mouse cursor on the image in My Computer or by opening the image in a graphics program and viewing its properties.

Specify Image Dimensions

① Open an HTML document that contains an `<img />` tag.

② Within the `<img />` tag, add `width` and `height` attributes.

● The values are in pixels.

③ Save the document.

④ Open the document in your Web browser.

● The Web browser uses the `width` and `height` attributes to allocate space for the image.

⑤ Open the document in your HTML editor.

⑥ Set the `width` and `height` attributes to new values.

⑦ Save the document.

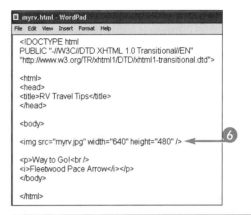

⑧ Open the document in your Web browser.

● Your Web browser displays the page with image dimensions that reflect your changes.

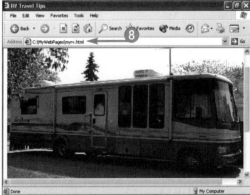

Why does my image appear distorted?

▼ You probably specified dimensions that changed one dimension disproportionately. For example, if an image is 320 x 240 pixels and you enter dimensions that decrease the height by 50 percent but decrease the width by only 25 percent, the settings distort the image. In most graphics programs, you can select an option to keep the dimensions proportional as you resize an image. If you decide to resize an image using the `height` and `width` attributes, enter settings that change the dimensions proportionally. See the section "Create Thumbnail Images" for more information about resizing images.

When I specify a smaller display size for an image, does the image display more quickly in my Web page?

▼ No. The entire image downloads, regardless of the size that you specify using the `width` and `height` attributes, so the images do not display any faster if you decrease the `width` and `height` values. You can make image files smaller by cropping out excess background, reducing the number of colors, decreasing image resolution, or resizing the image in your graphics program. Some digital cameras include a special setting that enables you to take smaller, low-resolution photos that are suitable for Web pages and e-mail.

Align Images

By default, inline images appear inside the line of text where you insert the <img /> tag. If you insert the <img /> tag in front of the source code for a paragraph, the image appears at the beginning of the paragraph. Insert it in the middle of a paragraph's source code, and the image appears in the middle of the paragraph, almost as if it were a typed character.

Unless you specify otherwise, the first line of text that follows the <img /> tag aligns with the bottom of the image. If the text wraps to two or more lines, those lines

wrap below the image. You can change the relative location of the text to the image by using the HTML align attribute. You can set align to equal "top", "bottom", "middle", "left", or "right". For example, align="right" moves the image to the right of the text.

Although the <img /> tag is still used in HTML 4.01 and XHTML 1.0, most of the attributes that control the appearance of the image on a Web page have been deprecated in favor of styles. This section shows you how to use styles to control the position of the image in relation to surrounding text.

Align Images

① Create a new HTML file that includes an <img /> tag and some text.

② Between the <head> tags, add opening and closing <style> tags to create an internal style sheet.

Note: See Chapter 4 for information about style sheets.

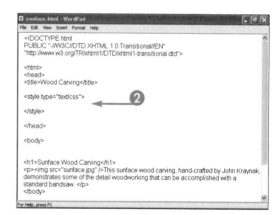

③ Define class selector styles for the img element to set vertical alignment.

④ Add the `class` attribute to the `<img />` tag to assign the class you want.

⑤ Save the document.

⑥ Open the document in your Web browser.

● The text aligns as you specified with the class that you assigned to the image.

Can I use the `style` attribute to position the image?

▼ Yes, you can add the `style` attribute to the image tag to set the image to an absolute position on the page. For example, type **`<img style="position: absolute; top:75px; left:100px; width:50px; height:50px" src="image.gif" />`** to position the image 75 pixels down from the top of the window and 100 pixels in from the left side of the window. As long as no other objects, such as text, occupy that space, this works fine. However, if another object occupies that space, the image may obscure it.

Can I set the dimensions of the image with style sheets?

▼ Yes, but you probably want to specify the dimensions for each image individually, so consider using the `style` attribute in the `<img />` tag to set the dimensions; for example, typing the code **`<img style="width:100px; height:75px" src="image.gif" />`** makes the image 100 pixels wide and 75 pixels tall.

How do I center an image at the top of a page?

▼ You can center an image at the top of a page, or anywhere else on the page, by embedding your `<img />` tag in a centered paragraph. To do this, type **`<p style="text-align:center"><img src="image.jpg" /></p>`**.

PART II

Add Space Between Images and Text

When you insert an `<img />` tag next to any text, the Web browser keeps the text and image separate; however, the text may appear too close to the image, making the page look crowded. To give your page a more professional look, you can create some white space around the image by using style sheet `margin` properties.

CSS features five margin properties: `margin`, `margin-bottom`, `margin-left`, `margin-right`, and `margin-top`. The `margin` property is a shorthand property that simply enables you to add an equal amount of space

around the entire object. Each of the other `margin` properties enables you to add space on one side of the object.

As with all CSS styles, you can apply these styles using external style sheets, internal style sheets, or by using inline style attributes. The example below uses an internal style sheet to add white space around all images in the document. To define the margins for each figure individually, you can use the `style` attribute or define and apply class selector styles. For more information about using CSS style sheets, see Chapter 4.

Add Space Between Images and Text

1 In your HTML editor, open an HTML document that contains one or more `<img />` tags.

2 Between the `<head>` tags, add opening and closing `<style>` tags to create an internal style sheet.

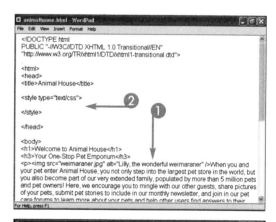

3 Define a style rule for the `img` element that adds white space to one side of the image.

- All images on the page are separated from adjacent text by the number of pixels that you designate.

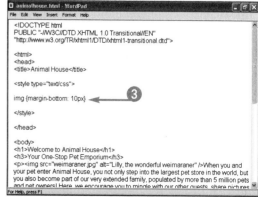

④ Add another `margin` property and specify the number of pixels you want for the margin width.

⑤ Ensure that you have text around the `<img />` tag, so that you can see the results of your settings.

⑥ Save the document.

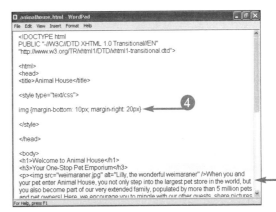

⑦ Open the document in your Web browser.

● Your Web browser displays the document, adding the specified amount of space between the image and adjacent text.

Can I use the HTML hspace and vspace attributes to add space around the image?

▼ Yes. Although HTML hspace and vspace attributes are deprecated, they still function in most Web browsers. However, because they are being phased out, you should use the CSS margin properties. Once you know how to take advantage of these properties, you soon realize how much control they provide. For example, using the hspace attribute adds an equal amount of space on both the left and right sides of an image. You can use margin properties to specify different amounts of space for each side.

Do the margin properties work for any other elements?

▼ Yes, you can apply the margin properties to various elements on a page, including paragraphs and headings. For example, typing **<p style="margin-left:20px; margin-right:20px">** creates a paragraph that is indented 20 pixels from the left and right sides of the Web browser window. An easier way to apply styles is to create style rules that govern the formatting of all occurrences of an element, as discussed in Chapter 4.

Can I decrease the default margin to produce less space?

▼ Yes, you can enter negative values for margin properties to create less space between two elements. This is very useful if your Web page has an image that directly follows an element that has a great deal of white space following it, such as a level-1 heading. By entering a negative value for the top margin, you can move the image closer to the heading.

Wrap Text Around an Image

In a word-processing or desktop-publishing program, you can wrap text around an image, just as it appears in a newspaper or magazine. You can also add this attractive formatting to your Web pages by using the CSS `float` property. By applying the `float` property to an image, you can position the image to either the left or right side of surrounding text and have that text wrap around the image.

You may find it useful to combine the `float` property with one or more `margin` properties to add some space between the image and the text that wraps around it. For example,

when you type **<img style="float:left; margin-right:10px; margin-bottom:10px" src="image.jpg">** it instructs the Web browser to display the image to the left of the text, add 10 pixels of space along the bottom and right side of the image, and wrap the text around the right side of the image.

The results vary depending on the image and its position relative to the text, so consider using the `style` attribute to customize the `float` property for each image.

Wrap Text Around an Image

① In your HTML editor, open a document that features a large block of text.

② Insert an <img /> tag with `src` and `alt` attributes after one of the opening paragraph tags.

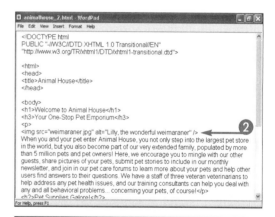

③ Add the `style` attribute, set equal to `float: left` or `float: right`, to the <img /> tag.

- The `left` attribute floats the image to the left of the paragraph, while the `right` attribute floats the image to the right.

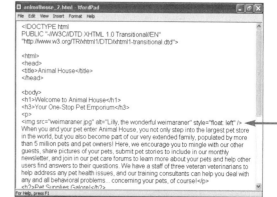

④ Add `margin` properties to create space between the image and adjacent text.

⑤ Save the document.

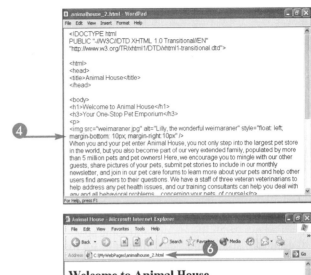

④

⑥ Open the document in your Web browser.

● Your Web browser displays the image with the text wrap and margins that you specified.

⑥

What happens if I do not specify a `float` property?

▼ If you decide not to float an image, it appears embedded in the text as if it were a typed character. The default setting for `float` is `none`, which gives you the same result as if you did not specify a float at all. A `float` property set to `none` is useful if you use an internal or external style sheet to set the `float` property for all images and you want to disable it for a particular image. To learn more about using external and internal style sheets to control formatting, refer to Chapter 4.

I want the text to form a clean box around the image, like in a magazine. How can I do that?

▼ For any text that wraps around the image, use the `style` attribute in the `<p>` tag to set the CSS `text-align` property to `justify`. For example, typing **<p style="text-align:justify">** spreads the text out as needed so it is flush against the left margin and flush against the image margin. If your document contains several images, consider creating a style definition for the `p` element to justify all running text. For example, the style rule `p {text-align:justify}` justifies all running text. For more on creating styles, refer to Chapter 4.

Add an Image Border

White space creates an invisible frame around an image that can significantly enhance the image's appearance on a Web page. If you want a frame that is more interesting, you can add a border to the image. Using various CSS border properties, you can add a border to any or all edges of an image, change the style and color of the border, and adjust its width.

The easiest and most common way to add borders is to use the `border` property; this adds a uniform border around the entire image. With this shorthand property, you can set the style, width, and color of the border. For example,

adding `style="border: thick solid blue"` to the `<img />` tag adds a thick, solid, blue border around the entire image.

Additional `border` properties give you even more control; `border-top`, `border-bottom`, `border-left`, and `border-right` enable you to set the border for each edge individually. `border-color`, `border-style`, and `border-width` enable you to set the color, style, and width of the borders. Several additional properties are available for setting the color, style, and width of each border individually. See Appendix B for these additional properties.

Add an Image Border

1. Open a document that contains one or more `<img />` tags and some text.

2. Between the `<head>` tags, add opening and closing `<style>` tags to create an internal style sheet.

3. Create a style definition that sets the `border` properties for the `img` element.

4. Save the document.

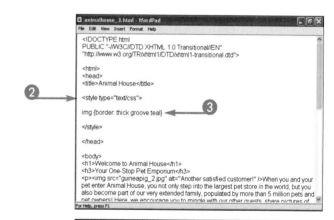

5. Open the document in your Web browser.

   ● A border appears around the image.

6 Open the document in your HTML editor.

7 Change the `border` properties to give the border a different look.

8 Save the document.

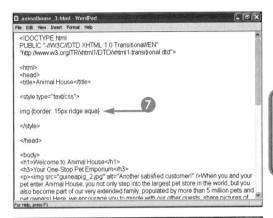

9 Open the document in your Web browser.

● The border's appearance reflects the changes you made to its properties.

Can I use a different color for each edge of the border?

▼ Yes, you can use the `border-color` property to define four different colors; for example, `img {border-color: red green blue yellow}` makes the top border red, the right border green, the bottom border blue, and the left border yellow. You can also use hexadecimal color codes instead of color names for more color choices.

Can I add a margin around the border?

▼ Yes. Add the `margin` property, as shown in the section "Add Space Between Images and Text," to add white space between the border and other surrounding elements. You can control the margin of each edge separately, which is useful if you want to keep the image flush left but increase space around the top, bottom, and right side of the image. Appendix B contains a complete list of `margin` properties.

I added the `border-width` property, but my borders do not appear. What should I do?

▼ Using a `border-width` property alone may not be sufficient to produce the borders. Try adding the `border-style` property before the `border-width` property. You can set the `border-style` property to `dotted`, `dashed`, `solid`, `double`, `groove`, `ridge`, `inset`, or `outset`. You may also need to enter a `border-color` property, but if you do not specify a color, the Web browser typically uses the default color black.

Create an Image Link

You can turn an image into a link by simply bracketing the `<img />` tag with opening and closing `<a>` tags. Just like text links, the opening `<a>` tag must contain the `href` attribute with its value set to the location and name of the destination page.

Image links, like text links, can use absolute or relative URLs. If you link to pages that are stored in the same directory or in the directory that you specified using the `base` attribute, you can set the `href` value to the name of the linked file. If the linked file is in a different directory on the same server, you can omit the domain name and type a path to the directory, followed by the filename. However, if the file to which you are linking is stored on a different Web server, you must enter an absolute URL, including `http://` and the site's domain name.

For more information about adding hyperlinks to other pages, internal page links, and mailtos, see Chapter 3.

Create an Image Link

1 In your HTML editor, open an HTML document that has an `<img />` tag.

2 Add an opening `<a>` tag with an `href` attribute set equal to the location and name of the linked file.

3 Add a closing `</a>` tag.

4 Save the document.

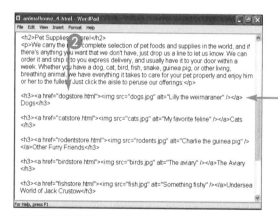

5 Open the document in your Web browser.

● A blue border appears around the image to indicate that it is a link.

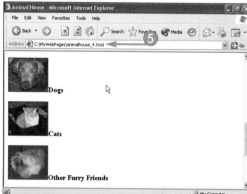

6 Rest the mouse cursor on the image.

● In this example, the linked URL appears in the Web browser status bar, and the mouse cursor appears as a hand icon.

7 Click the image.

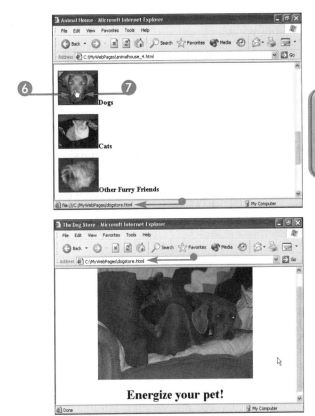

● Your Web browser opens the page to which the image is linked.

The border around the image does not appear blue. Is something wrong?

▼ If you used the CSS `border` property to set a border for the image, that setting overrides the automatic blue border that the `<a>` tag creates. If you want a blue border, remove the CSS `border` property from the image's style definition, or add the `style="border: thin solid blue"` property to the `<img />` tag. You can prevent a border from appearing by adding the `style="border: none"` attribute to the `<img />` tag.

Can I use image links to link to an e-mail or an FTP site?

▼ Because they use the `<a>` tag, image links are exactly the same as text links. To link to an e-mail address, add the `mailto:` protocol to the front of the e-mail address. To link to an FTP site, use the `ftp://` protocol in front of the FTP URL.

Can I have the URL pop up in a screen tip?

▼ Yes. In fact, this is a good idea, because it indicates to the user the address of the page that the link points to. The user can then decide, before clicking the link, if they want to visit the site or open the page. Just edit the `alt` attribute for the image to include the URL. For example, add `alt="Click here to go to www.mysite.com!"`

Create Thumbnail Images

Although pictures can make a Web page look very attractive, several large images can take a long time to download, especially for visitors who have a dial-up modem connection. This can often cause the user to skip your Web site or to view it without the images. One way to address this problem is to display thumbnail images — small versions of the original images that load much more quickly. Thumbnails are especially useful in online catalogues and photo albums. A user can quickly glance at the thumbnail image, and then, if the user wants to view a larger version, he or she can click the thumbnail.

To create a thumbnail image, you can use a graphics program to reduce the size of the original image and then save the thumbnail version as a separate file. Once you create the thumbnail image, you can insert an `<img />` tag to display the image on your Web page. You can then bracket the `<img />` tag with `<a>` tags and add the `href` attribute to link the thumbnail image to the original image. For more information, see the previous section, "Create an Image Link."

Create Thumbnail Images

① Open a large image in a graphics editor.

● This example uses Paint Shop Pro.

② Click the command or button for resizing the image.

● A dialog box appears, displaying controls for resizing the image.

③ Select the option to resize proportionally — the Lock aspect ratio check box in this example.

④ Type a width measurement.

● The height automatically changes to maintain the height-to-width ratio.

⑤ Click OK.

● The program resizes the image.

⑥ Save the image, giving it a different name.

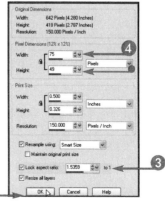

⑦ In your HTML editor, open an HTML file that has an `<img />` tag.

⑧ Change the `src` attribute to the thumbnail filename.

⑨ Add an opening `<a>` tag with an `href` attribute that links to the original image file.

⑩ Add a closing `</a>` tag.

⑪ Save the document.

⑫ Open the document in your Web browser.

⑬ Click the thumbnail image.

● Your Web browser loads the original, larger image.

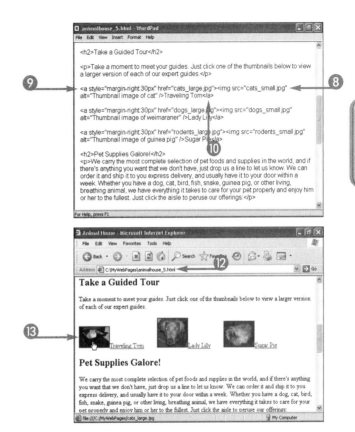

What size should I make thumbnail images?

▼ The size is entirely up to you, but anything smaller than the common setting for icons — 32 x 32 pixels — is not very useful. You can reduce the file size of your thumbnails by reducing the number of colors and the image resolution, but you should not degrade the quality so much that the image becomes unrecognizable; if so, users will have little incentive to click the link. Another option is to simply crop, or cut, a small section of the original image and use that as a thumbnail, especially if the image has a great deal of extraneous background.

Can I make the original image load in a separate window?

▼ Yes. Just add the `target="_blank"` attribute to the opening `<a>` tag. Many users appreciate having images open in a separate window, because they do not have to click the Back button to return to the image links. If you have several image links on a page, this approach is very effective.

Should I indicate the size of the original file?

▼ If the original file size is more than a few hundred kilobytes, then let your visitors know right away that the image is relatively large. If a user has a slow connection, he or she may want to avoid downloading the original image. If a user clicks an image link expecting the linked file to download in a matter of seconds, and it takes a minute or more, the person may choose not to return.

Insert and Position a Background Image

You can specify a background color for your page by creating a CSS tag selector style for the body element, as shown in Chapter 4. For example, body {background: yellow} generates a yellow background. You can also use the background or background-image property to add a background image to your Web page. This image can act like a watermark, adding a touch of elegance to your site. The Web page background is one of the first elements a Web browser loads and displays, so it provides visitors with their first impression of your site.

The most important aspect of using background images is to choose an image that is appropriate and that does not interfere with any text or other elements in the foreground. For example, if you choose a background image that contains a lot of dark purple, then black text in the foreground may become unreadable. Alternatively, you can change the font color to improve readability. Another option is to open the image in a graphics editor and increase the brightness of the image. This can often make the image appear more muted, like a watermark. Remember to use a fairly small image, so that it loads quickly for any visitor.

Insert and Position a Background Image

Insert a Background Image

① Display an internal or external style sheet.

- In this example, the style sheet controls the formatting for the document that contains the background that you want to change.

② Add a body tag selector style rule that contains the background-image property.

③ Save the document.

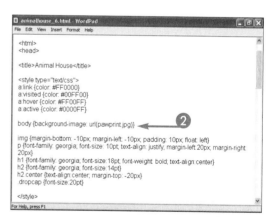

④ Open the document that uses the style sheet in your Web browser.

- The image loads into the background.

Note: *If the image does not fill the window, the Web browser repeats or tiles the image to fill the space. See the next section, "Tile a Background Image."*

Position the Background Image

① Display a style sheet that contains a `background-image` property in your HTML editor.

② Add the `background-position` property to the style rule.

- You can set the `background-position` to `top left`, `top center`, `top right`, `center left`, `center center`, `center right`, `bottom left`, `bottom center`, `bottom right`, or to an exact location.

③ Save the document.

④ Open the document that uses the style sheet in your Web browser.

- The background image is now centered at the top of the page.

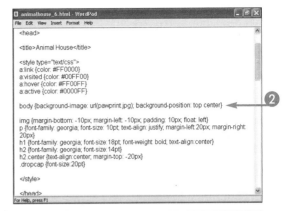

PART II

Can I use an image and a color for my background?

▼ Yes, you can specify an image and a color, but unless the image is transparent, it lays on top of the background color, obscuring it. Your graphics program may have options to transform a GIF or PNG file into a transparent image. The JPEG format does not support transparency. Even if the background image obscures the background color, setting a background color is a good idea in case the image fails to load in the visitor's Web browser.

How do I make my background image stay in place even when I scroll down the page?

▼ You can add the `background-attachment` property after the `background-image` or `background-position` property and set it to `fixed` to prevent your background image from scrolling. In addition to keeping the background in place, this usually makes the page scroll more fluidly.

Is there any property for setting the background image size?

▼ No. If the image is too small to fill the window, the Web browser automatically tiles it to fill the space, unless you instruct it not to. If the image is larger than the window, the Web browser displays as much of the image as possible. You can use your graphics editor to resize the image. For more information about tiling, see the section, "Tile a Background Image."

Tile a Background Image

If you use a background image that is smaller than the Web browser window, the Web browser repeats the image, like floor tile, to fill the window and create a consistent background for the Web page. This ensures that no matter what screen resolution a Web browser is using, and whatever the size of the Web browser window, the page has an unbroken background.

You can use this feature if you want a seamless tile image as your background. A *seamless tile* is one whose left edge matches its right edge and whose top edge matches its

bottom edge. This way the image, or pattern, repeats to look like one continuous background. Some clip art collections include seamless tiles designed specifically for this use.

Even if you are not using a seamless tile, a tiled background can look attractive, as long as the edges that meet do not clash. If you have an image that is questionable, consider adding a thin border in a solid color around the image so that the edges blend in better when the image is tiled.

Tile a Background Image

1 Display an internal or external style sheet.

- The style sheet in this example controls the formatting for the document that contains the background that you want to change.

2 Create a style rule for the body element that inserts a small image as the background image.

3 Save the file.

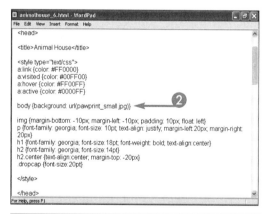

4 Open the document that uses the style sheet in your Web browser.

- The Web browser tiles the background to fill the screen.

Create Margin Backgrounds

A quick and easy way to add a professional touch to a Web site is to add a solid band of color to the left side of the page. This band of color acts as a margin background, providing a design element that holds the entire page together.

The example below uses Windows Paint to create an image with dimensions of 200 x 2000 pixels. It exaggerates the image height to ensure that the color band always reaches from the top to the bottom of the Web browser window displayed on most standard monitors.

You can then create a body style that defines the background using the image you created. After this, you can disable the scrolling feature by using the

`document-attachment: fixed` property, and disable the tiling feature with the `background-repeat: no-repeat` property. If the background image were allowed to repeat, it would fill the screen and make the entire background a solid color.

You can create similar designs using other techniques. For example, you can create a two-column table and add a style attribute to add color to the left column. You can also create a frameset that loads a page with a colored background in the left frame. See Chapter 7 for more information on improving navigation with frames.

Create Margin Backgrounds

① Display an internal or external style sheet.

● The style sheet in this example controls the formatting for the document that contains the background that you want to change.

② Create a style for the `body` element that inserts the background image you want, and that includes the `background-repeat: no-repeat` property.

③ Save the file.

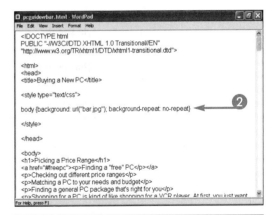

④ Open the document that uses the style sheet in your Web browser.

● A margin background appears on the left side of the Web browser window.

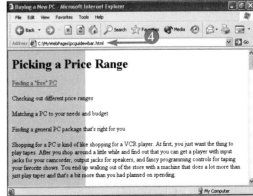

Explore Image Maps

Image maps are pictures that have two or more *hotspots*, which you click to access different Web pages. For example, a state tourism site may create an image map of the state with hotspots that represent state parks. When creating your own image map, you should use an image with clearly defined sections that you can easily select for hotspot regions. The most commonly used images are geographical maps or illustrations. Whatever image you select, it should be immediately obvious to users that they can click the image in order to obtain additional information.

Two attributes in the `<area>` tag specify the hotspot positions. The `shape` attribute defines the shape of

the hotspot: rectangle, circle, or polygon. The `coords` attribute specifies the coordinates that position the hotspot shape on the image. Coordinates are measured in pixels from the upper-left corner of the image and vary according to the shape that you define for the hotspot; for example, a rectangle's coordinates define the upper-left and lower-right corner of the rectangle, whereas a circle's coordinates define its center and radius.

This chapter focuses on *client-side* image maps, which rely on the client or Web browser to interpret the links. You can also create *server-side* image maps that rely on the Web server to interpret the links, but this requires you to program the server to interpret the links.

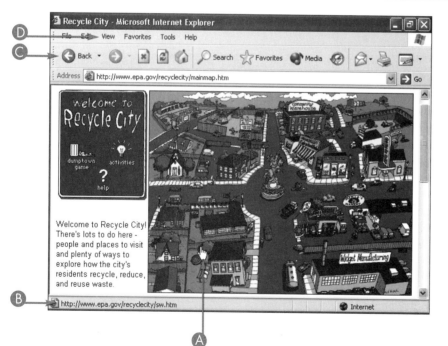

C Control buttons

You can click the Back (⊙) or Forward (⊙) buttons to navigate to the previous or next page. The Stop button (▣) stops whatever action you initiated, the Refresh button (▣) to update a page after you enter information, and the Home button (▣) takes you to the Web site's Home page.

D View Source Code

You can view the source code that creates the image map by clicking View Source.

A Hotspots

You can move your mouse cursor over different areas of an image map to reveal clickable, or *hot*, areas. When you click a hotspot, your Web browser loads the page to which it links.

B URLs

When you move your mouse cursor over a clickable area, the destination URL appears in the status bar.

When you click View and then click Source in the image map, the source code that created the map appears.

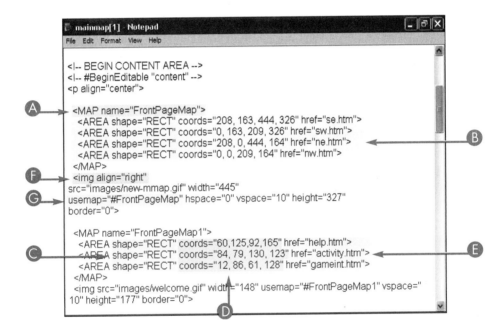

A `<map>` **tag**

This tag defines the image as a map.

B `<area>` **tags**

These tags mark sections of the image as hotspots and link them to other pages.

C `shape` **attribute**

The `shape` attribute defines the shape of the hotspot

D `coords` **attribute**

The `coords` attribute defines the hotspot's position, size, and dimensions.

E `href` **attribute**

The `href` attribute specifies the Web page to which the hotspot links.

F `<img/>` **tag**

The `<img/>` tag inserts the image that functions as the image map.

G `usemap` **attribute**

This attribute identifies the image as an image map so the `<map>` tag can refer to the image by name.

Create Client-side Image Maps

A client-side image map contains all of the source code necessary to display an image and to make it function as a clickable map. It contains the tag for loading the image as well as the tags that define the location, dimensions, and actions assigned to each hotspot that the user clicks to open a linked page.

You can add the usemap attribute to the <img /> tag to instruct Web browsers to treat the image as a map and to assign the image a map name. The paired <map> tags use the image's map name to identify it as a map, thus

enabling you to define hot spots within the map. You can insert <area> tags in between the <map> tags to define the shape, position, and size of the hotspots and to specify the location of the Web sites and pages to which you want each hotspot to link.

The example below shows you how to insert the necessary tags to add an image and to identify it as an image map. The section, "Specify Hotspot Shapes and Coordinates" guides you through the process of adding the <area> tags that define the hotspots on your image map, as well as showing you how to find X, Y coordinates on an image.

Create Client-Side Image Maps

① Open a document in your HTML editor.

② Add an <img /> tag that specifies the src of the image that you want to use as a map, as well as the image height and width.

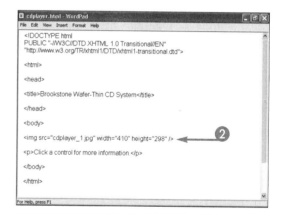

③ Add the usemap attribute and set it equal to the map name that you assigned to the image.

Note: Be sure to include the number sign (#) before the image map name.

④ Add the required alt tag and set it to equal the alternative text that you want to use for the image.

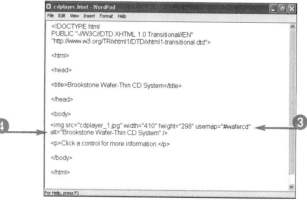

PART II

5 Add an opening <map> tag with the name attribute and set it equal to the map name.

6 Add the id attribute and set it equal to the map name.

7 Add a closing </map> tag.

8 Save the document.

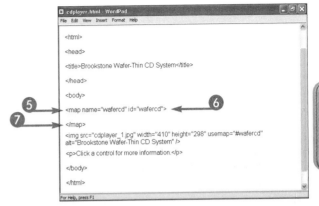

9 Open the document in your Web browser.

- The Web browser displays the image, but it looks and functions no differently than any other image.

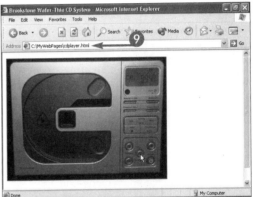

Why do I have to use both the id and name attributes in the <map> tag?

▼ Some Web browsers use the id attribute, while others use the name attribute. By including both attributes in the <map> tag, you ensure that most Web browsers can display and use the image map.

Can I use any other attributes to format the image map?

▼ Yes. You can use any of the attributes and style rules discussed in Chapter 5 to control the image map's position, margins, and the way text wraps around the image. You can also use CSS styles, as explained in Chapter 4 to control the appearance and position of the image.

Why do I need to add height and width attributes that match the size of the image?

▼ The height and width attributes create placeholders for images, enabling a Web browser to display the page without waiting for the images to download. To avoid distorting an image, do any resizing in a graphics program rather than relying on the height and width attributes to determine the image dimensions. This also helps when you identify and set image map coordinates in the following section.

Specify Hotspot Shapes and Coordinates

Before adding the `<area />` tags that define the image map hotspots, you can identify the areas on an image that you want to act as hotspots and determine the desired shape, size, and position of the hotspots. Most image-editing programs can display a point's coordinates in an image when you rest the tip of the mouse cursor on that point. You can then write down the coordinates, so you can specify them later in the `<area />` tags.

If you do not have access to an image-editing program, you can identify hotspot coordinates by using your Web browser.

To do so, you must add the `ismap` attribute to the `<img />` tag and surround the `<img />` tag with `<a>` tags. You can set the `<a>` tag's `href` attribute to anything and then delete these additions after you obtain the coordinates.

When you open the Web page file containing the `<a>` tags in a Web browser, the coordinates of the image appear in the status bar. You can then place the cursor over the hotspot and write down the hotspot coordinates for inclusion in the `<area />` tag.

Identify Coordinates in an Image-Editing Program

① Open an image file in an image-editing program.

- This example uses MS Paint.

② Position the mouse cursor over the image.

- The coordinates for the current cursor location appear on the status bar.

③ Position the mouse cursor to a different location on the image.

- The coordinates change as the mouse cursor moves.

④ Write down the values for each hotspot coordinate that you want to define.

   To set a rectangular hotspot, you need two sets of X, Y coordinates — one for the upper-left corner and the other for the lower-right corner.

Identify Coordinates in a Web Browser

① In your HTML editor, open a document that contains source code for an image map.

② Add an `ismap` attribute to the `<img />` tag.

③ Add an opening `<a>` tag with the `href` attribute set to equal `blank`.

④ Add a closing `</a>` tag.

⑤ Save the document.

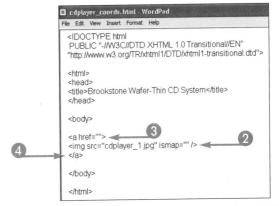

⑥ Open the document in your Web browser.

⑦ Position the mouse cursor over the image.

● In Internet Explorer, Netscape Navigator, and some other popular Web browsers, the coordinates appear in the status bar.

● Some Web browsers display the coordinates in a ToolTip, or not at all.

⑧ Write down the coordinates for the upper-left and lower-right corner of each hotspot.

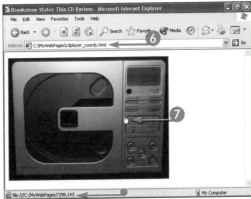

What does the `ismap` attribute do?

▼ The `ismap` attribute allows you to create server-side image maps, in which every pixel acts as a hotspot. This attribute determines the precise location of the tip of the mouse cursor when it is over an image. When a user clicks a point on the image, the page can send the coordinates to the Web server for processing. The addition of the `<a>` tags with the blank `href` value tricks the Web browser into treating the image as a link, and so it displays the coordinates in the status bar. This is an excellent way to determine precise X,Y coordinates.

If I want circular or irregularly shaped hotspots, which coordinates do I need?

▼ To define a circular area as a hotspot, you need an X and a Y coordinate to pinpoint the center of the circle and a number of pixels to specify the radius. To define an irregular shape, or polygon, you need an X and a Y coordinate for each point that defines its shape — for example, a pentagon requires five X,Y coordinates. Be sure to list the points in the sequence in which you want the connecting lines drawn, just as you would the points in a connect-the-dots image; otherwise, the coordinates may not define the perimeter of the area you want to mark.

Continued

Specify Hotspot Shapes and Coordinates *(Continued)*

Once you decide on the shapes that you want for your hotspots, and you know the coordinates required to define their size and position on the image, you can enter this information into your HTML document using `<area />` tags.

These tags use three attributes: `shape`, `coords`, and `href`. You can set the `shape` attribute to equal `rect` or `rectangle`, `circ` or `circle`, or `poly` or `polygon`. The `coords` attribute lists the coordinates that define the shape's position and size. Coordinates come in pairs because they need to define the exact position of a pixel in terms of the X- and Y-axes; contrary to what you may remember from school, numbers increase going down the Y axis. You must always separate these coordinates with a comma. The `href` attribute specifies the destination to which the hotspot links. You can specify another section of the same page, a different page on your Web site, or any page on the Web.

In addition to these standard three attributes, you can add the `target` attribute to specify the window in which the linked page opens. For example, the code `target="_blank"` opens the page in a new window.

The `<area />` tags depend on the `<map>` tags, so you must insert them between the opening and closing `<map>` tags.

Specify Hotspot Shapes and Coordinates *(continued)*

Define the Hotspot Position

① In your HTML editor, open the document that contains the `<map>` tags and `usemap` attribute.

② Insert an `<area />` tag for each hotspot and define the shape of each hotspot.

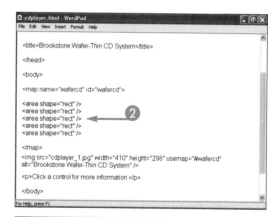

③ Add the `coords` attribute for each hotspot, and list the coordinates that define the hotspot's position and dimensions.

Note: *The coordinates are those that you wrote down when following the steps on the previous page.*

Note: *You must always type the X, Y coordinates of a point with the X value first followed by a comma.*

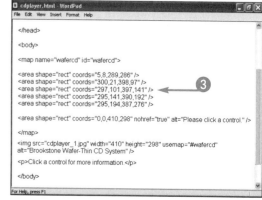

④ Add an `href` attribute for each hotspot.

- This attribute can point to a page in the same directory, or a URL of another page stored on your site or in another location on the Web.

⑤ Save the document.

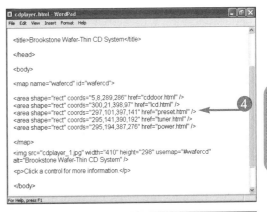

⑥ Open the document in your Web browser.

⑦ Position the mouse cursor over an image map hotspot.

- The URL of the linked page appears in the status bar.

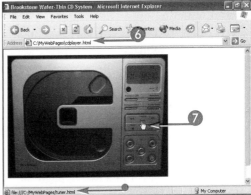

What happens if the coordinates of two hotspots overlap?

▼ If two hotspots overlap, the overlapped section links to the hotspot defined by the first `<area>` tag. Many image maps include hotspots that border one another, so the map has no dead space. This is fine if the hotspots are large and the clickable area is obvious. Otherwise, define your hotspots to include some space between them, to prevent users from accidentally clicking one hotspot when trying to click a different one.

The hotspots seem to be positioned differently when I point to them in my Web browser. What's going on?

▼ Coordinate values can be tricky to enter. An extra comma or space between coordinates can confuse a Web browser. Re-check your coordinates as you type them in the HTML file. Look for transposed numbers and for additional commas or spaces.

How big should I make my hotspots?

▼ Make your hotspots large enough to be a little forgiving if a user clicks outside the ideal area, and avoid crowding several hotspots into a small area. By spreading out your hotspots and making them as large as possible without overlapping them, you create an image map that is easier to navigate. You may also want to use your graphics program to highlight the hotspots in some way. For example, you can type names over the hotspots, brighten or darken the "hot" areas, or even circle or box the "hot" areas to make them more obvious.

Specify Alternative Text

If your image map contains distinct areas that the user can intuitively identify as hotspots, you can usually rely on the image to instruct the user on how to navigate your site. However, even relatively detailed image maps can be difficult to use.

To help users navigate your Web site using the image map, you can add alternative text to the `<area />` tag for each hotspot. This alternative text can describe the hotspot and indicate where the hotspot will take the user if they click the hotspot.

Using `alt` attributes with hotspot links works the same as `alt` attributes with normal images. You can include

descriptive text that the Web browser displays when the tip of the mouse cursor rests on the hotspot.

The `alt` attribute displays only the descriptive text for areas that make up a hotspot, but you can also add descriptive text that displays for the entire image. To do this, you can set the last `<area />` tag in the list to a rectangle shape whose coordinates include the entire image, and then add the `nohref` and `alt` attributes to the `<area />` tag and set the `alt` attribute to the descriptive text for the background.

Specify Alternative Text

Specify Hotspot Alternative Text

① In your HTML editor, open a document that has an image map with two or more `<area />` tags.

② Add the `alt` attribute to each `<area />` tag and set it equal to your descriptive text.

③ Save the document.

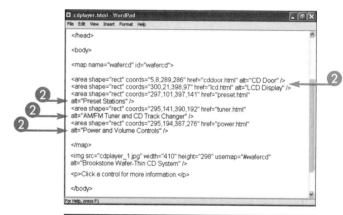

④ Open the document in your Web browser.

⑤ Position the mouse cursor over the image.

● The descriptive text that you entered for that hotspot appears in a screen tip in the status bar, or in the address bar, depending on the Web browser.

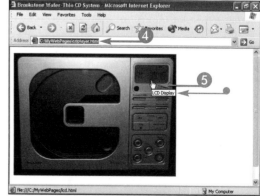

Specify Image Alternative Text

1 In your HTML editor, open a document that has two or more `<area />` tags.

2 Add an `<area />` tag that contains `nohref="nohref" shape="rect"` and `coords` set to the upper-left and lower-right corners of the image.

3 Add the `alt` attribute equal to the descriptive text that you want to display.

4 Save the document.

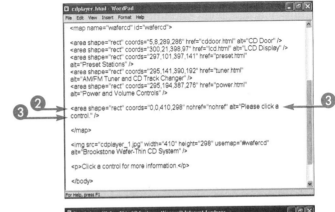

5 Open the document in your Web browser.

6 Position the mouse cursor over an area of the image that is not a hotspot.

- Descriptive text appears for the background.

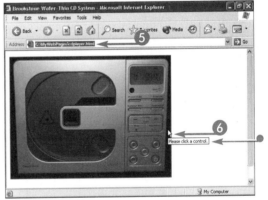

If you include an `alt` attribute as part of both the `<img />` and `<area />` tags, which descriptive text appears?

▼ If the `alt` attribute is included with both the `<img />` and the `<area />` tags, the description text for the hotspots takes precedence. Because the `alt` attribute is required in the `<img />` tag, you should keep the descriptive text in both the tags, even if the alternative text specified in the `<img />` tag does not appear.

Should I include the `alt` attribute with all `<area />` tags?

▼ Yes. It is a good idea to include the `alt` attribute and alternative text with every `<area />` tag. This precaution ensures that a description of the link is always available, even if the image cannot load. Although you cannot include links as part of your alternative text, you can include a list of links on your page that function as alternative navigational tools if the image map does not appear.

Do I have to link my image-map hotspots to other pages?

▼ No. You can also mark hotspots and use alternative text to identify various objects that appear in the image. For example, you could include a map of the United States that shows the capital of each state as a dot, designated as a hotspot. The user could rest the mouse cursor on the hotspot to view the name of the capital. Add the `nohref="nohref"` attribute to the `<area />` tag to exclude an address.

Build Image Maps
with Image Mapper

Writing down a list of coordinates and entering them correctly into your HTML document is a tedious process that can lead to errors. For example, if you mix up your coordinates, your image map may include hotspots that lead to dead ends. To eliminate possible errors, you can use one of the many image-map creation tools. One such tool is called Image Mapper, which is created by CoffeeCup Software. You can find this tool at www.coffeecup.com.

Image Mapper allows you to load images, select and edit hotspots using the mouse, and save the resulting image

map. It automatically generates the necessary HTML source code, complete with all of the required coordinates. You can then copy and paste this code into your HTML document. Image Mapper also provides a way to quickly preview the results of your image map.

The steps in this section use Image Mapper, a commonly used image-map creation software. If you are using another program, you may need to perform different steps. Please consult your program's help system for more information.

Build Image Maps with Image Mapper

① Start your image-map creation software.

② Click the command for creating an image map.

● In Image Mapper, you click File and then click Map Wizard, which leads you through the process.

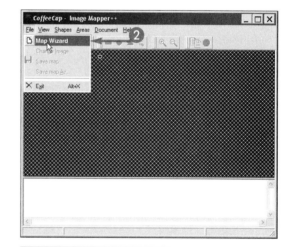

● The first page of the Map Wizard appears.

③ Click Create a new map (○ changes to ◉).

④ Click Next.

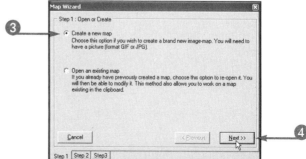

- The second page of Map Wizard appears.

⑤ Click Browse and navigate to the image you want to use as an image map.

⑥ Click Next.

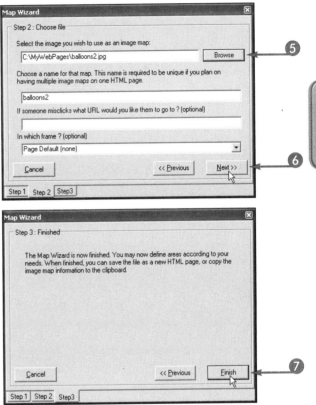

- The third page of the Map Wizard appears.

⑦ Click Finish.

PART II

Do I have to use the Map Wizard in Image Mapper?

▼ Yes, to create an image map with Image Mapper, you must run the wizard. After you create your image map, you can use additional tools to define or edit hotspots. Of the many image-map tools available, some include wizards and others do not. Image Mapper offers the Map Wizard as an easy way to open an image and specify the descriptive text that should accompany the image map. You can search for other available image-map utilities at www.download.com.

Can I test my image map before I copy the source code for it?

▼ Yes, Image Mapper includes an option for testing your image map. Select Document and then select Test Image Map. Image Mapper opens the image map in the Web browser that you specify. You can click the links to test them, but unless all of the linked pages are in the specified locations, you may encounter errors. Before testing links to external sites, make sure you are currently connected to the Internet.

What other image-mapping software can I use?

▼ Many different image-mapping programs exist, including MapEdit and Mini Mapper. In addition to shareware and stand-alone utilities, many of the major Web-editing applications, including FrontPage and HomeSite, offer image-mapping features. These features are built into the Web-editing interface. Photoshop includes a feature called ImageReady that is fairly easy to use. These built-in tools enable you to create image maps without having to learn a new program.

Continued

Build Image Maps with Image Mapper

(Continued)

Like other image-map creation programs, the Image Mapper work area includes two panes. The top pane displays the image, and the bottom pane displays the generated HTML source code.

Within the top pane, you define hotspots by drawing on various areas of the image. You simply select the desired shape and then define the hotspot area. For example, to mark a rectangular area, you select the Rectangle tool and then draw a rectangle starting at the upper-left corner of the rectangle and then moving your mouse to the lower-right corner of the rectangle. Different image-map creation

programs may require different steps, so consult the program's help system for details.

After you create a hotspot, a dialog box appears, asking you to type the destination URL for that hotspot. Each hotspot appears in the upper pane outlined in red and each coordinate point is marked with a square. By moving these squares, you can edit the position of each coordinate.

The source code in the lower pane immediately reflects changes that you make in the upper pane. When you finish editing the hotspots, you can select and copy the source code and paste it into your Web page file.

Build Image Maps with Image Mapper *(continued)*

- The image that you specified in step 2 of the Map Wizard appears in the top pane.

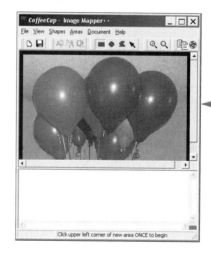

8 Click a shape button.

- This example uses the Polygon button.

9 Click each point that surrounds a hotspot area.

- A line connects each point that you click around the hotspot.

10 Double-click to complete the hotspot.

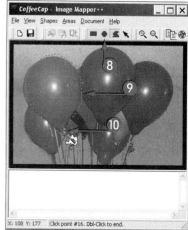

- After you define the hotspot, the Area attributes dialog box appears.

⑪ Type the destination link in the URL field.

⑫ Type the descriptive text in the ALT field.

⑬ Click the Cool! button.

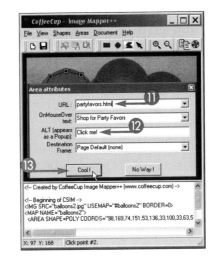

- The completed hotspot is highlighted in red with a square at each point.

⑭ Click and drag to select all the HTML text in the lower pane.

⑮ Click Document.

⑯ Click Copy map to clipboard.

⑰ Paste the map code into your HTML file.

- Your HTML file now has the source code required to display the image map.

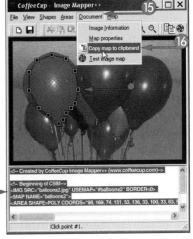

The output from Image Mapper listed some HTML tags in all capital letters. Is this correct?

▼ The creators of Image Mapper prefer the style of capitalizing all HTML tags. Most Web browsers do not require that you lower case HTML tags; your map appears the same and functions properly in almost all Web browsers. However, to comply with XHTML and to prepare your image map for future Web browsers, change all capitalized tags to lowercase. Also, add a space and a forward slash to the end of `<img>` and `<area>` tags.

Can I relate other events to my image map?

▼ Yes, you can include event-related attributes in the `<area>` tag, such as `mouseover` and `onmouseout`, to reference JavaScript methods and functions. These *event handlers* provide directives that enable the map to respond automatically when a user performs a specific action, such as moving the mouse over an area of the map or clicking an area. This can make your site much more dynamic and interactive. For more information about adding interactivity with JavaScript, see Part 3.

Can I add a border around my map?

▼ Yes. Using Image Mapper, you can add a border around the map. Click Document and then Map properties, then click in the Border around picture box. Type the border width you want in pixels, and click OK. This adds the `border="?"` attribute to the `<img />` tag, where *?* is the number of pixels you specified for the border width. If you already inserted the source code for the image map, you can can add the attribute at any time.

An Introduction to Frames

With HTML frames, you can divide a Web browser window into two or more panes, enabling the window to display a different Web page in each frame. For example, you can have three different HTML documents load into the same window by creating three frames: a vertical frame running down the left side of the window may contain a clickable table of contents for the Web site; a wider vertical frame on the right may display the text of the currently selected outline heading; and a short frame running along the bottom of the window can display a small banner advertisement.

Frames are easy to implement and require only three tags: <frameset>, <frame />, and <noframes>. The <frameset> and <frame /> tags define the layout of your frame document, while the <noframes> tag provides alternative content for Web browsers that do not support frames or that have frames disabled. In addition, Internet Explorer and Netscape Navigator 6 or later support the <iframe> tag, which embeds frames directly into the content of a standard HTML document. You can combine these tags and apply optional attributes to create simple or sophisticated frame layouts.

Using Frames

Before Cascading Style Sheets (CSS), tables and frames were the best way to divide your text into boxes and to position elements on a page. CSS has taken over these roles, and with much greater precision. However, frames are still useful for compartmentalizing text and providing some degree of interactivity to a Web site.

Many Web authors use frames to enhance Web site and page navigation and to set off banner ads and other unrelated material from the main window. In addition, frames can help you set off other content from the main page to display slide shows, animations, or objects that require programming scripts, such as JavaScript. For more information on JavaScript and frames, see Part 3.

Advantages of Using Frames

One advantage of using frames is that they are easier to maintain if you regularly update your Web site and add new directories or content pieces. For example, if your site navigation elements are contained within a single file on a frame-based Web site, then you can update that particular document rather than having to go through each page and edit the navigation elements. Another advantage of using frames is that they can make a Web page much more dynamic. For example, you can use inline frames to embed a slide-show presentation in a section of text.

Disadvantages of Using Frames

Frames do have a few drawbacks. First, when your Web site content is contained within a frameset, visitors cannot bookmark individual pages; they can bookmark only the top-level document containing the frameset. In addition, some search engine robots cannot index framed pages, so they may skip your Web site. You should also consider that by devoting a portion of your Web page real estate to one frame, you reduce the available window space for the remaining portion of your content.

The Great Frame Debate

Almost immediately after Netscape 2.0 introduced frames, Web designers began debating the merits of framed documents. Many designers object to the ways in which some Web sites use frames with little consideration of design and usability. After all, just because you can create a page with ten frames does not mean that you should. However, you have little reason to avoid frames completely when they are the best solution for your Web site. In fact, when you use them intelligently and sparingly, frames can significantly enhance your Web site's appearance and usability. Recent versions of Windows and MacOS have embraced frames, as well, as you can see in Windows My Computer and the MacOS X Finder.

Designing a Frame Layout

Using too many frames or making a frame too wide or too narrow can make your Web site difficult to navigate. This may ultimately discourage visitors, so you should always keep your frame layout in mind. When planning your frame layout, decide which page you want as the central page — the page that has the most relevant content — and place this in your largest frame. Typically, this frame appears on the right and takes up more than half the window space. Users who read from left to right look for navigation tools at the top or along the left side of the window. Users who read from right to left look for navigational tools on the right side of the window. Keep this in mind if you plan on including a table of contents or a list of links. Short frames along the top or bottom of the window are useful for displaying banner ads or supplemental content. Try to limit yourself to two frames, or three at the most.

Maximizing Frame Interactivity

Frames are powerful tools for adding interactivity to a Web site because they provide on-demand access to information. You can make your frames more interactive by adding links to a frame; when a user clicks them, these links can change the content in another frame. To do this, you must give each frame a name. When you add a link to another page, instead of having the linked page open in the current Web browser window or in a new window, you add the target attribute to open the page in the named frame. This chapter shows you how to create and name frames and change their target values.

Create a Frameset

You can create a frameset to divide the browser window into two or more frames. This requires the use of only two types of tags — the `<frameset>` tag set and the unpaired `<frame />` tag. The `<frameset>` tag set takes the place of the `<body>` tag set in standard HTML documents. The opening and closing `<frameset>` tags bracket the `<frame />` tags that define the frames and their contents. The `<frameset>` tag must include either the `rows` or `cols` attribute, which indicates the number and size of rows or columns contained in the frameset; see the section "Size Your Frames" for more information. You can use both `rows` and `cols` attributes together to create a grid.

Between the `<frameset>` tags, use the `<frame />` tags to define the pages that make up the frameset. Each `<frame />` tag must have a `src` attribute that indicates the location of the page that initially loads into the frame.

For each `<frame />` tag, you may include an optional `name` attribute and a unique name. After you assign each frame a unique name, you can include links throughout your Web site and have content load in specific frames. For more on targeting content using frame names, see the section, "Target Frames."

Create a Frameset

① Create a new document with the frameset DTD in your HTML editor.

② Add an opening `<frameset>` tag that includes the `rows` or `cols` attributes to specify the frame sizes.

● In this example, the top row is 100 pixels tall, the left column is 150 pixels wide, and the bottom row and right column consume the rest of the available window space.

Note: *For more information about sizing frames, see the section, "Size Your Frames."*

③ Add a closing `</frameset>` tag.

④ Add a `<frame />` tag for each frame you want to create, including the `src` and `name` attributes.

Note: *If you store your source pages in the same directory as the page that contains the frame tags, then you do not need to specify source locations, only the source filenames.*

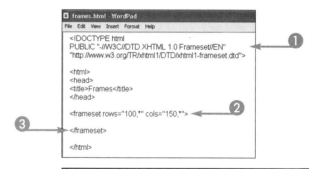

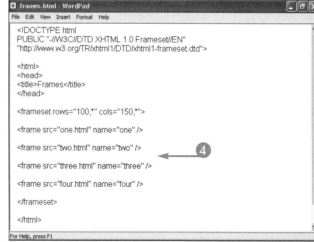

5 Create a separate Web page for each frame.

6 Save the Web pages, giving them names that correspond to the `src` names that you specified in your `<frame />` tags.

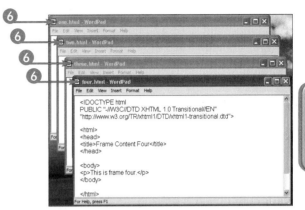

7 Open the page that contains the `<frame />` tags in your Web browser.

● Each of the source documents loads into an individual frame.

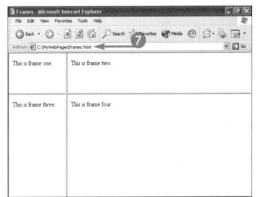

Can any other HTML tags appear within the frame document?

▼ When you create a frameset, you use the frameset DTD, which prohibits the use of any HTML tags except `<head>` and `<frameset>`. Omit any other tags, including the `<body>` tag that you use in most HTML documents. Documents that load into frames use either the strict or transitional DTD. You can use other HTML tags within those documents to mark the contents of the pages. Within the outermost `<frameset>` tags, you may include the `<noframes>` tags to display standard HTML content. For more information about using `<noframes>` tags, see the section, "Using `<noframes>` Tags."

If the `row` and `col` settings apply to all of the frames, why do the frames in this example differ in size?

▼ The numbers in the `rows="100,*" cols="150,*"` entries set the size of the first row and column. The asterisks instruct the Web browser to give any remaining window space to the second row and column. Instead of specifying row and column size in absolute terms using pixels, you can specify size in percentages; for example, `cols="25%,*"` gives the first column one quarter of the window width and the second column the remaining three quarters. See the section, "Size Your Frames" for additional information.

Using \<noframes\> Tags

Most Web browsers support frames, but to accommodate old Web browsers or devices that access Web pages that do not support frames, you can provide alternative content by including text between a pair of \<noframes\> tags. If you do not provide alternative content with the \<noframes\> tags, Web browsers that do not support frames display a blank page instead of your frame content.

You should place the set of opening and closing \<noframes\> tags within the \<frameset\> tags. If you have nested frames on your page, as explained in the section, "Nest Frames," you can place the \<noframes\> tags within

the top-level or outermost frameset. The \<noframes\> tags have no required attributes, but you can include optional class and style attributes for use with style sheets, as explained in Chapter 4.

Within the \<noframes\> tags, you must include a direct link to your Web site's main content frame in addition to a message. Of course, if portions of your Web site, such as the navigation elements, are contained within other frames, then visitors who have frame-disabled Web browsers may not have access to all of the features on your Web site. For this reason, repeating essential navigation within the body of the main content pages is a good idea.

Using \<noframes\> Tags

① Create a new document with the frameset DTD in your HTML editor.

② Add an opening \<frameset\> tag that specifies the percentage of window space for each frame.

③ Add a closing \</frameset\> tag.

④ Add \<frame /\> tags that specify the source and name of each frame.

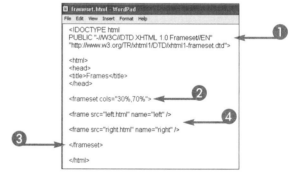

⑤ Between the \<frameset\> tags, add opening and closing \<noframes\> tags.

⑥ Between the \<noframes\> tags, add opening and closing \<body\> tags.

⑦ Between the \<body\> tags, add your alternative content.

⑧ Save the document.

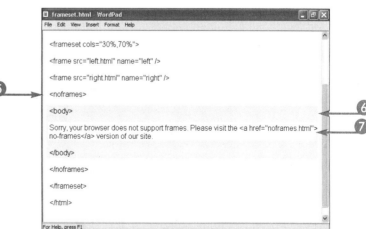

⑨ Open the document in a frame-enabled Web browser.

- The Web browser displays the frames, but does not display the content between the `<noframes>` tags.

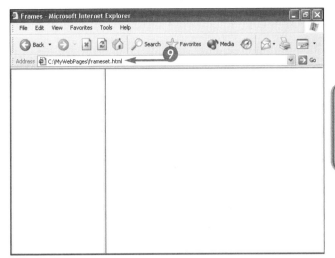

⑩ Open the document in a frame-disabled Web browser.

- The Web browser does not display the frames, but does display the content between the `<noframes>` tags.

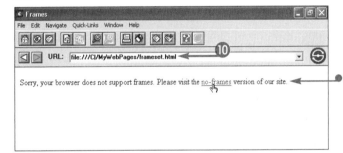

How can I access a Web browser that does not support frames?

▼ You can find links for downloading old versions of Web browsers at browsers. evolt.org, so that you can test your `<noframes>` content. Frame support came early to Web browsers, so you need to obtain a fairly old browser; Netscape Navigator 1.1, Mosaic 1.0, and Internet Explorer 1.0 and 2.0 do not support frames. A few early frame-supporting browsers included an option to disable frame support.

Can I use an image rather than an HTML document as my source?

▼ Technically, yes, but then the image does not contain a text description. Thus, if a non-visual visitor opens the frame, the visitor cannot obtain a description of the image. You can add the `longdesc` attribute to the `<frame />` tag to reference an HTML document that contains a description of the image, but most authors simply create a Web page that includes the image and description together.

Can I include any content within the `<noframes>` tags?

▼ You can include any content that you would normally include within HTML `<body>` tags, such as text, links, and images. In fact, to adhere to the XHTML specification, you must include a set of `<body>` tags between the `<noframes>` tags. All of your `<noframes>` content must be between the opening and closing `<body>` tags. Try to present information that is comparable to what you offer visitors in the framed version.

Size Your Frames

You can set the size of each frame by indicating a value for the `cols` and `rows` attributes of the `<frameset>` tag. You can make the value a number, a percentage, or an asterisk.

A number specifies the row or column size in pixels. For example, `cols="150,200"` displays a left frame 150 pixels wide and a right frame 200 pixels wide. A percentage value specifies a percentage of the window space. For example, `rows="20%,80%"` displays a top frame that takes up 20% of the window and a bottom frame that takes up 80%. The asterisk gives any remaining space to the frame. For

example, `rows="200,*"` creates a top frame 200 pixels tall and a bottom frame that takes up the rest of the window. `cols="150,*,*"` creates three columns: a left column 150 pixels wide and two additional columns that split the remaining screen space equally. `cols="*,3*"` creates two frames, with the frame on the right being three times wider than the frame on the left.

When your source document for a frame does not fit in the frame, the Web browser creates a scroll bar within the frame. This consumes additional screen space that can cause the browser to rewrap the content.

Size Your Frames

① Create a new document with the frameset DTD in your HTML editor.

② Add a pair of `<frameset>` tags.

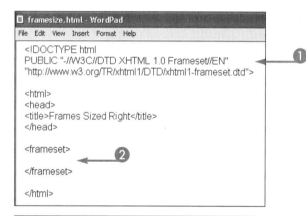

③ Add `cols` and `rows` attributes to define the frame dimensions.

● In this example, `*,35%` sets the second row to 35% of the window height, while the first row fills the rest of the available space. `5*,*` sets the width of the first column to five times the width of the second column.

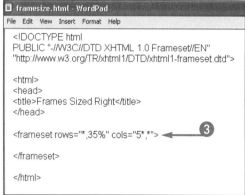

④ Add a `<frame />` tag for each segment of your frameset, including a `name` and `src` attribute for each frame.

⑤ Save the document.

⑥ Open the document in your Web browser.

● Your Web browser displays the frames in the sizes that the `rows` and `cols` attributes specify.

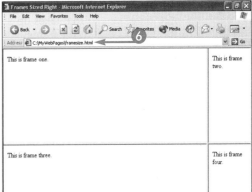

Can visitors to my Web site change the size of frame columns and rows?

▼ Yes. Users can position the cursor over a frame border and dynamically alter the dimensions of columns and rows. This resizes the frames temporarily and only in the user's window; your `rows` and `cols` settings remain unchanged. The exception is inline frames, which users cannot resize. You can prevent users from resizing frames by adding the `noresize` attribute to a `<frame />` tag; however, visitors may need to resize the frames, depending on the size of their Web browser window and their display resolution.

How do I prevent scroll bars from appearing?

▼ Add `scrolling="no"` to the `<frame />` tag. This prevents the Web browser from adding scroll bars, even if there is enough content to justify them. If you explicitly turn off scroll bars, keep in mind that if your content goes beyond the dimensions of the frame, the user has no way to access that content. Content may appear differently in a visitor's Web browser than it does in your Web browser; you should keep scrolling enabled if you want to make your pages more universally accessible.

Control Frame Borders

U nless you specify otherwise, Web browsers display a 3D border between frames. You can use the frameborder attribute to hide the borders so that multiple frames can appear as though they comprise a single page. This can give your page a more polished appearance, but it prevents users from having a visible divider that they can drag to resize the frames. Although users can still resize the frames, without a visible border, they may not realize that resizing the frames is an option.

You can add the frameborder attribute to the individual <frame /> tags to explicitly turn borders on or off.

Technically, Netscape Navigator and Internet Explorer accept different values for the frameborder attribute, but each supports the other's attribute value. To turn frames off, you must set the value to either "0" or "no." To explicitly turn them on, you must set the value to "1" or "yes."

In theory, the frameborder attributes should give you all the control you need. In practice, some Web browsers may still display borders even when you have the frame borders set to zero.

1 Create a new document with the frameset DTD in your HTML editor.

2 Add an opening <frameset> tag that includes the rows "and/" or cols attribute.

3 Add a closing </frameset> tag.

4 Between the <frameset> tags, add <frame /> tags, each with a frameborder attribute set to "0".

5 Save the document.

6 Open the document in your Web browser.

● Borders do not appear between the individual frames.

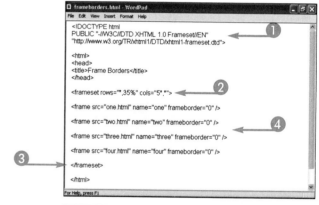

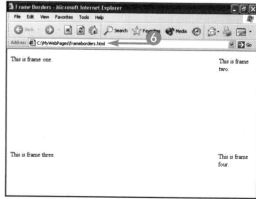

Nest Frames

Structurally, frames are very similar to tables. As a result, you can create a frameset using both `rows` and `cols` attributes to create a grid. However, if you want a frameset that is more sophisticated, you will need more than the `rows` and `cols` attributes — you may need to nest one frameset within another. For example, you can have two frames at the top, side by side, for navigating the main content of your Web site, and a single frame at the bottom that runs the width of the window to display supplemental content.

With nested frames, you still set the rows or columns using the top-level `<frameset>` tag. You can then

include additional framesets to add further sublevels. These sublevel framesets define the rows or columns that you set in the top-level frame. By creating a nested frameset for each top-level row or column, you can have varying numbers of frames in each segment, such as one row with two frames and another row with three.

Another option is to use nested framesets in combination with top-level frames. If you create a top-level frameset with two rows and then add one frame and a nested frameset, the single frame spans the width of the nested frameset.

Nest Frames

① In your HTML editor, open a document that contains a frameset.

② Add `<frameset>` tags between the existing `<frameset>` tags to set different dimensions for the rows or columns.

③ Add `<frame />` tags with `name` and `src` attributes to the nested frameset.

④ Save the document.

⑤ Open the document in your Web browser.

● Your Web browser displays the nested frames.

● This example shows a non-grid layout.

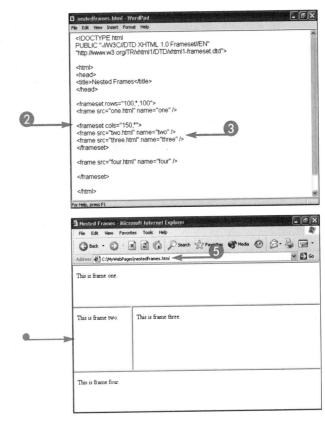

149

Create an
Inline Frame

ramesets act externally to instruct a Web browser window to divide the viewing area into frames. However, an inline frame appears as a boxed element on a Web page. It also behaves like an inline image, appearing *in line* with the text. Inline frames can contain various types of content, including text, images, and JavaScript.

You can create an inline frame by adding the `<iframe>` tag to any HTML document. You must indicate the URL of the frame's content with the `src` attribute. You can use the

optional `frameborder` attribute to explicitly turn the frame border on or off. In addition, you can control the height and width of the inline frame with the `height` and `width` attributes, which accept pixel values.

Inline frames are part of the HTML 4.0 specification and are supported by Internet Explorer 4.0 and Netscape Navigator 6. Because older Netscape Web browsers do not support inline frames, you should provide alternative content. To do this, you can include your alternative content inside the opening and closing `<iframe>` tags, instead of using the `<noframes>` tag as you do with regular frames.

Create an Inline Frame

① Create a new document with the transitional DTD in your HTML editor.

② Add an opening `<iframe>` tag that includes the `src` and `name` attributes and that sets the frame's dimensions.

Note: *You must place the `<iframe>` tags between the `<body>` tags.*

③ Add a closing `</iframe>` tag.

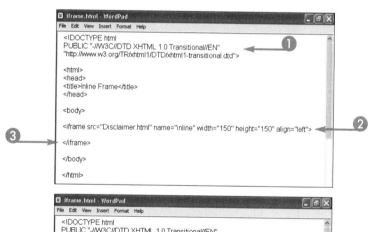

④ Add alternative content between the opening and closing `<iframe>` tags.

⑤ Save the document.

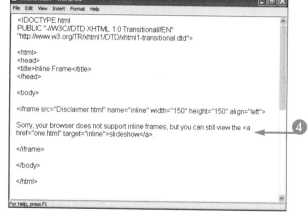

6 Create a document that contains what you want to load in the inline frame.

7 Save the document in the same directory as you did in step 5.

Note: *You must give the document the same filename that you assigned as the* `src` *attribute in step 2.*

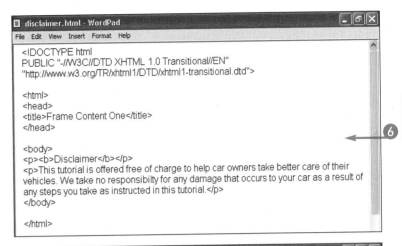

8 Open the document from step 5 in your Web browser.

● The Web browser displays the inline frame with the initial frame content.

Note: *If you view the page in a Web browser that does not support inline frames, the alternative text appears.*

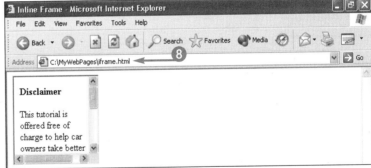

PART II

Can I use the `<noframes>` tags with inline frames?

▼ No. You must use the `<noframes>` tags only within `<frameset>` tags. To provide alternative content for inline frames, simply include the content between the opening and closing `<iframe>` tags. If the browser does not recognize the `<iframe>` tags, it displays the content in its current location on the page without displaying a frame around it. Users can still access the content, although it does not appear in the intended format.

How can I get text to flow around an inline frame?

▼ To have text flow to the left or right of an inline frame, you can use the HTML `align` attribute and set the value to `left` or `right`. Other values for the `align` attribute are `top`, `middle`, and `bottom`, and allow you to align the frame with any adjacent text. You can also create a CSS style rule for the `iframe` element that includes the `float` property, as shown in Chapter 4.

Can I prevent scroll bars from displaying within inline frames?

▼ Yes, you can explicitly prevent scroll bars by adding the optional `scrolling` attribute and setting the value to `"no"`. Other possible values are `"yes"` and `"auto"`. If you set `scrolling` equal to `"yes"` the scrollbars appear whether or not they are needed. Setting `scrolling` to `"auto"` displays the scroll bars only when the inline frame is too small to display all of the content in the frame.

Target Frames

I f you only want to display two or more blocks of content on a page in boxes, you can create the desired effect with CSS. However, frames are designed to add a degree of interactivity to Web pages, and they do this through the use of the `target` attribute. With the `target` attribute, you can specify that when a user clicks a particular link, the linked content appears in a specific frame. For the value of the `target` attribute, you must use the name that you assign to the frame within your initial frameset.

You can use the `target` attribute when you have specific frames for navigation and content segments. For all the

links within the navigation frame, you must set the target to the name of the content frame in order for content to load into that frame. For links within the actual content documents, you do not need to set the `target` attribute. Without an explicit target, the Web browser loads any new content within the current frame.

If the target that you indicate does not correspond to any frame or window that you have previously named, the Web browser opens a new window, assigns it the target name, and loads the content inside the window.

Target Frames

① Create a new document with the frameset DTD in your HTML editor.

② Add an opening `<frameset>` tag with the `rows` or `cols` attribute.

③ Add a closing `</frameset>` tag.

④ Add frames with the `<frame />` tag, giving each frame a `src` and `name` attribute.

⑤ Save the document.

⑥ Create the source documents for each frame.

- You must give the documents the same filenames that you assigned as the `src` attributes in step 4.

⑦ For each hyperlink that you add, include the `target` attribute, defining the frame in which you want the content to display.

⑧ Save the documents.

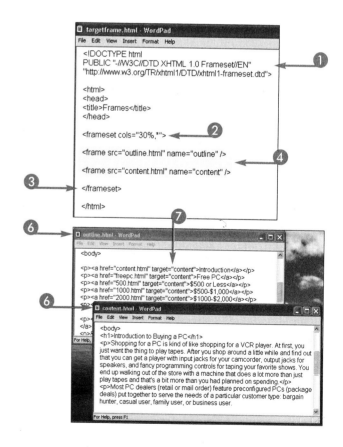

⑨ Open the document from step 5 in your Web browser.

● The content appears in the main content frame.

⑩ Click a hyperlink to display different content.

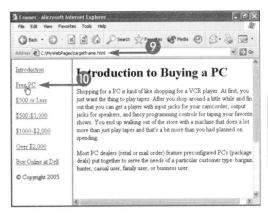

● The new content appears in the main content frame.

⑪ Click a link within the main content frame.

● Without the `target` attribute set, the new content appears in the currently active frame.

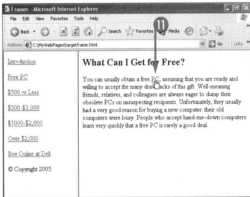

What other values can I use with the `target` attribute?

▼ Aside from the name of a specific frame or window, the `target` attribute accepts `_blank`, `_parent`, and `_top`. The `_blank` value displays the content in a new, unnamed window. The `_parent` value displays the content in the frameset that contains the frame with the hyperlink. The `_top` attribute causes the document to load into the main Web browser window. If your principal frame document contains only one frameset, the `_parent` and `_top` values lead to the same result. But if you have nested framesets, `_parent` indicates the immediate, nested frameset, and `_top` indicates the outermost frameset.

Can I use the `target` attribute to change the content of multiple frames at once?

▼ No, the `target` attribute accepts only one frame name. However, you can create functions with JavaScript that change the content of multiple frames at once. For more information about JavaScript, see Part III.

Can I target an inline frame?

▼ Yes, you can create links that change the contents of an inline frame. Typically, you place the links near the inline frame or inside it, and you must give the inline frame a name so that you can target it. You can create some interesting effects using inline frames in this way. For example, you can display links next to an inline frame that a user can click to change the content displayed in the frame.

Define a
Base Target

I f you have several links that you want to load into the same frame, you can do so without adding a `target` attribute and frame name to every link on your page. To set a global target for all links on a page, you must add the standalone `<base />` tag with the `target` attribute to your document. With the base target set, every link on the page loads into the same frame, unless you specify otherwise.

The `<base />` tag can include an `href` attribute, which defines the base URL for the relative links on the page.

However, if you store your frames document in the same directory as you store all the pages to which it links, you need not include the `href` attribute. If you store the pages in a different directory, you must add the `href` attribute to define the location of those pages. As a result, when you link to a particular source document, you simply enter its name without identifying its location.

For the value of the `target` attribute, you can indicate the name of the target frame just as you do for individual `<a>` tags. The base target then applies to every link on the page that does not have a defined target.

Define a Base Target

1 Create a new document with the frameset DTD in your HTML editor.

2 Add an opening `<frameset>` tag with the `rows` or `cols` attribute.

3 Add a closing `</frameset>` tag.

4 Add frames with the `<frame>` tag, and give each frame a `src` and `name` attribute.

5 Save the document.

6 Open the first frame document.

7 Add a `<base />` tag with the `target` attribute set to the name of the main content frame.

Note: If you store your source files in a different directory, then you need to add the `href` attribute and set its value to the URL for that directory.

8 Add a link to load other content into a `target="external"` frame.

9 Save the document.

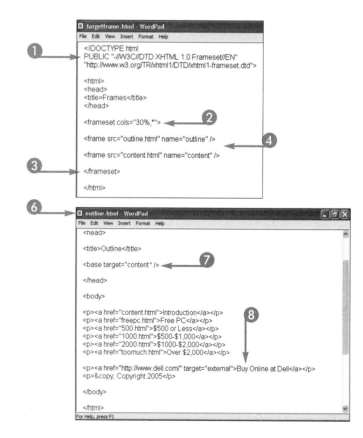

⑩ Open the document from step 5 in your Web browser.

⑪ Click a navigation link.

● The content loads into the content frame.

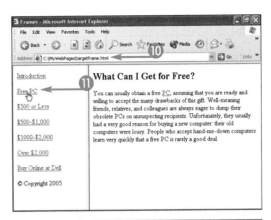

⑫ Click the link for loading external content.

● Because the document has no frame named "external," the Web browser creates a new window and loads the content into it.

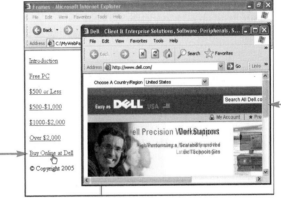

Can I still use the `target` attribute with `<a>` tags when I have the base target set?

▼ Yes, you can still use the `target` attribute with individual hyperlinks when you want content to load into a frame other than the one indicated through the base target. For example, a page may include links to other pages at your site that you want to load in a particular frame and links to external sites that you want to open in a new window. To open linked pages in a new window, add `target="_blank"` to the link's opening `<a>` tag. See the section "Target Frames" for more information.

Can I target frames from an image map?

▼ Yes, links in an image map can target specific frames. Simply add the `target` attribute to the links that you set up in your image map, and set the `target` attribute equal to the frame name that you want.

How do I ensure that links to external sites appear in a new window?

▼ To ensure that external links appear in a new window, include the `target` attribute within the `<a>` tag for any external links. Set the value to `"_blank"` to launch a new unnamed window, or create a new named window by setting the target value to a name you have not yet used. Then, use that name as a target value for all external links to ensure that they appear in the same secondary window.

Set Frame Backgrounds

U nless you set a Web page background color, all of your frames appear with the background colors that your browser uses — typically white — unless you specify otherwise. Sometimes, especially if you use one frame for navigating the Web site or if you hide frame borders, using a background color for the navigation frame helps visitors to differentiate between the two frames. Although you cannot set a color for the actual frame, you can set a background color for the Web page that displays in the frame.

To set a background color, you can create a style rule for the body attribute that sets the background color you want, as shown in this section.

I want to use a dark background, but doing so makes it difficult to read the text. Can I also change the font color?

▼ Yes. Using dark text on a light background or light text on a dark background ensures that the text contrasts against the background. For example, you can create a style rule for the body element to display white text on a green background: `body {background-color: green; color: white}`. You may also need to change link colors. For more information, as well as how to define hyperlink pseudo classes, see Chapter 4.

Set Frame Backgrounds

① In your HTML editor, open a Web page for which you want to change the background color.

② Between the <head> tags, type opening and closing <style> tags.

③ Add the body style definition to set the background color and text color.

● You can also change link colors.

④ Save the document.

⑤ Open the frames page that contains the document from step 4 in your Web browser.

● The background and text color reflect the styles that you defined.

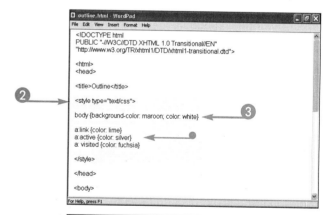

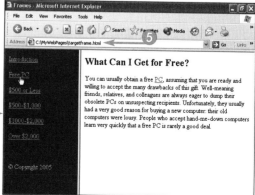

Using Frames for Banner Ads

Web sites often have a separate frame that is dedicated to banner advertisements. You may encounter this if you visit personal Web sites hosted on ISP member servers or networks that are composed of many independently run Web sites.

To create a separate frame for a banner ad, you must first define a two-row frameset. For the source of the banner frame, you must indicate the URL of the HTML document that contains the banner ad.

When you code banner ads directly into regular HTML pages, you can serve a new banner ad each time a visitor loads a new page. For example, five page views on your Web site can yield five banner impressions. However, when you place a banner ad within an independent frame, the banner rotation is independent of the content page views because the frame containing the banner does not reload each time the user visits a new page. To control banner impressions, you can use a <meta /> tag with a refresh attribute or create a script that rotates ads at specific intervals.

Using Frames for Banner Ads

① Create a new document with the frameset DTD in your HTML editor.

② After the </head> tag, add an opening <frameset> tag with a rows attribute.

③ Add a closing </frameset> tag.

④ Add two <frame/> tags, giving each frame a source and name attribute.

⑤ Save the document.

⑥ Create a new HTML document.

⑦ Between the <head> tags, add a <meta /> tag with the http-equiv attribute set to "Refresh".

⑧ Add a content attribute specifying the refresh interval and page URL.

⑨ Add a script to change the banner image each time the page reloads.

Note: See Part 3 for more information about adding scripts.

● A random banner ad appears each time the page reloads.

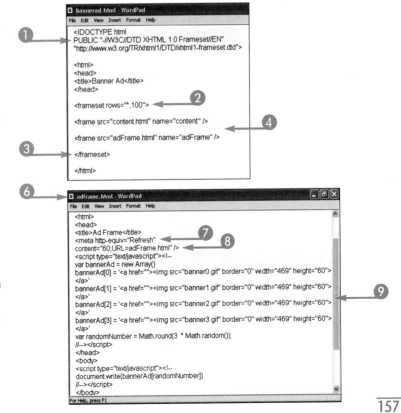

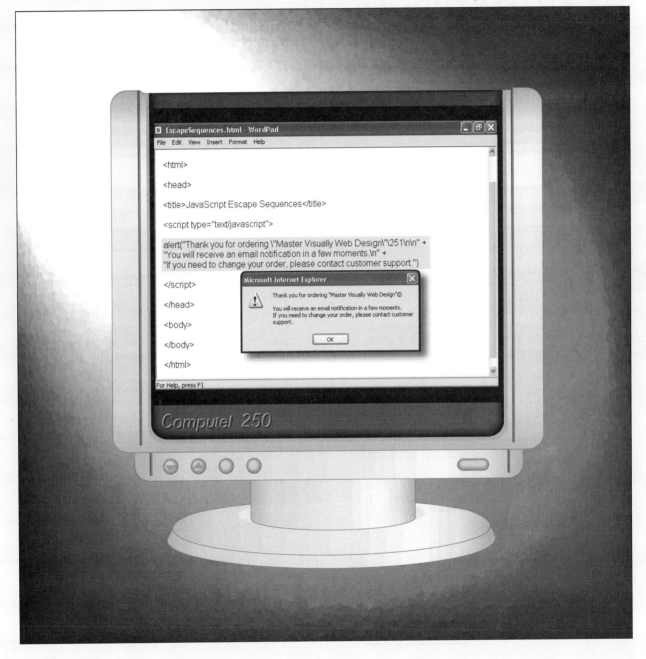

An Introduction to Client-Side JavaScript

The Web is an interactive medium that can respond to user events such as mouseovers, clicks, and keystrokes. You can add interac to use JavaScript, an object-based scripting language that allows you to create and execute procedures within a Web page. Unlike other technologies that add interactivity, JavaScript does not require additional plug-ins and is widely supported by most Web browsers.

This chapter provides a brief introduction to the lexical structure of JavaScript, while Chapter 9 describes how you can use JavaScript on your Web site. While these chapters should provide you with the skills necessary to create and edit simple JavaScript procedures, they do not fully explore the power and complexity of the JavaScript language. For more in-depth information, you can obtain a copy of *JavaScript: Your visual blueprint for building dynamic Web pages*, by Kelly Murdock (John Wiley).

JavaScript vs. Java

If you are completely new to programming, it may surprise you to find that JavaScript and Java are two completely different languages. In fact, despite the obvious similarities in their names, Java and JavaScript are entirely different species.

Java is a *compiled* programming language. Using a compiled programming language, you can write a program using instructions that you, as a human being, can recognize and understand, but that a machine cannot. When you finish writing your program, you must run the program through a compiler that converts the instructions into machine code, which a computer can recognize and interpret. For more information about Java applications for the Web, see Chapter 15.

JavaScript, like Perl, is an *interpreted* language. Once you write your instructions with JavaScript, the procedure is complete. The script can run in any JavaScript-enabled Web browser, and is checked for errors only at run-time, when the procedure is executed.

Versions of JavaScript

Netscape released the first version of JavaScript, now known as JavaScript 1.0, back in 1995, and the Netscape 2 Web browser was the first to support the language. Since then, Netscape has released several subsequent versions of the language, with the most recent Web browser supporting JavaScript version 1.5. At the same time, Microsoft has developed its own scripting language, called JScript. JavaScript and JScript are very similar, but they each have proprietary extensions to support their Document Object Models (DOMs).

In an effort to standardize the core language, the European Computer Manufacturers Association (ECMA) has developed a platform-independent version of JavaScript known as ECMAScript. Both JavaScript, 1.3 and higher, and recent versions of Jscript comply with the ECMAScript standard.

Client-Side JavaScript

JavaScript has three components: core, client-side, and server-side. Core JavaScript is the actual structure of the language, and is shared by both client-side and server-side JavaScript. Client-side JavaScript has additional features that apply only to the client, or Web browser. Server-side JavaScript has additional features that apply only to the Web server, such as database scripts. This chapter focuses primarily on core JavaScript. Chapter 9 deals more directly with client-side JavaScript, the core language as it applies specifically to the Web browsing environment.

Netscape Navigator, Internet Explorer, Opera, Safari and other Web browsers come with a built-in JavaScript interpreter that can process JavaScript statements. This means that you can add JavaScript to HTML pages by using `<script>` tags, external JavaScript files, or by adding JavaScript commands into `<a href>` tags and event handlers such as `onclick`. In addition, client-side JavaScript allows you to use the scripting language to interact with the Web browser's DOM to respond to user events and dynamically alter Web page content.

The DOM is a tree-like organizational structure that represents every element on a Web page, from windows and frames to form-field values. Because each Web browser has its own DOM, the ways in which you implement JavaScript applications can vary, depending on the Web browser type and version number. For more information about referencing the DOM, see Chapter 9.

Core Language Features

JavaScript has a number of core features, such as variables, arrays, and objects, which allow you to manipulate data within your scripts. A *variable* is a symbolic name that you assign to a particular value, such as $x = 3$, where x is the variable name and 3 is the value. While a variable is a single value, an *array* is a collection of values referenced by a single name and index. Within an array, each value is referenced using an index number, such as `car_model[0] = "Toyota"`. *Objects* are similar to arrays, but they allow you to reference values through named properties rather than numbers. For more information about variables, arrays and objects, see the sections, "Declare JavaScript Variables," "Create a JavaScript Object," and "Create a JavaScript Array."

JavaScript also has a number of *statements* that you can use to execute code. Some JavaScript statements, such as `for`, `while`, and `do while`, are loop statements, meaning they repeatedly execute code until a condition is no longer true. For example, you may use a loop statement to validate all of the fields in a form until it reaches the end of the form. Another statement that is common to JavaScript applications is the conditional `if` statement, which executes code only if a condition is true. For more information about conditional statements, see the section, "Create an `if` Statement."

Add Scripts to a Web Page

Because Web browsers are equipped with the interpreter that is required to process JavaScript statements, you can embed JavaScript directly inside your HTML source code. You simply need to identify the beginning and end of your script using opening and closing <script> tags. You can include these tags within the head or body of the document, and the Web browser executes the JavaScript statements in the order that they appear.

Within the opening <script> tag, you must specify the scripting language by using the type attribute. It is always important to specify the scripting language as *JavaScript* because there are other possible scripting languages, such

as JScript, that you can use on the Web. Many Web designers continue to use the language=JavaScript attribute, although this attribute is deprecated in favor of the type attribute. This book recommends that you use the type attribute, and set its value equal to "text/javascript".

Between the opening and closing <script> tags, you can include all of your JavaScript statements, as well as JavaScript comments. You can add single-line comments using the // sequence that is normally used in C++ programming. For multiple-line comments, you can use C-style comments that begin with a forward slash and asterisk (/*) and end with another asterisk and forward slash (*/).

Add Scripts to a Web Page

① Open an HTML document.

② Add a set of <head> tags.

③ Add a set of <body> tags.

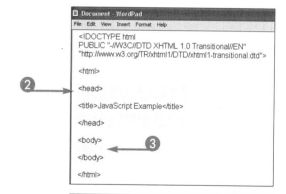

④ Within the head of the document, type an opening <script> tag with the type attribute set equal to "text/javascript".

⑤ Type a closing <script> tag.

● You can type the opening and closing <script> tags either between the <head> tags or between the <body> tags.

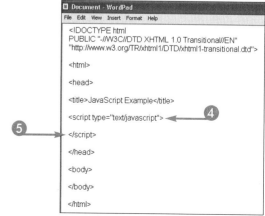

⑥ Add JavaScript statements.

● This statement causes a simple dialog box to appear on-screen.

Note: *For more information about statements, see JavaScript: Your visual blueprint for building dynamic Web pages, by Kelly Murdock (John Wiley).*

⑦ Save the document.

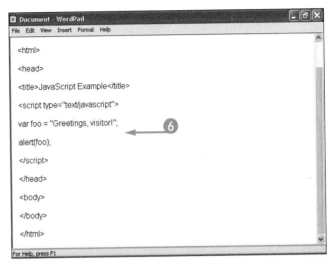

⑧ Open the document in your Web browser.

● Your Web browser executes the JavaScript statements embedded within the `<script>` tags.

Can I use regular HTML comments within scripts?

▼ No. JavaScript recognizes the opening HTML comment sequence (`<!--`) and treats it as a single-line comment, as it would for //. However, it does not recognize the closing comment sequence used in HTML. You should only use this opening HTML comment in order to hide scripts from old Web browsers. For more information, see the section, "Hide JavaScript from Old Web Browsers."

What other ways can I add JavaScript to HTML pages?

▼ In addition to the `<script>` tags, you can add JavaScript to URLs using the javascript: protocol or as an event-handler with an HTML attribute such as `onmouseover` or `onload`. Event handlers initiate a JavaScript function to respond to a particular action. For example, `onload` initiates a specified JavaScript when a browser opens a page, and `onmouseover` initiates a JavaScript when the user hovers the mouse cursor over an object.

Can statements in one set of `<script>` tags reference statements in another set of `<script>` tags?

▼ Yes. JavaScript is an object-oriented scripting language, meaning that each script is an object that can function independently or as a part of other scripts. With JavaScript, you can define a variable in one section of an HTML page, and then reference it elsewhere in the page using another set of `<script>` tags. By using JavaScript in this way, you need not repeat existing scripts to include them in other scripts on the same page.

Using Escape Sequences

JavaScript uses certain characters, such as apostrophes and quotation marks, as signals. If you want to use these characters in your JavaScript code, you must use *escape sequences*, which are snippets of code that indicate the signal characters are to be interpreted as themselves. You must also use escape sequences to create special characters, such as ampersands.

For example, you cannot use apostrophes with text that is enclosed inside single quotes because the apostrophe signals the end of the text string and causes an error.

Instead, you need to use an escape sequence, in this case a backslash and then an apostrophe (\'). All JavaScript escape sequences are composed in this way, with an initial backslash and a character or alphanumeric sequence.

You can also use escape sequences to insert line breaks. Because JavaScript does not recognize breaks that you add using a text editor, you can specify explicit line breaks using the new line sequence (\n). You may use this escape sequence if you have an alert dialog box and you want to format the text in a specific way.

Using Escape Sequences

① Open a document in your HTML editor.

② Add a set of <head> tags.

③ Between the <head> tags, type opening and closing <script> tags.

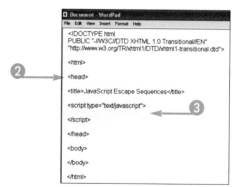

④ Add a script to generate an alert dialog box with a text message.

Note: *For more information about alert dialog boxes, see the section, "Script an Alert Dialog Box."*

⑤ Insert new-line escape sequences.

● Use multiple \n sequences to create additional line breaks.

6 Add additional escape sequences for quotation marks and special characters.

7 Save the document.

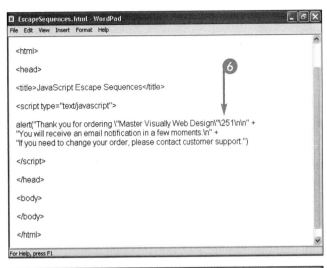

8 Open the document in your Web browser.

- The alert dialog box appears, displaying text formatted with the specified line breaks.

What other escape sequences can I use in my JavaScript?

JavaScript supports several escape sequences listed below. See Appendix A for a list of character entities you can create using three octal digits.

Escape Sequence	Represents
\b	backspace
\f	form feed
\n	new line
\r	carriage return
\t	tab
\'	single quote
\"	double quotes
\\	singe back slash

Escape Sequence	Represents
\???	character with Latin-1 encoding specified by three octal digits ???
\u????	character with unicode encoding specified by four hexadecimal digits ????
\x??	Character with Latin-1 encoding specified by two hexadecimal digits ??
\?	?, where ? is any character other than one of the characters specified for use in an escape sequence

Script an Alert Dialog Box

Y ou can communicate event-related messages to site visitors by using an alert dialog box. You create these simple dialog boxes with the `alert()` method associated with the Window object, the top-level object in the Web browser's DOM. See Chapter 9 for more Window-related methods. The `alert()` method causes the Web browser to pop up a small box that displays any message text you supply. The dialog box includes an OK button, so the user can close the dialog box after reading the alert. The syntax for the `alert()` method is:

```
alert("This is the alert message.");
```

When you are scripting alert boxes, you can make the text contained within the box plain text only, so you cannot include any HTML formatting in the message. In addition, you must use JavaScript escape sequences to add formatting elements such as new lines. For more information about escape sequences, see the section, "Using Escape Sequences."

Keep in mind that while you can format the text message using spaces, underscores, and line breaks, you cannot control the color or visual appearance of the dialog box.

Script an Alert Dialog Box

① Open a document in your HTML editor.

② After the opening <body> tag, add an opening <script> tag with the `type` attribute set equal to `"text/javascript"`.

③ Add a closing </script> tag.

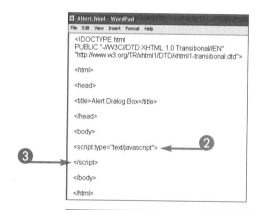

④ Type **alert** followed by your alert message enclosed in quotation marks and parentheses.

Note: Ensure that the parentheses are outside the quotation marks and that you add a semicolon after the closing parenthesis.

5️⃣ Add new-line escape sequences to format the message.

Note: *For more information, see the section, "Using Escape Sequences."*

6️⃣ Save the document.

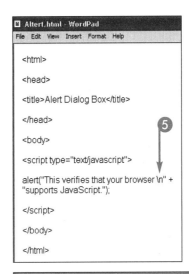

7️⃣ View the document in your Web browser.

● The Web browser launches an alert box displaying the message you created.

What other types of dialog boxes are possible in client-side JavaScript?

▼ In addition to the alert dialog box, the Window object in client-side JavaScript supports the `prompt()` and `confirm()` methods, both of which create dialog boxes that prompt the user to respond in some way. The prompt dialog box requests that the user type one or more entries. The confirm dialog box provides the user with two options: one to confirm and the other to cancel a given action. Refer to Chapter 9 for instructions on creating prompt and confirm dialog boxes.

Can I create an alert box with an option to cancel?

▼ The alert box only offers the user the opportunity to click OK to continue. To offer the choice to cancel an action, use the confirm dialog box, as shown in Chapter 9.

Do I have to reference the `Window` object when using the `alert()` method?

▼ No. It is not necessary to type **window.alert()** when calling this method. Because the `Window` object is a top-level object in the Web browser's object hierarchy, the Web browser automatically assumes that the alert method is referencing the `Window` object. However, including the reference to the `Window` object does not cause any errors, so you may reference it if you want.

Write to a Document

Y ou can use JavaScript to dynamically write HTML code to a Web page by using the document.write() method. When you include the document.write() method within <script> tags in the body of your document, the Web browser generates the HTML code as it displays the document. You can use this method to output variables or generate different content, based on user responses. For example, you can prompt a visitor to type his or her first name and then use the document.write() method to generate a Web page that greets the visitor by his or her name, and welcomes the visitor to your Web site.

Although you can use the document.write() method by itself when writing to the current document, if you use it to write content to another window or frame, you should use the document.write() method in conjunction with two other methods: document.open() and document.close().

The document.open() method tells the Web browser to open a new HTML document to write to, while the document.close() method signals that the output process is complete. The document.open() method is optional. If you omit it, the Web browser automatically opens a new HTML document. However, the document.close() method is required.

Write to a Document

① Open a document in your HTML editor.

② Add a set of <head> tags.

③ Add a set of <body> tags.

④ Add opening and closing <script> tags.

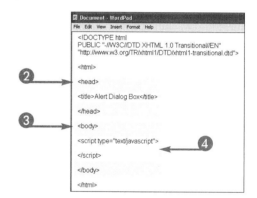

⑤ Declare a new variable and assign it a value.

Note: *See the section, "Declare JavaScript Variables," for more information.*

⑥ If the value is user-generated, add an if statement to check for the user's response.

⑦ Add the document.write() method to generate a message.

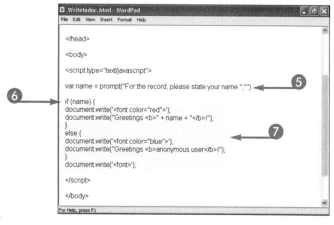

8 Save the document.

9 Open the document in your Web browser.

● In this example, the Web browser generates the `prompt()` dialog box.

10 Type a response.

11 Click OK.

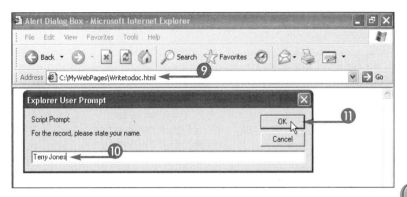

● The `document.write()` method dynamically writes the HTML code to the page.

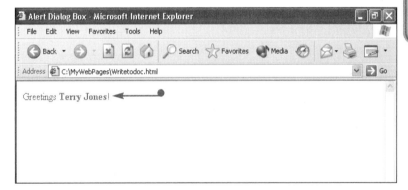

Can I call the `document.write()` method from an event handler?

▼ Yes, but realize that if you call the `document.write` method from an event handler, the method overwrites whatever is in the current document. In the example shown here, the `document.write` method is called before the page is finished loading, so any text the user enters is added to the rest of the content on the page. However, if you call the `document.write` method after the page is done loading, as an event handler would do, the method replaces the contents of the page. In most cases, this is not what you want.

Can the `document.write()` method take more than one argument?

▼ Yes it can. You can use plus (+) signs to *concatenate*, or link together, the various elements you want to write, or simply separate each element with a comma. In this way, you can write an entire page or a section of a page. You can achieve the same effect by using multiple `document.write` methods. You can include one `document.write()` method after another to write several HTML elements to a page. Simply type your HTML-tagged text inside the parentheses and enclose the text with quotation marks. Using multiple `document.write` methods can make the text more manageable.

Declare JavaScript Variables

You can store and manipulate information in your scripts by declaring *variables*. To declare variables, you create a variable name and assign a value to it. After you declare the variable, you can reference and use it throughout your scripts. To declare a variable, you can use the `var` keyword with the name of the variable:

```
var x;
```

The `var` keyword is optional, and you can declare a variable without it. If you omit the `var` keyword, JavaScript creates a global variable for you. You can also initialize the variable — that is, assign it an initial value — at the same time you declare it:

```
var x = 3;
```

If you declare a variable without giving it an initial value, the variable is defined but the value is undefined.

Variables you define can either be globally accessible to your entire JavaScript program, or local to a specific function. To define a local variable, you must declare it within the body of a function. For more information about functions, see the section, "Create a JavaScript Function."

Declare JavaScript Variables

① Open a document in your HTML editor.

② In the body of the document, add a set of `<script>` tags.

③ Declare a new variable by typing **var** and the name of the variable.

④ Use the `alert()` method to check for the value of the variable.

Note: For more information about alert dialog boxes, see the section, "Script an Alert Dialog Box."

⑤ Save the document.

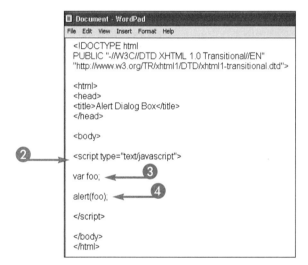

⑥ Open the document in your Web browser.

● The value of the variable is undefined.

⑦ Open the document in your HTML editor.

⑧ Initialize the variable by assigning it a value.

⑨ Save the document again.

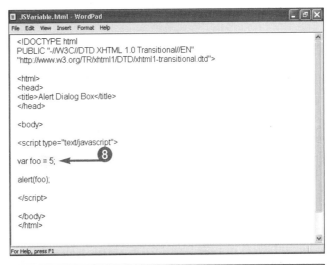

⑩ Open the document from step 9 in your Web browser.

● The variable now has an initial value.

Are there any words that I cannot use as variable names?

▼ You cannot use certain reserved words to name variables or functions because they are part of the JavaScript language and therefore carry special meaning. Reserved JavaScript words include the following:

break, case, continue, default, delete, do, else, export, for, function, if, import, in, new, return, switch, this, typeof, var, void, while, with

In addition, you should never name variables with words that are the names of properties or methods, such as alert or confirm.

If I assign a number value to a variable, can I later assign a text value to it?

▼ Yes you can. In JavaScript, variables are *untyped*, meaning that the value is not limited to one data type when you declare it. You can make JavaScript variables names, numbers, or a combination of characters and numbers, as long as the variable is unique, so your JavaScript can easily identify it. You can change the data type with no negative consequences. You can even have the variable change within a script; in the example in the steps, you can type **foo = 'five';** after var foo = 5; to change the value of foo to "five."

Create a JavaScript Object

With JavaScript, you can work with pre-existing objects, such as elements of the Web browser's DOM, as well as create new objects. By creating new objects, you can store and manipulate values by referencing the properties associated with an object.

You can create a new JavaScript object by defining a variable with the `new Object()` operator. You can then create and set properties for the object by using the object's name and adding a period (.) and the name of the property. The syntax for creating a new object is as follows:

```
var objectName = new Object();
```

The optional `var` keyword stores a reference of the object to a new variable. After you create the object, you can assign properties and values with the (`.`) operator:

```
objectName.property = value;
```

When you use objects, you create code that is better organized because it packages the data in a tree-like structure of properties. This also makes the JavaScript more modular, enabling you to reuse it more easily.

Create a JavaScript Object

① Open a document in your HTML editor.

② Within the body of the document, add an opening `<script>` tag with the `type` attribute set equal to `"text/javascript"`.

Note: *See the section, "Add Scripts to a Web Page" for more information about using `<script>` tags.*

③ Add a closing `</script>` tag.

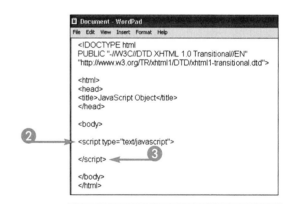

④ Type **var feature = new Object();**.

● An object called feature is created.

⑤ Add properties for the object.

Note: *This example has two properties, `feature.headline` and `feature.author`, with their assigned values in quotes.*

⑥ If you want, type **document.write()** and the name of a property you want to print.

Note: For more information about the `document.write()` method, see the section, "Write to a Document."

⑦ Save the document.

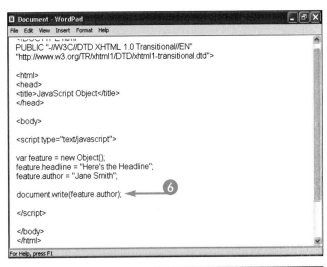

⑧ Open the document in your Web browser.

● The script writes the value of the object property to the page.

Is there a way to create objects without using the `new Object()` operator?

▼ Yes, you can also create objects by using a constructor function. To do this, you define a function, include properties as the parameters, and use the `this` keyword to initialize the object. The advantage to the constructor function is that it allows you to create a *class* of similar objects. For more information about this and other object-oriented programming techniques, see *JavaScript: Your visual blueprint for building dynamic Web pages,* by Kelly Murdock (John Wiley).

How can I delete a property of an object?

▼ You can delete a specific property of an object by using the `delete` operator, as in `delete objectName.propertyName`. Using the delete operator, you must always type the object's name and a period followed by the property's name. You cannot simply type the property's name. Another way to delete an object's property is to specify the object name first:

```
with(objectName)
delete propertyName;
```

The with statement specifies the object's name, so you can delete one or more of its properties.

How are methods related to objects?

▼ A method is essentially the same as a function, but it applies specifically to a given object. For example, the `alert()` method is invoked through the Web browser's `Window` object, and the `write()` method is invoked through the `Document` object. With custom objects, you can define methods by assigning a function to an object in the following way:

```
objectName.methodName =
functionName;
```

You can then invoke the method with the code `objectName.methodName()`. For more information, see the section, "Create a JavaScript Function."

Create a JavaScript Array

A JavaScript array acts as a storage area for data entries. You can think of it as a single column of mail slots, with each slot holding a single piece of data. Each slot has an assigned number, called an *index*, which identifies its location. Web authors commonly use arrays to store data that a user enters so that the data can be moved around and processed in various ways. You create a JavaScript array by using the `Array()` constructor. The syntax for creating an array is:

```
var arrayname = new Array("arrayvalue1",
"arrayvalue2", ...)
```

The optional `var` keyword stores a reference of the array to a variable.

When you first create an array, you can create an empty array with no data by leaving the parentheses empty, or you can set the values of the data within the parentheses. In some programming languages, you must specify the number of elements contained in an array, also known as the *length* of the array. However, in JavaScript, specifying an array's length is unnecessary.

When you reference elements in an array, keep in mind that in JavaScript the first element has an index of 0 (zero). For example, the fourth element in an array has an index of 3.

Create a JavaScript Array

① Open a document in your HTML editor.

② Add opening and closing `<head>` tags.

③ Add opening and closing `<body>` tags.

④ Add opening and closing `<script>` tags.

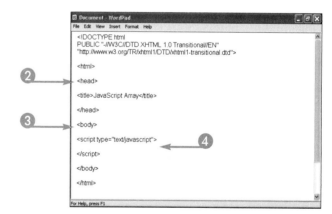

⑤ Create a new array.

● This example creates a new array named foo with 7 elements.

Note: *You must enclose strings, or text elements, within quotation marks.*

6 Add a `document.write()` method that references any element in the array using the `[ ]` operator.

Note: For more information, see the section, "Write to a Document."

7 Add another `document.write()` method using the `length` property to return the number of elements in the array.

8 Save the document.

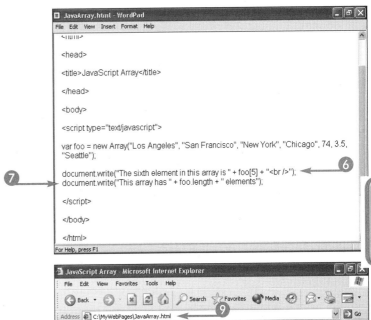

9 Open the document in your Web browser.

● The script writes the value for the specified array element, as well as the length of the array.

How do I add a new element to an array?

▼ To add an element to an array, simply use the `[ ]` operator with an index number to assign a value to the element. For example, for an array called cities, add an element with the following line of code:

```
cities[15] = "Houston";
```

How do I change the length of an array?

▼ The length of an array changes when you add new elements to it. In addition, you can change the length using the read/write `length` property. If the value you assign to the `length` property is smaller than the actual number of elements in an array, JavaScript deletes any element beyond the new length.

Can I create two-dimensional arrays in JavaScript?

▼ A JavaScript array typically contains a single column of entries. A two-dimensional array consists of two or more columns of entries, increasing the storage capacity of the array by a factor equivalent to the number of columns. For example, making a three-element array two-dimensional provides space for nine elements. You can create two-dimensional arrays by assigning a new array to an existing array element:

```
arrayname[0] = ("arrayvalue1",
"arrayvalue2");
```

You must then reference each element in the array using an index consisting of two bracketed numbers, such as `arrayname[0][0]`, `arrayname[0][1]`, and `arrayname[0][2]`.

Create an if Statement

By using `if` statements, you can create programs that respond differently, depending on conditions. For example, you can use `if` statements to direct users to particular pages, or issue different alert messages, depending on the actions the user takes.

The `if` statement consists of three parts: the *if* keyword, the *condition* enclosed in parentheses, and the *action statement*. When the Web browser evaluates the conditional statement and finds the result to be true, it executes the action statement. You can include action statements to execute if the conditional value is false by using the `else` clause:

```
if (condition) {
action statement;
action statement;
}
else {
action statement;
}
```

When only one statement is executed for a condition, you do not have to place the statements in curly brackets. However, many programmers always include the curly brackets around statements to make scripts easier to read and debug.

For more information about the action statements that you can use in `if` statements, consult *JavaScript: Your visual blueprint for building dynamic Web pages,* by Kelly Murdock.

Create an if Statement

1. Open a document in your HTML editor.

2. Within the head of the document, add opening and closing `<script>` tags.

3. Create a new function.

Note: *For more information about functions, see the section, "Create a JavaScript Function."*

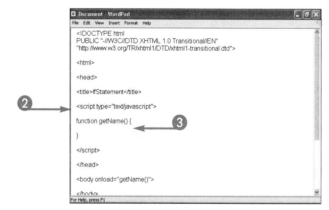

4. Create a new variable, and assign a value to the variable, or use the `prompt()` method to generate a user response.

Note: *See Chapter 9 for more information about the* `prompt()` *method.*

5. Add an `if` statement followed by a conditional expression.

- This example checks for a value for the variable that has been created.

⑥ Add statements to execute if the expression is true.

⑦ Add statements to execute if the expression is false.

⑧ Include an event handler to trigger the function.

Note: *This example uses the `onload` attribute with the `<body>` tag, which runs the script when the page loads.*

⑨ Save the document.

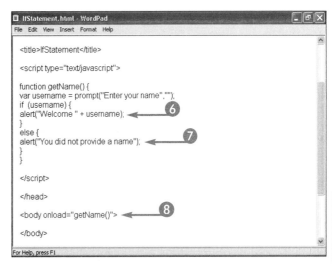

⑩ Open the document in your Web browser.

● In this example, the Web browser generates the prompt dialog box. When you type your name and click OK, the script evaluates the expression and executes the appropriate statement.

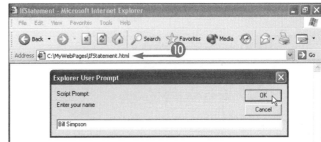

How can I use `if` statements when I have more than two possible outcomes?

▼ You can use the `else if` statement. In this case, the condition is still defined within the `if` clause, but the subsequent outcomes are defined using `else if`. The syntax of the statement is:

```
if (condition) {
action statement;
}
else if (condition) {
action statement;
}
else {
action statement;
}
```

For more information about these statements, refer to *JavaScript: Your visual blueprint for building dynamic Web pages,* by Kelly Murdock (John Wiley).

What other ways are there to evaluate conditions and perform operations in JavaScript?

▼ In addition to the `if` statement, JavaScript supports several other statements, including `switch`, `while`, `do/while`, and `for`. The `switch` statement is a particularly useful conditional operator for initiating any of several actions based on a user response or other condition, such as the current day or the Web browser being used to view the page. The `while` statement is a common looping structure used in JavaScript to instruct the script to continue performing an action as long as a certain condition remains. For example, you can have a script run indefinitely until the user clicks a button to stop it.

Create a JavaScript Function

Functions are collections of JavaScript statements that you define using a single name, so that you can invoke the function at any time by referring to its identifier. You can create functions to respond to specific user actions and invoke the functions through HTML event attributes such as `onclick`.

To create a function, you must use the `function` statement to give the function a unique name and an optional set of arguments, enclosed in parentheses. After the arguments, you can include the function's statements within curly brackets. Within the curly brackets, you can define local variables, set up conditional tests using `if` statements, and include any other statements to execute.

The syntax for creating a function is as follows:

```
function functionName(argument1, argument2) {
// JavaScript statements here;

}
```

When you invoke the function later in your HTML document, you must refer to the function's name, including the parentheses. For example, to invoke a function named `foo` when the user clicks a link, add a `javascript:` URL to the `href` attribute and indicate the name of the function. Otherwise, you can add the `onclick="foo()"` attribute to the `<a>` tag.

Create a JavaScript Function

① Open a document in your HTML editor.

② Add opening and closing `<head>` tags.

③ Add opening and closing `<body>` tags.

④ Within the head of the document, add opening and closing `<script>` tags.

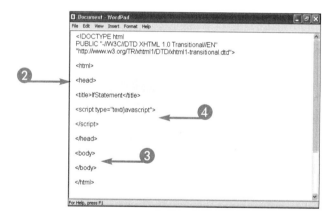

⑤ Create a new function.

⑥ Add JavaScript statements enclosed by a set of curly brackets.

Note: *For more information about conditional statements, see the section, "Create an `if` Statement."*

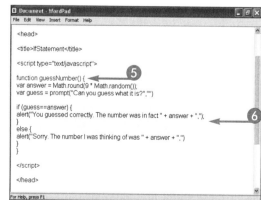

7 Within the body of the document, add code to invoke the function, and reference the function by name.

● This example uses a `javascript:` URL with the `href` attribute.

8 Save the document.

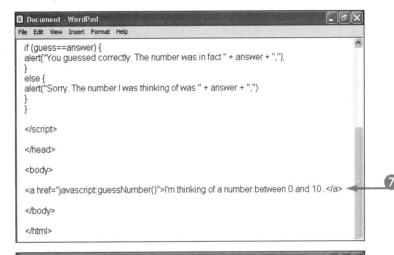

```
if (guess==answer) {
alert("You guessed correctly. The number was in fact " + answer + ".");
}
else {
alert("Sorry. The number I was thinking of was " + answer + ".")
}
}

</script>

</head>

<body>

<a href="javascript:guessNumber()">I'm thinking of a number between 0 and 10..</a>

</body>

</html>
```

9 Open the document in your Web browser.

10 Invoke the JavaScript function.

● In this example, clicking the link invokes the defined function.

Note: For more information about JavaScript functions, refer to JavaScript: Your visual blueprint for building dynamic Web pages, *by Kelly Murdock (John Wiley).*

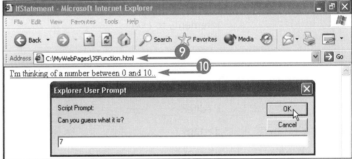

If a function contains only one statement, can I omit the curly brackets?

▼ No. Unlike `if` statements, where you may omit curly brackets in some cases, functions must always include them. Many Web page authors type each curly bracket on a line of its own, so they can readily see that they have typed the required number of brackets and identify the script between the brackets. For more information about `if` statements, see the section, "Create an `if` Statement."

How do I get a function to execute when the HTML page loads?

▼ To have a script execute after the HTML page has loaded, add the `onload` event handler to the HTML `<body>` tag and reference the name of the function you want to invoke. For example, to call a function named `greetuser` after a page loads, you type `<body onload="greetuser">`. Event handlers, such as `onload` and `onclick` trigger a response when a specified action occurs.

Can I nest functions within functions?

▼ JavaScript versions 1.0 and 1.1 do not allow nested functions. However, if you are using JavaScript 1.2 or higher, you can define functions within other functions. Because JavaScript 1.2 is only supported on versions 4 and higher of the Netscape Navigator and Internet Explorer Web browsers, you should use nested functions only if you are certain that your visitors are not using older Web browsers. In addition, you cannot define a function within an `if` statement.

Test JavaScript Code

Before you launch any new JavaScript features on your Web site, you should always thoroughly test your code to ensure that it works correctly. Small errors in syntax, logic, or typing can cause errors and prevent the script from running correctly. In addition, because the client-side JavaScript engine varies from Web browser to Web browser, code that works on one type and version of Web browser may not work on others.

Several techniques help you test and isolate errors in your JavaScript code. This process is called *debugging*, and is a necessary step in developing programming applications. You can use Internet Explorer or Netscape Navigator to identify bugs. In most cases, these Web browsers display any errors they encounter in the status bar, making them easy to overlook. This section shows how to set preferences in Internet Explorer so that error messages pop up when Internet Explorer encounters a JavaScript error. It also shows how to run the JavaScript console in Netscape Navigator to check your JavaScript for errors.

You can also use the JavaScript console to evaluate individual statements. To activate the JavaScript console in Navigator, you type **javascript:** into the Address bar. This divides the Navigator window into two panes. In the bottom pane, you type the expression you want evaluated.

Test JavaScript Code

Test in Internet Explorer

① In Internet Explorer, click Tools.

② Click Internet Options.

- The Internet Options dialog box appears.

③ Click the Advanced tab.

④ Click the options to enable script debugging and display notifications of errors.

⑤ Click OK.

⑥ Open a document that contains the JavaScript you want to test.

⑦ If necessary, perform the action required to execute the JavaScript.

- If an error occurs, Internet Explorer displays a dialog box that describes the error.

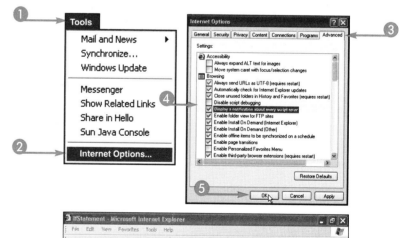

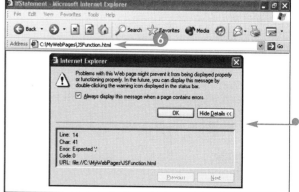

Test in Netscape Navigator

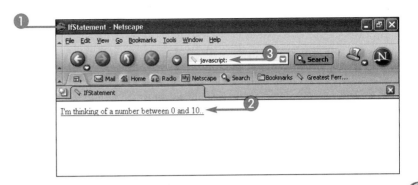

1 Open a document that contains the JavaScript you want to test in Netscape Navigator.

2 If necessary, perform the action required to execute the JavaScript.

● If possible, Netscape Navigator executes the JavaScript.

3 Type **javascript:** in the Address bar, and press Enter.

● Netscape Navigator opens the JavaScript console and displays any errors.

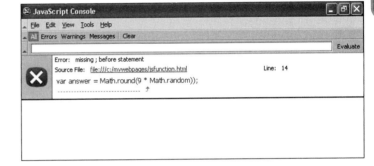

What types of errors occur in JavaScript?

▼ Some errors, called *load-time errors*, occur as the Web browser initially loads the JavaScript code, and usually result from a syntactical error, such as a missing curly bracket in a function. Other errors occur when the program is executed. These are called *run-time errors*. To locate and identify common errors, look for functions or variables in different scripts that use the same name. Look for typos, mismatched single or double quotes, or a single equal sign in an `if` statement instead of double equal signs (==). Another common error to look for is the use of a reserved JavaScript keyword as a function or variable name.

Are there other ways to debug JavaScript?

▼ Yes. because Web browsers read the code in a linear fashion, from beginning to end, you can insert JavaScript statements at various points to display alert dialog boxes indicating their position in the code. When an alert dialog box successfully pops up, you know that your code is fine up to that point.

Why do Web browsers hide JavaScript errors instead of displaying them?

▼ Early versions of Web browsers displayed all JavaScript errors. However, the warning boxes became more annoying than they were useful, so Web developers disabled error checking. Fortunately, developers did not entirely remove the error-checking capability from browsers, so with the proper knowledge you can use your browser to check for JavaScript errors.

Create an External JavaScript File

You can write scripts and reference them in multiple HTML pages by creating external JavaScript files. This technique is similar to using external style sheets — see Chapter 4 for more information about style sheets — and allows you to maintain your scripts more easily because you need to edit only one JavaScript file, rather than several HTML files. In addition, keeping scripts in an external file allows the Web browser to store them in the cache so that they load more quickly when used on subsequent pages.

To create an external JavaScript file, you must save a text file with the extension .js. Within this file, you can include all of your JavaScript statements and comments. To reference the external file in your HTML document, you can use the `<script>` tags with the optional `src` attribute. The value of the `src` attribute is the location of the JavaScript file on your Web server, so if the JavaScript file is located in the same directory as the current page, the tag becomes `<script src="`*NameofFile*`.js"></script>`. Even if you do not include any JavaScript statements within the `<script>` tags, you must still include the closing `</script>` tag.

① Open a new document in your HTML editor.

② Save the file as a plain-text document, giving it a filename with the .js extension.

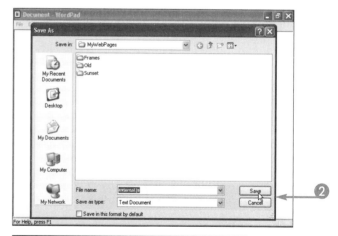

③ Add your JavaScript statements.

④ Save the document.

```
var name = prompt ("Enter name", "");

if (name) {
alert("Welcome" + name);
}
else {
alert("You did not provide a name.");
}
```

⑤ Open a document in your HTML editor that you want to reference the JavaScript file.

⑥ Type an opening `<script>` tag that includes the `src` attribute set to the location and name of the document from step 4.

⑦ Add a closing `<script>` tag.

⑧ Save the document.

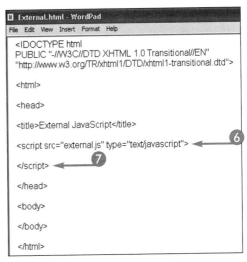

⑨ Open the document in your Web browser.

● The Web browser loads the external JavaScript file.

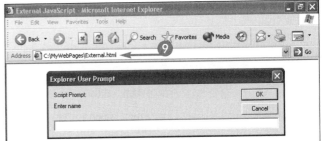

Do I need to use `<script>` tags within the external JavaScript file?

▼ No. Use the opening and closing `<script>` tags only when embedding scripts into the head or body of an HTML document or when referencing an external JavaScript file from an HTML document. The file you save as an external JavaScript file does not require the `<script>` tags.

Can external JavaScript files contain HTML code?

▼ No. External JavaScript files can only contain JavaScript code and JavaScript comments. Because you use a standard HTML document to call for an external JavaScript file, this is not a significant limitation. The page that calls the JavaScript into action can include all the HTML source code you want to use.

Do I need to configure my Web server to handle external JavaScript files?

▼ Yes. You should make sure that your Web server is able to handle JavaScript files by configuring the MIME type as application/x-javascript. If your Web site is running on an Apache server, you can add a MIME type by including the following code in the .htaccess file:

`AddType application/x-javascript js`

However, if you are unsure about the configuration of your Web server, you should contact the system administrator for assistance with MIME-type settings.

Hide JavaScript from Old Web Browsers

Y ou usually add JavaScript code to HTML pages using opening and closing <script> tags, but not all Web browsers support <script> tags. Instead, the browsers try to display the JavaScript code as HTML text, which is very confusing to anyone viewing the page. You can hide JavaScript elements from older Web browsers that do not recognize the <script> tag by bracketing your JavaScript with a combination of HTML and JavaScript comment sequences.

After the initial <script> tag, you add an opening HTML comment sequence (<!–). Before the closing </script> tag, you add a JavaScript comment (//) marker, and then the closing HTML comment (–>). Older Web browsers

disregard everything within the HTML comments, while Web browsers that support the <script> tag process the JavaScript statements.

Because JavaScript does not recognize the closing HTML comment sequence (–>), you must include the JavaScript comment marker (//) before the HTML comment sequence so that the Web browser does not interpret it as a JavaScript statement. This section demonstrates the correct placement of the comment sequences.

For a language other than JavaScript, the closing comment sequence depends on the scripting language. For example, for VBScript, the closing comment is ' —>, because the single quote (') is the comment indicator for that language.

Hide JavaScript from Old Web Browsers

① Open a document in your HTML editor.

② Type opening and closing <script> tags inside the document's <head> tags.

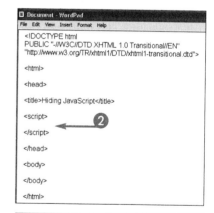

③ Add the type attribute and set it equal to "text/javascript".

④ After the opening `<script>` tag, add the opening element of an HTML comment.

⑤ Add your JavaScript statements.

⑥ Before the closing `</script>` tag, type a JavaScript single-line comment marker (`//`), followed by a closing HTML comment element.

⑦ Save the document.

● When you open the document in a Web browser that does not support JavaScript, the script remains hidden.

What happens if a Web browser recognizes the `<script>` tag but does not support JavaScript?

▼ The Web browser simply ignores all of the statements occurring between the opening and closing `<script>` tags. This is also the case for visitors that have JavaScript disabled in their Web browser. If you use external JavaScript files, you do not need to concern yourself with hiding the JavaScript. Older Web browsers that do not recognize the `<script>` tags do not recognize any calls to JavaScript files, either. As a result, they do not attempt to open the file or display the script.

If I use newer versions of JavaScript, do I need to hide my scripts from Web browsers that support only older versions?

▼ Yes. You can indicate the JavaScript version number using the `language` attribute of the `<script>` tag. For example, if your script uses JavaScript version 1.3, you can set the `language` attribute equal to JavaScript1.3. The language attribute is not supported by the XHTML specifications, so your page will not validate, but this is the only way to hide the script in such cases. Web browsers that do not support this version of JavaScript ignore any code contained within the `<script>` tags.

Using <noscript> Tags

You can use the <noscript> tags to provide a message or alternative content for Web browsers that do not support JavaScript or that have scripting disabled. Wherever you have scripts in your page, you must include the opening and closing <noscript> tags directly after the closing </script> tag. Web browsers that support scripting ignore anything contained within the <noscript> tags, while Web browsers that do not support scripting display the alternative content.

According to the HTML specification, Web browsers that support scripting can display the <noscript> content if the Web browser does not support the scripting language in use, or if the Web browser is configured with scripting turned "off." Keep in mind that some users have script-capable Web browsers but choose to disable JavaScript for a variety of reasons, such as reducing the number of pop-up ads or increasing security. If your Web site requires the use of JavaScript, you must include this information in your <noscript> tags and repeat it in the body of your HTML document. For example, if you use JavaScript extensively on your Web site, you may want to include a warning that visitors should enable JavaScript to experience all of the features that your Web site has to offer.

Using <noscript> Tags

① Open a document in your HTML editor.

② After the opening <body> tag, add <script> tags.

③ Add JavaScript statements.

④ Add a set of <noscript> tags.

⑤ Add any alternative content.

⑥ Save the document.

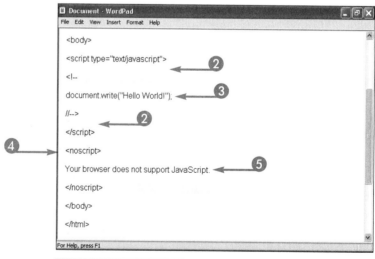

⑦ Open the document in a script-aware Web browser.

- The Web browser executes the JavaScript code but does not display the alternative content.

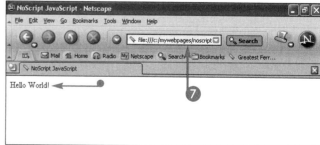

8 In your Web browser's Internet options or preferences, disable JavaScript.

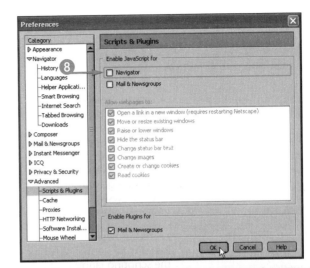

9 Reload the document in your Web browser.

● With JavaScript disabled, the Web browser displays the `<noscript>` content.

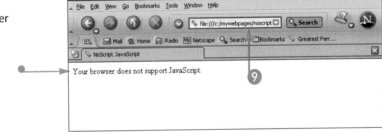

Do the `<noscript>` tags work on all Web browsers?

▼ No. Some older Web browsers do not recognize the `<noscript>` tag, although they represent a very small portion of the total Web browser market. In particular, Netscape 2 does not support the `<noscript>` tag, although it does support scripting. As a result, Netscape 2 Web browsers display the `<noscript>` content, even though they support JavaScript.

Are there any optional or required attributes for the `<noscript>` tag?

▼ No attributes are associated with the `<noscript>` tags. They simply bracket the alternative text. However, between the opening and closing `<noscript>` tags, you can include alternative text and HTML tags. For example, you can type

```
<noscript><b>Your
browser does not support
JavaScript!</b></
noscript>
```

to have your message appear bold. Using the `style` attribute, you can also format your text with CSS styles.

What sort of alternative content can I include within `<noscript>` tags?

▼ You can include any HTML tags and content within `<noscript>` tags. This enables you to offer alternative features that mirror your JavaScript functionality. For example, if you use JavaScript to implement a scrolling navigation list or to redirect to a new page, use the `<noscript>` tags to include a regular HTML drop-down menu or a `<meta>` refresh tag. For more information about HTML features, see Chapter 3.

PART III

Add Text to the Status Bar

A t the bottom of almost every Web browser window is a status bar that typically displays information about the current page or the page that is currently loading. Some Web browsers hid the status bar by default; you can choose an option, typically on the View menu, to display the status bar. Other browsers may display the status bar information in a screentip or somewhere else on the screen. Normally, when Web visitors rest their mouse cursor on a link or image-map hotspot, the status bar displays the URL of the hyperlink. However, you can change this behavior and have the status bar display a text message by setting the value of the Window object's status property.

To set the value of the status property, you can use the onmouseover event handler with the <a> tag. For more information about event handlers, consult *JavaScript: Your visual blueprint for building dynamic Web pages*, by Kelly Murdock (John Wiley). After the status bar text message, you must add the "return true" statement. This tells the Web browser that it should not perform the usual action of displaying the hyperlink URL, but should instead display your status bar text.

Most Web browsers erase the status bar message when the user moves the mouse off a link, but some Web browsers continue to display the custom text. You can explicitly clear the status message by adding the onmouseout event handler and setting the status property to an empty string.

Add Text to the Status Bar

① Open an HTML document.

② Add a set of <head> tags.

- Add a title between the <head> tags, if you want.

③ Add a set of <body> tags.

④ Between the <body> tags, add a hyperlink.

Note: *For more information about hyperlinks, see Chapter 3.*

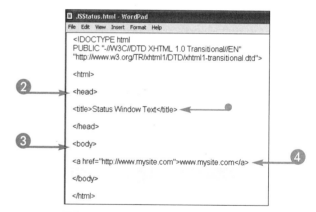

⑤ In the opening <a> tag, add the onmouseover event handler and set the value of the status property to the text you want to display in the status bar.

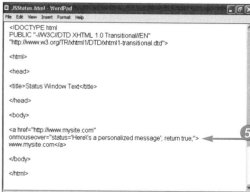

6⃝ Add the onmouseout event handler and set the value of the status property to display no text.

● The text disappears from the status bar when the mouse cursor moves off the link.

7⃝ Save the document.

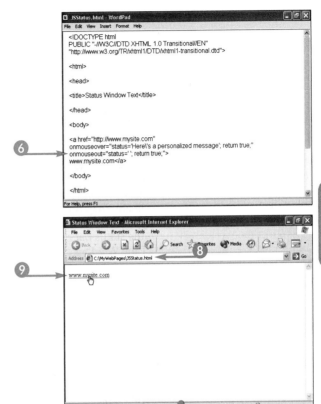

8⃝ Open the document in your Web browser.

9⃝ Position the mouse cursor over the link.

● Your custom message appears in the status bar.

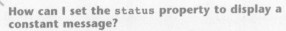

PART III

MASTER IT

How can I set the status property to display a constant message?

▼ Use the defaultStatus property to display a continuous message in the status bar. To set a defaultStatus message, add the onload="defaultStatus" attribute to the opening <body> tag:

```
<body onload="defaultStatus='message
here!';">
```

Any link-specific status bar messages temporarily override the default status bar message that you set with this property. For example, if you hover the mouse cursor over a hyperlink, the linked address appears in the status bar in place of the defaultStatus message. As soon as you move the mouse cursor off the hyperlink, the defaultStatus message reappears.

Do I have to use escape sequences when setting status bar text?

▼ If you want to include quotation marks or apostrophes within the status bar text, you must use JavaScript escape sequences. For example, to include an apostrophe in a status bar message of an <a> tag, add a backslash before the apostrophe:

```
<a href="#" onmouseover="status='Here\'s
a status message.';">click here</a>
```

If you do not, the Web browser interprets the apostrophe or quotation mark as the end of the string, which generates an error. For more information about using escape sequences, see Chapter 8.

Prompt the User for a Response

You can use the `prompt()` method to obtain a response from a user, and then issue a personalized message based on the response. Like the `alert()` and `confirm()` methods also associated with the Window object, the `prompt()` method generates a simple dialog box in which you can display a message that instructs the user what to do. The prompt dialog box also includes a text entry field along with two buttons, OK and Cancel. The user can choose to cancel the dialog box or type an entry and click OK. For more information about the `alert()` method, see Chapter 8; for more information about using the `confirm()` method, see the section "Get Confirmation."

This method takes two arguments — the message printed in the dialog box and the default value — for the response. The syntax for the `prompt()` method is:

`prompt("Message appearing in the dialog box", "");`

If you include a default value when calling the prompt method, this value appears in the text entry field. If you do not specify a value, the Web browser displays "undefined" in the field. To avoid this, you should include an empty string ("") as the default value.

Prompt the User for a Response

① Open an HTML document.

② Within the head of the document, add opening and closing <script> tags.

③ Declare a new variable, and set its value to the `prompt()` method, followed by the text message you want to display.

- The paired quotation marks " " keep the text entry field blank.

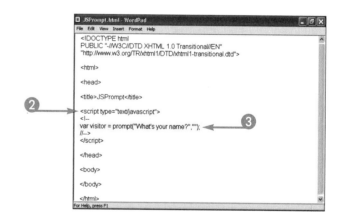

④ Between the <body> tags, add a set of <script> tags.

⑤ Add a `document.write()` method, including a reference to the variable that you declared in step 3.

Note: For more information about the `document.write()` method, see Chapter 8.

⑥ Save the document.

7 Open the document in your Web browser.

● Your Web browser generates the `prompt()` dialog box.

8 Type your response.

9 Click OK.

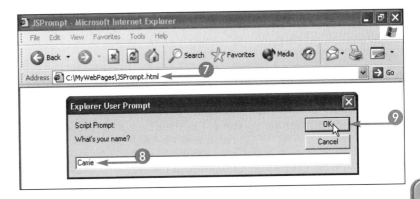

● Your Web browser inserts the value from your response into the `document.write` text and writes the result to the screen.

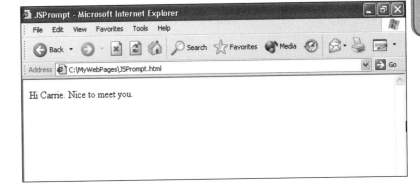

What if the visitor clicks OK without first typing an entry?

▼ If the user clicks OK without typing an entry, then no entry is inserted in place of the variable, and no change is made to the Web page. To prevent this from happening, include an `if` statement that writes a different message to the screen. See Chapter 8 for information about constructing `if` statements.

Can I include special characters in the text message?

▼ Yes. To include special characters, use JavaScript escape sequences with appropriate Latin-1 codes. For more information about escape sequences and Latin-1 codes, see Chapter 8. Appendix A provides a list of codes. Although you have control over the message and can include special characters, you cannot change the appearance of the dialog box. The appearance varies, depending on the Web browser that opens the page.

Can I use HTML to format the text message that appears in the prompt dialog?

▼ No. As with the other window dialog methods, the `prompt()` message cannot contain any HTML formatting and must be plain text. You can use spaces, underscore characters, and new-line sequences to add minimal formatting to the text message. You can use HTML tags and CSS styles to format the text that the script writes to the screen.

PART III

Get Confirmation

Y ou can enable visitors to confirm or cancel an action by using the confirm() method. This method, associated with the Window object, is similar to the alert() method discussed in Chapter 8 in that it generates a dialog box to which the user must respond before proceeding. However, while the alert() method has only the option of affirming the action, the confirm() method gives the user the choice of continuing or canceling. The syntax for a confirm() method is:

confirm("*dialog box message.*");

In addition, you can assign the dialog box message to a variable, and then reference that variable inside the parentheses of the confirm() method:

var msg = "*dialog box message.*";

confirm(msg);

Because the confirm() method allows for two possible responses, "OK" or "Cancel," Web authors use this method most often in conjunction with a conditional if statement. If the user clicks OK, the Web browser executes one statement; if the user clicks Cancel, the Web browser executes a different statement. One common application is to direct users to different destination pages, based on their response. For instructions on constructing if statements, refer to Chapter 8.

Get Confirmation

① Open an HTML document.

② Add a set of <script> tags to the head of the document.

③ Create a new function.

④ Declare a new variable and set its value to the message you want to display in the confirm dialog box.

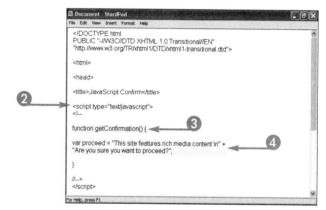

⑤ Add an if statement and type (**confirm()**) along with the name of the message variable you created in step 4.

● The if statement executes if the user clicks OK in the confirm dialog box.

⑥ Add a statement that you want to execute if the visitor confirms the message.

⑦ In the body of the document, add a hypertext link or event handler to trigger the confirmation function.

● This example uses a hypertext link with a `javascript:` URL.

⑧ Save the document.

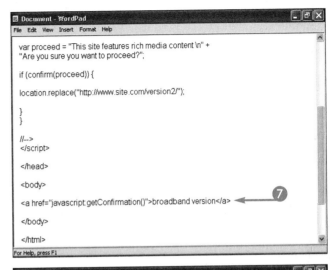

```
var proceed = "This site features rich media content \n" +
"Are you sure you want to proceed?";

if (confirm(proceed)) {

location.replace("http://www.site.com/version2/");

}
}

//-->
</script>

</head>

<body>

<a href="javascript:getConfirmation()">broadband version</a>

</body>

</html>
```

PART III

⑨ Open the document in your Web browser.

⑩ Click the link to invoke the event handler.

● In this example, clicking the link generates a dialog box that prompts the user to click OK to proceed or to click Cancel.

Is it necessary to create a new custom function in order to use the `confirm()` method?

▼ No, it is not necessary to create a new function that contains the `confirm()` method. You can also include the `confirm()` method and related statements on their own with `<script>` tags. In this instance, the Web browser executes the `confirm()` method as the HTML page loads.

What value does JavaScript return when a user clicks OK or Cancel in a confirm dialog box?

▼ If the user clicks OK, JavaScript returns a value of `true`, or 1. If the user clicks Cancel or closes the dialog box, the value returned is `false`, or 0. You can use these values in `if` statements to determine the direction that the script takes, depending on whether the user clicks OK or Cancel.

Can I have scripts running in the background while the user is responding to the confirm prompt?

▼ No, all three of the dialog prompts associated with the `Window` object — `alert()`, `prompt()`, and `confirm()` — are *modal*, meaning that they block the continuation of the script until the user responds to the dialog box. This enables the script to receive input from the user and then use the input in the script.

Add a
Last-Modified Date

You can use JavaScript to show your visitors when your Web site was last updated. The `document.lastModified` property, available since JavaScript version 1.0, allows you to automatically generate a timestamp, rather than altering your HTML code each time you update a page.

The `document.lastModified` property is a read-only string sent by the Web server that records the date and time of the last modification made to the file. To read the `document.lastModified` property, you can use the following JavaScript code:

```
document.lastModified;
```

You can write the value of this property to your page by using `document.write()`, discussed in Chapter 8, as follows:

```
document.write(document.lastModified);
```

When using the `document.lastModified` property, remember that not all Web servers provide this last-modified date. If no string is sent for this date, JavaScript assigns a value of 0 (zero) and records the date as midnight, January 1, 1970, Greenwich Mean Time (GMT). Therefore, you must include code to verify that the value of the `lastModified` string is not equal to zero. You can use the `Date.parse()` method, which converts a date string to milliseconds, to check for a zero value. For more on `Date()` methods, see *JavaScript: Your visual blueprint for building dynamic Web pages,* by Kelly Murdock (John Wiley).

Add a Last-Modified Date

① Open an HTML document.

② In the body of the document, add a set of `<script>` tags.

③ Add an `if` statement.

④ Within the parentheses, type **Date.parse(document.lastModified)**.

  ● `Date.parse` takes a date and converts it to a single number, which is the date in milliseconds.

⑤ Type **!= 0**.

  ● The `!=` operator tests to see that the date is not equal to zero.

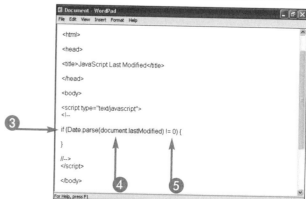

⑥ Add a `document.write()` method that includes a message leading up to the last modified date.

⑦ Add the `document.lastModified` property to the arguments for the method.

⑧ Save the document.

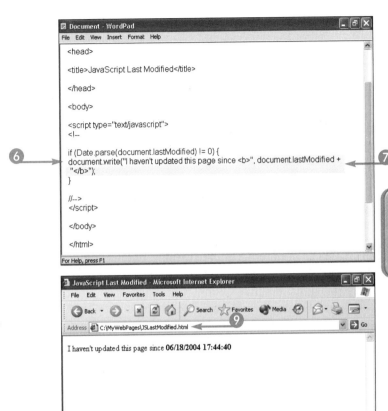

⑨ Open the document in your Web browser.

● The Web browser displays the date and time of the last update made to the page.

What is the format of the `document.lastModified` date?

▼ The date for the `document.lastModified` property is expressed in MM/DD/YYYY format. The time is expressed using the 24-hour clock and includes the hour, minutes, and milliseconds. The time zone is GMT. You can change the time zone when printing the last-modified date by converting the `document.lastModified` value to a `Date` object; you can use the `toLocaleString()` method to set the date to the local time zone.

Can I change the formatting of the date?

▼ Yes. You can use the `Date` object, the `Date()` constructor, and the associated methods to have the date print in a variety of formats. To create a variable for holding the `Date` object, type `var ? = new Date`, where ? is the name you want to assign to the variable. You can then call the various methods for this `Date` object.

Can I use the `document.lastModified` property on dynamically generated pages?

▼ Yes. You can use the property on both static and dynamic pages. However, on dynamic pages that use templates, such as a template for a product page, the date only indicates the last change to the template, not the last change to the page.

Script a Scrolling List

Y ou can use JavaScript to create a scrollable options list that automatically loads the page or Web site when the visitor makes a selection. By using JavaScript, you can avoid using Go buttons with your <select> fields and create a more seamless user experience.

In the Document Object Model, the Select object represents the HTML <select> tag and includes a property called selectedIndex. This property indicates the index number of a selected <option> within a drop-down or scrollable <select> list. See Chapter 10 for more on the <select> tag. If you set the value of each option to the destination URL, you can use the selectedIndex

property to determine the value of the selected option and redirect the user to that URL using window.location.href:

```
window.location.href = document.
formName.options[selectedIndex].value;
```

To initiate the code when the user selects an option, use the onchange event handler in the opening <select> tag. If you include the JavaScript code directly in the onchange handler — rather than referring to a custom function in the head of the document — you do not have to reference the document.formName.

Script a Scrolling List

① Open an HTML document.

② Within the body of the document, add a set of <form> tags.

③ Add a <select> menu, including a list of options.

Note: For more information about <select> menus, see Chapter 10.

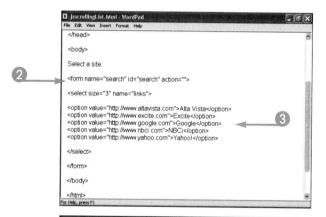

④ Add the onchange attribute to the <select> tag, followed by an if statement that checks for the selectedIndex value.

Note: For more information about if statements, see Chapter 8.

⑤ Set the location.href property to the selected option value.

Note: For more information about the location property, see the section "Redirect to a New Page."

6 Save the document.

7 Open the document in your Web browser.

8 Click one of the options.

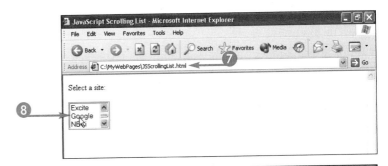

● Your Web browser replaces the window's location property with the value of the selected option.

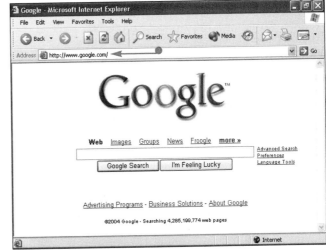

Is the selectedIndex property available in all versions of JavaScript?

▼ Yes, the property is supported by all versions of JavaScript, including JavaScript 1.0. In addition, in JavaScript 1.1 and later versions, selectedIndex is a writable property. This means that you can use the property to indicate which option should be selected. To deselect all options, set the selectedIndex property to -1.

Can I display a list with no scroll bar?

▼ Yes. As long as the <select> list is large enough to accommodate all options in the list, the list does not display scroll bars. In the <select> tag, set the the size attribute equal to the number of items in the list. To create some additional space at the bottom of the list, you can set the size attribute to a value greater than the number of items in the list.

How do I present the same information for Web browsers that do not support scripting?

▼ Because Web browsers that do not support scripting simply ignore the script elements, the code does not cause errors in Web browsers that do not support JavaScript. However, consider adding alternative content inside of <noscript> tags so that non-script Web browsers can still access the content. In this example, the <noscript> tags can include hyperlinks to the various search sites. For more on <noscript> tags, see Chapter 8.

Script Between Frames

hapter 7 shows you how to construct frames to provide visitors with easier navigational tools and to add a degree of interactivity. You can use JavaScript along with frames to generate additional interactivity between the frames.

Each Web browser window has a `frames[]` property that represents each frame in the frameset, so variables and functions defined in one frame are accessible from the other frames as well as from the parent frame. Because frames can communicate with each other and with the parent frameset, you can use frames to *maintain state*, or instruct the Web browser to "remember" data from one page to another.

When you reference frames contained within a frameset, you can use either the array index number or the ID of the frame, which you assign within the `<frame />` tag using the `id` attribute. If you reference a frame using its index number, keep in mind that the first element in an array has an index of 0 (zero).

If a window contains frames, the top-level window containing the frames is called the *parent*. Subframes can refer to other subframes by referencing the parent. For example, the first frame would access variables and objects in a second frame by referencing the `parent.frames[1]` property.

Script Between Frames

① Open an HTML document.

② Add opening and closing `<frameset>` tags.

Note: To learn more about creating framesets, see Chapter 7.

③ Add `<frame />` tags to create two frames, giving each frame a unique ID.

④ Create and save a document for each frame, giving them names that match the `src` names you specified.

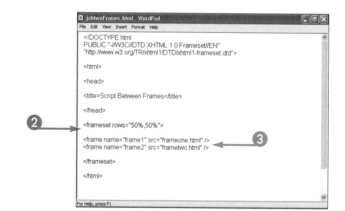

⑤ In the first frame document, add opening and closing `<form>` tags, giving the form an ID.

⑥ Add `<input >` tags for creating radio buttons.

⑦ Add an `onclick` event handler that invokes a JavaScript function.

● This example creates a submit button.

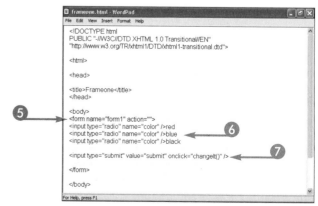

⑧ In the head of the first frame document, add `<script>` tags.

⑨ Create a new function and add `if` statements to specify actions based on visitor response.

● This example changes the background color of the second frame, which is referenced by `parent.frame2.document`.

⑩ Save all three documents to the same directory.

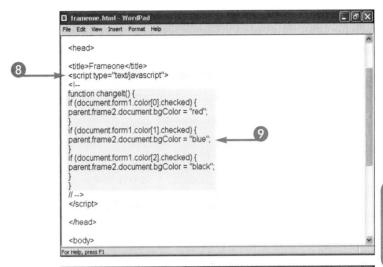

⑪ Open the document that contains the frameset tags in your Web browser.

⑫ Click a radio button (◯ changes to ◉).

⑬ Click the submit button.

● The script in the first frame accesses the `bgColor` property of the second frame to change the background color.

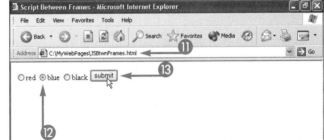

Can I use the `window.close()` method to close frames?

▼ No, you can only use the `window.close()` method to close top-level windows, not individual frames. However, you can use the `window.close()` method from within a frame to close the top-level window. Rather than using the `window.close()` or `self.close()` method in this case, you would use the `parent.close()` method.

Can I change the color of the text?

▼ Yes, in this example, you can add the `parent.frame2.document.fgColor = "color";` statement to change the text color; "fg" stands for "foreground." Refer to the color chart included in this book to determine the hexadecimal code for the desired color. Add this statement directly below the statement that changes the page's background color.

How else can I use JavaScript to maintain state?

▼ Normally in order to maintain state, you must use cookies (see the section "Set a Cookie"). Unlike frame-scripting techniques, which only store the values for variables while the window is open, you can set the expiration dates for cookies so that you can retrieve data the next time the user visits the site.

Script Around Frames

U sing the `length` property of the Window object's `frames[]` array, you can prevent other Web sites from placing your own page in a frameset. Although having your Web site appear within someone else's frameset is little more than a nuisance, it can disrupt your Web site's design and presentation. To prevent your Web site from being "framed," you use JavaScript code to read the length of the `frames[]` array and then force the Web browser to reload your Web site into the top window.

Every window has a `frames[]` array that references all of the frames that a frameset contains. In the object hierarchy,

the window containing the frameset is the *parent*, and the frames are the *children*. For more information, see the section "Script Between Frames." The `length` property indicates how many child frames are present. For example, if the `parent.frames.length` property is equal to 2, two frames are contained within the frameset. You can use this property to see if your Web site is contained within a parent window frameset by verifying that the `parent.frames.length` property is greater than zero. If it is greater than zero, you can replace the `location` property of the parent window with the `location` property of your own Web site.

Script Around Frames

① Open an HTML document.

② In the head of the document, add `<script>` tags.

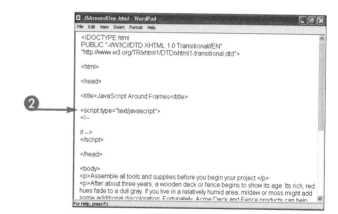

③ Type if (parent.frames.length >0) {.

● This determines whether the top window contains frames; if it does not contain frames, the `length` property is equal to zero.

④ Type **parent.location.href =location.href;}** to set the `location.href` property of the top window to the `location.href` property of the document.

⑤ Save the document.

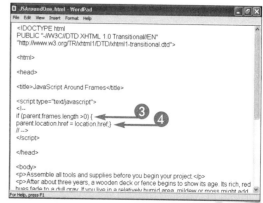

6 Open or create another HTML document.

7 Add opening and closing `<frameset>` tags.

Note: For more on creating HTML frames, see Chapter 7.

8 Add two `<frame />` tags, including one that contains a `src` attribute equal to the document from step 5.

9 Save the document.

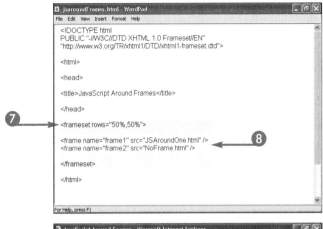

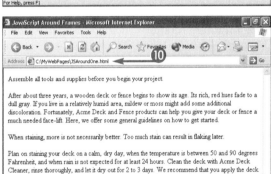

10 Open the document from step 9 in your Web browser.

● The script overrides the frameset to load the frame page into the top window.

Can I use JavaScript to force my Web site to load into a new window rather than the top Web browser window of the frameset?

▼ Yes. Rather than setting the `parent.location.href` property, you can use the `window.open()` method to display the Web site in a new Web browser window:

```
if (parent.frames.length > 0) {
window.open(location.href);
}
```

Of course, you can open a page in a new window by adding the `target="_blank"` attribute to an `<a>` tag, but the `window.open()` method gives you more control over the way the window presents itself. For more information about using the `window.open()` method, see the section "Open a New Window."

In JavaScript, I sometimes see a reference to a `top` property. Is the top frame the same as the parent frame?

▼ Not exactly. The parent is the document that contains the current frame; it contains the `<frameset>` tags that define the frame structure and names the source file that loads into each frame. The `top` window contains the parent document, which defines the frames, along with each of the child frames. In most cases, the parent and top window are the same, and you can use them interchangeably. However, if the document contains nested framesets — frames within frames — the parent may not represent the top-level window.

Capture Keystrokes

J avaScript includes several event handlers that can capture keyboard events, such as a user pressing a key. You can use this feature to determine which key a user pressed and have the code respond accordingly. However, different versions of Netscape Navigator, Internet Explorer, and other Web browsers support keystroke events differently. In order to achieve cross-browser compatibility, you must use object or Web browser detection. For more information, see the section "Check for Web Browser Versions."

In order to capture keystrokes, you can use the HTML `onkeypress` event handler to create a custom function to print the code that corresponds to the key. The proper syntax for the `onkeypress` event handler is as follows:

`onkeypress="`*`functionName`*`(event)"`

Within your function, you can add JavaScript code for both Internet Explorer and Netscape Navigator to translate keystroke events. Internet Explorer Web browsers allow you to determine which key a user pressed by referencing the `event.keyCode` property. This property returns the character code that is generated by pressing a particular keyboard key. Netscape Navigator Web browsers have a similar property, `event.which`, which also returns the Unicode character code for the key. If you want to convert the code back into the keyboard character, you can use the `String.fromCharCode()` method.

Capture Keystrokes

① Open an HTML document.

② Add opening and closing `<frameset>` tags.

③ Add two `<frame />` tags.

Note: *For more information about frames and framesets, see Chapter 7.*

④ Save the document.

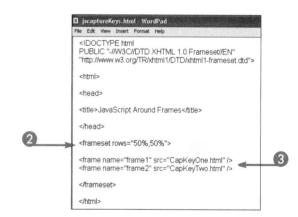

⑤ Create and save a document for each frame, giving them names that match the `src` names that you specified.

⑥ In the body of the first document, add opening and closing `<form>` tags.

Note: *See Chapter 10 for more information about HTML forms.*

⑦ Add a text entry field with an `onkeypress` event handler that invokes a function to capture the keystroke event.

● This function captures the code that corresponds to the keystroke.

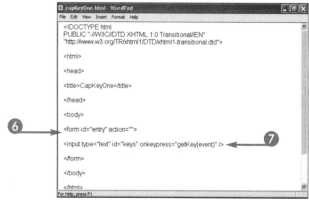

8. Create a function called `getKey()`.

9. Declare a new variable with `if` and `else` statements to customize the script for different Web browser types.

   - For Internet Explorer, you can define the variable as `event.keyCode`. For other Web browsers, you can use `event.which`.

10. Add the `document.write()` method to write the keystroke and character code to the second frame.

11. Save the document.

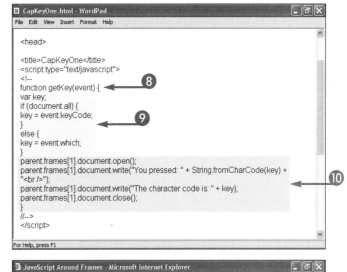

12. Open the frameset document from step 4 in your Web browser.

13. Click in the form field and type a character.

   - The script writes the key and corresponding character code to the second frame.

Must I pass the event argument from the event handler to the function?

▼ Netscape Web browsers require that the script pass the event argument to the function when using event handlers. If you omit the event argument, Netscape Web browsers do not register the keystroke. Because Internet Explorer stores events differently, it still processes the event if you omit this argument.

Is it easier to capture keystrokes using a form?

▼ Yes, but you can use `onkeypress` in a variety of ways, for example, to enable users to respond during interactive lessons, or to control which action occurs when a visitor presses a special key, such as the Escape key.

What other event handlers are associated with keystroke events?

▼ In addition to `onkeypress`, there are also event handlers for when the user presses a key (`onkeydown`), releases a key (`onkeyup`), presses a mouse button (`onmousedown`), and releases a mouse button (`onmouseup`). The `onkeypress` handler is actually a combination of `onkeydown` and `onkeyup`. Note that when you use event handlers as HTML attributes, the name of the event handler is case insensitive, so that `onkeypress` is synonymous with `onKeyPress`, but XHTML requires all lowercase characters. For more information about event handlers, consult *JavaScript: Your visual blueprint for building dynamic Web pages,* by Kelly Murdock (John Wiley).

Open a New Window

You can create links on your Web page that load into new windows by using the `window.open()` method associated with the Window object. HTML also allows you to do this, by adding the `target` attribute to the `<a>` tag and setting its value to `"_blank"`; however, the JavaScript method provides additional control over the presentation of the new window. For example, the `open()` method sets the size of the window and disables certain elements such as toolbars and resizing.

The `window.open()` method can take several optional arguments, including the link URL, the name of the new window, and a list of features. For the window's features, you can specify the width and height of the window in pixels, include or remove scroll bars, hide the Web browser toolbar, and indicate whether or not the user can resize the window by dragging the border. The syntax for using the `window.open()` method is as follows:

```
window.open("URL","windowName","width=x,
height=y,scrollbars,toolbar,resizable");
```

If you omit any features in the `window.open()` method's arguments, the new window excludes those features. Also, you cannot omit the reference to the `Window` object and use the `open()` method as a shortcut because another `open()` method is associated with the Document object. For more on the `document.open()` method, see Chapter 8.

Open a New Window

① Open an HTML document.

② In the head of the document, add `<script>` tags.

③ Create a new function, including arguments.

- This function takes arguments for the URL, window name, height, and width.

④ Type **win = window.open** followed by arguments and optional features.

- The arguments allow you to pass values for the URL, window name, width, and height.

- Optional features include `scrollbars`, `menubar`, `toolbar`, and `resizable`.

⑤ In the body of the document, add a hypertext link, including an **href** attribute set equal to a **javascript:** URL that invokes the function and specifies values for the arguments.

⑥ Save the document.

⑦ Open the document in your Web browser.

⑧ Click the link.

● The Web browser opens a new window that reflects the values that you entered for the window in step 4.

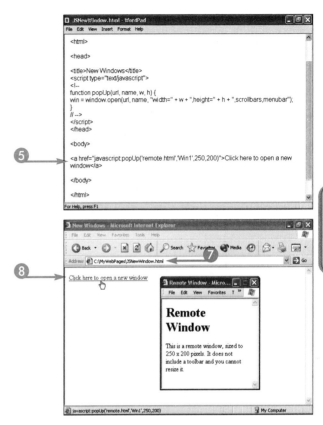

What if I assign a window a name that is already in use with another window?

▼ If a window with the assigned name already exists, the Web browser loads the URL into that window. It creates a new window only if no window with that name is already opened or if no name is specified. If you have multiple links set up to open in the same window, a user might click a link and think it is not working because the window in which the content appears is behind the current window.

What are the features available for the window.open() method?

▼ In addition to the standard features such as menubar, toolbar, and scrollbars, you can specify the status bar text with the status attribute. See the section "Add Text to the Status Bar." You can also set the position of the window using top and left for Internet Explorer Web browsers and screenX and screenY for Netscape Navigator. Many unscrupulous adware authors use window positioning to move the popup window far to the right, so the user has to move the window in order to gain access to the Close button.

Close a Window

Whenever you open a remote or *popup* window, you should always provide the user with a link or button to close the window and return to the main page. While the user can always close the window using the Web browser's Close button, it is a courtesy to provide the user with the means to do this from within the actual Web page.

To provide a link to close a remote window, you can use the `window.close()` method. You can reference this method using a `javascript:` URL in the `href` attribute of an `<a>` tag, as follows:

```
<a href="javascript:window.close()">close
this window</a>
```

You can also include this method with an event handler, such as `onclick`, with both hyperlinks and form buttons:

```
<input type="button"
onclick="window.close()">
```

For more information about using form fields, see Chapter 10.

Alternatively, you can use the `self.close()` method, which is synonymous with `window.close()` and which simply tells the current window to close. Unlike the `window.open()` method, the `window.close()` method does not take any optional arguments and does not have any features associated with it.

---

① Open an HTML document.

② Between the `<head>` tags, add `<script>` tags.

③ Add a function to create a popup window.

④ In the body of the document, add a hypertext link for opening a page in a new window.

⑤ Save the document.

⑥ Create a new HTML document to load into the remote window.

⑦ Add a hypertext link with the `href` attribute set equal to `"javascript: self.close()"`.

⑧ Save the document.

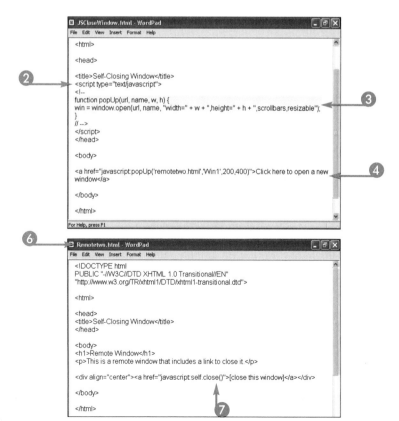

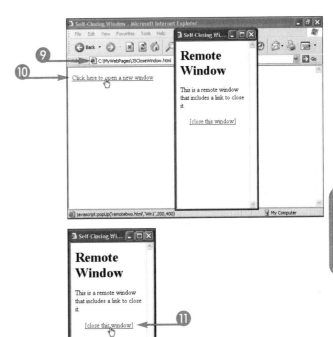

9 Open the document in your Web browser.

10 Click the link to launch a remote window.

● The Web browser loads the document into a remote window.

11 In the remote window, click the link to close the window.

● The Web browser closes the window.

Can I close other windows that I did not create using JavaScript?

▼ Yes, however, if you try to close a window that you did not create with JavaScript, the Web browser presents the user with a confirmation dialog box. This is a security measure to prevent you from closing the user's Web browser window without permission. As long as your script makes sense, the user will likely click the button to confirm and close the window.

Can I have a window close automatically after a period of time?

▼ Yes. The easiest way to do this is to add the onload attribute to the `<body>` tag of the remote window:

`onload="setTimeout(window.close, 5000)"`

5000 in this example represents 5000 milliseconds, or 5 seconds.

Can I check if the user has closed one of the remote windows?

▼ Yes. Use the `window.closed` property to verify a window's status. If you assigned the window a name, you can use this name to read the `closed` property, which returns a value of `true` if the window is closed or `false` if it is open. See the section "Open a New Window" for more information. For example, you can execute JavaScript code, such as writing to a remote window, if the remote window is still open, or create a new window if the remote window is closed.

Redirect to a New Page

You can use the `location` property in the Web browser's Document Object Model to redirect users to a new page. The `location` property stores the URL of the current page that is displayed in the user's Web browser. When you assign a new value to this property, the URL changes and the user is redirected to the new page.

When Web authors reorganize their Web sites, they commonly use the `location` property to redirect users to the new locations of their pages. To use the `location` property to direct the user to a new page, you can add the following code to your script:

```
location = "newPage.html";
```

or:

```
location.href="newPage.html";
```

In addition, you can use the `location` property to direct users to different pages, based on elements such as Web browser version, plug-ins present, or user responses to form fields or dialog boxes. When you set the value of the `location` property, the previous value still remains a part of the Web browser's history. As a result, using the Web browser Back button to navigate returns the user to the original page. To have the Web browser overwrite the original URL with a new URL, you can use the `location.replace()` method.

Redirect to a New Page

① Open an HTML document.

② Between the <head> tags, add <script> tags.

③ Type **location.replace();** including the filename of the destination page.

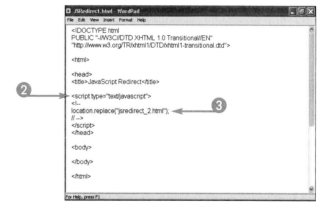

④ Add a pair of <noscript> tags.

Note: *See Chapter 8 for more information about* <noscript> *tags.*

⑤ Between the <noscript> tags, add a hypertext link to the new page.

Note: *See Chapter 3 for more information about hypertext links.*

⑥ Save the document.

⑦ Create another HTML document.

⑧ Save the new document, giving it a name that matches the filename you typed in step 3.

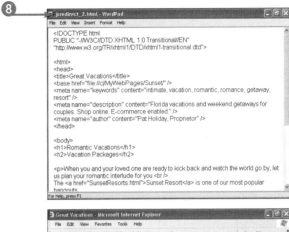

⑨ Open the document from step 6 in your Web browser.

● The Web browser redirects you to the destination page.

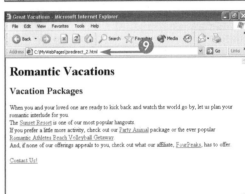

PART III

Do all versions of JavaScript support the location.replace() method?

▼ JavaScript 1.0 does not support the location.replace() method, but all subsequent versions do support it. You can enclose the location.replace() code in script tags with the language set to "JavaScript1.1" to ensure that it does not execute on JavaScript 1.0 Web browsers. For those Web browsers, add another set of <script> tags and use the location.href property.

Can I redirect pages using HTML?

▼ Yes. You can use the <meta /> tag with the http-equiv attribute set to "refresh" and the content attribute set to the URL of the page to which you want to redirect the browser. Any text you include in a <meta /> tag does not appear on the page but is available to the browser. For more information about using <meta /> tags, see Chapter 3.

What is the difference between using location and location.href?

▼ They perform the same function and contain the same value — the URL for the current Web page. You can use either location or location.href when redirecting users to different Web pages. The location object contains four additional properties that store references to different parts of the complete URL: protocol (such as FTP or HTTP), host (the domain name), pathname, and search (the query string, or any information after a question mark).

Reference the DOM

You can access and dynamically manipulate elements on a Web page by using JavaScript to reference the *Document Object Model* (DOM). While the Window object refers to the top-level Web browser window or frame, the Document object contains references to properties of the HTML document, such as the background color and all of the objects contained within the document, such as forms, images, and links.

In the Document Object Model, all of the elements on a Web page are grouped as arrays. Each specific element is one object within the array. For example, on a Web page containing two <form> tags, the `document.forms[]` array contains two Form objects.

Because array index numbers always begin with 0 (zero), you can access the first form using the expression `document.forms[0]` or `document.formName` if you have assigned the form a name. Moving down the Document Object Model, you can access individual form elements and their values in the same way:

`document.formName.inputName.value;`

You can also reference one of the form's *elements* via the `elements[]` array:

`document.formName.elements[x].value;`

Similarly, you can access the third image in an HTML document with the expression `document.images[2]`. For more information on manipulating images, see the section "Script Image Mouseovers."

Reference the DOM

① Open an HTML document.

② In the body of the document, add a form.

Note: For more information about HTML forms, see Chapter 4.

③ Name the form using `name` and `id` attributes.

- `name` and `id` values allow you to reference the objects by name.

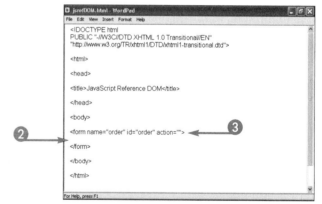

④ Add form fields that specify the `type` and `name` of each field.

- This example uses text entry fields. For more information, see Chapter 10.

⑤ Add a submit button to invoke a new function that reads the value of the form elements.

- This example uses the `onclick` attribute to invoke the function.

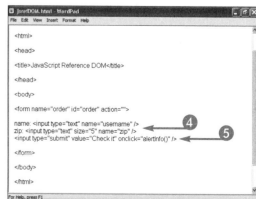

6 Within `<script>` tags, create a new function to read the form values through the Document Object Model.

7 Declare variables set to the values of the form fields, and type **document.forms[0].elements[0].value** to access the value of the first form element.

8 Add an optional `alert()` method to test the values of the variables.

9 Save the document.

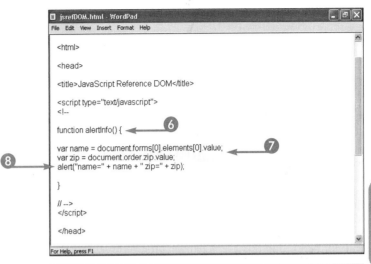

10 Open the document in your Web browser.

11 Type text in the form fields.

12 Click the submit button.

- The Document Object Model allows you to read the values of the form fields.

- In this example, the alert box prints the values of the form fields.

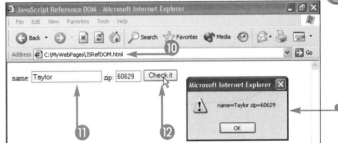

Are there different version numbers of the Document Object Model?

▼ Yes. DOM level 0 contains the standard references to windows, documents, forms, and other HTML elements. DOM level 1, completed in 1998, adds support for HTML 4.0 and XML 1.0. DOM level 2, completed in 2000, adds support for CSS. DOM level 3, completed in 2004, extends DOM's XML support.

Is the Document Object Model consistent across Web browser types and versions?

▼ No, each Web browser type and version implements its own version of the DOM, and even among Netscape Navigator and Internet Explorer Web browsers, the DOM can differ significantly, depending on the Web browser version number. These differences make it difficult to compose JavaScript that functions properly for different Web browsers.

What other properties of the `Document` object are accessible?

▼ In addition to color properties such as `bgColor` (background color), `fgColor` (text color), `linkColor`, `alinkColor`, and `vlinkColor`, you can access the title of the document, the URL, and the referrer. The `document.referrer` property indicates the URL of the document that contains the link to the current document. The `Document` object also contains several different arrays of objects that you can reference. These arrays include `anchors[]`, `applets[]`, `embeds[]`, `forms[]`, `image[]`, `links[]`, and `plugins[]`.

Validate a Form

You can use JavaScript to validate your HTML forms and to ensure that visitors fill out required fields. You can use form validation to check for responses in text input fields, check boxes, and radio buttons, as well as any other type of form entry field. You can also use JavaScript to ensure that responses such as postal codes, telephone numbers, and e-mail addresses are formatted correctly. You can accomplish this type of form validation through an application on the server, such as a CGI, but JavaScript validation is more efficient because the processing occurs on the client side and does not require data to be sent to the server.

To validate a form using JavaScript, you can define a function in the head of your document that checks for required fields. You can use `if-else` statements to return error messages for missing fields. After you have defined your validation function, you must invoke it using an HTML event handler such as `onsubmit`. For more information about HTML event handlers, consult *JavaScript: Your visual blueprint for building dynamic Web pages,* by Kelly Murdock (John Wiley).

Validate a Form

① Open a document with form fields in your HTML editor.

Note: *For more information about creating HTML forms, see Chapter 10.*

② Invoke a new function to validate the form.

- This example invokes the function through the `onclick` event handler.

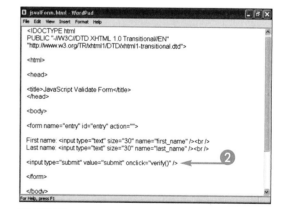

③ In the head of the document, add opening and closing `<script>` tags.

④ Create a new function.

⑤ Define variables for the form values.

⑥ Define a variable to hold the error message.

⑦ Define an empty variable for the second error message.

- The script will add text to the empty variable each time it encounters an empty form field.

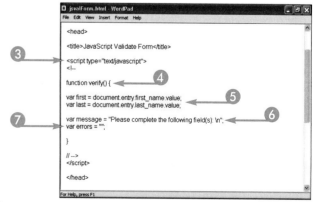

8 Add `if` statements that check for the presence of a value and generate a text message if a value is not present.

- The `!` operator executes the statement if the value is not present.

- The `+=` operator adds the string to the error variable.

9 Add an `if` statement to display a dialog box with the error message if a value is not present.

10 Save the document.

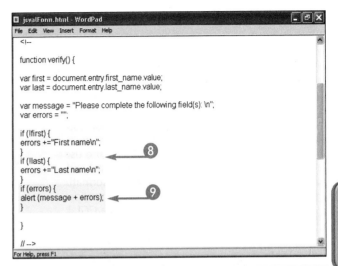

11 Open the document in your Web browser.

12 Enter a value in only one of the form fields.

13 Click the submit button.

- The Web browser generates the alert dialog box with the error message.

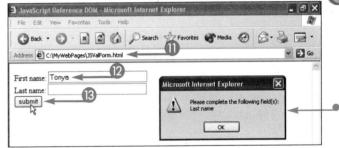

How do I use JavaScript to verify that form responses are formatted correctly?

▼ You can verify that responses are formatted correctly in several ways. You can use methods associated with the String object, such as `String.indexOf()` and `String.length()`, to search for particular characters and to ensure that responses contain a certain number of characters. `String.length()` is especially useful for testing the validity of phone number and ZIP code entries.

How do I submit the form if it contained no errors?

▼ Use the `"return true"` statement to process the form if it contained no errors. Use the `"return false"` statement to prevent the form from being submitted if errors were discovered on validation. If errors are discovered, a dialog box appears informing the user that the form contains errors, so the user can correct the errors and try to submit the form again.

How do I validate form fields such as radio buttons and check boxes?

▼ You use the `checked` property. Each radio button and check box is stored in an array and has a `checked` property that returns `true` if the element is selected and `false` if it is not selected. For example, to verify that the first radio button is selected, you use this code:

```
if (document.formName.
radioName[0].checked)
```

For more information, consult *JavaScript: Your visual blueprint for building dynamic Web pages,* by Kelly Murdock (John Wiley).

Preload Images

You can use JavaScript to load images into the Web browser cache, and then reference them later when swapping images with `mouseover` events. Preloading images into the Web browser's cache allows for instantaneous image swapping. If you fail to preload your images, a slight delay occurs on the `mouseover` event, because the Web browser must retrieve the image from the server.

To preload images, you can use the `Image()` constructor to create a new `Image` object and assign its URL to the image's `src` property. This creates an off-screen image that you can reference later when you create image mouseovers.

For more information, see the section "Script Image Mouseovers."

The following example uses a technique called *object detection* to prevent errors from occurring on Web browsers that do not support the `document.images` property. This property is a reference to the array of images contained within the HTML page. Because the `Image()` constructors are contained within an `if` statement, the JavaScript executes only if the Web browser's Document Object Model contains the `document.images` property. Object detection is a useful way to prevent errors without resorting to Web browser detection techniques. For more information, see the section "Check for Web Browser Versions."

Preload Images

① Open a graphics editor.

● This example uses Paint Shop Pro.

② Create two navigation graphics for the "on" and "off" states of a rollover.

Note: For more information about Web graphics, see Chapter 5.

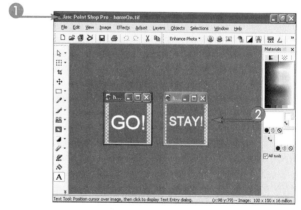

③ Open an HTML document.

④ In the head of the document, add a set of `<script>` tags.

⑤ Add a JavaScript `if` statement to test for the `document.images` object.

Note: For more information about `if` statements, see Chapter 8.

6 Use the `Image()` constructor to create a new image with the `src` property set equal to the location and name of the image.

7 Save the document.

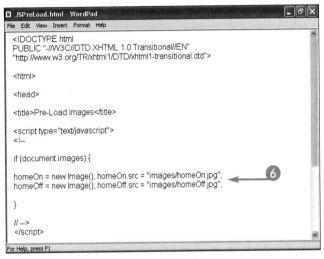

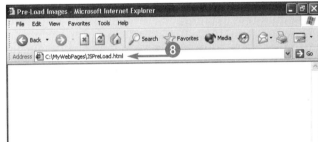

8 Open the document in your Web browser.

● The `Image()` constructor does not display the image on a page, but instead loads it into the Web browser's cache.

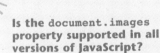

Is the `document.images` property supported in all versions of JavaScript?

▼ The `document.images` property, which tests for the presence of the `images[]` array, is supported in JavaScript versions 1.1 and higher. This means that versions 3 and higher of Netscape Navigator and Internet Explorer support `document.images`. In the example shown in the steps, the Web browser executes the JavaScript only if its DOM contains the `document.images` property.

When I preload images, can I make the `src` property either a relative or absolute URL?

▼ Yes. You can use either relative or absolute URLs when setting the `src` property for images. To use relative URLs, indicate the location of the image file relative to the current document:

```
imageName.src =
"../directoryName/
imageName.gif";
```

Can the `new Image()` constructor take any arguments?

▼ Yes. There are two optional arguments, `width` and `height`, that you can use to specify the dimensions of the image. To do this, use the following syntax:

```
imageName = new
Image(width, height);
```

However, because image dimensions are usually specified within the HTML `<img />` tag, it is not necessary to define the width and height using the `new Image()` constructor.

Script Image Mouseovers

One way to add an interactive element to your Web page is through *image mouseovers*, also referred to as *rollovers*. Within the Web browser's Document Object Model, every image has a read/write `src` property, meaning that you can use JavaScript to change the source of any image on the Web page.

When scripting image mouseovers, the first step is to ensure that all the images are preloaded in the Web browser's cache (for more information, see the section "Preload Images"). After the images are preloaded, you can use the `onmouseover` and `onmouseout` event handlers to invoke a function to swap in the new image. Within the `<img />` tag, you can add the following code to invoke a mouseover function:

```
onmouseover="functionName()"
```

Inside the parentheses, you must specify the *name* of the image — as set using the `name` attribute — and use it in the image-swapping functions to point to a different image. You must ensure that the images that you are swapping share the same name but have `on` and `off` suffixes:

```
document[imageName].src = eval(imageName + "On.src");
```

The `eval()` function takes the name of the image, adds the `"On.src"` suffix, and matches it to the preloaded image.

Script Image Mouseovers

① Open an HTML document with a script to preload images.

Note: *For more information, see the section "Preload Images."*

② Define a function to change the image source on rollons.

③ Define a function to change the image back to its original source on rolloffs.

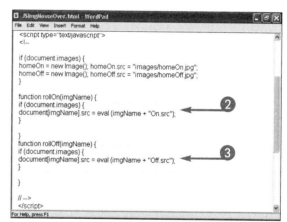

④ In the body of the document, add source code to insert an image that acts as a hyperlink.

- The `<img />` tag must include the `name` attribute set equal to the name of the preloaded image without the `on` or `off` suffixes.

Note: *For more information about hyperlinks, see Chapter 3.*

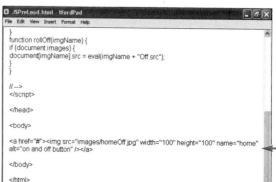

5 Add the onmouseover attribute and type the name of the on function that you created in step 2.

● Inside the parentheses, type the name of the image.

6 Add the onmouseout attribute and type the name of the off function that you created in step 3.

7 Save the document.

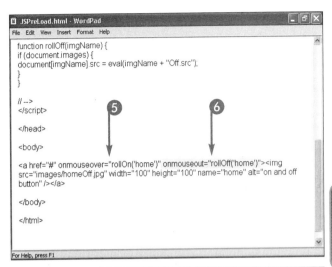

8 Open the document in your Web browser.

9 Move the mouse cursor over the image.

● The function alters the src property of the image to create an image-swap effect.

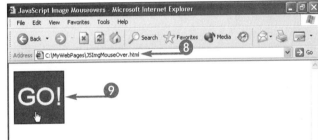

Can the images that I use for the on and off states be different sizes?

▼ Yes, however, for a seamless rollover effect, the on and off state images should be the same size. If you use an image for the on state that is twice as wide as the image for the off state, the change can be jarring, especially if the images are near any text that must shift to accommodate the change in size.

Are there other ways that I can use to code mouseovers?

▼ Yes. You can change the source property for individual images by adding JavaScript code to the onmouseover and onmouseout attributes. Reference the image by its array index number, such as document.images[0].src, or by its name. Then set the src property to reference the image you want to swap in or out.

What happens if I use only the onmouseover attribute and do not include the onmouseout attribute?

▼ If you do not use the onmouseout attribute to switch the src property back to the original image, the image remains in the on state even after the user moves the mouse cursor off the image. To prevent this from happening, always use both the onmouseover and onmouseout attributes.

Check for Web Browser Versions

To make your Web site accessible to a variety of Web browser types and versions, you can create different versions of code that apply to different Web browsers. However, you must also automatically determine which Web browser and version each visitor uses. You can use JavaScript to check for Web browser type and version number, as well as other information such as Java or plug-in support.

The `Navigator` object contains several properties that store information about the user's Web browser. You can check the Web browser type by reading the `navigator.appName` property, which typically returns "Netscape" for Netscape Navigator Web browsers and "Microsoft Internet

Explorer" for Microsoft Internet Explorer Web browser. The `navigator.appVersion` property contains the Web browser version number in addition to other information, such as platform and encryption data. To extract the version number from this string, you can use the `parse.Int()` or `parse.Float()` methods, for example:

`parse.Int(navigator.appVersion);`

These methods evaluate a string and return only the integer or floating point number. Keep in mind that the Web browser version number in the `appVersion` property is sometimes the version with which the Web browser is compatible, rather than the actual version number. For example, Internet Explorer 5 returns a value of "4," and Netscape Navigator 7 shows up as "5."

Check for Web Browser Versions

① Open a new HTML document.

② In the body of the document, add a set of `<script>` tags.

③ Define a new variable to store the version number.

- `parseInt (navigator.appVersion);` obtains the version number to assign to the variable.

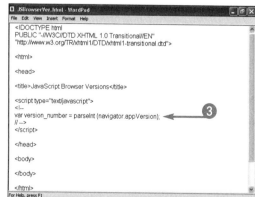

④ Add `document.write()` methods, if you want to display the information.

Note: For more information, see Chapter 8.

⑤ Save the document.

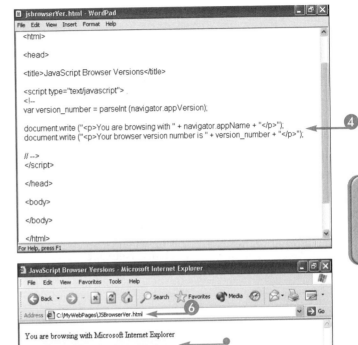

④

⑥ Open the document in your Web browser.

● The Web browser name and version number appear.

What other properties are associated with the Navigator object?

▼ In addition to `navigator.appName` and `navigator.appVersion`, other properties include `navigator.platform`, which returns the operating system, and `navigator.language`, which returns a two-letter language code, such as "en" (English). Modify the script you created by following the steps to include these other properties and see what the script reports as your system's platform and Web browser language code.

How can I use the Navigator object to test for plug-ins?

▼ The Navigator object includes the `plugins[]` array that contains all of the plug-ins installed in the Web browser. This enables you to automatically determine if Netscape Navigator is equipped to play a particular file type included on your Web page. However, in Internet Explorer 4 and more recent versions, this array is always set to `[0]`, and so it is empty.

Are there other ways to handle Web browser incompatibilities?

▼ Yes. Use object detection to determine whether a user's Web browser supports an object that you are using in your script. This is sometimes more efficient because you need not write different code for numerous Web browser versions. To check for an object, use a conditional `if` statement and include the object, such as `document.images`, in parentheses. If the object exists, the Web browser executes the code. For more on object detection, see the section "Preload Images."

Set a Cookie

You can use client-side JavaScript to set cookie values that you can later retrieve to personalize a visitor's experience on your Web site or to pass information from one Web page to another. *Cookies* are small pieces of data that Web browsers store and use to identify you on various Web sites or pages. You can think of a cookie as an identification tag that helps a Web site recognize your Web browser.

By storing data that a Web browser can pass back to a server, cookies allow you to *maintain state*, meaning that the Web browser can remember specific data that are normally stored temporarily while the user visits a particular Web page.

You can set a cookie by using the `document.cookie` object to assign name-and-value pairs. The *name* is the name you assign to the cookie, and the *value* is the value of the named cookie. For example, in a cookie called `login`, the value is the visitor's login name:

`login=visitorLoginName;`

Because values cannot contain commas, semicolons, or spaces, you may have to use the `escape()` function to properly encode the cookie value before setting it. For more information on encoding special characters, see *JavaScript: Your visual blueprint for building dynamic Web pages,* by Kelly Murdock (John Wiley).

Set Cookie Values

① Open an HTML document.

② In the head of the document, add a set of `<script>` tags.

③ Define a new function to set a cookie.

Note: *For more information about JavaScript functions, see Chapter 8.*

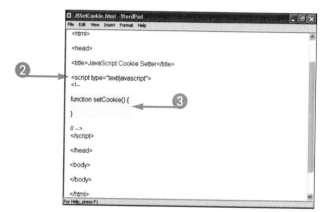

④ Define a new variable to prompt for user input using the `prompt()` value.

Note: *For more information about using the `prompt()` method, see the section "Prompt the User for a Response."*

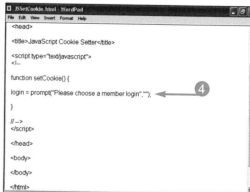

5 Type **document.cookie =** followed by a name for the cookie and the variable generated by the user's response.

● This example creates a cookie called Login that uses `escape(login)` to insert the login entry.

6 Type **onload="setCookie()"** in the opening `<body>` tag to invoke the function.

7 Save the document.

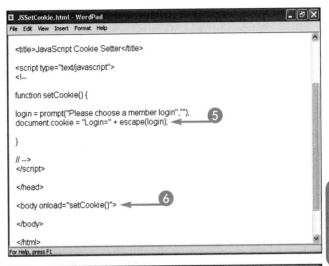

8 Open the document in your Web browser.

9 At the prompt, type a login entry.

10 Click OK.

● The Web browser stores the entry in a cookie so that the Web browser can "remember" it when the visitor returns to the Web site and logs in.

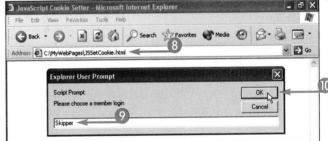

When must I use the `escape()` and `unescape()` methods to read and write cookies?

▼ When you set a cookie, the value stored in a name-and-value pair cannot contain commas, semicolons, or spaces. If the user-generated value is a piece of data such as a member name or other string, use the `escape()` method to encode the value, because the value may contain spaces. If you retrieve the value without using the `unescape()` method, any spaces are represented with the code `%20`. Using the `unescape()` method converts the string back to regular characters, replacing `%20` with a space.

Is there a limit on the number of cookies I can set?

▼ Yes. Some Web browsers limit the number of cookies that they can store per Web site. This is a particularly important restriction if you have more than one Web site on your Web server. However, when a cookie exceeds the limit, the browser removes the least-used cookie, so the restriction's effect is usually minimal.

Can I use cookies to store other information that a visitor enters?

▼ Yes, but storing some types of information, such as credit card information, can make transactions less secure. Most cookies store only an ID number that the Web site uses to identify a user. Store any data that a user entered at your Web site on a secure server.

PART III

Set a Cookie
(Continued)

When you set cookies, you can include several optional attributes to extend the cookie's capabilities. For example, the `expires` attribute sets an expiration date for information that you store with the cookie. This allows the Web browser to "remember" a login name for a specified amount of time. You can add the expiration date after the name-and-value pair in the cookie:

```
document.cookie="cookieName=value;expires=
expirationDate";
```

To set the cookie to expire in a certain number of months, you can use the `new Date()` constructor to create a reference to the current date, and then add a specific number of months and set the new date:

```
var expirationDate = new Date();
expirationDate.setMonth = (expirationDate.
getMonth + x);
```

You must set expiration dates in the GMT format. For more information about using JavaScript dates, consult *JavaScript: Your visual blueprint for building dynamic Web pages,* by Kelly Murdock (John Wiley).

The `path` attribute allows directories other than the original one to access a cookie. By setting the path to `"/"`, you make a cookie accessible from any page on the Web site. The `domain` attribute allows you to use the same cookie across multiple Web sites that use the same domain name.

Set a Cookie *(continued)*

Set Cookie Expiration Date

① Open an HTML document that contains a cookie script.

② Within the function to set a cookie, create a new variable set equal to `new Date()`.

- The `Date()` constructor creates a `Date` object set to the current date and time.

③ Add a statement to set the expiration date.

- `getMonth() + 6` obtains the current month and adds six months to it.

- `myExpire.setMonth` sets the value of the expiration date.

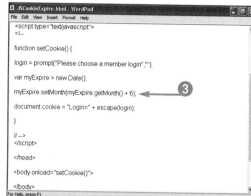

④ Type **expires=" + myExpire. toGMTString();** at the end of the `document.cookie` string.

● The `toGMTString()` ensures that the expiration date is in the correct format.

⑤ Save the document.

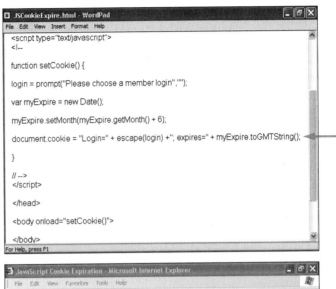

⑥ Open the document in your Web browser.

⑦ At the prompt, type a login entry.

⑧ Click OK.

● The Web browser stores the entry in a cookie until the cookie expires.

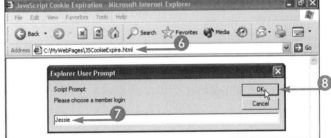

Can I be sure that my cookie always executes in a visitor's Web browser?

▼ No. Visitors can disable cookies in their Web browser to prevent the Web browser from accepting cookies. In addition, visitors can delete cookies at any time. Most Web browsers also store a limited number of cookies, so a Web browser with many cookies may delete your cookie before its expiration date if it has not been modified for some time.

What happens to a cookie if I do not set an expiration date?

▼ The cookie expires when the session ends — after the visitor closes her or his Web browser. You can set extremely long expiration dates, and some Web page authors even attempt to set dates that keep the cookie alive for the life of the computer, but most of these attempts are futile — users often choose to delete any cookies stored on their computers as part of their regular maintenance.

Is the data transmitted in cookies secure?

▼ No, cookies pass through a regular HTTP connection and are insecure. To ensure that your cookie transmits only with a secure connection between the Web browser and the server, use the `secure` attribute:

`cookieName=value; secure`

You can add the `secure` attribute to the cookie, along with any other optional attributes, such as `expires`, `path`, or `domain`. Simply separate each attribute with a semicolon.

Read a Cookie

After you store user data in a cookie, you can retrieve the stored values by using JavaScript. A cookie enables a Web browser to use stored data to pre-populate form fields or to remember purchase information as the visitor completes an e-commerce transaction.

To read and retrieve data from a cookie, you must search the `document.cookie` property for the specific name-and-value pair of your cookie data, and then extract the appropriate value. See the section "Set a Cookie" for more information. To search the cookie to find the beginning and the end of the value, you can use the `String.indexOf()` method:

```
document.cookie.indexOf("cookieName=");
```

After you locate the value, you can extract it using the `String.substring()` method. The `substring()` method extracts a part of a string according to two values, *start* and *end*. Within a cookie, the start position is the character after *cookieName=*, and the end position is the semicolon that separates each individual cookie. If only one cookie is present, the end is simply the end of the cookie string, represented by `document.cookie.length`. If you used the `escape()` method when setting the cookie, you can use the `unescape()` method to decode the cookie data's value.

Read a Cookie

① Open an HTML document.

② Type **function readCookie() {**.

③ Create a new variable, setting its value to the position of the cookie name within the string.

④ Add an `if` statement to test for the presence of the cookie name.

● If the name is not present, the statement returns a value of "-1".

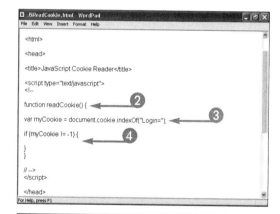

⑤ Search the string for the start and end points of the value.

● The start value is equal to the position of the name plus the number of characters in the name.

● The end value is the semicolon.

⑥ Create a new variable to store the cookie value.

● The `substring()` method extracts the value, and the `unescape()` method decodes Latin-1 characters.

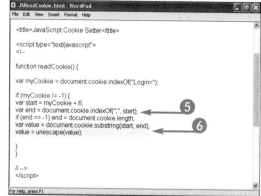

⑦ In the body of the document, add a form with a text input field.

Note: For more information about HTML forms, see Chapter 10.

⑧ Within the script, set the value of the text input field to the value of the cookie data.

⑨ Add the onload attribute and the function name to the <body> tag.

⑩ Save the document.

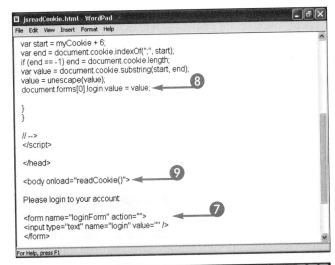

```
var start = myCookie + 6;
var end = document.cookie.indexOf(";", start);
if (end == -1) end = document.cookie.length;
var value = document.cookie.substring(start, end);
value = unescape(value);
document.forms[0].login.value = value;        ⑧


}
}

// -->
</script>

</head>

<body onload="readCookie()">        ⑨

Please login to your account:

<form name="loginForm" action="">        ⑦
<input type="text" name="login" value="" />
</form>
```

⑪ Open the document in your Web browser.

● The form field is populated with the cookie value.

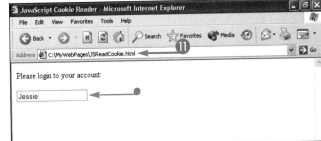

Why are string methods such as indexOf() and substring() used when reading cookies?

▼ When you retrieve a cookie using the document.cookie property, JavaScript returns a string value containing all of the cookies for that Web page. This string is a collection of name-and-value pairs, separated by semicolons. This means that if you read the entire document.cookie property, JavaScript returns a string in the following form:

cookieName=value; cookieName2=value

You can use any of the methods associated with strings to search and extract only the part of the string that you need.

What other methods can I use to extract the cookie value?

▼ Rather than using String.indexOf() and String.substring(), use the String.split() method to break the string into discrete pieces, based on the delimiter that separates each element, such as a semicolon.

Can I see the information a particular cookie stores on my computer?

▼ Yes, but Web browsers use different methods for storing cookies. Internet Explorer stores cookies as TXT files in a Cookies folder. You can double-click a file to open it in a text editor and view its contents. In Netscape Navigator you can view cookies by clicking Edit, Preferences, Privacy & Security, Cookies, and then clicking the Manage Stored Cookies button. Check your Web browser's help system.

FormTextInput.html - WordPad

File   Edit   View   Insert   Format   Help

```
<title>Form Text Input</title>

</head>

<body>

<form action="./cgi-bin/form_processing.pl" method="get"
name="myform" id="myform">

<p>Please type your email address:</p>

<input type="text" name="email" size="30" maxlength="64" />

<p>Enter your 5-digit zip code:</p>

<input type="text" name="zip" size="5" maxlength="5" />

</form>

</body>

</html>
```

For Help, press F1

Please type your email address:

Enter your 5-digit zip code:

12345

POSTDATA.ATT - Notepad

File   Edit   Format   View   Help

```
drama
----------------------------7d42a43f6024e
Content-Disposition: form-data; name="genre"

action
----------------------------7d42a43f6024e
Content-Disposition: form-data; name="price"

6-8
----------------------------7d42a43f6024e
Content-Disposition: form-data; name="view"

theater
----------------------------7d42a43f6024e
Content-Disposition: form-data; name="info"

Please enter a list of all your top 5 favorite movies
1. Blade Runner
2. Goodfellas
3. The Deer Hunter
4. Chariots of Fire
5. Pulp Fiction
```

Set Up a Form

Y ou can use forms to search the Web, send feedback, request information, post messages to bulletin boards, navigate Web sites, and make purchases. You add a form to your Web site using the HTML `<form>` tag. The opening and closing `<form>` tags contain all of the form elements, such as text entry boxes and buttons. You can also include other HTML elements within `<form>` tags to properly format the form and provide text directions to help users.

You must include two attributes with every opening `<form>` tag: the `action` attribute and the `method`

attribute. Within the `action` attribute, you can indicate the location of the program that processes the form — for example, the cgi-bin directory for a Common Gateway Interface (CGI) program.

The `method` attribute determines how the Web browser sends the form data to the server. You can make the value for the `method` attribute either `post` or `get`, but your decision depends on a variety of factors, including the complexity of the form, the security of the transmission, and whether you need to pass parameters to the server. If your forms are fairly small and security is not an issue, you can use the `get` method.

Set Up a Form

① Open a new HTML document.

② After the opening `<body>` tag, add an opening `<form>` tag.

③ Add the required closing `</form>` tag.

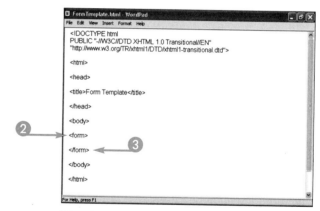

④ Within the opening `<form>` tag, add the `action` attribute set equal to the URL of the form-processing application on the server.

Note: *See Chapter 11 for details about using CGI applications to process form data.*

⑤ Add the `method` attribute set equal to `"get"` or `"post"`.

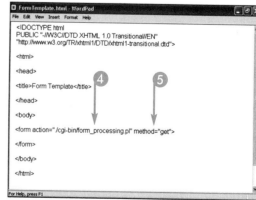

6 Add name and id attributes set equal to the name you want to give the form.

7 Inside the opening and closing `<form>` tags, type **`<input type="text" />`**.

Note: *For more information about text input fields, see the section "Add a Text Input Field."*

8 Save the document as a text-only file, with the .html extension.

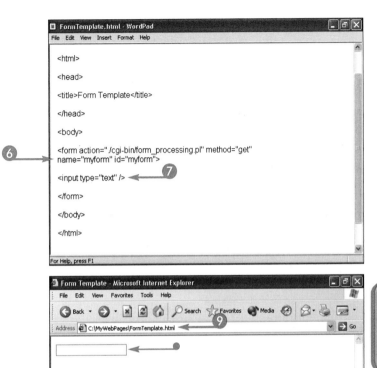

9 Open the document in your Web browser.

● Your Web browser displays the Web page, complete with the text entry field you added.

What is a CGI program?

▼ A CGI program receceives incoming data that conforms to the CGI specification and passes that data along to other programs that request it. CGI is not the only system for handling form data. Microsoft's Active Server Pages perform a similar function but enable developers who are familiar with programming in Visual Basic to use a familiar set of programming tools.

What is the difference between the post and get methods?

▼ The post method first contacts the server and then sends the data in a separate transmission. The get method contacts the server and sends the data in a single transmission with the data added onto the end of the action URL. Because the get method sends the data as a single transmission, it is a less secure way of passing data to the server.

What optional attributes can I include within the `<form>` tag?

▼ Optional attributes include the enctype attribute, which indicates how the Web browser encodes the data, the lang attribute, which sets the language in the form, and the name and id attributes, which identify the form by name, so that you can reference it in JavaScript. You can also include a variety of event attributes such as onsubmit. You often use the event attribute to invoke JavaScript functions to validate forms. For more information, see Part III.

PART IV

Add a Text Input Field

You can add single-line text fields with the `<input />` tag and the `type="text"` attribute. Text fields are ideal when you need to prompt users for individual information such as a name or address. When adding a text input field, you must specify a name for the field by using the `name` attribute.

The size of the text input field varies from Web browser to Web browser, but you can indicate the character length of the visible field with the `size` attribute. For example, setting the `size` attribute to 2 limits the visible space of the text input field to two characters. This is particularly useful when prompting visitors for information with specific character lengths, such as state abbreviations.

The `size` attribute controls only the appearance of the field, and not the maximum number of characters that a user may enter. If you want to ensure that users do not enter more than a certain number of characters, you must add the `maxlength` attribute. If users type the maximum number of characters allowed, the Web browser prevents them from entering additional text.

Add a Text Input Field

① Open a document in your HTML editor.

② Add an opening `<form>` tag, including the `action`, `method`, `name`, and `id` attributes.

③ Add a closing `</form>` tag.

Note: *For more information about `action` and `method` attributes, see the section "Set Up a Form."*

④ Add instructional text for the user.

⑤ Add the `<input />` tag, including the `type`, `name`, `size`, and `maxlength` attributes.

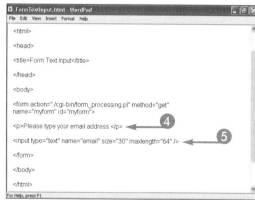

6 Add instructions for the next input field.

7 Add a second `<input />` tag, including the `type`, `name`, `size`, and `maxlength` attributes.

8 Save the document as a text-only file, with the .html extension.

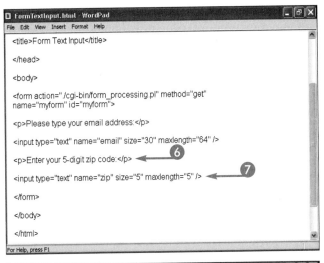

9 Open the document in your Web browser.

10 Position your cursor within a text entry field.

11 Type several characters.

● The Web browser does not allow you to type characters beyond the `maxlength` value.

What are the default values for the `size` and `maxlength` attributes?

▼ If you do not include the `size` and `maxlength` attributes in the `<input />` tag, their default values are used. The default size for a text field is about 13 characters, and the default `maxlength` value allows an infinite number of characters.

What if the `maxlength` value is smaller than the size of the input field?

▼ The `size` attribute still dictates the appearance of the form, but users cannot type additional text after they reach the maximum length allowed. If you set the `size` to a specific value and the user types a number of characters that exceeds that value, the input field scrolls as the user continues to type additional text.

Can I have text appear inside the input field over which the user can type?

▼ Yes. Use the `value` attribute with text enclosed in quotation marks to have the value appear within the input field. Although the user must erase the message to type new text, prepopulated values on form fields help guide the user through the data entry process. For example, to display the required format for a phone number, you can add `value="555.555.5555"` to the `<input />` tag for a text entry field.

Add a Password Field

By using the `type="password"` attribute, you can add a form field that masks the text that the user types. The password field is essentially the same as a regular single-line text entry field, except that the text characters appear obscured, usually as a series of asterisks or bullets. This prevents someone nearby from reading the password as the user types it.

All of the attributes that apply to the text input field apply when you set the type to `password`, so you must include the required `name` attribute. The `name` attribute gives the data entry an identifiable name, so that the entry can be

processed. In addition, you can use all of the other optional attributes available to the input field, including `value`, `size`, and `maxlength`.

You can use the password field in conjunction with a standard text entry field when you need users to enter a username and password to gain access to private or member sections of your Web site. Be aware, however, that the password type field only obscures the appearance of text on a Web browser window; it does not provide any additional security when the data is transmitted to the server.

Add a Password Field

1. Open a document in your HTML editor.
2. Add an opening `<form>` tag, including the `action`, `method`, `name`, and `id` attributes.
3. Add a closing `</form>` tag.
4. Add text to prompt the user for a password.
5. Add an `<input />` tag for the password, including the `type`, `name`, `size`, and `maxlength` attributes.
6. Save the document.

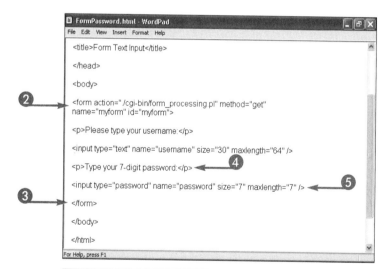

7. Open the document in your Web browser.
8. Type a password in the input field.

   ● The text is obscured on the Web page.

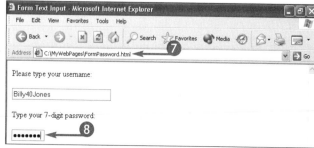

Add a Text Area

To give your users the opportunity to submit feedback, you can use the `<textarea>` tag with your form. Unlike text input fields that allow for only a single line of text, the `<textarea>` element creates a field with multiple lines so that users can enter entire paragraphs of text.

You can set the visible size of the text area with the `rows` and `cols` attributes. The `rows` attribute specifies the height of the box, expressed as lines of text, and the `cols` attribute specifies the width. A text area with `rows="4"`

and `cols="30"` accommodates about four lines of text with approximately 30 characters per line. If the user types additional text, the Web browser creates a vertical scroll bar to accommodate the additional rows.

The `<textarea>` element has both an opening and closing tag. You must always include the closing tag. Any text that you add between the opening and closing tags appears in the field as default text. You can use this text to prompt the user to enter specific information, but keep in mind that your default text cannot contain any additional HTML formatting such as font or emphasis elements.

Add a Text Area

① Open a document in your HTML editor.

② After the `<body>` tag, add opening and closing `<form>` tags.

③ Add a text label for your form field.

④ Add `<textarea>` tags, including the `name`, `rows`, and `cols` attributes in the opening tag.

⑤ Save the document.

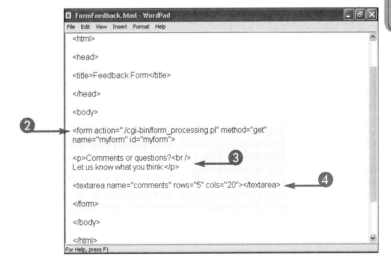

⑥ Open the document in your Web browser.

● Your Web browser opens the document and displays the text area in which you can type a message.

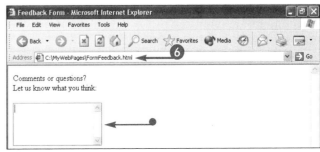

Add a Submit Button

The form fields that you include on your Web page are of little use if your visitors cannot send the form data to you. To enable visitors to transmit form information, you must include a Submit button. When the user clicks the button, the Web browser sends the data to the URL indicated in the form's `action` attribute. The Submit button can have any label you choose, for example, "Submit," "OK," or "Done." However, it still serves the same function of passing the data from the form to a server. For more information about passing data from a form to a server, refer to Chapter 11.

To create a Submit button, you can use the `<input />` tag and set the `type` attribute to `"submit"`. The submit `<input />` tag requires no additional attributes, but you probably want to use both the `name` and `value` attributes. Your form-processing application uses the `name` attribute to identify which button the user clicks, and it uses the `value` attribute to control the button label that is visible to the user. If you do not include a customized value, the Web browser displays the button with the default "submit" label.

Add a Submit Button

① Open a document in your HTML editor.

② Add an opening `<form>` tag, including the `action`, `method`, `name`, and `id` attributes.

③ Add a closing `</form>` tag.

④ Between the `<form>` tags, add `<input />` tags to create two text input fields.

Note: *For more information about text fields, see the section "Add a Text Input Field."*

⑤ Add explanatory text for each form field.

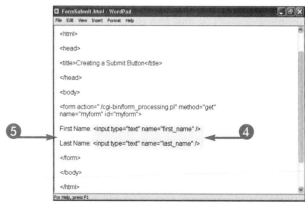

6 Add another `<input />` tag with the `type` attribute set equal to `"submit"` and `value` set to the name of the button.

7 Save the document.

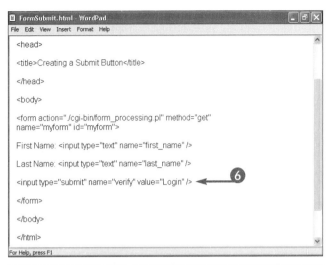

8 Open the document in your Web browser.

● Your Web browser opens the document and displays the button.

● When a user clicks the button, the Web browser transmits the data to the specified server.

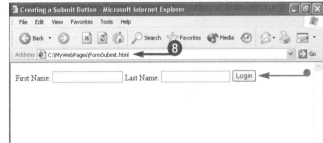

Can I include more than one Submit button?

▼ Yes, you can include multiple Submit buttons within the same form. For example, you may have distinct Submit buttons for editing a certain field, saving to a shopping cart, or proceeding to a checkout. If you include more than one Submit button, give each button a unique name or value so that the processing application can identify the button that the user clicks. You can add space between the buttons using CSS style rules to set their positions or add margin space around them. See Chapter 4 for details.

How do I create Submit buttons that provide more flexibility in terms of customizing the buttons?

▼ You can use the `<button>` `</button>` tags. Set the `type` attribute to `"submit"` and include formatted text or images within the `<button>` tags. This content appears on top of a standard Web browser button. Older Web browers do not support the `<button>` tag.

Can I use an image as a Submit button?

▼ Yes. The `<input />` tag accepts the `type="image"` attribute as well as `name` and `src`, which you use to indicate the location of the image file. When included within your form, the image appears as a clickable button. Many clip art collections include ready-made graphic buttons designed specifically for Web pages.

Add Check Boxes

Y ou can add check boxes to your form by using the `<input />` tag and setting the `type` attribute to `"check box"`. Check boxes are useful when you want to present the visitor with multiple choices and enable them to select more than one option.

For each check box, you must include the `name` and `value` attributes. When you have a group of related check boxes, you can assign the same name to all of the check boxes and then give each a specific attribute. For example, if you want visitors to indicate newsletter subscriptions, you can

name all check boxes "subscriptions" and then assign each value the name of a specific newsletter. When the user submits the form, the Web browser transmits any checked values associated with the check box name.

The value that you indicate for each check box is not visible to the user, so you should include a text description or image with each `<input />` tag. You can insert descriptive text or images to the right or left of a check box. If the descriptive text or image and the `<input />` tag have no breaks between them, the elements are aligned vertically on the baseline.

Add Check Boxes

① Open a document in your HTML editor.

② Add an opening `<form>` tag, including the `action`, `method`, `name`, and `id` attributes.

③ Add a closing `</form>` tag.

④ Add an `<input />` tag with the `type` attribute set equal to `"checkbox"`.

⑤ Add several more check box input fields.

⑥ Add a `name` attribute to each check box, giving each check box the same name.

⑦ Add a `value` attribute to each check box, assigning a unique value to each check box.

⑧ Add text labels for each check box.

⑨ Save the document.

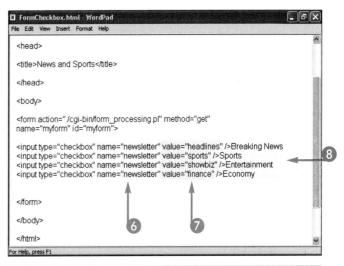

⑩ Open the document in your Web browser.

● Your Web browser displays the page, as well as the check boxes that you added, which are unchecked by default.

How do I prevent visitors from selecting more than one check box?

▼ Check boxes allow for multiple selections. If you want to have users select only one choice, then use radio buttons instead. For more information, see the section "Add Radio Buttons." You can also include a check mark in a box by adding the `checked` attribute to a check box. This is a good idea if your visitors are more likely to select one check box in the list than the others. The `checked` attribute is a standalone attribute; however, set it equal to `"checked"` to remain consistent with the XHTML specification.

How can I prevent users from selecting a particular check box?

▼ You do this by adding the `disabled` attribute to the `<input />` tag. You may want to do this for nested checkboxes that are available only if users select other fields. A disabled element does not allow user input, and the Web browser may change the appearance of the check box to signal that the option is unavailable.

Can I group the check boxes that I create?

▼ Yes, by assigning the check boxes identical names, you place them in the same group. This provides no real advantage except to organize the check box options.

Add Radio Buttons

When you want to limit users to only a single choice in a multiple-choice field, you can use radio buttons. *Radio buttons* are similar to check boxes, except that a user can select only one radio button option; selecting an option deselects any other option in the group. Radio buttons are most useful when you need users to choose from mutually exclusive choices or yes/no responses.

You can add radio buttons with the <input /> tag and the type attribute set to "radio". For each radio button,

you must include the name and value attributes. To define a group of radio button options, you can assign each radio button an identical name. To distinguish between the radio buttons in a group, you must assign a unique value to each button.

For each radio button, you must include a descriptive label to the right or left of the option. Like other form elements, radio buttons include limited built-in formatting options. You can use paragraph or line break tags to format buttons, place them within a table to fix their positions, or use CSS styles to control their appearance and positions on a page.

Add Radio Buttons

① Open a document in your HTML editor.

② Add an opening <form> tag, including the action, method, name, and id attributes.

③ Add a closing </form> tag.

④ Add several <input /> tags, each with a name and value attribute, and the type attribute set equal to "radio".

● This example sets type equal to "radio" and gives each radio button the same name but a unique value.

⑤ Add descriptive text for each button.

⑥ Add a <br /> tag following each <input /> tag to place each radio button option on a line of its own.

● You can use CSS style rules to change the layout or appearance of the buttons.

⑦ Save the document.

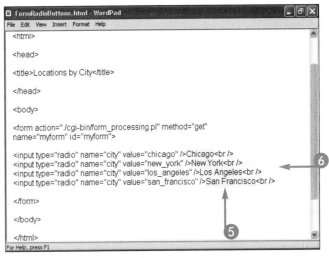

⑧ Open the document in your Web browser.

● Your Web browser displays the document, including the radio buttons that you created.

● You can click the various options to see how the buttons respond.

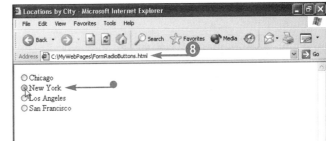

Can I use the checked attribute with radio buttons?

▼ Yes, you can use the checked="checked" attribute to preselect one option. Without the checked="checked" attribute, no option initially appears to be selected. However, keep in mind that because radio buttons are mutually exclusive, you should never preselect more than one option. Preselect the option that a user is most likely to click.

Can I change the color of radio buttons?

▼ Yes, you can change the background color of a radio button by using the style attribute with the background-color style property. This changes the color of the box that contains the radio button. For more information about using style sheets with form elements, see the section "Add Style to Form Elements." Refer to the color chart for hexadecimal color values.

Can I give the buttons different names?

▼ No. If you want the options to appear as a group in which users can select only one option, you must give all the options the same name. If you give each option a separate name, the options will appear as radio buttons but function as check box options, enabling the user to select more than one option in the group.

Create
a Menu

You can create a menu or a scrolling list of options with the `<select>` tag. For every menu that you create, you must add the required `name` attribute to the opening `<select>` tag. In addition, you can use the `multiple` attributes to allow users to select more than one option at a time. You must add the `size` attribute to create a scrolling list with several visible options. For example, setting the `size` attribute to 5 creates a list with the first five options visible; for more than five options, a scroll bar appears, enabling the user to bring additional options into view.

Within the opening and closing `<select>` tags, you can add options using the `<option>` tag. Though many Web authors often omit the closing `</option>` tag, include it to adhere to XHTML guidelines. If you do not use the optional `value` attribute with the `<option>` tag, the Web browser sets the value to the text content of the selection.

You can list options on menus rather than as check box or radio button options in cases where you have a limited amount of space but want to give the user numerous options. Menus are a great way to provide Web site navigation or search parameters.

Create a Menu

1. Open a document in your HTML editor.

2. Add opening and closing `<form>` tags.

3. Add an opening `<select>` tag, including the `name` attribute.

4. Add a closing `</select>` tag.

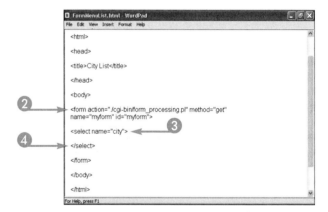

5. Between the `<select>` tags, add several `<option>` tags, giving each option a unique value.

● The `<option value=""></option>` tag inserts a separator between groups of options.

⑥ Add another opening <select> tag, including the size and multiple attributes.

⑦ Add a closing </select> tag.

⑧ Add several <option> tags, assigning a unique value to each option.

⑨ Save the document.

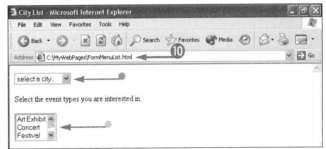

⑩ Open the document in your Web browser.

● Your Web browser displays the document.

● A menu appears when no size attribute is specified.

● A list appears when a size attribute sets the size to 2 or more.

Can I have certain options preselected in a menu?

▼ Yes. Add the selected attribute to an <option> tag to preselect a choice. Set the selected attribute equal to "selected" to comply with the XHTML specification. If no <option> tags contain the selected attribute, the Web browser displays the first option as the preselected choice.

How do I make the initial option a blank field?

▼ To make the initial option blank, add an additional <option></option> tag set directly below the opening <select> tag, but do not assign it a value. If you create a menu, the other options remain hidden until the user opens the menu; otherwise, blank space appears at the top of the list.

How do I control the width of menus?

▼ Most Web browsers expand the width of menus to accommodate the maximum number of characters presented in the option values. To make the menu wider, you can lengthen one or more of your options or add non-breaking spaces to the end of the longest option; type ** ** for each space you want to add.

Add Style to Form Elements

You can enhance the appearance of forms and specific form elements by using style properties. You apply inline styles using the `style` attribute or create tag-selector, class-selector, or ID-selector style rules for the various form elements, just as you can for other HTML elements.

To specify the background color for all form elements, you can create a tag-selector style rule for the `<form>` tag that sets the `background-color` property to the color you want. The style rule uses the following syntax:

`form {background-color: color}`

You can also use the `style` attribute with individual form fields, such as `<input />`, `<select>`, or `<option>` tags, to add color to specific elements. For example, to add color to an entire menu, you add the `style` attribute with a specified color to the opening `<select>` tag. To have alternating colors for each choice, you apply the `style` attribute to each of the `<option>` tags, with a different color for each option.

To create global style settings that you can reference repeatedly, consider creating an internal or external style sheet with defined form selectors or classes. For more information about creating style sheets and defining style rules, see Chapter 4.

Add Style to Form Elements

① Open a document that contains a form in your HTML editor.

② Define a tag-selector style rule to control the formatting for an HTML form element.

- This style rule sets the background color for the section of the document that is defined as a form.

Note: *Refer to Chapter 4 for more information about creating tag-selector style rules.*

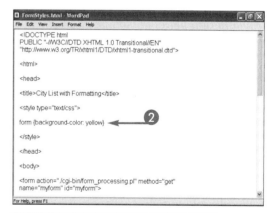

③ Define a class-selector style rule for an HTML form element.

- Class-selector style rules enable you to assign a style to individual elements.

Note: *Refer to Chapter 4 for more information about creating class-selector style rules.*

④ Add the `class` attribute to a tag set equal to the class-selector style name to apply the class selector style.

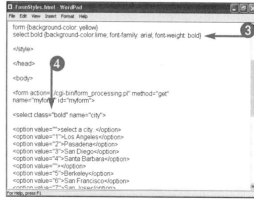

5 Add the `style` attribute to a form tag and set it equal to the formatting you want.

● This creates an inline style that overrides any tag- or class-selector styles.

6 Save the document.

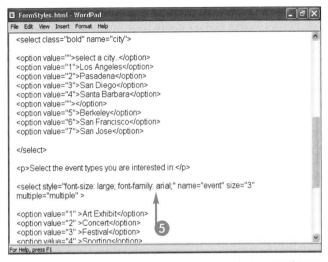

7 Open the document in your Web browser.

● The tag-selector style applies the formatting you specified.

● The class-selector style applies the formatting you specified.

● The inline style applies the formatting you specified.

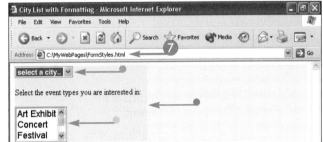

Can I apply style properties to the text that appears for each menu option?

▼ Yes. You can include font properties such as `font-weight` and `font-size`, as well as the `color` property, to change the appearance of text options. This is particularly useful if you change the background color of the `<select>` element or the individual `<option>` tags to a dark color to make the text legible on the dark background.

How do I change the appearance of the text on the form?

▼ The text that describes the various form elements is standard HTML text, so format it as you would any other text on the page. Because most of the HTML presentation attributes have been deprecated, use CSS style rules, as discussed in Chapter 4. If a Web browser does not support style sheets or certain style properties, it simply ignores the style attributes.

Can I use style properties to specify the color of radio buttons and check boxes?

▼ You can use the `background-color` property to add color to the immediate area around a radio button. You can also use the `color` property to change the color of the text. However, you cannot change the color of the actual radio button or check box.

Using Fieldsets and Legends

You can organize related form elements by using `<fieldset>` and `<legend>` tags. A fieldset groups related options together. A legend assigns a label to a group of options. For example, an order form may have three groups of options labeled "Ordered Items," "Billing Information," and "Shipping Information." This creates visual breaks in the form, but it also provides contextual information for users who are vision-impaired, as well as improving keyboard accessibility.

To group a section of form components together, you can enclose the elements within opening and closing `<fieldset>` tags. The Web browser may display the fieldset differently, perhaps creating a box around the grouped options. You can add a label to the fieldset by including summary text within opening and closing `<legend>` tags. Neither the `<fieldset>` nor the `<legend>` tags include any implicit formatting instructions, but you can apply `style` attributes to both. For information about using style sheets with forms, see the section "Add Style to Form Elements."

Older Web browsers do not recognize the `<fieldset>` and `<legend>` tags. However, this should not prevent you from implementing them because Web browsers that do not support the tags simply ignore them and display the form elements normally.

Using Fieldsets and Legends

① Open a document that contains a form in your HTML editor.

② Add opening and closing `<fieldset>` tags around a group of options.

③ Add a description of the group, bracketed by opening and closing `<legend>` tags.

④ Save the document.

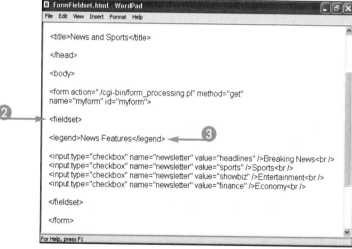

⑤ Open the document in your Web browser.

● Your Web browser displays the fieldset as a labeled group of options.

Note: *The fieldset may appear differently in a different Web browser.*

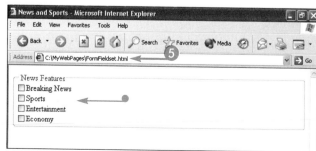

Using Labels

With some form elements, such as the Submit button, you can add a `value` attribute to give the element a name or *label*. Other form elements, such as text entry fields, check boxes, and radio buttons, do not support labeling in this way. However, you can label these elements by using the `<label>` tag. The `<label>` tag provides Web browsers with contextual information that associates the label text with a specific element. This is important for visually impaired visitors using special Web browsing applications. In addition, the `<label>` tag allows users to select options by clicking the label text; without a label, the user must click the actual control — the check box, option button, or text box.

The easiest way to add labels is to enclose your label text and form element within opening and closing `<label>` tags. You can also associate labels with form elements by using the `for` attribute with the `<label>` tag and the `id` attribute with the target form element. When the user selects the label text, the Web browser jumps to the form element that has the corresponding `id` value.

Using Labels

1 In your HTML editor, open a document that contains form elements that you want to label.

2 Add the `name` and `id` attributes to identify the elements that you want to label.

3 Add opening and closing `<label>` tags around the text that describes each form element.

● The `for` attribute identifies the element being labeled.

4 Save the document.

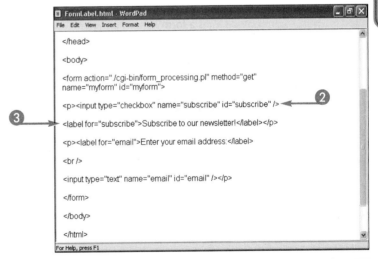

5 Open the document in your Web browser.

● Your Web browser displays the document, complete with the labeled elements.

● You can click a text label to select an option or position the cursor inside a text box.

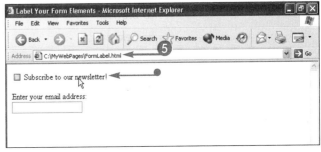

Disable Form Fields

Y ou can make form fields inaccessible to users with the `disabled` and `readonly` attributes. The `readonly` attribute is useful for displaying informative text on a form that you do not want the user to modify — for example, a license agreement or disclaimer. You can use the `disabled` attribute to prevent a user from selecting an option unless the user has typed a particular entry or selected another required option. When you disable form fields or designate them as read-only, the user cannot select the option or enter a new value, and the Web browser often displays the fields differently, usually graying them out.

This section shows how to mark a text area as read-only and how to use the `disabled` attribute together with

JavaScript to disable a Submit button unless the user chooses to agree with a license agreement. The JavaScript, not shown in the section, appears before the form:

```
<script type="text/javascript">
function codename() {
if(document.myform.agree[0].checked)
{document.myform.okay.disabled=false;}
else
{document.myform.okay.disabled=true;}
}
</script>
```

For more information about JavaScript, see Part III.

① In your HTML editor, open a document that contains form fields that you want to disable.

② Add the `readonly` attribute to any text input fields that you want to prevent the user from changing.

③ Add the `disabled` attribute to any fields that you want to disable.

④ Save the document.

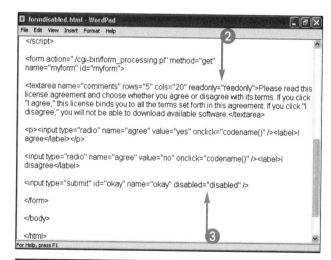

⑤ Open the document in your Web browser.

● Your Web browser displays the Web page, but you cannot select any disabled options or type in any read-only text fields.

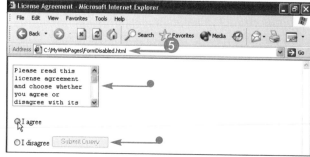

Using Hidden Fields

When you want to include form fields to process a form, but you do not want the user to alter or even view the information, you can use *hidden fields*. Hidden fields are simple `<input />` elements with the `type` attribute set to `"hidden"`. With hidden fields, you must also include the `name` and `value` attributes. The `name` attribute identifies the data being submitted with the form and the `value` attribute specifies the data entry being sent.

You use hidden fields if your form-processing application receives several different forms and you need to distinguish the processing action that takes place. For example, you may have an application that creates new records as well as updating existing ones. For forms with new record information, include a hidden field with the `value` set to `"new"`. In another location, you may have another form with a hidden field where the `value` is set to `"update"`. Based on the transmitted hidden values, the form processing application decides how to handle the data.

You can also use hidden fields to pass along the current date and time, cookie information, or other data without requiring the user to enter that data or to see what is being sent.

Using Hidden Fields

① Open a document in your HTML editor that contains a field that you want to hide.

② Add `type="hidden"` to the opening tag of the field that you want to hide.

● Ensure that the tag also includes the `name` and `value` attributes.

③ Save the document.

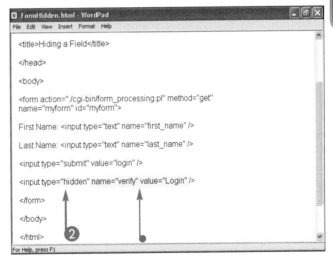

④ Open the document in your Web browser.

● Your Web browser displays the document but does not show the hidden field.

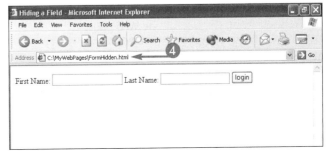

Allow Users to Send Attachments

You can enable visitors to send you attachments by using an <input /> tag with the type set to "file". This creates both a text entry field where the user can enter in the path of a file, and a button that allows users to browse their local drive and select the file they want to attach.

When using file-selection input fields, you must include the enctype attribute within the opening <form> tag and set the value to "multipart/form-data". If you do not include this attribute, the form simply transmits the value

entered into the text entry field, namely the location of the file on the user's drive. In addition, you must set the method attribute to "post".

The way in which the file attachments are processed depends entirely on your form-handling application on the server. Because you cannot verify the size or content of a file that the user sends, you must ensure that your CGI or other application can cope with large files, a variety of formats, and possible file corruption. You should also have an anti-virus program in place to scan incoming files for potential virus infection and to block any suspect files.

Allow Users to Send Attachments

① Open a document in your HTML editor that contains a form in which you want to include an option for attaching a file.

② In the opening <form> tag, set the action attribute to an e-mail address or the location of a CGI program, and set the method attribute to "post".

③ Add the enctype attribute.

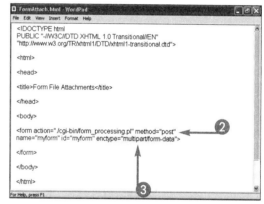

④ Add an <input type="file" /> tag, including the name attribute.

⑤ Save the document.

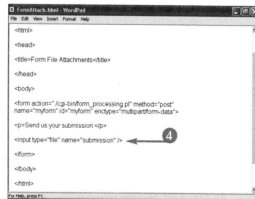

6 Open the document in your Web browser.

● The file selection element creates a text input field and a Browse or Choose File button, depending on the browser.

7 Click the Browse or Choose File button.

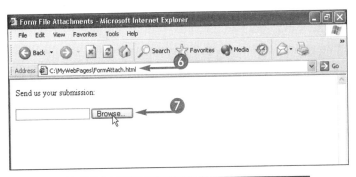

● The Web browser opens a platform-specific file selection dialog box.

8 Click the file you want to attach.

9 Click Open.

● Your Web browser inserts the path to the file that you selected.

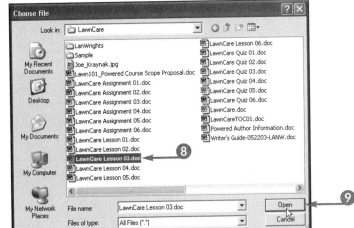

Can I limit the types of files that users can send?

▼ Yes. You can include the `accept` attribute within the `<input />` tag to restrict the types of files that users may attach. The value of the `accept` attribute should specify MIME types. To limit the file selection to images, set the value of the `accept` attribute to `"image/*"`. The asterisk tells the Web browser to accept all file formats with the `image` MIME type. You can limit the acceptable images by specifying the file format; for example, type **accept="image/gif jpg jpeg"** to accept only GIF and JPEG images. To limit the selection to text files, include the `"text/*"` MIME type.

Can I have file attachments sent to an e-mail address rather than a CGI program?

▼ It is possible. In theory, you can include a `mailto:` URL within the form's `action` attribute to send attachments to an e-mail address. However, in practice, this is not a very reliable or secure way to process file attachments.

How do I indicate where the file should be stored on my server?

▼ This directive should be a part of your form-processing application. For example, if you use a CGI program to process your form data, the program should include a directive on where to store any incoming files. For more information about form processing, refer to *PHP: Your visual blueprint for creating open source, server-side content* by Paul Whitehead and Joel Desamero (John Wiley).

Understanding Form Data Collection

Forms provide Web pages with various elements that enable users to enter data. You can use the data that users enter in two ways: the first way is to write scripts that provide immediate feedback to users, based on the data that they enter. For example, you can use a form to prompt a user for their name and then use a script to generate a page that greets the user by name.

The second way is to collect data from users and then pass the data back to you, either packaged in an e-mail message or by sending the data to a program on the server. For example, you can collect data in this way to create membership rosters, collect order and billing information, and log feedback.

Process Forms

If you need to actually receive and process the form data, you can have the Web browser send values to an e-mail address or to a form-handling application on the server. The last section of this chapter, "E-mail Form Results," demonstrates how to deliver simple form data to an e-mail address, but for more robust form handling, you can use server-side applications, such as Active Server Pages (ASP), PHP: Hypertext Preprocessor (PHP), or Common Gateway Interface (CGI) applications. These applications receive the form data and process it to make the data suitable for storage in a database and for other uses.

CGI and other server-side applications add a dynamic element to Web sites by executing requests from Web browsers rather than simply serving up requested pages. For example, most Web search sites use server-side applications to execute search requests. When you enter a search phrase describing a topic of interest and execute the search, the Web page passes the information that you entered to a server-side application, such as a CGI application. The server-side application processes the request and creates a custom Web page that displays results extracted from the search site's database.

Regardless of the scripting language you use, the interface communicates between the client and server by passing data using *headers*. Data is passed to the server as a *request header* and is received from the server as a *response header*.

These headers store data as environment variables. For example, with CGI, the REMOTE_HOST environment variable holds the hostname of the client; REQUEST_METHOD lets you know whether the form was submitted using the get or post method; and QUERY_STRING holds the form name=value pairs if the form was submitted using the get method.

This chapter provides a brief overview and basic examples of CGI scripts and programming. Many other books are available for learning CGI and Perl, including *Perl for Dummies*, by Paul Hoffman (John Wiley).

Implementing CGI Applications

CGI applications run on the server where you store your Web pages, and provide an interface between the client, usually a Web browser, and the server. With CGI, you can run the client and server on different hardware configurations or on different platforms and still exchange data. CGI applications are a popular way to process forms, and you can script them in a variety of programming languages, including Perl, C, Visual Basic, or even AppleScript.

Many Web-hosting services support the use of CGI applications for processing form data. They may even supply ready-made CGI scripts. You can also download scripts from any of several online libraries. Some of the most popular libraries are scriptsearch.com, www.scriptarchive.com, and hotscripts.com. At these and other related sites, you can often find free scripts that are easy to use and customize to fit the forms that you build for your Web site.

Before installing scripts, you should ensure that your Web server or hosting company supports the technology that you are using. You also need to know in which directory you should store your scripts. Many hosting services require that you store scripts in the /cgi-bin directory, but others allow you to place your scripts in any directory, as long as the script files end with the .cgi extension.

Secure Form Data

When implementing forms, carefully consider what level of security you need to implement. If you request private information from users, be sure to secure the transmission of the data from the user's Web browser to your Web server. In addition, you need to ensure that your Web server is adequately protected against malicious attacks. To find out what sort of security your server offers, talk to your system administrator or host provider.

Give Visitors Confirmation

HTML forms enable visitors to send feedback and process orders, but you must not forget that communication on the Web is a two-way street. Each time a visitor submits a form, they want to know that the transmission was successful and that you received the data. Not only does confirmation improve the user's experience on the Web site, but in the case of online transactions, it is also a necessary element in establishing a reputation of trust and reliability. Confirmation can take the form of an e-mail response or a specific confirmation page that loads after the user submits the form. For forms that process online purchases, you should have both. The section, "Script an HTML Response" shows you how to provide instant feedback.

Handle Form Data

To send form data to a server for processing, the form must include a submit button, as explained in Chapter 10. When a user clicks this button, the Web page passes the form data to the server.

You can use two attributes to provide instructions on how to handle the form data: the `action` and `method` attributes, which you include in the opening `<form>` tag. The `action` attribute specifies the destination of the data, and the `method` attribute specifies how the form data is sent.

You can set the `action` attribute to an e-mail address, as explained in the section, "E-mail Form Results" or you can

set it to the URL of an application that processes the form data. These applications are typically CGI programs that are stored in a directory on your server. See the section, "Understanding Form Data Collection" for information on where to obtain CGI scripts, and consult with your Web-hosting service to determine where to store them on the Web server.

The CGI application that the `action` attribute calls on processes the data on a server, not on your local machine. To do this, you must upload your Web page to the server, as shown in Chapter 18.

Handle Form Data

① In your HTML editor, open a document that contains a form.

② Set the `action` attribute of the opening `<form>` tag to the CGI application's location and filename.

③ Save the document.

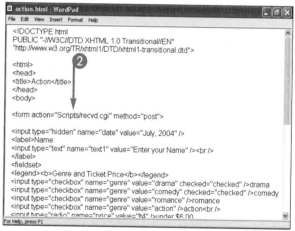

④ Upload the CGI application to the directory that your Web-hosting service specifies.

Note: *See Chapter 18 for details on uploading files to Web servers.*

⑤ Upload the document from step 3 to the server.

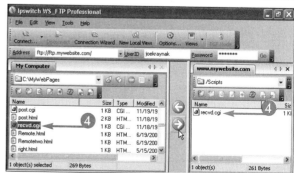

⑥ Open the HTML file in your Web browser.

⑦ Complete the form.

⑧ Click the submit button.

● The form data is sent to the specified CGI application.

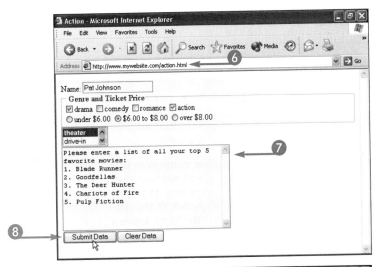

● The CGI application processes the form data and returns a message to the Web browser.

Note: To view the script for generating this message, see the section, "Script an HTML Response."

Can I test CGI applications on my local machine?

▼ If you install a Web server on your local machine, you can test CGI applications locally. Many Web editing tools, including Microsoft FrontPage and Macromedia Dreamweaver, include a stripped-down version of a Web server that you can install on your local machine for this purpose. If you have Windows XP Pro, you can install Internet Information Services (IIS) from the Windows installation CD to enable your computer to act as a Web server. Windows XP Home edition does not include this component. Earlier versions of Windows call the component Personal Web Server. For Mac users, OS X includes the Apache Web server.

Can I set the message that appears when my Web server receives data?

▼ The CGI application that accepts the form data returns the message that the Web browser displays. See the section, "Script an HTML Response" for more on how to script a CGI application that generates the response that you want to display on the user's screen.

Can I place any CGI application on my Web server?

▼ Probably not. Because the CGI application runs on the server, many Web-hosting services are careful about which CGI applications they allow on their servers. In some cases, you may be restricted to using only those applications that the Web-hosting service supplies. Contact your Web hosting service to determine which options are available.

Get Form Data

The `method` attribute defines how the Web browser passes form data to the CGI application specified in the `action` attribute. You can set the `method` attribute to one of two values, `get` or `post`. With the `get` method, the Web browser appends the form data to the end of the URL that the Web browser sends back to the server. This makes it fairly easy to return data to the server.

If your form data is short, straightforward, and contains no sensitive information, the `get` method is sufficient. However, if the form calls for a great deal of data or

sensitive information, you should use the post method, as discussed in the section "Post Form Data."

W3C recommends that you use the `get` method only when a form is *idempotent*, that is, when the form makes no changes to the data. For example, most Web search sites use the `get` method for the forms that users fill out when they search for Web sites. The form requests data from the database but does not change or add information to the database. A form that is not idempotent may add shipping information to a database or register a user to subscribe to a Web site.

Get Form Data

① In your HTML editor, open a document that contains a form.

② Set the `action` attribute to the name of the form-handling CGI application.

③ Set the `method` attribute to `get`.

④ Save the document.

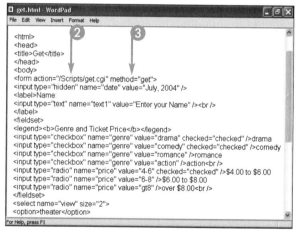

⑤ Upload the CGI application that you specified in step 2 to the directory that your Web-hosting service specifies.

Note: To script the CGI application shown in these steps, see the section, "View Environment Variables."

⑥ Upload the document from step 4 to the server.

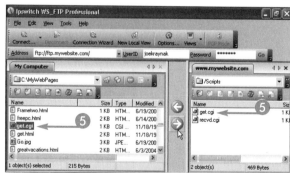

⑦ Open the document from step 6 in your Web browser.

⑧ Complete the form.

⑨ Click the submit button.

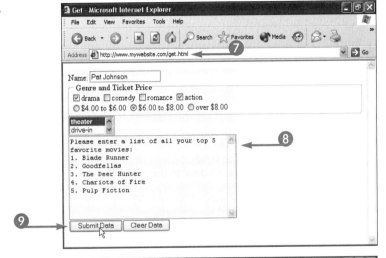

● The CGI application specified in the `action` attribute receives the data and processes it.

● In this example, the CGI application sends the data it received back to the Web browser, to display the form in which the data was sent.

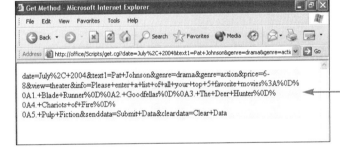

What exactly does the `get` method send to the server?

▼ The Web browser sends data to the server as a `name=value` pair, in which `name` is the name assigned to the form element using the `name` attribute, and `value` is the data entered in that field. For text input fields, the value is what the user types. For check box options, radio buttons, and submit buttons, the value is whatever the `value` attribute specifies for that option.

After the CGI runs, the URL in my browser's address bar contains additional text. Where did it come from?

▼ Using the `get` method, the form data is attached to the end of the URL, which appears in the Web browser's address bar. A question mark (?) separates the actual URL address and the name/value pairs. Each name/value pair is separated from the other with the ampersand symbol (&).

What default method does the Web browser use if I omit the `method` attribute?

▼ If the `method` attribute is missing from the `<form>` tag, the Web browser uses the `get` method to submit the form data. To use the `post` method you must include the `method="post"` entry, as discussed in the section "Post Form Data." The `method` attribute is optional, but the `<form>` tag requires the `action` attribute.

Post Form Data

When you create a form that calls for a large quantity of data — more than 200 characters — or when you need to exchange data more securely, you can use the post method. The post method instructs the Web browser to connect to the server and transfer the form fields and data directly to it. The post method sends the data in a structured format that pairs the field names with the values that the user enters.

Because the post method sends the form data to a standard input channel, you do not need to worry about

the form data exceeding the Web browser limits. The post method can handle a large amount of data. The post method also ensures that the returned URL is uncluttered, and is typically a more reliable way to transmit data.

You can change the method type without changing any other attributes of the opening <form> tag, because the method type merely specifies the way in which the data is passed. If you decide to change the method from get to post, you do not need to change the value of the action attribute; you can send the data to the same CGI application.

Post Form Data

① In your HTML editor, open a document that contains a form.

② Set the action attribute to the name of the form-handling CGI application.

③ Set the method attribute to post.

④ Save the document.

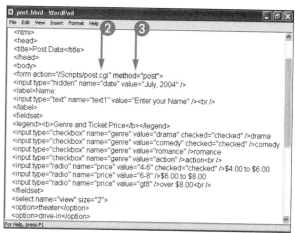

⑤ Upload the CGI application specified in step 2 to the directory that your Web-hosting service specifies.

Note: *To script the CGI application shown in these steps, see the section, "View Posted Form Data."*

⑥ Upload the document from step 4 to the server.

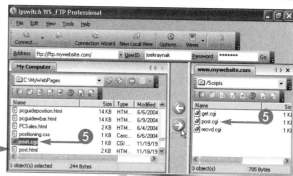

⑦ Open the document from step 6 in your Web browser.

⑧ Complete the form.

⑨ Click the submit button.

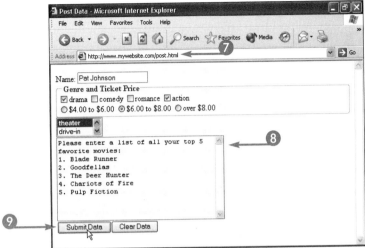

- The CGI application specified in the action attribute receives the data and processes it.

- In this example, the CGI application sends the data that it received back to the Web browser, to display the form in which the data was sent.

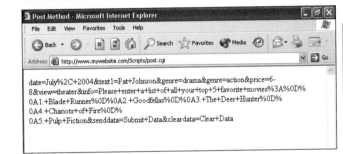

How can a CGI application determine whether the Web browser sends the form data using the get or post method?

▼ CGI applications can obtain information about the form data from the environment variables that are passed along with the form data. These environment variables tell the CGI application the parameters of the form data. One of these environment variables, REQUEST_METHOD, tells the CGI application whether the value of the method attribute is get or post. See the section, "View Environment Variables" for more information.

Can I use both the get and post methods on the same form to pass data?

▼ No. You must set the method attribute to either get or post. A single Web page can have multiple forms, and each form can use a different method, but most Web pages use one method or the other.

Some of the data I entered on the form is not included in the message that the server received. What happened?

▼ Web browsers successfully transmit only name=value pairs from a form. If you do not name a form control or if a particular control is disabled, any value associated with it is not sent to the server. Check the source code for your form.

PART IV

Parse Form Data

Whenever a Web browser uses the `get` or `post` method to send data to a server, it encodes that data before sending it. This enables it to present the data in a standard format and prevent it from becoming corrupted during the transmission. If you do not specify an encoding type, Web browsers use the default encoding method: `application/x-www.form.urlencoded`, commonly called *URL encoding*.

When a Web browser uses URL encoding to encode data, it changes spaces to plus signs (+). In place of any characters that may cause problems, the Web browser inserts a percent symbol (%), followed by the hexadecimal ASCII value that identifies the character. This tells the Web browser to replace the character with the specified symbol. For example, a Web browser interprets the URL http://www.myfamily.com/Favorite%20Videos as having a space between Favorite and Videos.

To present the data in a more easily recognizable format, you can use a CGI script to *parse* the data. Parsing essentially decodes the URL-encoded data, replacing the plus signs with spaces and replacing any special symbols and ASCII values with the characters they represent. You can download parsing scripts at any of several Web sites, as explained in the section, "Understanding Form Data Collection."

Parse Form Data

1. In your HTML editor, open a document that contains a form.

2. Set the `action` attribute to the name of the form-parsing CGI application.

3. Set the `method` attribute to `post`.

4. Save the document.

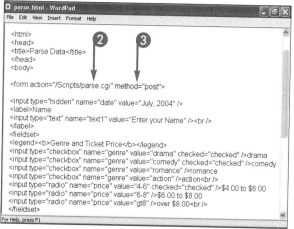

5. Upload the CGI application specified in step 2 to the directory that your Web-hosting service specifies.

Note: *See Chapter 18 for details about uploading files to Web servers.*

6. Upload the document from step 4 to the server.

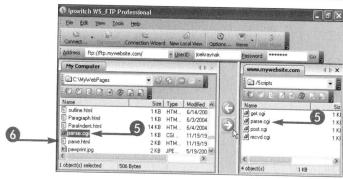

⑦ Open the document from step 6 in your Web browser.

⑧ Complete the form.

⑨ Click the submit button.

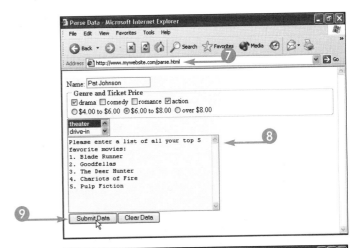

● The CGI application specified in the `action` attribute receives the data and parses it.

● In this example, the CGI application sends the data that it received back to the Web browser to show how a parsing application presents the data.

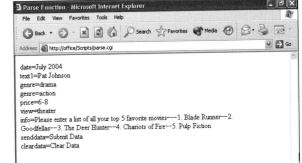

Apart from spaces, which other symbols are encoded, and what are their encoded values?

▼ Most of the nonstandard symbols are encoded when they are passed as part of the URL line. Some of these symbols and their encoded values include the ampersand (%26), the question mark (%3F), the percent (%25), quotation marks (%22), the number sign (%23), the @ sign (%40), the colon (%3A), the forward slash (%2F), and the equal sign (%3D).

Does URL encoding make a URL secure?

▼ URL encoding does not make a URL or a Web site secure. URL encoding only puts the URL in a form that the server can recognize and easily interpret. To secure a Web site and data transfers, the site must support Secure Socket Layers (SSL) or employ another security protocol for data transmissions.

Can I specify a different encoding type?

▼ Yes. You can add `enctype="multipart/form-data"` to the opening `<form>` tag to handle encoding for file attachments and any form data that contains characters not included in the standard ASCII set. The encoding type is an agreed-upon way of presenting data that enables data to be exchanged across an Internet connection. See Chapter 10 for more information.

Script an HTML Response

CGI is intended to be dynamic and interactive. If a user submits data and receives no response, the user is likely to wonder whether the server received the data. To provide the user with feedback, you can script an HTML response that indicates to the user that the server successfully received the data. The script produces a plain-text file that includes HTML tags and your text message. This creates a dynamic Web page by writing source code to a new document.

Using the Perl scripting language, you can send text back to the user by using the `print` keyword. For the Web browser to recognize the response text as HTML, you need to specify the Multipurpose Internet Mail Extensions (MIME) type before any text. The `Content-type:` label, followed by the MIME type, enables you to do this. The MIME type for standard HTML is `text/plain`.

At the end of every HTML line, you should include the new line (\n) command, except for the `Content-type:` line, which should include two new line (\n) commands. You should place a semicolon (;) at the end of every line.

Script an HTML Response

① Open a new document in your HTML editor.

② Type **#!/usr/bin/perl** at the top of the document.

Note: `#!/usr/bin/perl` *is the UNIX shell's cue that the script should be executed by the Perl command.*

③ Add the `print` keyword, followed by `"Content-type: text/plain\n\n"`.

④ Add several additional `print` statements with HTML statements in quotes.

⑤ Save the document as a text-only file, adding the .cgi extension.

⑥ Upload the CGI application from step 5 to the directory that your Web-hosting service specifies.

Note: See Chapter 18 for more information about uploading files to Web servers.

⑦ Upload the Web page that references the CGI application to the server.

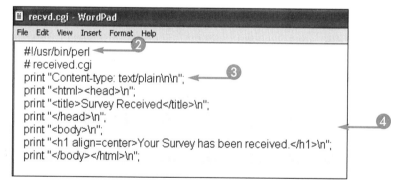

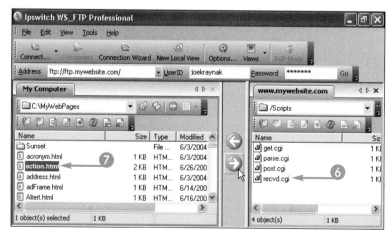

8 Open the document from step 7 in your Web browser.

9 Complete the form.

10 Click the submit button.

● The form data is sent to the specified CGI application.

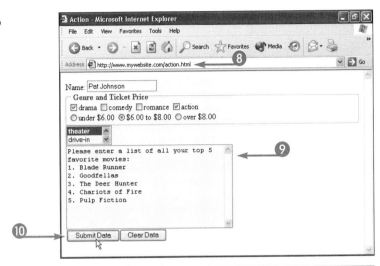

● The CGI application processes the form data and returns a message to the Web browser.

What exactly are MIME types?

▼ *MIME types* are defined extensions that enable different types of data to be sent over standard e-mail protocols. These same extensions are incorporated into HTML as a way to include alternative data in a Web page. By specifying a MIME type, you identify to the Web browser or other program that receives the file the type of file that you are sending.

Can I set the content type to `text/html` instead?

▼ Yes. Either `text/html` or `text/plain` creates a plain text file that a Web browser can read. However, you must add the .cgi extension to the filename — not the .html extension — because the Web browser must execute the file, and not simply open it.

Can I script a response that sends something other than an HTML document?

▼ A CGI script responds back to the Web browser using any number of content types, if you specify a different MIME type. Sample MIME types include: `video/quicktime image/gif` , `image/jpeg`, `audio/x-wav`, or `video/x-msvideo` for AVI video files. Leave a blank line after specifying the MIME type. Follow this with the binary contents of the file to send. You display the binary contents of a file, such as an image, by opening it in a text editor.

View Environment Variables

Whenever a client calls on a CGI script, usually by completing and submitting a form, the server generates *environment variables*. These variables store the data that the user submitted, along with additional data, such as the IP address of the remote host that is making the request. Environment variables can also store information about the server that the client may request, such as the server name.

You can use these variables to interface with the client. For example, the REMOTE_ADDR environment variable can identify the Web address of the Web page that called the CGI script, and the REQUEST_METHOD environment variable identifies the method attribute of the form.

Common environment variables include REMOTE_ADDR, REMOTE_HOST, HTTP_ACCEPT, HTTP_USER_AGENT, REQUEST_METHOD, CONTENT_LENGTH, QUERY_STRING, and PATH_INFO.

When a form is passed to a CGI script using the get method, the form data is stored in the QUERY_STRING environment variable.

To look at the environment variables in the Web browser, you can print the ENV keyword, followed by the environment variable in brackets and single quotes. A dollar sign ($) in front of the ENV keyword identifies Perl variables. For example, the statement $ENV{'REMOTE_ADDR'} accesses the remote address environment variable.

View Environment Variables

① Type **#!/usr/bin/perl** at the top of a new HTML document.

② Type **print "Content-type: text/html\n\n"**.

③ Add print statements.

④ Add a **print "$ENV{'QUERY_STRING'}"** statement.

⑤ Save the document as a text-only file with the .cgi extension.

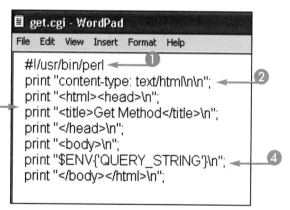

⑥ Upload the CGI application from step 5 to the directory that your Web-hosting service specifies.

Note: *See Chapter 18 for information about uploading files to Web servers.*

⑦ Upload the Web page that references this script to the server.

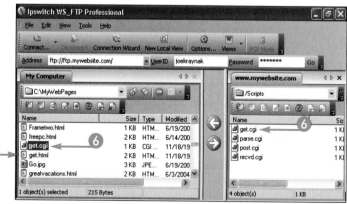

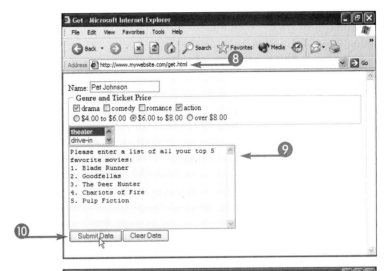

⑧ Open the Web page from step 7 in your Web browser.

⑨ Complete the form.

⑩ Click the submit button.

● The CGI application processes the form data and displays the contents of the `QUERY_STRING` variable.

How can I easily see all of the environment variables?

▼ All of the environment variables are stored in the `%ENV` array. You can print all of these variables by looping through this array. For example, you can enter the Perl statements `foreach $env_vars (keys %ENV) { print "$env_vars = $ENV{$env_vars}\n";`.

Which environment variable is used most often?

▼ The `QUERY_STRING` environment variable is probably used more than the other environment variables because it contains the form data that is passed from the Web page. The form data for each form element consists of the form element's name and its associated value.

I tried to view the `Query_String` environment variable, but the Web page appears blank. What happened?

▼ If your form uses the `post` method to transmit data, the Web browser sends the data to the standard input (STDIN) stack rather than to the `Query_String` environment variable. The `Content_Length` variable stores the length of the data entry when the `post` method is used, and the CGI script that processes the data uses the statement `read(STDIN, $buffer, $ENV{'CONTENT_LENGTH'});` to read data from the STDIN stack. See the section, "View Posted Form Data" for more information.

View Posted Form Data

W hen a Web browser passes data to a CGI script using the `post` method, the Web browser sends the data to *standard input* (STDIN) rather than to the `Query_String` environment variable. By accessing the form data through the STDIN, you can manipulate and use the data as needed to tabulate the results or log the information into a database.

All scripting languages have a standard input and a standard output (STDOUT). STDIN is the stream (file) that holds the data on which the CGI script acts. The CGI script writes any response to the STDOUT. For the Perl scripting language, you can access form data using the STDIN keyword.

To view the encoded form data, you must read the data into a temporary variable and then output the contents of that variable to the Web browser.

The CONTENT_LENGTH environment variable holds the length of the form data. You can use this environment variable to read the form data. For example, in Perl you would read the standard input into a buffer with a statement like this: `read(STDIN,$buffer, $ENV{'CONTENT_LENGTH'})`. You can then use a `print` statement to display the contents of the buffer in a Web browser window.

View Posted Form Data

① Type **#!/usr/bin/perl** at the top of a new HTML document.

② Add `print` statements.

③ Add the `read` statement to read the standard input.

④ Add a `print` statement that prints the variable.

⑤ Save the document as a text-only file, adding the .cgi extension.

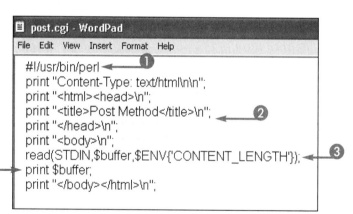

⑥ Upload the CGI application from step 5 to the directory that your Web-hosting service specifies.

Note: *See Chapter 18 for information about uploading files to Web servers.*

⑦ Upload the Web page that references this script to the server.

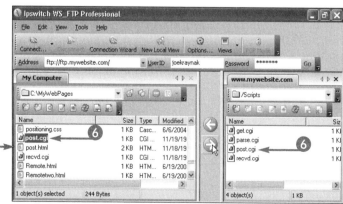

⑧ Open the document from step 7 in your Web browser.

⑨ Complete the form.

⑩ Click the submit button.

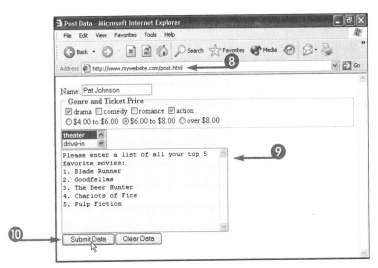

• The CGI application processes the form data and displays the contents of STDIN.

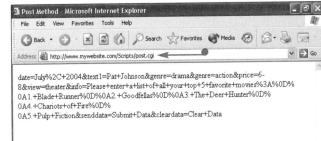

I see the data, but where did all of those plus signs and strange symbols come from?

▼ By default, all data passed to a CGI script is URL encoded. You can include the statements within the CGI script to decode the form data. This process is handled by parsing the data. You can download CGI parsing scripts from any of several script libraries on the Web. For more on how parsing script decodes the data, see the section, "Parse Form Data."

Is URL-encoded data any easier to manage if I use the post method rather than the get method?

▼ No. When a Web browser uses URL encoding to encode form data, it encodes the data in the same way whether you use the get or post method to send the data. The data arrives in an unbroken stream consisting of *name=value* pairs separated with ampersands (&), which the CGI script must then process.

What does the CONTENT_LENGTH environment variable do?

▼ When a Web browser sends data to the STDIN, it provides no indication of where the data ends. Instead, it specifies the length of the data transmission in the CONTENT_LENGTH environment variable. When receiving data, the CGI script checks this variable to determine how much data to read.

Create a Page Hit Counter

You can use a CGI script to keep track of the number of times visitors have opened a particular Web page. You can also have the script store a running count on the server, where you can access the information at any time. This can give you an indication of the popularity of your Web site. Web authors refer to these scripts as *page hit counters*.

A page hit counter executes every time a visitor opens a particular page. This script includes statements that open a file on the server that contains the current page hit count.

The script reads the current page hit count from the file, adds one to the count, and saves the file back to the server. Every time a visitor opens the page, the script repeats the process, keeping a running tally of page hits.

You can find the count value by looking at the count variable in the server file or by printing the value to the Web browser. You can even create a script that generates an HTML document indicating to the visitor how many times users have visited the page since a particular date.

Create a Page Hit Counter

① Open a document in your HTML editor and type **#!/usr/bin/perl** at the top of the file.

② Declare a local variable for the count, as well as a filename.

③ Type the remaining code shown in the figure to open the file, increment the count variable, and display the count value in the Web browser.

④ Save the document as a text-only file, adding the .cgi extension.

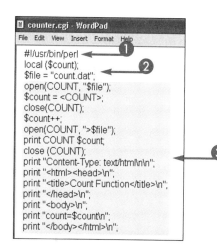

⑤ Upload the CGI application from step 4 to the directory that your Web-hosting service specifies.

Note: *See Chapter 18 for more information about uploading files to Web servers.*

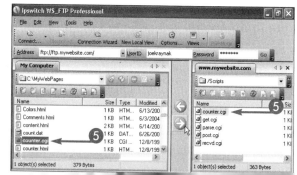

6 Open the CGI script in your Web browser.

● The CGI application runs and displays the count value.

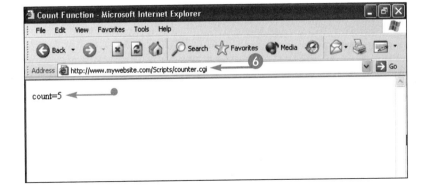

7 Click your Web browser's Refresh button.

● The CGI application updates the count value and displays the new page hit count.

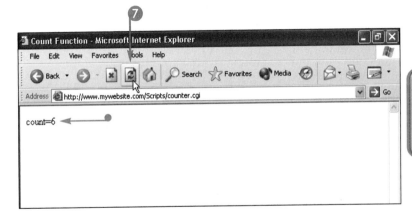

How can I add the counter CGI script to a Web page?

▼ You can add the counter CGI script to your Web page by using a server-side include statement. This statement includes the #exec keyword followed by cgi= and the path and filename in quotes. You need to make the entire statement into a comment so that it does not display in the Web browser. For example, type **<!— #exec cgi="/cgi-bin/ counter.cgi"** —> at the place in the Web page where you want the counter to appear.

Can I format my page hit counter?

▼ Yes. You can add formatting to the page hit counter by using HTML formatting tags or by scripting CSS styles into your CGI page hit counter script. An easier way to incorporate eye-catching page hit counters is to download free counters from the Web. Use a Web search site such as Google to search for "cgi page hit counter."

Does the page hit counter tell me the number of different visitors to my Web site?

▼ No. It only indicates the number of times a page was opened. For example, one visitor may open the page many times. You can try this yourself. With your CGI script loaded in the Web browser, click the Refresh button several times and watch the number of hits increase.

Restrict Site Access

Because CGI scripts run on the server, you can use them to restrict access to certain sections of your Web site. For example, you can write a script that checks the domain name from which a Web browser is trying to access your site and grant access only if it detects an approved domain name. This section shows you a sample script that reads the REMOTE_HOST variable to determine the visiting Web browser's domain name and whether to allow or prevent access to a site.

Another common approach is to create a form that enables users to enter a username and a password, which you store on the server. When users then wants to access the site, another form prompts them to enter their username and password. The script compares the username and password to valid username/password pairs on the server to determine whether to allow the user access to the site. The form enabling users to enter a username and password is fairly basic; see Chapter 10 for more information. You can obtain CGI password scripts from the Web.

Restrict Site Access

① Open a new document in your HTML editor, and type **#!/usr/bin/perl** at the top.

② Define a local variable and set it equal to the REMOTE_HOST environment variable.

③ Type the script shown in the figure to check the variable with the valid host name and display the appropriate message.

④ Save the document as a text-only file, adding the .cgi extension.

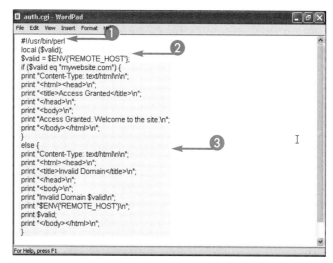

⑤ Upload the CGI application from step 4 to the directory that your Web-hosting service specifies.

Note: *See Chapter 18 for information about uploading files to Web servers.*

⑥ Open the CGI script from step 5 in your Web browser.

● For this domain, the Web site is valid and a valid message appears.

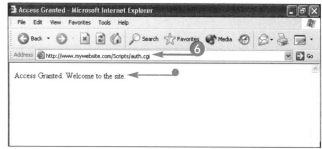

⑦ Open the CGI script you just created in your HTML editor.

⑧ Change the valid host name.

⑨ Save the document with a new filename.

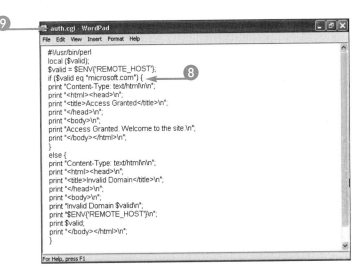

⑩ Upload the CGI application from step 9 to the directory that your Web-hosting service specifies.

⑪ Open the new CGI script in your Web browser.

● For this domain, the Web site is invalid and an "invalid" message appears.

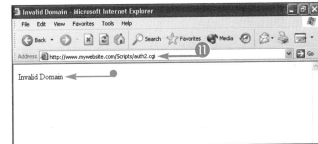

Managing usernames and passwords seems complicated. Is there an easier way?

▼ Yes. You can purchase software that is specially designed to help you manage usernames and passwords and increase security for your Web site. Most of these software packages use scripting to control site access, but they are a little more user-friendly and may even include documentation. MTopsoft offers a utility called HTML Password Lock that provides a graphical interface for managing passwords for up to 1,000 users. You can find it at www.mtopsoft.com.

How else can I use CGI scripts?

▼ This chapter shows only a few simple examples of how you can use CGI scripts. More complex examples include integrating with databases, processing orders, site search engines, and form validation. CGI is especially useful for creating custom HTML content based on a user's input and displaying it in a user's Web browser.

Where can I learn more about scripting and the various programming languages used on the Web?

▼ The primary focus of this book is creating and formatting Web pages using HTML, XHTML, and CSS, and to introduce you to some of the more powerful tools available. Many other books are available for learning CGI and Perl, including *Perl for Dummies*, by Paul Hoffman. Several tutorials are available on the Web, as well; use your favorite Web search tool to search for "cgi tutorial."

E-mail Form Results

If you have a form that calls for only a few data entries, and you do not need to transfer those entries to a database or use the data to script a response, you can avoid CGI scripts altogether and have the form data e-mailed to you. You can do this by adding the `mailto:` value to the `action` attribute in the opening `<form>` tag and typing the destination e-mail address after `mailto:`. You should also set the `method` attribute to `post`.

When you use URL encoding to have form data e-mailed to you, the Web browser replaces spaces with plus signs and special symbols with ASCII codes, which can make the data difficult to decipher. You can add the `enctype` attribute and set it to `multipart/form-data` to have the Web browser return the data in a more readable format. However, this spreads the data out quite a bit, creating a fairly long document attachment that can be difficult to read. When you obtain data through e-mail, you generally do not parse the data. For more information about encoding, see the section, "Parse Form Data."

E-mail Form Results

① In your HTML editor, open a document that contains a form.

② Add the `action` attribute set equal to `mailto:` followed by your e-mail address.

③ Set the `method` attribute equal to `post`.

④ Set the `enctype` attribute equal to `multipart/form-data`.

⑤ Save the document.

⑥ Open the document in your Web browser.

⑦ Complete the form.

⑧ Click the submit button.

● The Web browser sends the form data to the specified e-mail address.

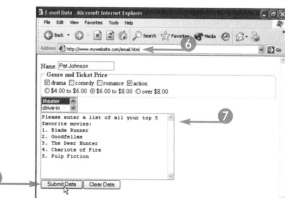

9 Run your e-mail program and check for incoming mail.

Note: The message may take several minutes to arrive.

10 Open the e-mail message as you normally do.

Note: If you are prompted to select an application to open the attachment, select a text editor, such as Notepad.

● The specified application opens and displays the attachment.

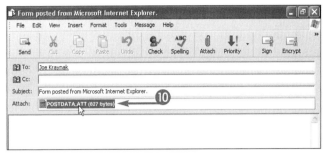

How is the e-mail sent to my e-mail address?

▼ If you include an e-mail address in the `action` attribute, the server automatically sends the form data to the e-mail address by using the server's `sendmail` function. If you load the page locally, the submit button attempts to open the e-mail client with the e-mail address listed. The server routes the form data to the e-mail address specified in the `action` attribute. This address can be any valid e-mail address.

What happens if the specified e-mail address does not exist?

▼ If the e-mail address does not exist, the server generates an error that appears in the server logs. However, no information is sent to the Web client, and the form data is lost. After you upload your Web pages to your Web server, test the e-mail address by entering and submitting some data to ensure that the form can successfully send data to your e-mail address.

Can users send me file attachments through e-mail?

▼ Yes, but be sure to include the `enctype="multipart/form-data"` attribute, so that the user can send you binary files in addition to plain-text files. Otherwise, the user cannot send file attachments. For more information about specifying an encoding type, see the section "Parse Form Data" in this chapter and refer to Chapter 10.

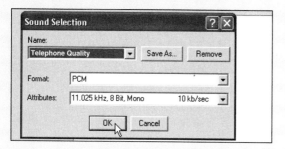

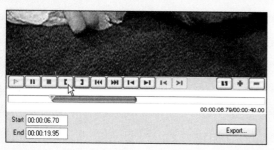

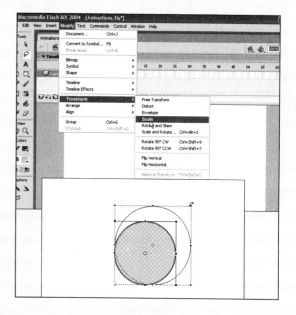

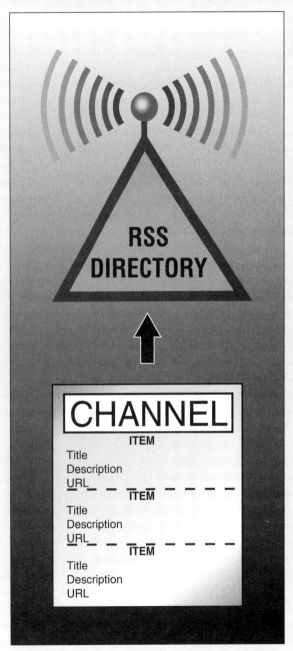

Introduction to Audio

You can add music and other audio elements to your Web page to make it more engaging. Ambient music playing softly in the background can set the mood for your Web site, and audio feedback associated with specific actions, such as mouse clicks and logins, can also make your Web site more dynamic and interactive.

You can add an audio dimension to your Web pages in several ways, all of which are fairly easy. However, before you add audio clips to your Web pages, you should become familiar with the various audio file formats that are available and the trade-offs that you must make between file size and sound quality.

Big Sound = Big File

Because multimedia files — audio and video clips and interactive presentations — are some of the largest elements in a Web page, you should be careful when deciding which ones to include. Packing your Web pages with large audio and video clips can drive away Internet users who still use dial-up modems.

The reason audio files are so large is that high-quality sound requires a high sampling rate. The *sampling rate* is the number of times per second a sound is recorded, or sampled. This means that data for every audible frequency needs to be stored in the file many times each second.

You can control the size of your audio files by choosing to record 8-bit, 16-bit, or 32-bit sound clips. 8-bit sound is of relatively low quality, and is suitable for beeps and other basic sounds that you use to provide feedback. 16-bit sound is suitable for CD-ROM-quality stereo output. When working with audio clips, be prepared to compromise. For voice narrations, 8-bit recordings are sufficient. For songs and music, you may want higher quality recordings, but keep in mind that one minute of high-quality audio requires more than one megabyte of storage space and takes more than 2 minutes to download with a 56Kbps modem.

Audio File Types and Players

When you record an audio clip, you must save it as a file in order to add it to your Web page. You can save the file in various formats, including WAV, AU, AIFF, MIDI, MP3, and RA. The file type can help you control the file size to some degree. The file type also determines which Web browsers and plug-ins are required to play the audio.

Most Web browsers can play at least one type of audio file. For example, Internet Explorer can play WAV files without the need for a special plug-in or ActiveX control. If a user's Web browser cannot play a particular file, it usually automatically downloads the required player or displays an error message indicating that it cannot play files of the type selected.

AU Format

The AU audio format is the default audio format that UNIX and Linux systems use. The AU format is common on the Internet because it requires relatively small audio files; however, the resulting sound quality is low.

AIFF Format

The AIFF audio format is used with Macintosh computers and offers a high-quality audio option, but the file sizes can be very large.

WAV Format

The WAV audio format is commonly found on Windows machines, and is another high-quality audio option with large file sizes. AIFF and WAV are essentially the same format with different names and filename extensions.

MIDI Format

The MIDI format is different from the other audio formats. Instead of storing sound frequencies, this format stores the notes that are played. The audio output consists primarily of synthesized music, which is common on the Web. The main advantage of this format is that it produces relatively small files. The disadvantage is that MIDI is not suitable for recording speech or CD-ROM-quality music.

MP3 Format

The MP3 format is a digital compression format for recording entire songs or audio tracks. MP3 is a popular format for exchanging audio files across the Internet, and is becoming increasingly more common for embedding audio clips in Web pages. Many companies that sell tracks and CD-ROMs offer downloadable audio clips in the MP3 format that you can burn to a CD-ROM or transfer to a portable MP3 player.

Other Audio Formats

As you browse the Web, you may encounter several other audio file formats, including RA, WMA, VOC, SND, RAW, and RAM. Most of these audio file formats require a special media player. For example, to play RealAudio (RA) files, you need Real Player. WMA files require Windows Media Player, which is included with Microsoft Windows, or another player that can handle WMA files.

Record and Save Audio Files

To add an audio file to a Web page, you must acquire the audio file. The Web has audio files, which you can find with your favorite Web search tool; searching for "free audio clips" or "free sound files" or other phrases that may return a list of Web sites that feature audio clips. You can also record the audio using your computer's sound card, recording software, and a microphone or other input device.

Most operating systems, such as Windows and Mac OS, include utilities that record audio files. A typical audio utility resembles a tape recorder, and allows you to record a brief voice message at a reasonable level of quality. Other audio software *rips* tracks from CD-ROMs, however you may be legally prohibited from including copyrighted CD-ROM tracks on your Web site. Ripping converts a track on a CD-ROM into a file that you can play on a computer.

This section shows you how to record a voice message using Windows Sound Recorder. If your computer runs a different operating system, use its audio recorder instead, as most audio recorders are very similar, both in appearance and operation. Note that for this section, you must ensure that a microphone is connected to your system.

Record and Save Audio Files

Record an Audio Tile

1 Click Start.

2 Click Programs or All Programs.

3 Click Accessories.

4 Click Entertainment.

5 Click Sound Recorder.

● The Sound Recorder window appears.

6 Click the Record button (●).

7 Speak into the microphone.

8 Click the Stop button (■) when you are finished.

Save an Audio File

⑨ Click File.

⑩ Click Save As.

- The Save As dialog box appears.

⑪ Navigate to the folder in which you want to save the audio file.

⑫ Type a filename for the file.

⑬ Click Change.

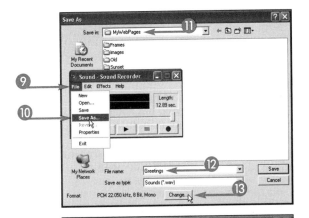

- The Sound Selection dialog box appears.

⑭ Click here and select Telephone Quality.

⑮ Click OK.

⑯ Click Save.

- The file is saved.

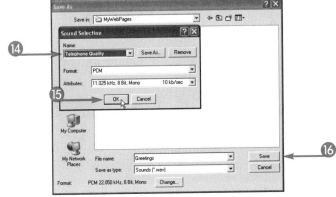

Can I use Sound Recorder to save the audio file in another format, such as AU and AIFF?

▼ No. Sound Recorder is a program that works only with WAV files, but many other programs can convert between the various audio formats. These programs include Adobe Audition, Sound Forge, and Goldwave. You can download a trial version of Full Audio Converter by visiting www.dandans.com/FullAudio Converter/index.htm.

Can I record from a CD-ROM?

▼ You obtain better results by ripping the track from the CD-ROM. This preserves the sound quality and enables you to save the audio clip in a compressed file format that requires less storage space. If your computer runs Windows, you can use Media Player to rip tracks and save them as WMA files. Before including a sound track, however, make sure you have permission to use it on your site.

Can I use a CD-ROM track as background music?

▼ Files created from CD-ROM tracks may be too large for use as background audio. Consider using a MIDI file instead. MIDI audio clips are synthesized versions of tunes that do not include vocals. MIDI recordings are not as rich as recordings of actual musical instruments, but the files are much smaller. See the section, "Add Background Music" for more information.

Add Audio Files as Links

You can add an audio file to a Web page to add variety to the page. The easiest way to do this is to use the <a> tag to create a link that the user can click to play the audio clip. This works just like linking to another Web page, except the audio filename replaces the Web page filename as the value for the href attribute.

When a user clicks the link, the Web browser, or one of its plug-ins or ActiveX controls, starts to play the file. If the Web browser does not recognize the audio file type, it

displays a message prompting the user to select a program that is already installed to play the clip, or to download and install a player from the Internet.

As with any link, you can use text or an image to represent the link that the user clicks. If you use text, type the text between the opening and closing <a> tags, as shown in the steps in this section. If you use an image, you can insert the <img /> tag between the opening and closing <a> tags, and set its src equal to the location and name of the image on the Web server.

Add Audio Files as Links

① Open a document in your HTML editor.

② Add an opening <a> tag with the href attribute set equal to the location and name of the audio file.

③ Add descriptive link text.

④ Add a closing </a> tag.

⑤ Save the document.

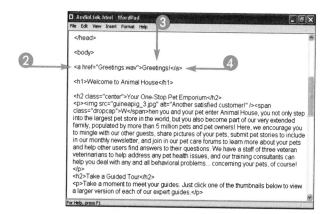

⑥ Open the document in your Web browser.

⑦ Position the mouse cursor over the link.

● The status bar displays the location and name of the audio file.

⑧ Click the link.

Note: If you are prompted to select or download a player, you can follow the on-screen instructions.

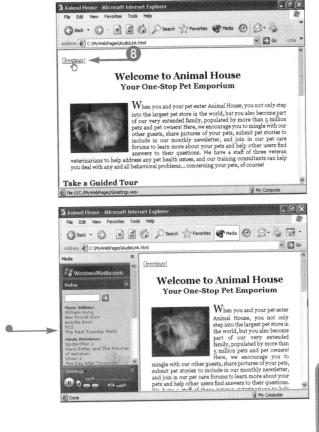

● The Web browser or player associated with the linked audio file runs and starts playing the file.

How can I check that both Mac OS users and Windows users can play my audio clips?

▼ On both platforms, most Web browsers, including Internet Explorer, Netscape Navigator, and Safari can play audio clips saved in the more popular file formats, such as AU, AIFF, MIDI, and WAV. Free plug-ins are available for playing audio files that you save in less common formats. As a result, most users should have no trouble playing your audio clips. A bigger concern is the size of the file. Remember to keep your audio files as small as possible.

My Web browser plays an audio clip, while my friend's Web browser runs a different program to play the clip. Why?

▼ The operating system determines the default program for opening audio files. When you install a player, such as Windows Media Player or Real Player, the installation routine assigns different programs to play particular types of file. You can choose which program plays each file type. For example, in Windows, you open My Computer, click Tools, click Folder Options, and click the File Types tab to access the file associations and then select the program you want to associate with a selected file type. Mac OS uses a different scheme, but allows you to override the operating system's program assignment on a case-by-case basis.

Add Background Music

In addition to exciting visuals and an engaging Web page design, background music can complement your page and draw visitors to your site. However, unlike linked audio clips, users do not choose whether they want to listen to background music; it plays automatically when they open a Web page. To accommodate users who have relatively slow Internet connections, consider using MIDI files for your background music. This format stores musical notation that the Web browser interprets, thus allowing for very small audio files.

You can add background music to a Web page with the `<object>` tag. You must include the `data` attribute set equal to the location and name of the audio file, and the `type` attribute set equal to the file's MIME type, for example, audio/midi for MIDI files.

Before you embed audio or video clips or other types of media files into your Web pages, decide whether you want to include embedded media. Because these files play automatically and may be quite large, embedded media can turn some users away from your Web site, especially those users who have dial-up connections. Users who commonly listen to music from other sources while they browse may also find the background music annoying.

Add Background Music

① In your HTML editor, open a document in which you want to embed an audio clip.

② Add an opening `<object>` tag that includes the `data` and `type` attributes.

Note: The `data` attribute specifies the location and name of the file, and the `type` attribute specifies the file's MIME type.

③ Type a closing `</object>` tag.

④ Save the document.

⑤ Open the document in your Web browser.

● The Web browser initially displays an area reserved for the object.

● In this example, the Windows Media Player window appears embedded on the page.

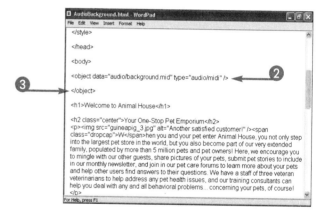

- In this example, the Web browser displays a warning message.

6 Click Yes to confirm that you want to run the application.

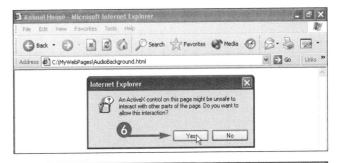

- The Web browser starts playing the audio clip.

- If the Web browser cannot play the audio file, it runs the application that is associated with the audio file's type.

Can I resize or hide the audio player that appears on the Web page?

▼ Yes. When an `<object>` tag embeds an audio file on a Web page, the player appears on the Web page. For example, Windows Media Player appears in a 240 x 180 pixel window. You can resize this icon by adding the `width` and `height` attributes to the opening `<object>` tag. You can also make this icon disappear by setting the `width` and `height` attributes to 0. The player still plays the audio file, but the control window does not appear on the page. Between the opening and closing `<object>` tags, add `<param name="autoplay" value="true">` to enduce that the audio begins to play.

Which MIME type should I use?

▼ Multipurpose Internet Mail Extensions, or MIME, indicate the data type for the application that is associated with the file. Use the right MIME type for the audio file type: `audio/basic` for AU files, `audio/aiff` for AIFF files, `audio/wav` for WAV files, and `audio/midi` for MIDI files. If the MIME type is not listed here, you can search for MIME types on the Web. If you omit the `type` attribute that specifies the MIME type, a Web browser cannot identify the file type or run the right application for playing the file.

Embed and Loop Background Music

W3C recommends using the `<object>` tag to add background music to a Web page. However, the `<object>` tag is not the ideal solution, because it does not play the audio clip in the background. A player appears on the Web page or pops up in a separate window, and both of these effects can distract a user.

Internet Explorer supports the `<bgsound />` tag that actually plays music in the background without displaying a separate player window, but it works only in Internet Explorer. Netscape Navigator and Internet Explorer both

support the `<embed />` tag for playing background audio. Neither of these tags conforms to the HTML 4 or XHTML 1.0 specifications, but they both play in the background without displaying a separate window for an audio player. In addition, they both support the `loop` attribute, which enables you to replay an audio clip continuously.

Unlike the `<object>` tag set, which requires an opening and closing tag, the `<bgsound />` and `<embed />` tags are self-terminating. In addition, you do not need to specify a MIME type with these tags. You can simply use the `src` attribute to specify the location and name of the audio file that you want to play in the background.

Embed and Loop Background Music

Embed Background Music

1. In your HTML editor, open a document in which you want to embed background music.

2. Add the `<embed />` tag with the `src` attribute set to the location and name of the audio file you want to play as background music.

3. Save the document.

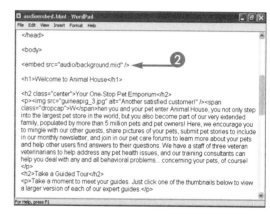

4. Open the document in your Web browser.

- The background music plays, and a small control bar appears on the page to allow the user to stop the music.

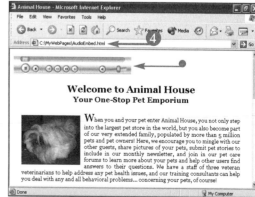

Loop Background Music

1. Open a document that contains an `<embed />` tag for playing background music.

2. Add the `loop` attribute set to `"true"`.

Note: If you set the attribute to `loop="false"`, then the tune only plays once.

3. Save the document.

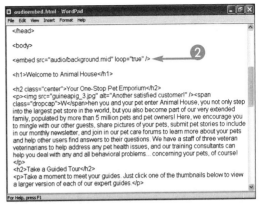

4. Open the document in your Web browser.

   ● The music begins playing in the background and replays until you click your Web browser's Stop button.

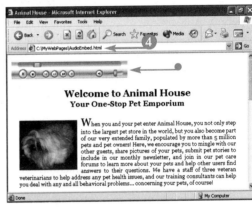

Can I make the background music loop a certain number of times?

▼ Yes, but the setting varies, depending on the Web browser. In Internet Explorer, to play the clip a certain number of times, add the `playcount` attribute set to the number you want; for example, `playcount="2"` plays the audio clip twice and then stops. In Netscape Navigator, to specify the number of times you want the clip to repeat, set the `loop` attribute to the number of repetitions you want, minus 1; for example, if you set `loop="1"`, the Web browser plays the clip a total of two times. Add both attributes to your `<embed />` tag.

Does the `<bgsound/>` tag work in Netscape Navigator?

▼ No. Because the `<bgsound>` tag is proprietary, it works only in Microsoft's Internet Explorer browser.

I opened the page that contains the `<embed>` tag, but the music does not start playing. What should I do?

▼ Try adding the `autostart="true"` attribute to the `<embed />` tag to force the Web browser to start playing the clip as soon as it downloads. If that does not work, check that you typed the correct location and name of the audio file. If you misspell the value of the `src` attribute, the Web browser cannot find the file.

Edit Audio Files with Sound Forge

udio files can be quite large, but you can edit them to trim their size and use only a portion of a clip. Many companies offer audio-editing programs for free or as shareware that provides tools for trimming audio clips. These tools decrease the sampling rate and compress the audio files so that files require less storage space. Audio-editing programs also commonly offer features to adjust the volume, add special effects such as echoes, and even speed up the tempo. The audio editor that is featured in this section is Sound Forge.

When you open an audio file in Sound Forge, it appears as a graph of sound volume or amplitude over time. This makes it easy to identify any blank areas in the audio

recording, which you can trim without losing much of the clip. These dead-air sections typically appear before and after the recorded sound, because there is usually a slight delay when you click the Record and Stop buttons while recording.

You can follow the steps in this section using almost any sound-editing program, but if you want to use Sound Forge, you can go to www.mediasoftware.sonypictures. com/products/ and follow the links to download a trial version of the program.

Edit Audio Files with Sound Forge

① Run your audio-editing program.

● This example uses Sound Forge.

② Click File.

③ Click Open.

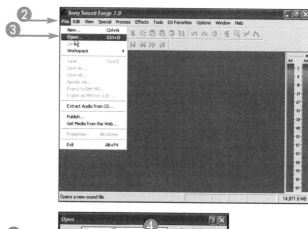

● The Open dialog box appears.

④ Navigate to the folder that contains the audio file you want to edit.

⑤ Click the name of the audio file you went to edit.

⑥ Click Open.

● The audio clip appears as a wave signal.

⑦ Click and drag the mouse cursor over the segment of the audio clip you want to keep.

⑧ Click the Play button (⊠) to listen to the selected audio segment to verify that it is the segment you want to keep.

⑨ Click the Trim/Crop button (⊞).

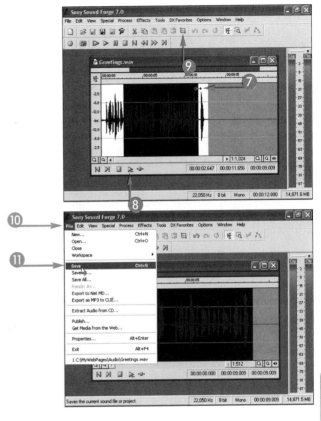

● Sound Forge removes any segment of the audio clip to the left or right of the selected area.

⑩ Click File.

⑪ Click Save.

● Sound Forge saves the edited audio clip.

Besides deleting unwanted audio segments, can I also add audio segments?

▼ Yes. By using the Cut, Copy, and Paste functions, you can select an audio segment from one audio file, copy it, and paste it into another audio file. However, you may find it difficult to achieve a smooth transition from one audio clip to the next. Full-featured audio editors provide options for fading out at the end of a clip and fading in to the next clip.

Can I layer one audio clip on top of another?

▼ Yes, you can layer audio by *mixing* two or more audio clips. Sound Forge, Adobe Audition, and Goldwave are examples of audio-editing programs that include tools for mixing and doing voice-overs.

What other sound-editing tools are available?

▼ Another popular sound-editing tool is Adobe Audition. You can download a demo from www. adobe.com/products/audition/. Goldwave is another popular audio editor, and you can learn more about it by visiting www.goldwave.com. Some sound cards come with software that includes audio-editing features, so the program you need may already be installed on your computer. You can also upgrade QuickTime to the QuickTime Pro version. All of these audio editors enable you to trim audio clips, layer sounds, convert files to other formats, and adjust the sound quality, but the steps for using the tools may vary between programs.

Convert an Audio File to a Different Format

You can use sound-editing tools, such as Sound Forge, to convert audio files from one format to another. Saving an audio file in several different formats enables users of many different types of systems to access your audio files. You can add a separate link for each file format, so that users can select the format they want, or you can add all available formats to a single <object> tag.

In the Save As dialog box, the Save as Type menu has different formats. The most common audio formats for the Web include the WAV, AU, and AIFF formats. Sound Forge

can also save audio files in the RealAudio (RA) format and Advanced Systems Format (ASF), which enables audio to stream across the Web. With *streaming audio*, the Web browser starts playing the clip as soon as it begins receiving it, rather than waiting until the entire file downloads. See the section, "Using Streaming Audio" for more information.

Most audio editors enable you to convert between various formats by using the Save As command; as a result, the steps in this section work in most audio-editing programs, although the available file formats may differ.

Convert an Audio File to a Different Format

① Open the file you want to convert in your audio editor.

② Click File.

③ Click Save As.

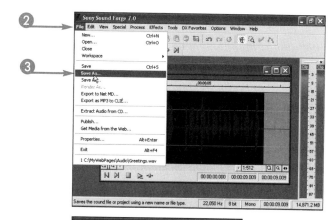

● The Save As dialog box appears.

④ Click here and click the file format you want.

● You can change the name of the file.

⑤ Click here and select the template you want.

Note: The template specifies the sampling rate and whether you want mono or stereo output.

⑥ Click Save.

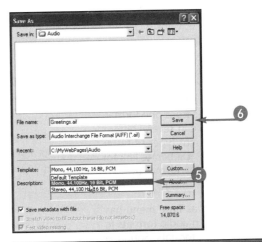

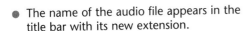

● The name of the audio file appears in the title bar with its new extension.

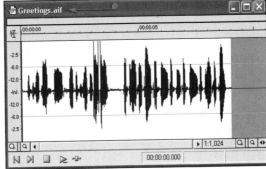

When should I use the streaming audio formats?

▼ If you embed an audio clip that is 50KB or larger using the `<object>` tag, use a streaming audio format. This enables users who have a dial-up modem connection to start listening to the audio clip and continue navigating the Web page before the Web browser completely downloads the clip. A user is unlikely to wait for an audio clip to download, especially if the user does not want to listen to the clip.

Can I have music that plays over and over again — or loops — in my Web pages?

▼ Yes. To do this, consider using MIDI files. MIDI files are typically very small, and you can set them to loop indefinitely or a specified number of times. See the section, "Add Background Music," for more information. However, keep in mind that after a certain point, a continuously playing tune can annoy users.

When I convert an audio file from one type to another, does the file size change?

▼ Yes, when you convert a file, this can alter its size. However, the sampling rate has a bigger influence on size. You can reduce file size by decreasing the sampling rate, although this can reduce sound quality. Experiment with different file types and sampling rates to obtain the optimum balance between file size and audio quality.

PART V

Using Streaming Audio

When playing most types of audio files, a Web browser must download the entire file before it plays the file. If a user clicks a link to play an audio clip that is more than a few seconds long, he or she must wait for the file to download before doing anything else. *Streaming audio* enables a Web browser or other audio player to play an audio file as soon as the Web browser or player receives it. This enables users to experience audio without having their browsing interrupted.

Although users may experience choppy playback, streaming audio is generally smooth, because it continuously feeds the audio data to a buffer on the user's computer. This buffer

sends a steady flow of data to the player to ensure that the player does not wait for the data it requires to create the sound.

Several streaming audio formats are available, including Real Audio, QuickTime, and Windows Media. Many Web sites use similar streaming formats for video media, as well. Many streaming audio formats require a proprietary audio player to play the audio. Both Internet Explorer and Netscape Navigator browsers can automatically detect some of these formats and launch the appropriate audio player, provided that you have it installed.

Using Streaming Audio

① Open a large audio file in your audio editor.

② Click File.

③ Click Save As.

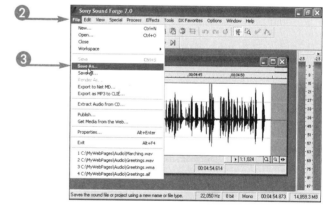

● The Save As dialog box appears.

④ Click here and select one of the streaming audio file types.

● This example shows a file being saved in the Real Media format.

⑤ Click Save.

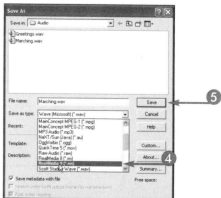

- In this example, a prompt appears, asking you to run the player that is associated to the file type that you just saved.

6 Click Yes.

- Sound Forge can save some file types but cannot open or edit them.

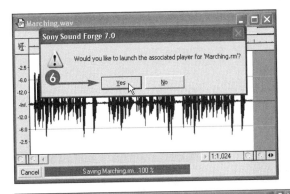

- If you saved a file in the Real Media format, and Real Player is installed on your computer, Sound Forge runs Real Player, which starts playing the file.

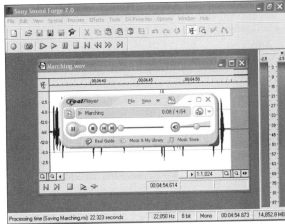

What are the most popular streaming formats?

▼ RealAudio (RA or RM) is the most popular streaming audio format on the Web. You can visit www.real.com to learn more about the format and to download a free copy of Real Player. Real Player can play RealAudio files along with many other popular formats. Microsoft has worked with many different companies in the industry to develop the Advanced Systems Format (ASF). Apple QuickTime also supports streaming audio. You can save your audio files in any of these popular formats to ensure that most Web users can play your files.

Can I use these same streaming formats to stream video as well as audio?

▼ RealNetworks has a related product called RealVideo that you can use to stream video files. The Advanced Systems Format and QuickTime formats also support streaming video. Apple's QuickTime video is very impressive. For more about video, see Chapter 13.

When I upload my page and streaming audio file to the server, the audio file does not play. Why not?

▼ Streaming formats typically require that you install extensions on the server to stream the content. Contact your Web-hosting service to determine if you must do anything special to have your streaming audio files download and play.

Introduction to Video

Few Web components are as dynamic and engaging as video clips, and with the proliferation of quality hand-held video cameras and broadband Internet services, an increasing number of Web authors and developers are incorporating video into their Web pages.

You can easily add video clips to your Web pages. All you need to begin is a video camera, a video capture device or some other method for converting video into files, and a video-editing program to divide video into manageable clips.

Video Cameras

To include video clips on your Web pages, you must first record original video. You can do this with any camcorder, but a digital camcorder is best. Older camcorders capture video in an analog format, which is suitable for producing VHS tapes. To save the video in a digital file format, you must then use a video capture card or device, such as Canopus Advanced Digital Video Converter, to convert the analog video into a digital format. In most cases, you lose video quality during the process. With a digital camcorder, the original video is already in a digital format, so conversion is not necessary. Many digital cameras, designed primarily for taking snapshots, also include digital video capabilities. Some can even capture audio. However, digital cameras typically capture low-resolution video at a lower frame rate than you can obtain from even a VHS capture.

Capturing Video

After recording your video, you can transfer it from the camera to your computer so that you can store it in one or more files, edit it, and then distribute it in various ways — on CDs or DVDs, through e-mail, or on the Web.

If you recorded the video using an analog camcorder, you can purchase an analog-video capture device that converts the analog signal into a digital signal. The device typically plugs into a USB or FireWire port or comes with its own video capture board that you install in your computer. You must connect the camera to the device with three composite video cables — one for video, one for left audio, and one for right audio. The device typically includes the software that you need to capture and edit the video.

If you recorded your video using a digital camcorder or a digital camera, the process is much easier and requires no additional hardware, assuming your computer is equipped with a FireWire or USB port that is compatible with the digital camcorder or camera. In most cases, the camcorder comes with digital-editing software for capturing and editing the video. You simply plug a cable from the camcorder or camera into your computer's USB or FireWire port, and play the video into the computer. The software captures the video, enables you to edit it, and then saves it to a disk. FireWire is also commonly referred to as IEEE-1394, or i.Link.

Editing Video

As you play video into your computer, the digital video editor typically divides the video into clips to make them more manageable. You can group the clips together in whatever order you like, and edit the clips individually to remove any video segments that you want to exclude from your final video. Fire Wire is also commonly referred to as IEEE-1394, or i.Link.

Digital video editors also include a selection of tools to enhance your video. In most editors, you can add a title and other text to your video clip to introduce it, and you can add credits at the end. If you group some clips together and the transitions between the clips are abrupt, you can fade out at the end of one clip and fade in at the beginning of the next to smooth the transition. Most editors also enable you to layer music and other sounds over the video.

Saving and Compressing Video

After you splice together your clips and add any enhancements, you can save the finished video as a file. Because video requires so much data to play both the video and audio components, video files can be quite arge. To reduce the file size, you can use any of several techniques, alone or together: save the file in a compressed file format, such as MPEG; decrease the dimensions of the playback area; decrease the number of colors; or shorten the duration of the video.

Adding Video to Web Pages

To add video to your Web pages, you can place a link to the video file on a Web page using <a> tags. You can also use the <object> tag, which is the same tag that you use to add audio clips to Web pages. The <object> tag includes the data attribute set equal to the location and name of the video file, and the type attribute set equal to the MIME type of the video file. If you add the video file using the <object> tag, the video clip plays directly on the page or in a separate player window.

However you choose to add video to a Web page, the Web browser does not actually play the video. Instead, it calls a video player into action, which then opens the file and plays the video. The video player that the Web browser calls depends on the video file format. Common formats include MPEG (Motion Picture Experts Group); AVI (Audio Video Interleave), which is the default video format for Windows; MOV (QuickTime format); and ASF (Advanced Systems Format).

PART V

Add Video Files as Links

E ven a relatively short video clip can be several megabytes in size. Broadband users generally do not have any trouble downloading and playing longer video clips, but these same clips may slow down dial-up modem connections. This is why very few Web sites contain video clips that run automatically on a Web page. Most Web authors add video to their Web sites by creating links to the video files. This gives users a choice of whether or not to download and play the clips.

You can add a link to a video clip using the same tag that you use to link to another HTML document — the <a> tag with the href attribute. Instead of setting href equal to an HTML document file, you can set it equal to the video file. Between the opening and closing <a> tags, you can add a title or description of the video clip or use the <img /> tag to display a representative frame from the video to act as a link. In any case, you should also add text that indicates the size of the video clip so users can decide whether they want to download it.

Add Video Files as Links

① Open an HTML document in which you want to add a link to a video file.

② Add an opening <a> tag with the href attribute set equal to the location and name of the video file.

③ Type a title or description of the video clip.

Note: You can use the <img /> tag to display an image as a link.

④ Type a closing </a> tag.

⑤ Save the document.

⑥ Open the document in your Web browser.

⑦ Click the link that points to the video file.

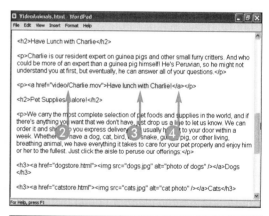

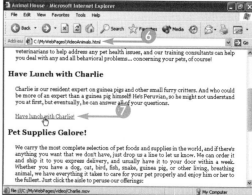

- In this example, the logo for the QuickTime Player appears briefly.

- A dialog box may appear, prompting you to save the file or select a player for this file type.

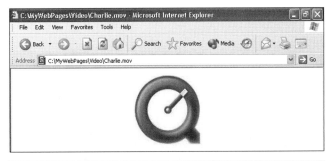

- The appropriate video player runs, opens the file, and plays the video.

Note: In this example, QuickTime plays the clip inside the Web page; other players may open a separate window.

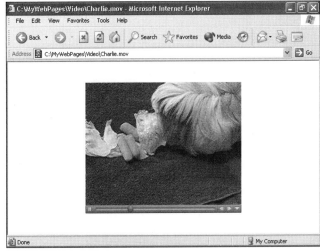

What happens if a user does not have the application required to play my video clip?

▼ Many media players support several video file formats. For example, QuickTime supports the MOV, MPEG, and AVI formats. Windows Media Player supports the AVI, MPEG, WMV, and older MOV formats, as well as others. Most users have QuickTime or Windows Media Player installed. If a user's Web browser cannot find the application required to play the video clip, the Web browser typically displays a dialog box that alerts the user and often prompts the user to download the required player.

Why is QuickTime playing Windows AVI files on my computer?

▼ Your computer determines which application should open a particular file type through file associations. When you install most applications, the installation process automatically associates files of a particular type with the application that you are installing. For example, the QuickTime installation associates the filename .mov extension with QuickTime. The installation may also take the initiative to associate the program with other file types. QuickTime probably associated itself with AVI files when you installed it. You can change file associations in Windows by opening My Computer, clicking Tools, Folder Options, and then File Types, and entering your preferences.

Add Video Files as Objects

You can use the `<object>` tag to add a video clip to a Web page so that the clip plays directly on the Web page, next to the page's other contents. Although the QuickTime Player is particularly suited for playing video clips on a Web page, the source code for inserting a QuickTime movie is lengthy:

```
<object width="320" height="260"
classid="clsid:02BF25D5-8C17-4B23-BC80-
D3488ABDDC6B"
codebase="http://www.apple.com/qtactivex/
qtplugin.cab">
<param name="src"
value="directory/filename.mov" />
<param name="autoplay" value="true" />
<param name="controller" value="true" />
<embed src="directory/filename.mov"
```

```
width="320" height="260"
autoplay="true" controller="true"
pluginspage="http://www.apple.com/quicktime/
download/">
</embed>
</object>
```

You can replace the `width` and `height` values with dimensions, in pixels, that match or exceed the dimensions of your video; experiment with different values to ensure that both the window and controls display completely. You can replace *"directory/filename.mov"* with the location and name of the QuickTime movie file. The second and third lines of code designate the QuickTime Player as the preferred application and enable the Web browser to download the player if it is not installed on the computer. The `<embed>` tags play the same video on Web browsers that do not recognize the tag.

Add Video Files as Objects

① Open the HTML document in which you want the video to play.

② Add an opening `<object>` tag that includes the `classid` and `codebase` attributes.

● `classid` specifies the player you want to use, and `codebase` indicates the Internet location from which your browser can download the player if it is not installed.

③ Type a closing `</object>` tag.

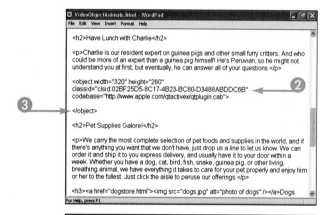

④ Add a `<param name />` tag to specify the location and name of the video file.

⑤ Add a `<param name />` tag to specify whether or not the video starts playing automatically.

⑥ Add a `<param name />` tag to specify whether the QuickTime Player controls are visible.

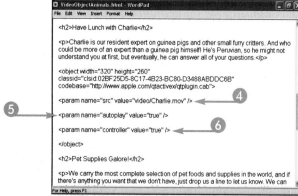

7️⃣ Add <embed> tags along with the source code, as shown, to play media types that the browser does not directly support.

● XHTML does not support the <embed> tag, but you need to use it so that browsers that do not support the <object> tag can play the video.

Note: Visit www.apple.com/quicktime/authoring/ embed.html for a discussion of additional parameters and other considerations.

8️⃣ Save the document.

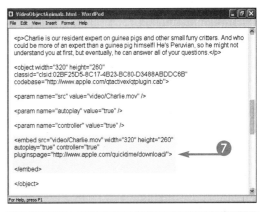

9️⃣ Open the document in a Web browser.

● The Web browser displays the document and runs the QuickTime Player, which then plays the video on the page.

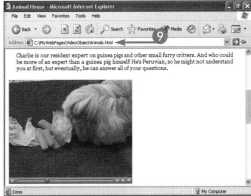

Can I load several different formats of a video file using several `<object>` tag sets?

▼ Yes. To support a wide range of systems, you can include several `<object>` tags within one another. Each `<object>` tag can specify different video files in different formats. The Web browser then looks at each `<object>` tag in order from top to bottom and displays the first format that it recognizes.

Can I specify which player to use for playing my video clip?

▼ No. The file associations set up on the user's computer determine which player the operating system runs when the user chooses to open a particular type of file.

Is there an easier way to make videos play automatically?

▼ Yes and no. The `<object>` tag is designed to replace the `<embed>` tag, but right now, it is not the perfect replacement. You can use the `<embed>` tag to play videos on a page by using the following syntax: `<embed src="directory/filename" width=640 height=480 autostart=true />`. You can use a streamlined version of the `<object>` tag in the following syntax: `<object data= "directory/filename" type="video/ mimetype"></object>`. However, this does not always work, and when it does work, it plays the video in a separate player window.

Reduce Video File Size

A 20-second MPEG-1 video clip that plays in a 320 x 240 dpi window requires approximately 3MB of storage space. Over a 56Kbps modem connection, this file takes more than two minutes to download, severely limiting the user's ability to play the video clips on your Web page. To minimize these problems, you can use several techniques to decrease the size of your video files.

The most obvious way to make video files smaller is to make them shorter. For example, you can remove any extraneous content. Also, if your video clip is more than a few minutes in length, you can divide it into multiple clips.

You can also reduce the file size by reducing the dimensions of the playback area. For example, most monitors are set up to display a full screen at 800 x 600 dpi or greater. You can resize your video to play in an area that is 400 x 300 pixels or even 200 x 150 pixels.

This example shows how to use River Past Video Slice to reduce the file size of a video. You can download a trial version at www.riverpast.com. Other video-editing software requires you to follow a similar procedure.

Reduce Video File Size

1 Open a video-editing program.

- This example uses River Past Video Slice.

2 Click File.

3 Click Open Video.

4 Click the video file that you want to edit.

5 Click Open.

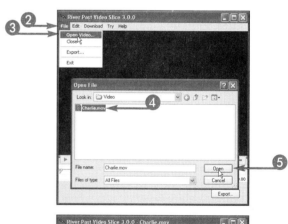

- The selected video appears.

6 Click and drag the scrubber bar to the point on the timeline where you want the video to start.

7 Click the Set Start Time button ([ ]).

8 Click and drag the scrubber bar to the point on the timeline where you want the video to end.

9 Click the Set End Time button ([ ]).

10 Click Export.

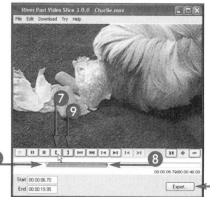

● The Export dialog box appears.

⑪ Click here and click Video Settings.

⑫ Click the Size Specify option
(○ changes to ⊙) and type the
dimensions you want for the
playback area.

⑬ Click the Frame rate Specify option
(○ changes to ⊙) and decrease the
frame rate to 15 fps or less.

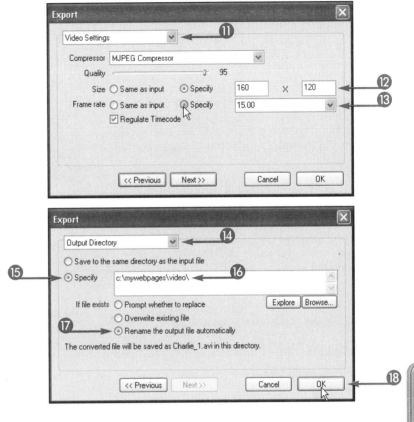

⑭ Click here and click Output Directory.

⑮ Click Specify (○ changes to ⊙).

⑯ Type the path to the directory in which
you want to save the new file.

⑰ Click the Rename the output file
automatically option (○ changes
to ⊙).

⑱ Click OK.

● The program exports the shortened
version of the video clip to the
specified directory and gives it a
new filename.

**What effect does decreasing the
frames-per-second setting have on
my video clip?**

▼ Decreasing the frames-per-second setting can make
the video play a little less smoothly, especially on a
computer. For nearly a decade, the standard for
movies has been 24 frames per second. Television
uses 30 frames per second in the U.S. and Japan or
25 frames per second in other countries, including
Australia and most of Europe. Due to the nature of
computer screens, you need about 60 frames per
second for high-quality video. However, Web-page
videos play in a relatively small window and are not
a very high quality. Experiment to determine
whether the trade-off is worthwhile.

**I know about streaming audio, but
is streaming video available?**

▼ Yes, streaming video is available, and you can find
it at most of the popular network news sites,
including www.foxnews.com and www.cnn.com.
With streaming video, such as Real Video, ASF, and
QuickTime, the player begins playing the video clip
as soon as it begins receiving the clip, rather than
waiting until the clip is completely downloaded.
You can view some impressive movie trailers that
use QuickTime's latest technology by visiting www.
apple.com/trailers/. If your Web-hosting service
supports streaming video, you can save your video
file in a streaming video format and include it on
your Web site.

Convert Video to Animated GIFs

One drawback of video files is that they require a video player or a plug-in to work within a Web browser. However, this is not a problem for animated GIF files. They can play in a Web browser without any help from an external program such as a separate video player.

You can convert your video file to an animated GIF file to ensure that others can view the video even if no video player is installed. Many animated GIF programs, such as GIF Animator, allow you to convert files from standard video formats to animated GIF files. After you perform the conversion, you can add the animated GIF file to your Web page using the `<img />` tag.

Animated GIF files support only 256 colors, which can appear coarse on screen, so they are not the best option if you need fine detail. However, if you want a file that plays directly on your Web page without the help of a media player, GIF animation is an excellent option. This example uses GIF Animator to convert a video file to an animated GIF file. Other GIF converters require you to perform similar steps.

Convert Video to Animated GIFs

1 Run GIF Animator.

● The Startup Wizard dialog box appears.

2 Click Open an existing video file.

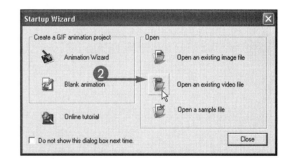

● The Open Video File dialog box appears.

3 Navigate to the directory where the video file is stored.

4 Click the video file you want to convert.

5 Click Open.

- GIF Animator loads each of the frames that comprise the video clip.

⑥ Click and delete any unnecessary frames.

⑦ Click File.

⑧ Click Save As.

⑨ Click GIF File.

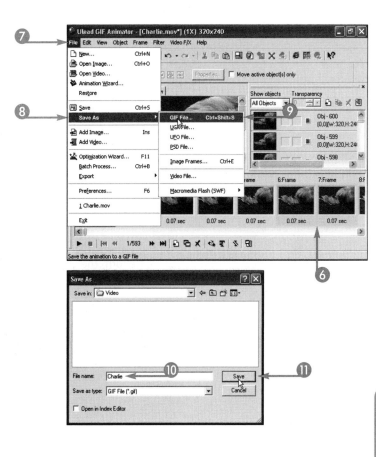

- The Save As dialog box appears.

⑩ Type a name for the file.

⑪ Click Save.

- GIF Animator saves your GIF animation.

How do animated GIF file sizes compare to video file sizes?

▼ Video files are compressed using algorithms that detect changes between various frames of the video file, but animated GIF files consist of multiple images all attached to each other. For this reason, a compressed video file with little motion is much smaller than the same file converted into an animated GIF file. Animated GIF files are the best choice for animations with relatively few colors and large sections of similar color. For most types of video shot with a camcorder, video files are the preferred choice.

Can I decrease the size of the GIF file?

▼ Yes. You can decrease the size of the resulting GIF file by deleting as many frames as possible. Even a short video may consist of hundreds of frames. Also, before you save the file, click File, then click Optimization Wizard, and follow the wizard's instructions to optimize the file. The Optimization Wizard creates a custom color palette for your animated GIF that enables the GIF file to describe changes in color from one frame to the next, rather than storing all of the details for each frame. This can significantly reduce the file size.

Download and Install the Flash Plug-in

With a Web browser and the Flash ActiveX control or plug-in, you can play interactive, multimedia Flash movies on your computer. Flash is a software package created by Macromedia that enables developers to create multimedia presentations, or *movies*. These movies can include animated graphics, sound, and interactive controls, making them engaging additions to any Web site.

Flash movies are popular not only because they are animated and interactive, but also because they enable developers to keep file sizes to a minimum by using *vector* graphics. Unlike raster graphics, such as JPEG files, which define an image as a collection of colored pixels, vector graphics use mathematical formulas to define the lines and shapes that comprise an image. This keeps the files small and enables you to resize the graphics without losing any resolution.

To view Flash content in a Web browser, you need to download and install the Flash player. Macromedia offers the Flash player in two forms: as an ActiveX control for Internet Explorer and as a plug-in for Netscape Navigator and other Web browsers.

You can download the Flash plug-in from Macromedia's Web site at www.macromedia.com. Once downloaded, the player automatically installs for use with your Web browser.

Download and Install the Flash Plug-in

① Type **www.macromedia.com** in your Web browser address bar and press Enter.

② Click Downloads.

③ Click Get Flash Player.

● The Get Flash Player page appears with instructions for downloading and installing the Flash Player.

④ Read the download and installation instructions.

⑤ Click Install Now.

● Your Web browser may display a message prompting you to confirm the download.

⑥ Click Yes.

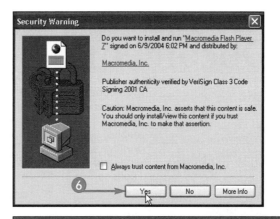

● The Flash plug-in player automatically downloads and installs.

● A test Flash file on the Macromedia Web site appears when the plug-in is fully installed.

What happens if I try to view a Web page with Flash content if the Flash player is not installed?

▼ When you encounter a Web page that includes Flash content and you have not installed the Flash player, your Web browser detects that the plug-in is missing and asks if you want to download and install the plug-in. Clicking Download in this dialog box automatically begins the download process. After the download is complete, you can view the Flash content.

Can I install the Flash player from anywhere else?

▼ Web sites that include Flash content typically have a button or icon that you can click to download the Flash player. Because of its popularity, the Flash player comes pre-installed on all Macintosh computers and on most newer PCs. However, a newer version may be available, so perform the steps in this section to ensure that you have the latest version.

I do not use Internet Explorer to browse the Web. Does that mean that I cannot play Flash movies?

▼ No. Internet Explorer uses the ActiveX version of the Flash player. However, if you open the Flash download page with a different Web browser, such as Netscape Navigator, the page enables you to download and install the plug-in version. You can also access plug-ins at www.download.com and other similar sites.

PART V

Create a New Flash Document

You can add Flash movies to your own Web pages to make them more entertaining and engaging. To start producing your own Flash movies, you can purchase the program — approximately $500 for the full version or $200 for the upgrade — or you can download a 30-day free trial version from www.macromedia.com. The installation file requires about 78MB of storage space. You can also create Flash animations using Adobe ImageReady CS, which is part of the Photoshop CS package.

After you install and run Macromedia Flash, the program creates a new file for you and presents you with a workspace in which you can begin to construct your

animated movie. Before you begin piecing together the various components of your movie, you should define the movie settings, including the background color, dimensions, and play speed. The movie dimensions refer to its vertical and horizontal size on the Flash Stage. The movie's play speed determines the number of frames per second, or fps, at which the animation plays.

You can adjust all of these settings through the Movie Properties dialog box. After entering the settings you want and saving the file, you have an overall framework for your Flash movie.

Create a New Flash Document

① Launch the Flash program.

② Under the Create New column, click Flash Document.

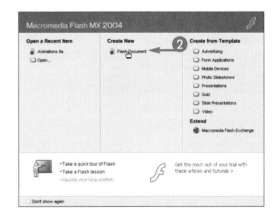

● A new, blank document appears.

③ Click the Document Properties button.

● The Document Properties dialog box appears.

④ Type the width and height you want for your Flash movie.

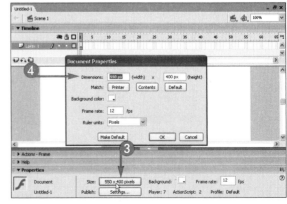

⑤ Click here and click the background color you want.

⑥ Click here and type the frame rate you want.

⑦ Click here and click the measurement unit you want.

⑧ Click OK.

⑨ Click File.

⑩ Click Save.

⑪ Navigate to the folder in which you want to save the file.

⑫ Click here and type a name for the file.

⑬ Click Save.

● Flash saves the file with the document properties you specified.

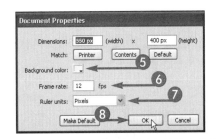

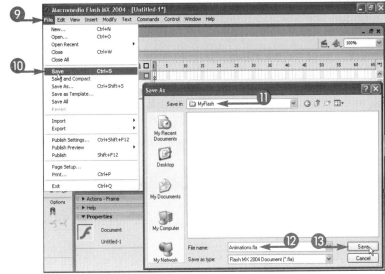

What frame rate should I use?

▼ Frame rates for the Web should be between 8 and 12 fps. A value in this range is sufficient to see the motion of the Flash objects. You may find higher values more difficult to maintain on lower-bandwidth connections.

Does a movie with larger dimensions download more slowly than one with smaller dimensions?

▼ High-resolution movies do not necessarily take longer to download. Because Flash content is vector-based, a movie's dimensions have little effect on the file size. The number of objects included in a Flash movie has more influence over file size.

My screen is cluttered. What can I do to create more work space?

▼ Each window frame has a button displaying a solid triangle (⬚▾⬚). Click the button to collapse the pane. The button remains on-screen, but the triangle points in the opposite direction. Click (⬚▾⬚) again to bring the pane back into view. You may be able to fit more on the screen by increasing your display resolution in Windows. Right-click a blank area of the Windows desktop, click Properties, click the Settings tab and drag the Screen Resolution slider to the right to set the resolution to 1024 x 768 or higher.

Create a Flash Document from a Template

lash includes several document templates that you can use to begin creating your own Flash document without having to create a completely new design. Flash groups the templates based on how you would probably use them on a Web page. These groups include Advertising for use with Web page marketing, Form Applications for providing a response to form entries, and Mobile Devices for targeting your Flash movie to various mobile Internet devices. They also include Photo Slideshows, Presentations, Quiz, Slide Presentation, and Video.

You can create a Flash Document from a template using the New Document dialog box. The Templates tab lists the available template groups and displays a brief description

and a preview of each template, so you can explore your options. You can simply select the template you want to use. Flash creates the document for you based on the template's settings. You can then adjust the settings, if you want.

Below each new Flash document, Flash displays its Property Inspector. You can use the controls in the Property Inspector to adjust the settings for the template, or click the Document Properties button, as shown in this example, and enter your preferences.

Create a Flash Document from a Template

1. In the Flash program, click File.

2. Click New.

3. In the New from Template dialog box, click the Templates tab.

4. Click the template group you want.

5. Click the template you want.

6. Click OK.

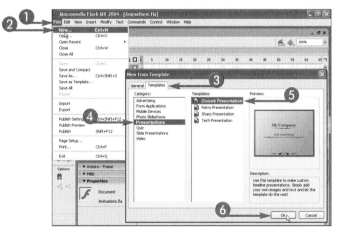

- A new document appears, reflecting the template's document settings.

7. Click the Document Properties button.

- The Document Properties dialog box appears.

8. Type the width and height you want for your Flash movie.

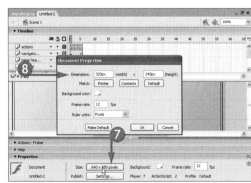

⑨ Click here and click the background color you want.

⑩ Click here and type the frame rate you want.

⑪ Click here and select the measurement unit you want.

⑫ Click OK.

⑬ Click File.

⑭ Click Save.

⑮ Navigate to the folder in which you want to save the file.

⑯ Click here and type a name for the file.

⑰ Click Save.

● Flash saves the file with the document properties you specified.

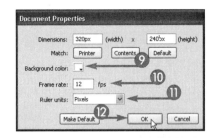

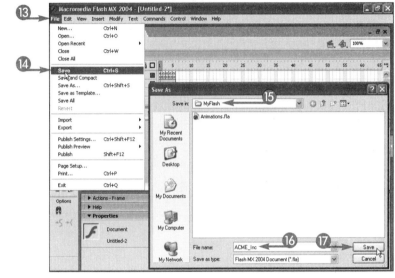

Can I use the files I create as templates for new files?

▼ Yes. When your Flash document is at a stage where you want to save it as a template, click File and click Save As Template. The Save As Template dialog box appears. Type a name for the template, click the category in which you want it to appear, and then highlight the text in the Description text box and type a description of the template. The description is optional, but it provides additional information about the file to help you identify the template later. Click Save. Your new template appears along with the other templates.

Are any other templates or samples available?

▼ Yes. One of the best ways to learn how to create your own Flash movies is to study those that other experienced Flash users have created. Click Help and click Samples to access links to some sample Flash movies. Click Help and click Flash Exchange to visit Macromedia's Flash forum, where Flash users can post their movies for others to download. You can view the movie in your Web browser or open the file in Flash to study the author's techniques. For additional samples, use your favorite Web search site to search for "flash samples".

PART V

Draw Objects

Like most graphics programs, Flash provides a collection of tools you can use to create, format, and manipulate the various objects that comprise your Flash movie. The primary drawing tools appear in a toolbar on the left side of the window. This toolbar includes tools for drawing lines, ovals, and rectangles; selecting the line and fill colors you want; zooming in and moving the image; selecting objects; adding text; and erasing objects.

To draw an object, you can click the button for the drawing tool you want to use. An Options area below the tools displays any options available for the tool you selected.

For example, if you select the Brush tool, the Options area displays settings for the brush size and shape, along with other options. When you select some tools, such as the Text tool, a Properties panel appears with additional options. You can change the options either before or after drawing your object. To create an object, you click and drag in the drawing area.

With vector graphics, objects exist as defined shapes, not as a collection of colored pixels, so you cannot edit individual pixels. Instead, you layer shapes on top of each other to create an illustration.

Draw Objects

Draw a Text Object

1. Launch the Flash program and create a new file.

   - To provide additional workspace, you can click the name of a panel to collapse the panel.

2. Click the Text tool (A).

3. Click where you want to place your text.

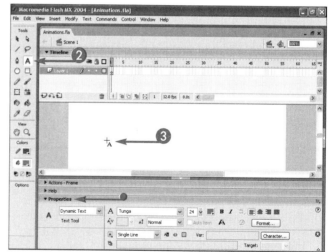

4. Click and drag a corner to resize and reshape the text box.

   - You can change the font, text size, color, and formatting options here.

5. Type the text.

   - If you want, you can change other properties.

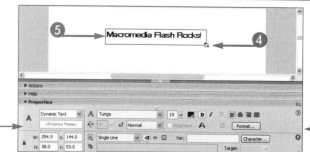

Draw a Shape

1️⃣ Click a Shape tool.

● This example uses the Oval tool (🔘)

2️⃣ Click here and click the stroke color you want.

3️⃣ Click here and click the fill color you want.

4️⃣ Select the line thickness and style you want.

5️⃣ Click and drag to create an oval.

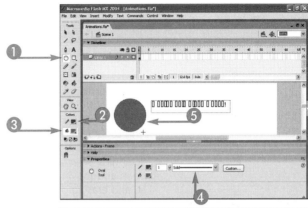

Draw a Line

1️⃣ Click the Line tool (📏)

2️⃣ Click here and click the stroke color you want.

3️⃣ Click here and type the line thickness you want.

4️⃣ Click here and click the line style you want.

5️⃣ Click and drag to define the length of the line.

● Flash displays the objects you created.

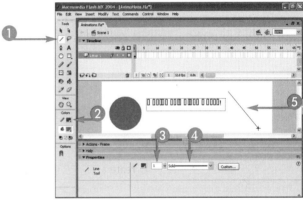

Can I draw a perfectly horizontal line, a perfect circle, or a perfect square?

▼ Yes, you can draw perfect circles or squares by holding down the Ctrl key while dragging to create the shape. When you hold down the Ctrl key while dragging a line, you can draw a perfectly vertical or horizontal line, as well as one that is on a 45-degree angle.

Why does my text appear as tiny rectangles?

▼ To save system resources, Preview mode may display characters as rectangles. Click View, then click Preview Mode, and then click either Fast or Antialias. Antialias is a software technique designed to smooth the jagged edges of curves, but you can use it here to make the text visible. This may, however, slow down your system slightly.

What is the difference between the Pencil tool and the Pen tool?

▼ The Pencil tool (📏) is a free-form drawing tool that you can use to draw a line of any shape on the screen. Using the Pen tool, you can draw a line by defining several points on the line and then drag the points to define smooth-flowing arcs and curves. This takes a great deal of practice to master.

Select Objects

You can select a drawn object at any time to change its position, shape, or properties. You may think that you can click the Selection tool and then the object to select it. However, Flash provides several selection tools, each with unique options: the Selection tool, the Lasso tool, and the Subselection tool.

You use the Selection Tool to select any component of an object, either its stroke or fill. An object's *stroke* is the line that defines its shape. An object's *fill* is the color inside the stroke. You can also draw a marquee around an object or multiple objects, to select everything inside the marquee.

This is useful for selecting neighboring objects, although you must be careful not to select objects or portions of other objects that you do not intend to select.

The Lasso tool is more precise because you can draw irregular marquees around any object or objects. Flash selects any objects that are completely inside the lasso.

Flash's Subselection tool enables you to completely reconfigure a shape by dragging the points that define it. You can use this tool along with the tools for drawing shapes to create some interesting effects.

Select Objects

Using the Selection tool

1 Click the Selection tool (🔧).

2 Click and drag a marquee around the object or objects you want.

● Flash selects all objects that fall inside the selection marquee.

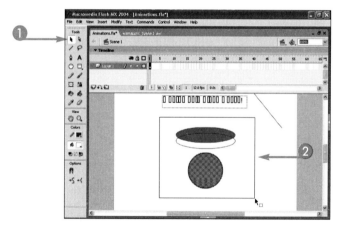

Using the Lasso tool

1 Click the Lasso tool (🔾).

2 Click and drag around the object you want to select.

● Flash selects all objects that are completely inside the lasso.

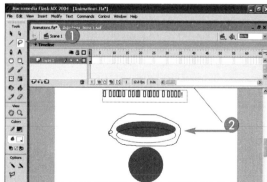

Using the Subselection tool

1️⃣ Click the Subselection tool ().

2️⃣ Click the object you want to manipulate.

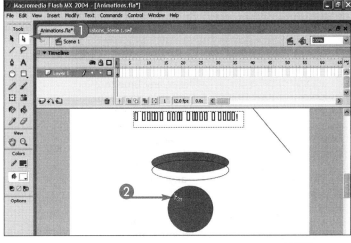

● Flash displays various points that define the object's shape.

● You can click and drag these points to redefine the shape of the object.

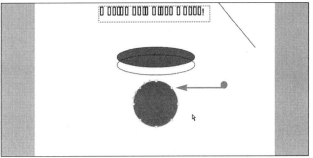

Can I reshape objects using the Selection tool?

▼ Yes, but not if you select the object with the Selection tool (🔲). First, click the Subselection tool (🔲) and click the object to select it. Then, click 🔲. The points that define the object's shape disappear, but you can drag the border to reshape the object. A better way to reshape objects is to use the Subselection tool 🔲 as shown in the steps above.

Which is the best selection tool to use for moving an object?

▼ If you want to move a single object without moving any neighboring objects, the Lasso tool (🔲) gives you the most precise control. You can draw a lasso around an object without selecting neighboring objects and then drag the object where you want it.

I placed one object on top of another one, and they seem to have merged into a single object. What did I do wrong?

▼ You did nothing wrong. This is the nature of vector graphics. When you place an object on top of another object, the points that make up the object become a set of points, and any similarities the objects have, such as fill color, merge. To keep drawn objects from merging, you must place them on separate layers, as shown in the section, "Work with Layers."

Resize, Reshape, and Move Objects

You can change the size, shape, and position of objects, rotate them, flip them, and manipulate them in other ways to create the visual effects you want. If you are familiar with graphics programs, you may still need to learn some new techniques when working with objects in Flash. When you select an object using either the Selection or Lasso tool, Flash does not display selection handles around the object for resizing or reshaping the object. You can drag a selected object to move it, but you cannot redefine the shape of the object.

If you use the Subselection tool to select an object, you can drag the object to move it. You can also drag one of the points that define the object's shape to reshape it. Dragging

a point away from the center of an object forms a protrusion, while dragging a point toward the center forms an indentation.

By using the commands on the Transform submenu of the Modify menu, you can further manipulate objects. This submenu contains commands for rotating objects clockwise or counterclockwise, flipping objects horizontally or vertically, scaling or resizing objects, skewing objects, and creating other effects.

Resize an object

1 Select the object you want to resize using ![k] or ![p].

Note: *For more information, see the section, "Select Objects."*

2 Click Modify.

3 Click Transform.

4 Click Scale.

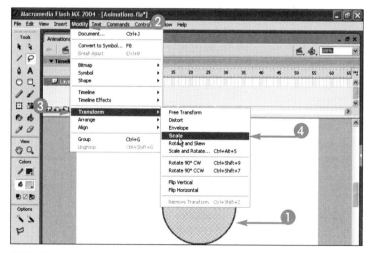

● Selection handles appear around the object.

5 Drag a corner selection handle to change the size of the object.

● Dragging the selection handle toward the center of the object makes the object smaller.

● Dragging the selection handle away from the center to makes the object larger.

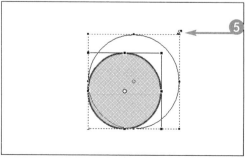

Reshape an object

① Click .

② Click an object.

③ Click and drag one of the points that define the object.

- Dragging toward the center indents the object.

- Dragging away from the center creates a protrusion.

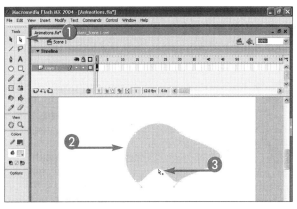

Move an object

① Click ⬉.

② Click the object you want to move.

③ Click and drag the object's perimeter — not one of its points — and drop the object in the position you want.

- The object moves to the new position.

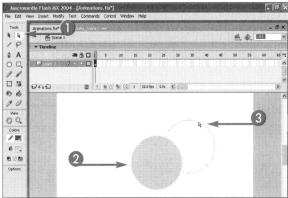

Can I rotate an object?

▼ Yes. In addition to Rotate 90° CW (clockwise) and Rotate 90° CCW (counter-clockwise), several options on the Transform submenu of the Modify menu enable you to rotate an object. They are Free Transform, Rotate and Skew, and Scale and Rotate. Select an object, select one of these commands, and then move the cursor near one of the corner handles. When the cursor changes to a counterclockwise arrow, you can click and drag to rotate the object. If you select Free Transform, a small white circle appears on the object; you can drag the circle to the point around which you want the object to rotate.

What does the Envelope option do?

▼ The Envelope option displays handles around the object that you can drag to change the object's shape. This is very similar to the way you can change an object's shape after using the Subselection tool to select it. With the Envelope option, however, you can can click and drag tangents as you can with the Pen tool to create smooth curves.

I really messed up my original object. Can I return it to its original condition?

▼ Yes. You can click Edit, then click Undo several times until all of the transformations are reversed. You can also click Modify, then click Transform, and then click Remove Transform, to reverse all of the transformations.

Work with Layers

W hen you create a new Flash document, the drawing area consists of a single layer on which you can draw your objects. You can draw objects on top of other objects to form your illustration. However, when you place one object on top of another, common points merge and you cannot separate the objects. To keep objects separate, you can create additional layers. Each layer acts as a transparency that covers any layers below it. Assuming you do not place any objects on a new layer, you can see through it to the layer below and even select objects on lower layers. As you place objects on the new layer, they can overlap objects on lower layers while remaining entirely separate from those objects.

You can create new layers at any time. Flash places each new layer on top of the layer that is currently selected. You can select a layer in order to create or manipulate objects on that layer. When you select a layer, Flash selects and highlights all objects on that layer. This example shows you the basics of creating, selecting, activating, and deleting layers.

Work with Layers

① Click Insert.

② Click Timeline.

③ Click Layer.

● A new layer, called Layer 2, appears on top of the currently selected layer.

④ Repeat steps 1 to 3 to create two more layers.

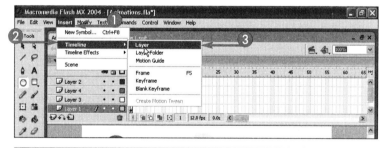

⑤ Click Layer 1 to select it.

● Flash outlines and highlights all of the objects that are on Layer 1.

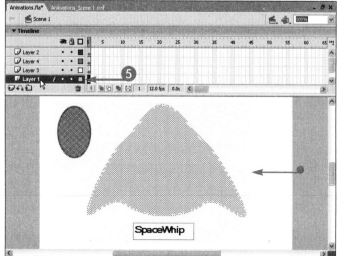

⑥ Click .

⑦ Click and drag a marquee around an object to select it.

⑧ Cut the object from the layer by clicking Edit and then cut.

⑨ Click Layer 2.

⑩ Click Edit.

⑪ Click Paste in Center.

● The selected object appears on Layer 2.

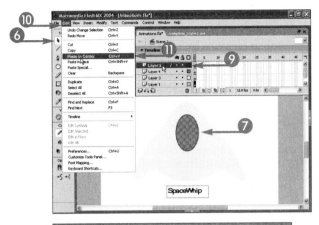

⑫ Click Layer 1.

● The objects on Layer 1 are outlined and highlighted.

● The object on Layer 2 is deselected.

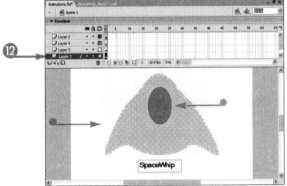

Can I rename or rearrange layers?

▼ You can rename a layer by double-clicking the layer name and then typing a new name. As your documents get larger and more complex, you may want to rename your layers to help you remember which graphics are on which layer. You can rearrange layers by clicking and dragging the Layer buttons up or down, to place one layer beneath or on top of another.

What is the purpose of the icons and dots to the right of the layer names?

▼ You use the icons to the right of and above the layer names to hide, lock, and display an outline for each layer. The dots indicate whether the layer is visible, locked, or displayed in outline mode. The legend displayed above the Layer buttons indicates the purpose of each dot.

I click an object to select it, but it does not appear or behave as though it is selected. What happened?

▼ The object you are trying to select may be on a lower layer. Click the layer that holds the object and then try clicking the object again. Also, if the object has no fill, clicking inside the object does not select it, and so you must click the line that defines the object's border.

PART V

Create a
Motion Tween

You can animate a scene in Flash by creating a *motion tween* in which objects move across the screen. You can do this by designating *keyframes* to mark the beginning and end of the action. You then select the command for creating a tween. During the tweening process, Flash fills in the frames between the keyframes to create the illusion of motion or change.

A simple example of using keyframes is to create a block of text that moves smoothly from the left side of the Web browser window to the right side. To create the animation,

you can create two keyframes: one with the text displayed on the left side of the Flash stage, and the second displaying the text on the right. Flash can fill in the frames in the middle to make the text glide across the screen from left to right.

When creating a motion tween, keep in mind that the objects you place in motion move on their layer. Objects moving on upper layers pass in front of objects on lower layers, and objects on lower layers pass behind objects on upper layers.

Create a Motion Tween

① Create a scene containing two or more layers with objects in position for the end of the movie.

② Click and drag over empty frames for all layers under the ending frame count you want.

● This example creates a 25-frame movie.

③ Click Insert.

④ Click Timeline.

⑤ Click Keyframe.

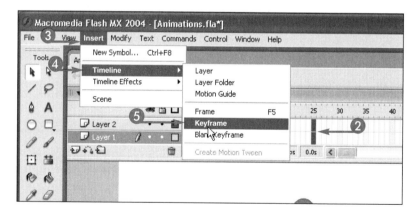

● Flash marks this as the ending keyframe.

⑥ Click and drag over the beginning and ending keyframes and all frames in between.

⑦ Click Insert.

⑧ Click Timeline.

⑨ Click Create Motion Tween.

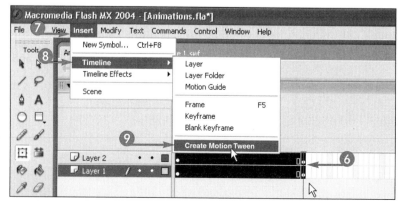

● Arrows appear between the beginning and ending keyframes.

⑩ Click and drag the red timeline marker to the starting frame.

⑪ Click and drag the objects to the positions where you want them to appear at the beginning of the movie.

Note: You may need to select the layer on which the object appears before moving the object.

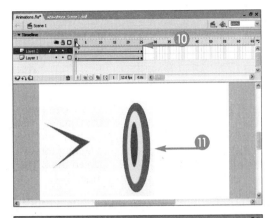

⑫ Drag the red timeline marker from left to right across the timeline.

● As you drag the marker, Flash displays the movement of the objects across the screen.

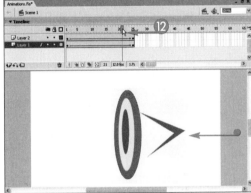

Can I have an object follow an irregular path?

▼ Yes. You can tween motion along an irregular path. First, create your animation and click the layer that contains the animated object. Click Insert, click Timeline, and then click Motion Guide. Flash inserts a new layer above the selected layer with the Motion Guide icon to the left of the layer name. Use the drawing tools to plot the path you want. Drag the object so that its centerpoint is over the beginning point in the first keyframe, and the ending point in the last keyframe, so that it snaps to these points. For more on the drawing tools, see the section "Draw Objects."

Can I make an object spin?

▼ Yes. You can make an object spin in place or as it moves across the screen. Click any frame in the timeline that is part of the animation. In the Properties panel, click Rotate, and then click the rotation direction you want. Click in the Rotate text box and type the number of times you want the object to rotate. Drag the red timeline marker across the timeline to preview the animation. If you want to partially rotate an object in place, you can create a shape tween, as shown in the next section, "Create a Shape Tween."

Create a
Shape Tween

You can create a shape tween to make an object change shape, color, or size or to transform into another object through the course of a Flash animation. To create a basic shape tween, you define two keyframes — one that displays the image at the beginning of the animation and another that displays the image at the end of the animation. Flash fills in the frames between the beginning and ending frames to produce an effect that makes the first object appear to smoothly morph into the second object.

If the beginning and ending images are drastically different, the effect may not be as smooth as you want. Flash is not a morphing program. You can smooth the transformation by increasing the number of frames.

Shape tweens are especially effective at creating objects that fade in or out or change color over time. Shape tweening works best when you tween one shape at a time. You can tween multiple shapes, but you must place them all on the same layer. To use shape tweening with text, groups of objects, or bitmapped graphics, you must break the elements into separate objects.

Create a Shape Tween

① Click the layer that contains the shape you want to tween.

② Click or create a keyframe in which you want the animation to start.

③ Click here and click Shape.

④ Click Ease and drag the slider up or down.

● A negative setting accelerates toward the end of the animation.

● A positive setting decelerates toward the end.

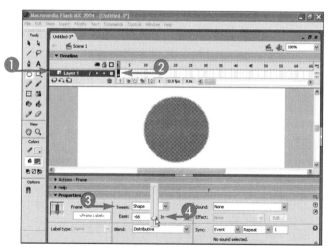

⑤ Click the frame in which you want the animation to end.

⑥ Click Insert.

⑦ Click Timeline.

⑧ Click Keyframe.

● Flash marks this as the ending frame.

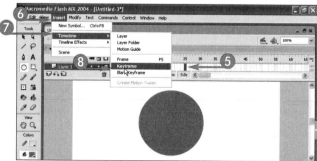

⑨ Alter the object's color, size, shape, or position, or replace the object with another image.

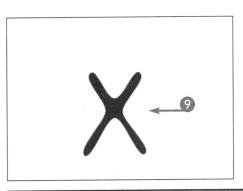

⑩ Drag the red timeline marker from left to right across the timeline.

● As you drag, Flash displays the starting object morphing into the ending object.

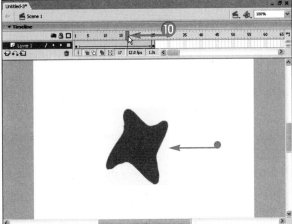

Can I make an object spin as it morphs?

▼ It is better to spin, or rotate, an object with a motion tween, as discussed in the previous section, "Create a Motion Tween." However, you can create a slight rotating effect by rotating the object in the ending keyframe. You can rotate the object, flip it vertically or horizontally, skew it, or even distort it. Select the object and then use the commands on the Transform submenu of the Modify menu to create the modifications you want. See the section, "Resize, Reshape, and Move Objects," for more information. This can make the object appear as though it is moving in place as it morphs.

I do not see the Properties panel with the Tween menu. How do I bring it into view?

▼ Click Window and then click Properties. This brings the panel into view. If the Properties panel is minimized, click Properties in the panel's title bar. Creating enough screen space to display all of the available options and provide sufficient room to work on your animation can be difficult. Refer to the tips in the section "Create a New Flash Document" for some suggestions.

What is the difference between a Distributive and Angular Blend?

▼ In the Properties panel, the Blend options are Distributive and Angular. Angular is only for shape tweens that need to have sharp angles blended. Otherwise, use Distributive blending for smoother effects.

Preview Your Animation

After you create a motion tween or a shape tween, you can immediately preview the objects in motion by dragging the red timeline marker back and forth across the timeline. You can also choose options in the Publish Preview submenu of the File menu to preview your animation in Flash or in your Web browser. These commands actually process the source code and load the resulting code in your default Web browser, so you can see how it should play on the Web.

The Control menu contains several commands for previewing your Flash animations. Using the commands on the Control menu, you can play your movie, rewind it, go to the end, step through it one frame at a time, test your movie, debug it, test a scene, play multiple scenes, and loop playback. Looping instructs Flash to continue playing the animation repeatedly until you choose to stop it.

By previewing your animations, you can ensure that they work as you intend before using them on your Web pages. You can also test your animations without leaving Flash and tweak them to perfect their appearance and performance.

Loop Your Preview

1. Click and drag the red timeline marker to the first frame.

2. Click Control.

3. Click Loop Playback.

   ● Clicking Loop Playback toggles this option on or off.

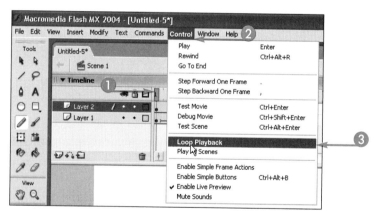

4. Click Control.

5. Click Play.

   ● Flash plays and continues to replay your animation.

   ● To stop playing your animation, click Control, and then click Stop, or press Enter.

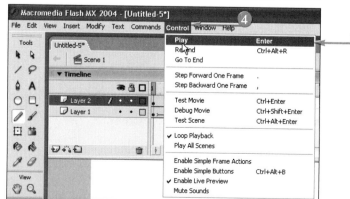

Test Your Animation

1 Click Control.

2 Click Test Movie.

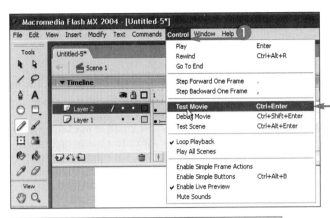

● Flash displays your animation on a separate tab that plays the animation continuously.

● To pause the Animation, press Enter.

● To restart the movie again, press Enter again.

When I am finished testing my movie, how can I return to editing it?

▼ When you test a movie, Flash displays it on a separate tab. You can return to the previous screen by clicking the tab for the previous screen, which is usually the tab to the left of the current tab.

Can I view the animation in slow motion?

▼ Yes. Click Control and then click either Step Forward One Frame or Step Backward One Frame. To step forward, type a period. To step backward, type a comma. You can press either of these keys repeatedly and change directions when you want.

When I test my movie, does the test simulate how other users should experience the animation?

▼ Not initially, but the View menu that appears when you test your movie displays options that can provide a more accurate simulation. Click View, and then click Simulate Download (☐ changes to ☑). Click View, click Download Settings, and then click the modem speed you want to use for the simulation. For example, to see how users with 56Kbps dial-up connections experience the animation, click 56K (4.7 KB/s). You can also test your Flash movie after you upload it to the Web server along with the HTML document on which it appears; see Chapter 18 for more information.

Create Symbols

You can identify objects that you create as symbols and reuse them in your presentations without increasing the size of your file. Flash uses two types of objects, instances and symbols. An *instance* is an object you create that acts as a unique entity. A *symbol* is an object that you create and identify as a reusable object. When you designate an object as a symbol, Flash adds it to the library for the document, enabling you to reuse it. Because your Flash animation has all the information required to display the symbol, you can reuse it in a movie without adding to the file size.

Symbols also provide greater control when you are creating animations. In fact, before you create an animation, Macromedia encourages you to designate objects as symbols if you intend to move them. This provides the object with a unique identity, giving you more control over its motion.

Symbols offer several advantages in addition to helping you reduce file sizes. For example, when you edit a symbol, your changes appear wherever you use that symbol. If you change an instance, the changes appear only in that particular use of the object.

Create Symbols

① Click ▣.

② Click and drag a selection loop around the object that you want to convert into a symbol.

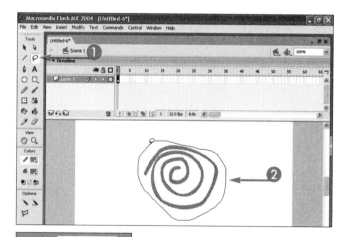

③ Right-click the object.

④ Click Convert to Symbol.

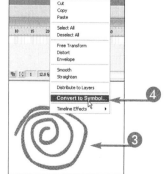

- The Convert to Symbol dialog box appears.

5 Type a name for the symbol.

6 Click the option that best describes the object's behavior (○ changes to ●).

7 Click OK.

- Flash displays the object as a symbol and adds it to the library, so you can easily reuse it.

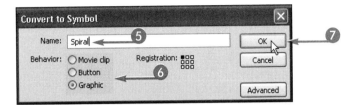

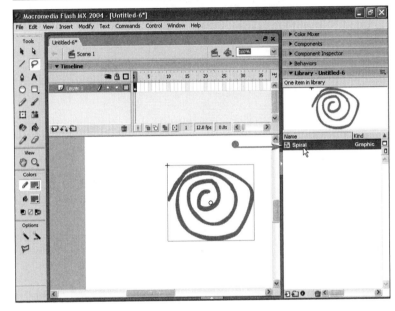

How do I convert an animation into a movie clip symbol?

▼ Click and drag over all of the frames that make up your animation to select them. Right-click one of the highlighted frames and click Copy Frames. Click Insert, and then click New Symbol. Type a name for the symbol, and ensure that the Movie Clip option is selected (○ changes to ●). Click OK. Right-click the first frame in the timeline and click Paste Frames. The new movie clip symbol appears in the library with a small Play button (▶) next to it. Click the Play button to preview the clip.

How do I add a movie clip symbol to another movie?

▼ Drag and drop the movie clip symbol from the library to the position in the Flash scene where you want it to begin playing. This adds an instance of the movie clip from the library to the existing movie. To preview the animation, you can use the options on the Control menu.

Do I need to convert an instance into a symbol before using it in an animation?

▼ No. You can animate instances of an object with motion tweening. However, if you want to tween the color of a group, you must first convert the objects in the group into symbols.

Add a Button from the Library

You can add objects from the Flash libraries to further enhance your presentations and make them more interactive. Flash includes a well-stocked library of sample buttons, scripts, and source code. The sample buttons are particularly useful. Exploring these options in detail is beyond the scope of this chapter, but you should know how to access the libraries.

The Flash library appears on-screen by default. However, it typically displays only the symbols you have created and the objects that are currently inserted in any Flash document that you presently have open. If the library does not appear, you can bring it into view by clicking Window and then clicking Library.

The Flash library enables you to reuse symbols without adding significantly to the size of your Flash file. You simply drag symbols from the library to the Flash scene and drop them where you want them to appear. See the section, "Create Symbols" for more information.

You can display additional libraries by selecting them from the Common Libraries submenu. This example shows you how to access the Buttons library and how to copy a button to your presentation.

Add a Button from the Library

1. Click Window.
2. Click Other Panels.
3. Click Common Libraries.
4. Click Buttons.

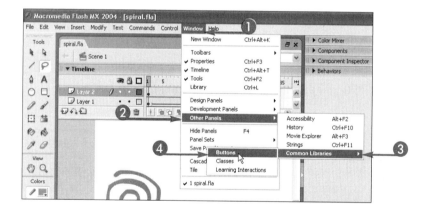

- A list of button folders appears.

5. Double-click a button folder.
   - A list of available buttons appears.

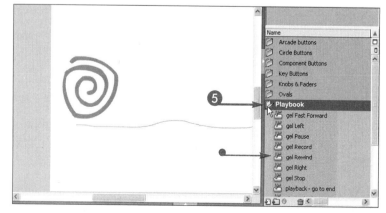

6 Click Insert.

7 Click Timeline.

8 Click Layer.

● A new layer appears, on which you can place buttons.

9 Click and drag a button from the Library window and drop it on the Flash stage.

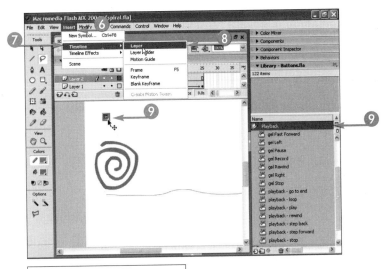

● The button appears on the stage.

● You can resize and reposition the button.

Note: For more information, see the section, "Resize, Reshape, and Move Objects."

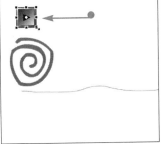

How are the libraries organized?

▼ Each library can include folders and objects. You can add objects to a folder by dragging them onto the folder. Double-clicking a folder opens it and reveals its contents. You can delete objects and folders using the Delete icon (🗑) at the bottom of the window. However, be careful not to delete any items you might need in the future.

Can I make my own buttons?

▼ Yes. When you convert an object into a symbol, as shown in the section, "Create Symbols," the dialog box that appears contains a Button option. Click the Button option (○ changes to ◉). By giving an object button status, you can assign button properties to the object later.

Are other libraries available?

▼ Yes. To view components for interacting with various Web services, click Window, click Other Panels, click Common Libraries, and then click Classes. To view form controls designed specifically for online quizzes, click Window, click Other Panels, click Common Libraries, and then click Learning Interactions. Click the Components bar to check out a list of components that enable you to easily add form elements to your Flash movie.

Activate Buttons

You can assign actions to a button to make it perform a specific action when a user interacts with it, for example, by clicking it. Simply inserting a button does not associate it with any other objects in a scene or with any movie clips. However, through the Actions-Buttos panel, you can choose any of several user responses to activate a button, such as on (press), on (release), or on (rollover).

You can also assign a button an action that you want it to perform when activated. For example, if your movie contains multiple scenes, you can create a button that a user clicks

to go to the previous or next scene. When you choose actions for a button, Flash inserts the script required to execute the action; however, it still needs some additional input from you. Fortunately, Flash provides script hints that pop up after Flash inserts the boilerplate script. The script hints can help you determine what to type.

The options for activating and enabling buttons are too numerous to describe here in great detail. This example guides you through the process of activating buttons by showing you how to create buttons that start and stop a movie.

Activate Buttons

① Create a new layer and add the buttons you want to activate to the new layer.

- This example uses the Playback-play and Playback-stop buttons from the Buttons library.

Note: See the sections, "Work with Layers" and "Add a Button from the Library," for more information.

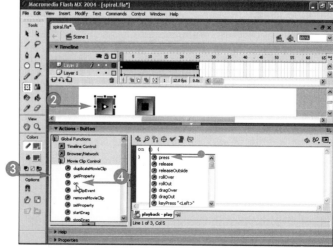

② Select the button you want to activate.

③ In the Actions-Button panel, navigate to the function you want to assign to the button.

④ Double-click the function.

- You may need to double-click the specific function.

- This example shows the on (press) function that executes an action when the user clicks the button.

⑤ Click between the opening and closing curly braces.

⑥ Navigate to the action that you want the button to perform.

⑦ Double-click the action that you want the button to perform.

⑧ Type any necessary parameters as instructed in the script hint.

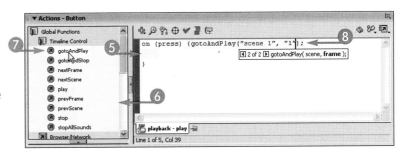

⑨ Repeat steps 2 to 8 to insert the script for each additional button.

● Flash activates the button.

● This example shows the Playback-stop button set to activate on a mouse click and to perform the stop action, which requires no parameters.

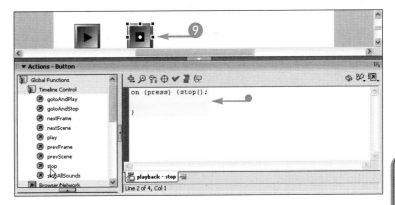

When I select a button, the Actions-Button panel does not appear. How do I bring it into view?

▼ If a panel is not visible, it is usually minimized to provide more screen space for working on your movie. Look below the Flash stage area for a bar with a *disclosure triangle* (⟶) on it. The disclosure triangle points right when the panel is collapsed and down when the panel is expanded. Click the ⟶ and then click Actions-Button. If the Actions panel is visible but it does not display "Button," then you have not selected a button. The panel should appear when you select a button.

How do I test my buttons to ensure that they function properly?

▼ Click Control and then click Test Movie. This plays your movie in Flash on a separate tab. If the script has any errors, Flash displays a dialog box describing the errors and the line number for each error, so that you can go back and edit the script.

Can I remove actions that I associated with a button or other object?

▼ Yes. Click the button or other object, display the Actions-Button panel, drag over any script that is associated with the button or object, and press Delete. This removes the actions but leaves the button or other object intact, so you can assign different actions to it.

Add Links
to Objects

You can add navigational tools to your Flash movie that link to other Web pages and content. By selecting an object and choosing the getURL function from the Actions panel, you can transform any object into a live link that opens another Web page when a user clicks the object or when a designated frame triggers the Web page to load.

If you use the getURL function to associate a URL with a graphic object, the page that the URL designates automatically loads when the object appears, which is usually what

most Web authors want to avoid. To enable an image to act as a link, you must first convert it into a symbol, as shown in the section, "Create Symbols." In the Convert to Symbol dialog box, you can click the Button option to assign button properties to the object. This enables you to associate the object with a user action that triggers the object to load the linked document.

Using the Actions panel, you can insert the getURL command and type the URL of the page to which you want the object to link. To test the link, you must be connected to the Internet.

Add Links to Objects

① Click the button symbol that you want to appear as the clickable link.

② In the Actions panel, click Global Functions.

③ Click Movie Clip Control.

④ Double-click the on action.

⑤ Double-click the action that you want the user to take to activate the link.

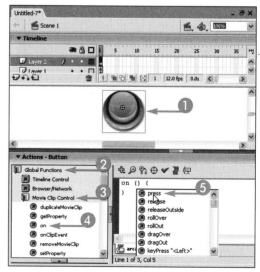

● Flash inserts the necessary script.

⑥ Click between the two curly braces.

⑦ Under Global Functions, click Browser/Network.

⑧ Double-click the getURL action.

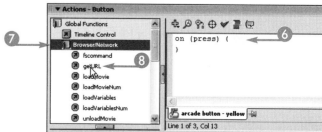

● Flash inserts the necessary script.

9 Type the URL of the Web page that you want this object to open.

Note: It is important to enclose the URL in quotation marks.

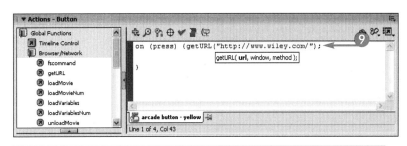

10 When previewing your movie, rest the mouse cursor on the link.

● The mouse cursor changes to a pointing hand icon.

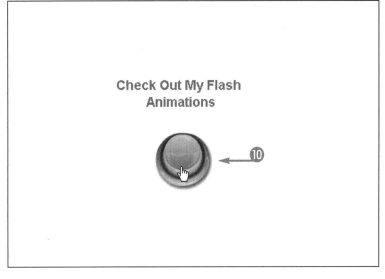

Check Out My Flash Animations

Can I use the `getURL` action to create an e-mail link?

▼ Yes. Instead of using an http:// address to link to a Web page, type **mailto:** followed by your e-mail address. When a user clicks the button, the user's e-mail program runs and displays a new message window addressed to you. See Chapter 3 for more information about creating hyperlinks and mailtos.

Are there other actions that I can associate with objects?

▼ Yes, Flash has many options available for various components, form elements, buttons, and other objects. When you click a component, element, button, or other object, the Actions panel displays options for the selected item. Explore the options in the Actions panel and use the Flash Help system to learn more about these options.

When a user clicks a link in my movie, does the Web page load alongside my movie?

▼ No. When a user clicks a link, the linked page loads in the Web browser, replacing the page that is playing your movie. The user can click the Web browser's Back button to return to your page. You can have the linked page appear in a new window by adding the `"_blank"` parameter to the `getURL` statement. Type a comma after the closing quotation mark for the URL, type a space, and then add the `"_blank"` parameter to avoid syntax errors.

Add Sound Clips

J ust as you can add background audio to your Web page, you can have an audio clip play in the background while your Flash movie plays. The audio clip can play independently of your movie's timeline, or you can synchronize the sound and movie so that the audio portion follows the timeline. You can also associate audio clips with certain events, such as mouseovers and mouse clicks, to provide valuable feedback to users and to make your Web site more interactive.

To incorporate audio in your movie, you import the audio clips that you want to use to the library to make them available. To have the audio clip play in the background,

you can create a blank layer and drag the audio clip from the library to the new layer. Placing audio on a separate layer generally provides you with more control over how the audio clip plays.

Flash supports two types of sounds: *event* sounds and *stream* sounds. Event sounds must download completely before Flash can begin playing them, whereas stream sounds begin as soon as the movie begins to play. You can modify sounds using the Sound Properties panel, which appears whenever you select a sound object.

Add Sound Clips

1 Click File.

2 Click Import.

3 Click Import to Library.

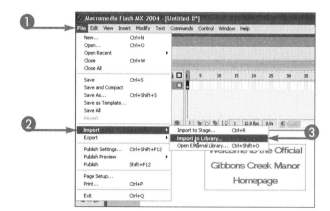

● The Import to Library dialog box appears.

4 Navigate to the folder in which the audio file is stored.

5 Click the name of the audio file.

6 Click Open.

- Flash adds the audio file to the library.

7 Create a new layer for your movie.

Note: See the section, "Work with Layers" for more information.

8 Click and drag the audio clip over the new layer and drop it anywhere on the layer.

- The wave form for the audio clip appears in the frames.

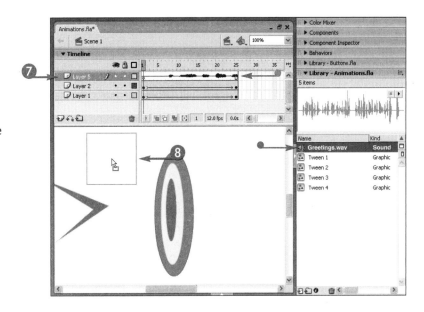

9 Click here and click the sync option you want.

- To have the audio clip play in sync with your movie, you can click Stream.

- The audio clip is set to synchronize with the movie according to the selected option.

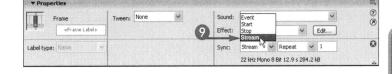

Can I modify the audio clip in any way?

▼ Yes. When you select a frame that contains audio, the Properties panel displays properties for the audio clip. Click Edit to display the Edit Envelope dialog box, which enables you to adjust the way the sound fades from one speaker to another. Fading sounds from one speaker to the other in sync with a motion tween can significantly enhance the feeling of phyiscal movement.

How do you make a sound loop several times?

▼ By default, Flash is set to play an audio clip once. To have the clip play continuously, click the Repeat box and click Loop. Keep in mind, however, that looping sounds can become annoying and that some people like to listen to other sounds, such as online radio stations or audio CDs as they browse the Web.

Can I associate a sound with a button?

▼ Yes. Right-click the button in the library and click Edit. In the button's timeline, add a new layer. Create a keyframe that corresponds to the button state with which you want the sound associated. Display the Properties panel and then click the new keyframe that you created. Open the Sound menu and click the sound you want.

Save and Publish Your Presentation

You can save and publish your Flash document to give it a name and to save it in one or more formats that are suitable for distribution on the Web. Flash can publish your document in several file formats, including Flash, HTML, QuickTime, JPEG, and Windows Movie Projector, so you can use them in various ways.

If you choose to publish before saving your Flash document, all files are saved using the name "untitled," so consider saving and naming your document first. You should also check your Publish settings in Flash to

ensure that Flash is set up to publish your files in the format or formats you prefer. When you enter the command for publishing your Flash document, Flash automatically creates the files based on the settings in the Publish Settings dialog box. You can view the Publish Settings dialog box by using the Publish Settings command.

By default, Flash is set up to publish documents in the Flash and HTML file formats. Each of these formats has a separate tab that you can click to enter additional preferences. If you select another format, a tab appears for that format, as well.

Publish Your Presentation

Save a Flash document

1. Click File.

2. Click Save As.

3. In the Save As dialog box, navigate to the folder in which you want to save the document.

4. Type a name for the document.

5. Click Save.

   ● Flash saves your document.

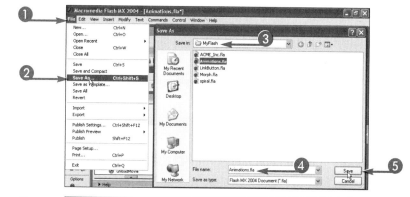

Enter Publish Settings

1. Click File.

2. Click Publish Settings.

3. In the Publish Settings dialog box, click the check box next to each file format you want (○ changes to ◉).

   ● You can click a tab to enter additional options for that format.

4. Click OK.

   ● Flash saves your settings.

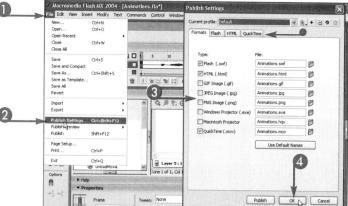

Publish a Flash movie

1 Click **File**.

2 Click **Publish**.

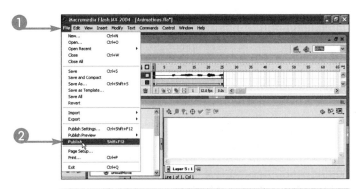

● Flash publishes the movie in the specified file formats and stores them in the same folder in which you saved the file.

Can I convert a movie I made in Flash into a different format?

▼ Yes. You can do this by selecting the format you want to use during publishing, as shown in this example. You can also click File, click Export, and then click Export Movie. When you choose to export a movie, Flash displays the Export Movie dialog box. Type a name for the exported file and then open the Save as type list and click the file format you want. Click Save to save the file in the selected format.

When Flash publishes my files, what names does it use? Can I change the names?

▼ By default, Flash gives each published file the same name you gave the original Flash file when you saved it, although it appends a different filename extension, based on the published file type. You can click File and then click Publish Settings to provide different names for the files.

Can I publish my files directly from the Publish Settings dialog box?

▼ Yes. Click File and then click Publish Settings, enter your preferences, and then click Publish. Of course, you need a Web hosting service in order to gain access to a Web server. Chapter 18 discusses Web page publishing in greater depth and reveals various Web hosting options.

Understanding Java Applets

You can make your Web site more dynamic by embedding small programs called *Java applets* in your Web pages. Java applets load, along with your HTML source code, and play directly inside the Web browser window. You can write the applets using the Java programming language. Java is a robust programming language that is similar to C++, but which includes many unique capabilities that make it ideal for writing programs that run on the Web.

This chapter provides a brief introduction to Java programming, in order to highlight its potential and to provide you with the knowledge you need to start using it. However, programming in Java can be very complex and is beyond the scope of this book. Several excellent books discuss Java programming in greater depth, including *Beginning Programming with Java for Dummies* by Barry Burd and Rich Tennant (John Wiley).

Understanding Java's Benefits

One of the traits that make Java suitable for the Web is its portability. You can write a Java program and run it on different platforms without having to modify it in any way. On the Internet, which is essentially a global network of different operating systems, Java programs can run on a wide variety of computer platforms, including Windows, Mac OS, and Linux.

Java is also *object oriented,* a programming paradigm that enables developers to create reusable *objects* — data structures and dedicated functions called *methods* that operate on the data structures. This saves programmers a great deal of time because they can re-use programming code they have already written.

Java has built-in security restrictions that work along with Web-browser security settings to prevent Java applets from gaining unauthorized access to programs, files, and other resources on a user's computer. These security restrictions enable users to execute Java programs knowing that the programs are unlikely to damage their system in any way or gain unauthorized access to their data.

How Java Works

You can write Java programs in any text editor using a programming language that you can recognize and understand with the proper training. You must then run the program code through a *compiler*. The compiler converts the programming code into language that a Java interpreter, such as Java Virtual Machine, can understand. The code that the compiler generates can run on any computer, as long as a Java interpreter is installed on the computer. The Java interpreter translates the code produced by the compiler into machine code that the computer running a particular operating system can understand.

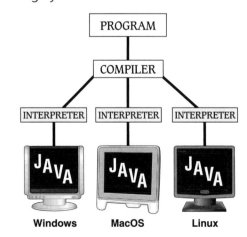

Compiling Java Applets

After writing your Java program, you save it as a text-only file with the .java filename extension. This is
your *source* file. You then run your source file through a compiler to convert it into a *bytecode* file that has the .class filename extension. The compiler examines the source file for errors before producing the bytecode file. If errors exist in the source file, the compiler reports the errors. After you eliminate all syntactic errors from the source file, the compiler can generate the bytecode file.

Embedding Java Applets

You can embed Java applets in a Web page using the <object> tag, which calls the applet into action. When a Web browser encounters an <object> tag that includes a call to a Java class file, the Web browser launches the Java Virtual Machine or another virtual machine, which then interprets the bytecode file so the applet can run in the Web browser.

Between the opening and closing <object> tags for an applet, you can insert one or more <param /> tags to modify the appearance of the applet, such as the background color and dimensions of the area in which it runs.

Running Java Applets

Because Java is such a powerful and popular way of incorporating dynamic content into Web pages, most computers have Java Virtual Machine or another type of virtual machine installed. Sun Systems distributes a runtime version of Java Virtual Machine, called the Java Runtime Engine (JRE). Recent versions of Microsoft Windows include the Microsoft Java Virtual Machine (VM), but Microsoft is no longer distributing it and plans to phase out support for it by December of 2007. You can embed Java applets on your Web pages with the confidence that most users should be able to run them.

Download the Java SDK

You can download the Java Software Developer's Kit (SDK) from Javasoft's Web site and install the kit on your computer so that you can compile your Java programs after writing them. You can write your Java programs in any text editor, or by using a Java program editor. The examples in this chapter use Windows WordPad. Many Java program editors, commonly called integrated development environments (IDEs), are more robust, featuring menu-based commands, a text editor, and a debugger.

James Gosling at Sun Microsystems invented the Java technology, and as Java grew in popularity, Sun Microsystems created a separate Web site to promote and support Java development. You can visit java.sun.com to obtain information about its various products and download a Java SDK for free.

The Java SDK includes many different components that can help you as you develop Java applets. It includes the compiler, several libraries of Java code that you can use to write new programs, and the Java Virtual Machine so that you can test your programs after compiling them.

Separate SDK versions are available for a variety of platforms, including Windows, Macintosh, Solaris, and UNIX, so you must be sure to download the right version for your system.

Download the Java SDK

① Type **java.sun.com** and press Enter.

② Under Popular Downloads, click the link for the latest version of the SDK.

- This example downloads Java 2 Standard Edition (J2SE) version 1.4.2.

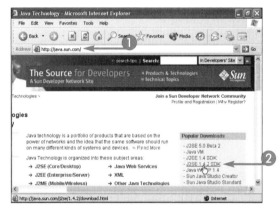

③ Scroll down the Web page and click the link for the Java SDK version that you want.

④ Read the license agreement.

⑤ If you agree to the conditions in the agreement, click Accept.

⑥ Click Continue.

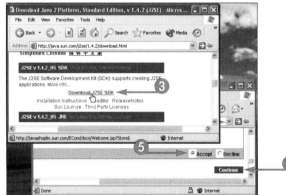

7 Click the link for downloading the appropriate version for your processor and operating system.

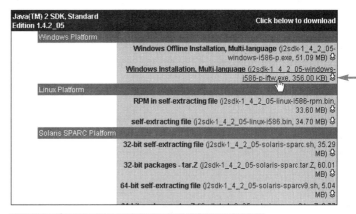

- A dialog box appears, prompting you to save the installation file or to run the installation utility.

8 Follow the on-screen instructions to download and install the SDK.

- The Java SDK installs on your computer.

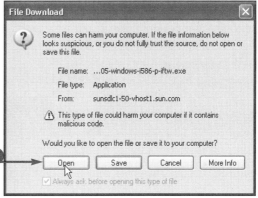

Where else can I find the Java SDK?

▼ You can download the Java SDK from several Web sites; however, downloading it from Sun's official Web site ensures that you obtain the most current version of the SDK. You can find a link for downloading the SDK at www.download.com, which connects you to Sun's Java site. For information about transitioning from Microsoft Java Virtual Machine to Java Virtual Machine, go to www.microsoft.com/mscorp/java/.

Which SDK version should I use?

▼ Several versions of the SDK are available. This book recommends that you start with the Standard Edition. Javasoft also offers an Enterprise Edition, which features additional tools and Java support, along with a version that includes netBeans, which are Java applets that are similar to ActiveX controls.

Do I need any additional tools?

▼ No. With a text editor and the Java SDK, you have the tools required to write and compile Java programs. However, many additional tools are available. You can explore many of the more popular tools by visiting Download.com at www.download.com. Under Software Developer, click the Java link to view a directory of shareware, freeware, and trialware, including class libraries, utilities, source code, and tutorials. Click the Tools & Utilities link for Java program editors, compilers, decompilers, and other useful tools. If your system runs MAC OS X, XCode tools, which come bundled with it, include an extensive Java Development Environment. Spare distributions also include complete sets of Java development tools.

Create a Java Source File

Several advanced Java tools enable you to work in an integrated environment. These tools include Sun's Forte for Java, Microsoft Visual J++, Symantec Visual Café, and Borland JBuilder. However, these tools are not really necessary; you can write Java applets using a standard text editor, such as WordPad. All you need are the Java SDK and a text editor, and you can start developing your own Java applets.

Java code begins with `import` statements that allow access to specific Java libraries. These libraries include functions that are used within the code. For example, the Abstract Window Toolkit (AWT) library includes functions such as

`drawString`, which is used to by the applet to display text to the user.

The simplest Java applets consist of the definition of a single class, the smallest independent unit of the Java source code, consisting of the `class` keyword and a pair of curly braces. You can declare the class as public by preceding the `class` keyword with `public`.

After you enter the code, you can save the Java applet source file with the .java filename extension. The .java filename extension identifies the file as a Java applet source file to the compiler.

Create a Java Source File

① Open a new document in a text editor.

Note: You can compose Java code in a Java editor or text-based HTML editor.

② Add `import` keywords to begin your applet.

● This example uses two `import` keywords.

③ Type the name of each library you want to import followed by a semicolon (;).

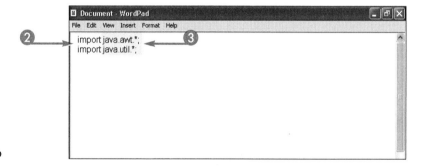

④ Add a `public class` name that extends the `java.applet.Applet` class.

Note: Java is case-sensitive, so type the code exactly as it is presented here.

⑤ Add opening and closing curly braces.

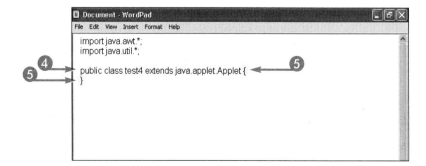

⑥ Within the `class` brackets, add a `public` function named `paint` with the `Graphics screen` parameter type.

⑦ Add opening and closing curly braces after the function declaration.

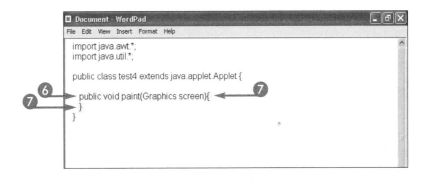

```
import java.awt.*;
import java.util.*;

public class test4 extends java.applet.Applet {

    public void paint(Graphics screen){
    }
}
```

⑧ Declare and set three color variables.

⑨ Declare a `newColor` variable of type `Color` with the color variables.

⑩ Use this `newColor` variable to reset the background color using the `setBackground` method.

⑪ Add the `drawString` method to draw some text.

⑫ Save the file as *?.java*, where *?* matches the class name from step 4.

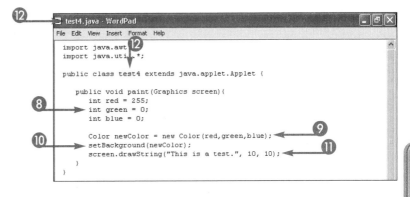

```
import java.awt.*;
import java.util.*;

public class test4 extends java.applet.Applet {

    public void paint(Graphics screen){
        int red = 255;
        int green = 0;
        int blue = 0;

        Color newColor = new Color(red,green,blue);
        setBackground(newColor);
        screen.drawString("This is a test.", 10, 10);
    }
}
```

This seems complicated. Where can I go to learn more about Java development?

▼ One of the best places to go to learn about Java is from the source of Java itself: Sun Microsystems. The site where you downloaded the Java SDK features a development area for Java novices at http://java.sun.com/learning/new2java/. You can check out a wide variety of Java applets at http://java.sun.com/applets/. Another great place to learn about Java and explore sample Java applets is Jars at www.jars.com.

What do the import statements do?

▼ The import statements at the top of the document allow access to specific Java libraries. These libraries include functions that are used within the code. For example, the AWT library includes functions like `drawString`, which the applet uses to display text to the user.

Does a Java program differ in any way from a Java applet?

▼ A Java program is a standalone application — a program that runs just like other programs on your computer. A Java applet runs only in a Java-enabled Web browser or in a runtime environment, such as Applet Launcher, which is included with OS X and the various applet *wrappers* that Sun provides. You write programs and applets in much the same way, but when you compile a program, the compiler creates an executable file.

Compile
Java Code

After you write a Java applet, you can save it as a source file with the .java filename extension. You can then run the source file through a Java compiler to convert it into a bytecode file with the .class filename extension. Compiling the code produces a small, portable file that the Java Virtual Machine can interpret and execute in a Web browser window.

The Java SDK includes a program called javac.exe that compiles the Java programming code for you. You can find javac.exe in the \bin directory under the main directory where you installed the SDK.

You can run the compiler command from a command line. If your computer runs Windows, you must first display the Command Prompt, which enables you to type commands at the MS-DOS prompt. To compile your Java programming code, you type the **javac.exe** command, followed by the location and name of the file that contains the code you want to compile.

If the Java file has any errors, the compiler recognizes them and displays descriptions of these errors. If the Java file does not have any errors, the compiler creates a class file, giving it the same name as the Java source file but changing the filename extension from .java to .class.

Compile Java Code

1 Click Start.

2 Click Programs or All Programs.

3 Click Accessories.

4 Click Command Prompt or MS DOS Prompt.

● The Command Prompt appears.

5 Type **cd** followed by the path to the directory where the javac.exe file is stored.

● In this example, the file is stored in c:\j2sdk1.4.2_05\bin.

6 Press Enter.

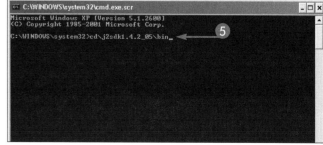

⑦ Type **javac**.

⑧ Type a space followed by the path and filename of your Java source file.

⑨ Press Enter.

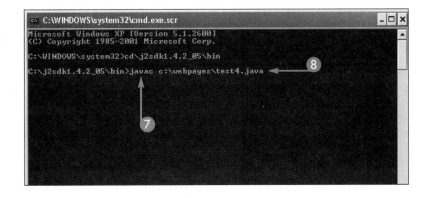

● If the code is error free, the compiler generates a class file and returns you to the command prompt.

● If the code contains errors, the compiler displays a description of each error and does not generate a class file.

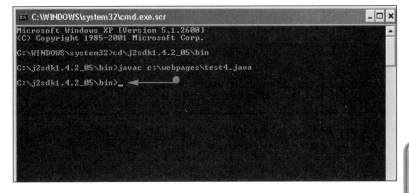

How can I fix a Java program that has errors?

▼ If an error message appears while you compile a Java file, the message displays the line and place where the error occurred. It also gives you a brief error description that helps you identify the problem. From this information, you can return to the Java file, correct the error, resave the file, and then try to compile it again. The compiler cannot generate a class file until the source file is error free.

If the compiler does not detect any errors in the source file, does it display a message stating that the process was successful?

▼ No, it simply creates the class file and displays the DOS prompt as if nothing happened. Because no confirmation appears, you may think nothing did happen, but if you display a list of files in the directory, you see the name of the new class file.

Where does the Java compiler store the resulting class file?

▼ The compiler saves the resulting class file to the same directory in which the source file is stored. If the compiler does not display any error messages, then at the Command Prompt, type **cd** followed by the path to the source file's directory. Press Enter, type **dir *.class** and then press Enter to see a list of files with the .class extension.

Embed an Applet in a Web Page

You can embed a Java applet in a Web page by using <object>, HTML's universal tag for embedding objects. The opening <object> tag specifies the location and name of the Java class file. When the Web browser receives the applet, the Java Virtual Machine interprets and executes the applet in its own display area on the Web page.

You can include the classid and codetype attributes within the opening <object> tag. The classid is set to the keyword java: followed by the class filename. The codetype attribute defines the MIME type to the Web

browser. For Java files, codetype is set to application/octet-stream.

The <object> tags can also include other attributes, including width and height to set the applet dimensions, and the align attribute to align the applet with the left or right margin.

If you store the class file in a directory other than the directory in which your Web page is stored, you can use the codebase attribute to indicate the name of the subdirectory. For example, <object codebase="classes/myJava.class" locates the class filename myJava.class in the classes subdirectory.

Embed an Applet in a Web Page

① Open an HTML document and add a set of <object> tags within the <body> tags.

② Type **classid=** and set it equal to **java:** followed by the class filename, in quotes.

③ Type **codetype="application/octet-stream"**.

④ Add some alternative text between the <object> tags.

⑤ Save the document.

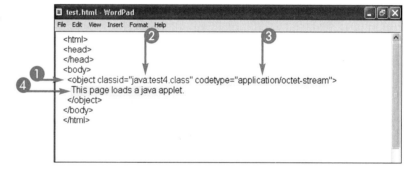

⑥ Open the document in a Web browser.

● The applet loads and runs in the Web browser.

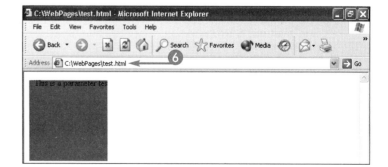

⑦ Open the document in your HTML editor.

⑧ Add the `width` and `height` attributes to the opening `<object>` tag, and set them equal to the height and width you want.

● In this example, height and width are set to 200 pixels.

⑨ Save the document.

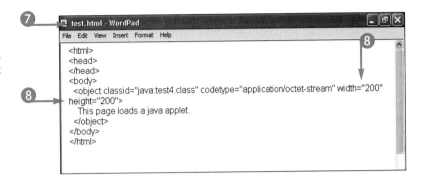

⑩ Open the document in a Web browser.

● The applet loads and plays in an area with the dimensions you specified.

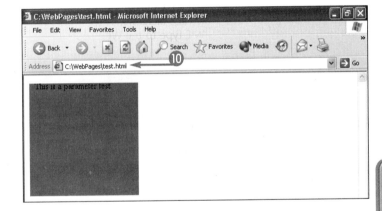

Can I use applets without writing the Java code?

▼ You only need the Java files to compile the class files. If you have the class file, you do not need the source files unless you make changes to the applet. Many Java applet repositories on the Web, such as Java Boutique at http://javaboutique.internet. com, let you use precompiled Java applets. To embed files from these repositories, you do not need to download the SDK and compile the code; simply embed the applet as shown in this section.

Can I determine if an object in the Web browser is an applet?

▼ This depends on the Web browser. If you open your Web page in Netscape Navigator, the status bar displays "Applet test4 started." Other Web browsers may display the applet name if you rest the mouse cursor on the applet. Some Web browsers do not indicate that an applet is running.

I cannot run any Java applets in my Web browser. What is wrong?

▼ Some Web browsers do not support the current Microsoft Java Machine or Java Runtime Environment and may not be able to run Java applets. Most Web browsers that do support current JVM/JRE have security settings that allow you to disable Java. Check your Web browser's help system to determine how to change the security settings.

Change Applet Parameters

You can make Java applets that include variables and that you can modify within the Web page file by adding parameters. If a Java applet is coded correctly, you can specify applet parameter values within the Web page file that can affect the output of the applet.

You can add one or more <param /> tags between the opening and closing <object> tags. The <param /> tags send values from the HTML document to the applet. Each <param /> tag includes two attributes, name and value. The name attribute is the name of the parameter, and the

value is the value that the <param /> tag sends to the applet.

The name attribute needs to match the name of the variable included in the Java code. The applet receives all parameters that the <param /> tags send as a string. You must convert these strings to a number type if you intend to use them in calculations.

This example adds parameters to a Web page, and the applet uses those parameters when it runs to modify its output.

Change Applet Parameters

① Open the Java source file in which you want to add or change parameters.

② Modify the code to accept a parameter using the getParameter function.

③ Save the source file.

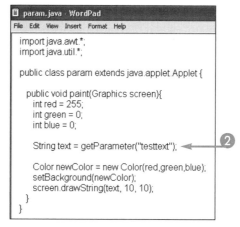

④ Display the Command Prompt.

Note: For more information, see the section "Compile Java Code."

⑤ Change to the disk drive and directory in which the Java source code file is stored.

⑥ Type **javac** followed by a space and then the name of your Java source file.

⑦ Press Enter.

⑧ Open the HTML document that references the class file you modified.

⑨ Add a <param /> tag with the name attribute set equal to the Java code and the value attribute set equal to the value that you want.

⑩ Save the document.

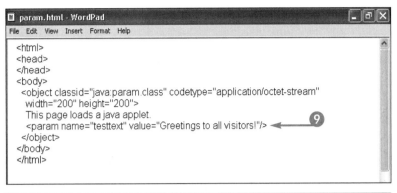

⑪ Open the document in a Web browser.

● The Web browser displays the Web page, revealing the effects of the <param /> tags on the output.

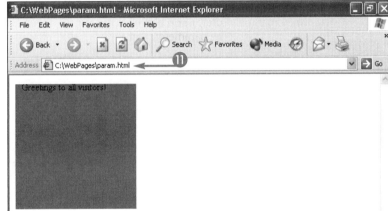

If I download an applet from a Web repository, how do I find out the acceptable parameters?

▼ When you download an applet from the Web, you can find out what the acceptable parameters are by searching the Java file for the getParameter method. If you do not have access to the Java source file, the applet probably includes a Read Me file or some other form of documentation that lists the acceptable parameters. Return to the site from which you downloaded the applet and look for additional information. The site may include a link you can click to contact the developer or a discussion group where you can post a question.

What is the benefit of using the <param /> tag?

▼ Using the <param /> tag, you can control the applet with parameters that are sent from the Web page. This functionality does not require you to recompile the Java class for a subtle change. For example, if you send a color as a parameter, you can program the applet to use the color parameter as the background color. If you want to change the background color, you can change the value in the <param /> tag instead of modifying the Java class file.

Understanding RSS Feeds

You can distribute Web content and increase traffic to your Web site by using RSS feeds. RSS, short for Rich Site Summary or Really Simple Syndication, enables you to summarize Web content and distribute the summaries with links to the original, complete content. News organizations commonly use RSS feeds to make their content available to a wide audience of users.

RSS feeds also make it easy to link to Web page content. Web sites that feature RSS feeds usually offer source code that Web authors can copy and paste into their Web pages to link their sites to the original content. You can think of RSS as a way of advertising what is new at your Web site and broadcasting your content to users who decide to view it.

Subscribing to RSS Feeds

You can subscribe to existing RSS feeds to see how they function from a user's perspective. Many news organizations, including CNN and ESPN, feature RSS feeds that allow users to subscribe, often for free, to obtain up-to-the-minute news and information. For example, with an RSS feed from CNN, you can access the latest headline news and feature stories.

To subscribe to RSS feeds, you can download and install an RSS reader or *newsreader*. One of the more popular newsreaders is Awasu, and you can find it at www.awasu.
com. When you run Awasu, it displays a collection of channel packs from which you can choose. A channel pack is a news category that contains multiple channels with related content. You select the channel that you want and then choose the headline of a story that you are interested in reading. You can also use online newsreaders, such as the Rocket RSS Reader, which you can find at http://reader.rocketinfo.com.

Automated Publications

RSS enables Web authors to create automated publications that pull content from multiple sources and present it on a Web page. A good example of an automated publication is Google News, which you can find at http://news.google.
com. Google News gathers news and information from approximately 4,500 news services worldwide to create an online newspaper that is constantly updated. It does this by using Atom, which is another news-feed standard similar to RSS. You can learn more about Atom at its official Web site, www.atomenabled.org.

Syndicating Your Content

You can syndicate the content on your Web pages by creating and publishing an RSS feed. The overall process consists of four steps: creating an RSS file, validating the file, uploading the file, and registering your RSS feed with one or more RSS directories.

Creating RSS Files

You can create an RSS file using a text editor, such as WordPad. An RSS file contains source code, including tags that are very similar in structure to the tags that you use to create Web pages. RSS files use some standardized XML tags to mark the content that you want to include in your feed.

As a whole, the RSS file defines your feed as a *channel*. Each channel can have from 1 to 15 items. Each item consists of a title, a description or summary of the content, and a link to the content. In most cases, you create an item based on content that is already included on a Web page. As a result, creating an item in an RSS file is usually a simple matter of copying and pasting the content that you want to include.

Validating Your RSS File

Every RSS file must contain a document declaration identifying it as an RSS document and specifying the RSS version number. Several versions of RSS are available, including RSS 0.91, a very basic version that is quite popular. Versions 1.0 and 2.0 also have wide support. A competing standard, called Atom, is quickly gaining support and has been embraced by Google for its blog-hosting service, Blogger.

Before publishing your RSS file, you should run it through a validator, such as the one at http://feedvalidator.com. This ensures that your source code is error free and conforms to the RSS or Atom standard that is specified in the document declaration.

Uploading and Registering Your RSS File

To make your RSS feed accessible to Web users, you first upload your RSS file to your Web server. You can then include a link on your Web page that enables visitors to access the RSS feed. By registering your RSS feed with RSS directories, users can find and access your Web site content using an RSS reader, and other Web developers can display your content on their pages.

Enter RSS Information

Y ou can create an RSS file to list the items that you want to include in your RSS feed. Each item in your list requires a title, a description or summary of an article, and a link to the complete article. In place of the text description or summary, you can include a link to an image file, such as a logo. Every RSS file must contain at least 1 item and no more than 15 items.

The item title does not need to match the title of the article, nor does the description or summary need to match text from the original article. However, you can often save

time by cutting and pasting text from the original source. You should make your headline and description both engaging and clear, to attract users to your Web site.

Version 0.91, an early and very popular version of RSS, placed strict limitations on the length of each element that comprised an item. For example, each title was limited to 100 characters, you could not make a description longer than 500 characters, and you could not make a link URL longer than 500 characters. Since the introduction of version 0.92, these limitations are no longer in effect.

Enter RSS Information

① Open a new document in your HTML editor.

② Type a title for the item that you want to syndicate.

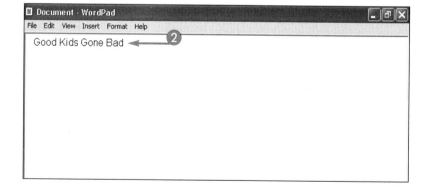

③ Type a brief description or summary of the item that you want to syndicate.

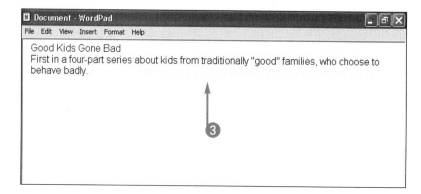

4 Type the URL of the Web page that contains the item that you want to syndicate.

- It is important to start the URL with `http://`.

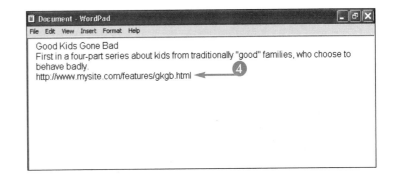

5 Save the document as a plain-text file with the .xml filename extension.

- Your document is saved to disk.

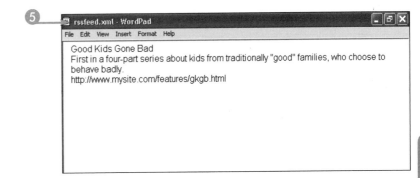

What do I enter to insert an image instead of a text item?

▼ You type a title whose URL specifies the location and name of the image on the Web, the URL of the Web page on which it appears, and the height and width of the image, in pixels. Instead of using the `<item>` tag to mark this entry as an item, use the `<image>` tag. For more on inserting the `<image>` tag and setting image dimensions, see the section, "Code an RSS Item."

When an item changes, do I need to create a new RSS file?

▼ No. You can edit your file instead of creating a new file. Editing an RSS file typically consists of removing outdated items and inserting items for new content. Any newsreaders or aggregators that reference your feed automatically scan the file for changes and notify users that subscribe to your Web site of any updates, so you should ensure the filename remains the same.

I have seen some RSS files with the .rss filename extension. Are those different types of files?

▼ No. You commonly use three filename extensions for RSS files: .xml, .rss, and .rdf. If your RSS file does not pass validation, you can try changing the filename extension and testing it again. See the section "Declare XML and RSS Version," to learn where to go to validate an RSS file.

Code an RSS Item

Y ou can code the data that you enter in an RSS file to identify the various elements that comprise an item, such as its title, description, and URL. RSS uses four XML tags to mark the text. You bracket each item with an opening and closing `<item>` tag, insert a `<title>` tag before and after each title, insert a `<description>` tag before and after the description or summary, and insert a `<link>` tag before and after each URL. Each item in your RSS file must employ the proper syntax:

Unlike HTML tags, which are strictly defined in the HTML standard, you can make XML tags anything you want to make them. However, in RSS, the XML tags are defined, so they can function as a standard way of referencing the various elements in the file. You must use the tags as specified. Any variations can result in a file that is invalid.

```
<item>
<title>Article Title</title>
<description>This is a description or
summary of the article that the user sees
when previewing the feed.</description>
<link>http://www.website.com/directory/
subdirectory/article.html</link>
</item>
```

Code an RSS Item

① Open a document in your HTML editor that has the item or items that you want to code.

② Type **<item>**.

③ Type **</item>**.

④ Type **<title>**.

⑤ Type **</title>**.

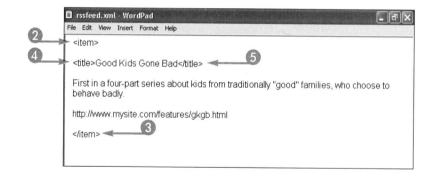

⑥ Type **<description>**.

⑦ Type **</description>**.

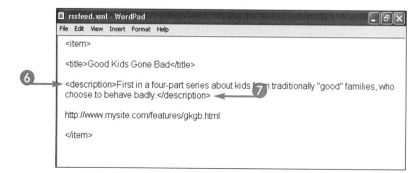

⑧ Type <**link**>.

⑨ Type </**link**>

⑩ Repeat steps 2 to 5 to code additional items.

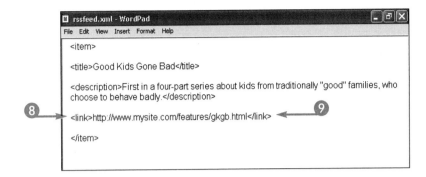

⑪ Click File.

⑫ Click Save.

● Your HTML editor saves the file with your changes.

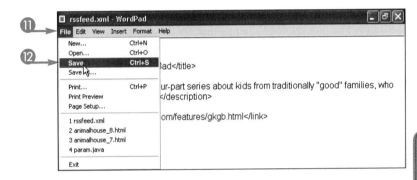

Can I automate the process of creating an RSS feed?

▼ Yes. Many blog authoring programs and services can automatically generate RSS feeds, based on the content of your Web pages. (A *blog*, or *Web log*, is a Web site, typically updated daily and commonly used to express personal insights and observations.) You can also use an RSS generator to have the necessary tags inserted for you. For example, using the ListGarden RSS Feed Generator, you type the title, URL, and description of each item in a form, and the program generates the RSS file for you, complete with the required codes. You can learn more about this program at www.softwaregarden.com.

I added a URL to include an image in my RSS feed. How do I code the entry?

▼ Instead of using the `<item>` tag to mark this entry as an item, bracket the entire entry with opening and closing `<image>` tags. Use the `<title>` , `<description>`, and `<link>` tags the same way that you use them to code an item. Bracket the URL that links to the image, with an opening and closing `<url>` tag. You can specify the image dimensions using opening and closing `<width>` and `<height>` tags, but these tags are optional.

Define a Web Site
as a Channel

You can group the items in your RSS feed as a channel to make the entire collection of items available to newsreaders or aggregators as a single unit. Whenever an item in the channel changes, the newsreader or aggregator can then detect the change in the channel and notify a subscriber of available updates.

Defining a Web site as a channel requires you to create another entry that consists of a title, description, and URL. However, you must omit the `<item>` or `<image>` tags, so that the entry is not identified as an item or image within the file. You should also add the `<language>` tags to specify the language of your Web site content. In most cases, an RSS file contains only one channel entry that must follow the proper syntax:

```
<title>Site Title</title>
<description>This is a description of the Web site.</description>
<link>http://www.website.com/</link>
<language>language</language>
```

Items can contain additional elements, including: a Platform for Internet Content Selection (PICS) rating, to specify whether or not content is appropriate for children; a copyright date; a publication date; and a list of hours when RSS readers should not access the content. However, the example in this section addresses only the required information — the title, description, link, and language.

Define a Web Site as a Channel

① Open an RSS file in your HTML editor.

② Type **<channel>**.

③ Type **<title>**.

④ Type a title for your Web site.

⑤ Type **</title>**.

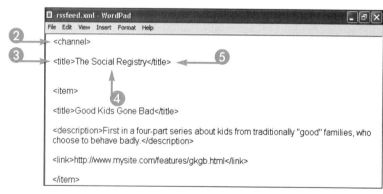

⑥ Type **<description>**.

⑦ Type a description of your Web site.

⑧ Type **</description>**.

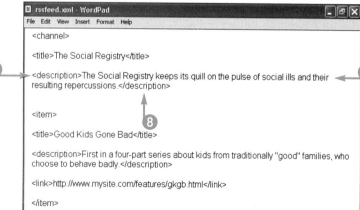

9 Type **<link>**

10 Type the URL of your Web site's home page.

11 Type **</link>**.

12 Type **<language>**.

13 Type the code that identifies the language in which your Web site content is written.

14 Type **</language>**.

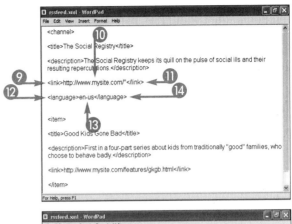

15 Scroll to the end of the document and type **</channel>**.

16 Save the document.

● All items in the document are now part of a channel.

Can I use character entities in my RSS file?

▼ Yes, the RSS standard enables you to include character entities in your source code. For example, you can type **©** to include the copyright symbol. For instructions on how to add character entities to a Web page, see Chapter 3. See Appendix A for a list of character entity codes.

Can I use HTML tags in my RSS file?

▼ Most versions of RSS do not allow HTML tags. To keep RSS simple, its developers focused on content rather than formatting. The aggregator that presents the information in your RSS feed may add its own formatting to display information from all feeds in a consistent format.

Where can I learn more about other tags that I can use in my RSS file?

▼ Netscape originally developed the RSS specification to manage news feeds at the Netscape NetCenter. Although Netscape no longer plays a central role in the development of the RSS specification, it does provide a description of the 0.91 specification, which is one of the most popular versions. You can view it at my.netscape.com/publish/formats/rss-spec-0.91.html. This page displays a complete list of available tags.

Declare XML and RSS Version

You can create an RSS file that conforms to various RSS specifications, but you must add a document declaration at the top of the document indicating which specification you are following. In addition, you must specify an XML version. You can type the tags that specify the XML and RSS version numbers at the top of your RSS file in the proper syntax:

```
<?xml version="1.0"?>
<rss version="2.0">
```

You must also type a closing `</rss>` tag at the end of the document:

```
</rss>
```

The examples in this chapter are very basic and conform to most RSS specifications. However, as developers began to realize the potential uses of RSS, they expanded on the early versions. UserLand (www.userland.com), which took over development of the RSS specification after Netscape, has released versions 1.0 and 2.0. The newer specifications remove some of the limits imposed on RSS coding, but generally adhere to the basic RSS philosophy of keeping RSS coding simple. RSS 2.0 contains some additional tags, but it is backward-compatible with RSS 0.91; that is, RSS 0.91 feeds are valid RSS 2.0 feeds.

Declare XML and RSS Version

① Open an RSS file in your HTML editor.

② At the top of the document, type **<?xml version="1.0"?>**.

③ Press Enter to create a new line.

④ Type **<rss version="?">** where **?** is the RSS version to which this document conforms.

⑤ Scroll to the end of the document.

⑥ Press Enter to create a new line.

⑦ Type </**rss**>.

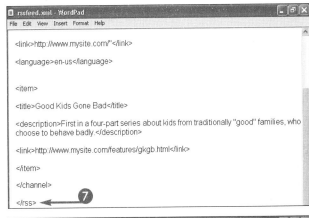

⑧ Click File.

⑨ Click Save.

● Your RSS file is now complete.

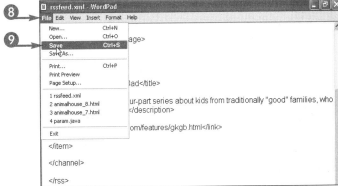

Do I need to be aware of any differences in XML versions?

▼ As long as you enter the tags as instructed, you need not concern yourself with XML versions. Most RSS files specify XML 1.0 as the version. If you limit your RSS file to include only basic elements, the file is more likely to be universally accepted.

Where can I go to learn more about the differences between the various RSS versions?

▼ SourceForge.net provides an excellent overview of the differences between the various RSS versions. For more information, visit http://rss-net. sourceforge.net/documents/ version_comparison.html. Here, you can find comparisons of versions 0.90, 0.91, 0.92, 1.0, and 2.0. The site also provides information about which tags are required, optional, and not supported in each version.

Where can I go to have my RSS file validated?

▼ To validate your RSS file, first upload it to your Web server. Chapter 18 provides instuctions on how to upload files. After uploading the file, you can go to http://feedvalidator.org or http://rss.scripting.com to validate it. Validating ensures that the file is coded properly so that newsreaders and aggregators can access the items described in the file. At http:// feeds.archive.org/validator/, you simply type the URL to your RSS feed file and click the Validate button.

Display RSS Feeds on a Web Site

After you create your RSS feed, you can add a button on your Web page that links to the RSS feed file. The button shows that your Web site contains syndicated content, and it enables visitors to quickly access your RSS file. When a user opens your RSS file, the Web browser displays the URL of your RSS file, so that the user can copy it and then paste it into a newsreader or aggregator to subscribe to your Web site.

You may have seen RSS buttons on other Web sites that contain syndicated content. The buttons typically appear orange or blue and are labeled RSS, XML, or RDF.

To link to your RSS file, you can create a link using opening and closing `<a>` tags that bracket an `<img />` tag for the button that you want to use. In place of the `<img />` tag, some users create a button using CSS styles, as follows:

```
<a href="subdirectory/rss.xml"><span
style="border:2px solid;border-
color:rgb(255,225,0) rgb(60,60,60)
rgb(60,60,60) rgb(255,225,0);padding: 1px;
font: bolder 10px verdana,sans-serif;
color:white; background:rgb(255,100,0);
text-decoration:none; ">RSS</span></a>
```

Display RSS Feeds on a Web Site

① Open an HTML document that you want to link to your RSS feed file.

② Add an opening `<a>` tag with the `href` attribute set equal to the location and name of the RSS file.

③ Add a closing `</a>` tag.

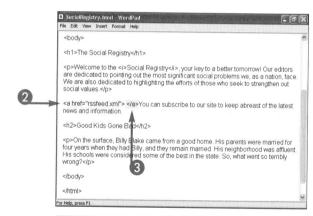

④ Between the opening and closing `<a>` tags, insert an `<img />` tag that links to an RSS button image.

● You can find button images on the Web or create one in a graphics program.

⑤ Save your HTML document.

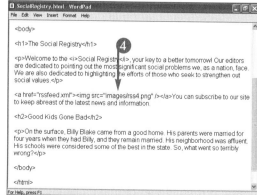

⑥ Open the document in a Web browser.

⑦ Click the RSS button.

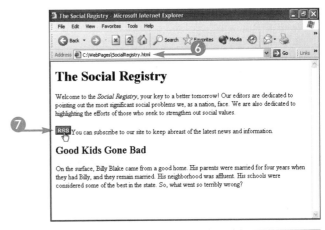

● The Web browser displays your RSS file.

● The RSS file's URL appears here.

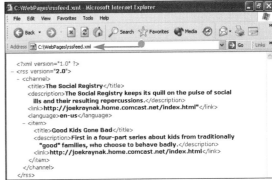

I want to design my own button. What color should I make it?

▼ RSS buttons are typically blue, and XML buttons are typically orange. This enables users to quickly identify the graphic as a button that they can click to view an RSS feed. You can create your own button in any graphic program, such as Window Paint, and save it as a PNG file. Simply set the background to the color that you want and add white text for the button label.

Can I simply include a text link to my RSS file?

▼ Yes, you can add a text link, but many users who subscribe to Web sites look for the easily identifiable buttons. If you decide to use a text hyperlink, make it descriptive, for example, "Syndicate this site."

How can I include syndicated content from other Web sites on my Web pages?

▼ This typically requires the use of a JavaScript or other type of script to convert the XML content into HTML and display it on a Web page. Many Web sites that provide syndicated content, such as the BBC site, provide instructions complete with source code that you can copy and paste into your document.

The W3C Markup Validation Service - Microsoft Internet Explorer

File   Edit   View   Favorites   Tools   Help

Back   ·   ×   🗋   🏠   🔍 Search   ⭐ Favorites   🐾 Me

dress 🔗 http://validator.w3.org/

--- **VALIDATE BY URL** ---------------------------------------

Address: [   ]   Check

Enter the URL of the page you want to check. Advanced
available from the Extended Interface.

--- **VALIDATE BY FILE UPLOAD** -----------------------------

Local File: C:\MyWebPages\animalhouse_8.htr Browse...

Select the file you want to upload and check. Advanced o
available from the Extended File Upload Interface.

THIS PAGE IS **NOT** VALID   TRANS

are the results of attempting to parse this document with an SGML pa

Line 28, column 3: **element "H3" undefined**

`<H3 > Your One-Stop Pet Emporium</h3>`

*You have used the element named above in your document,
but the document type you are using does not define an
element of that name. This error is often caused by incorrect
use of the "Strict" document type with a document that uses
frames (e.g. you must use the "Frameset" document type to get
the "<frameset>" element), or by using vendor proprietary
extensions such as "<spacer>" or "<marquee>" (this is usually
fixed by using CSS to achieve the desired effect instead).*

Available

☑ **pizzacake4u.com**

☐ **pizzacake4u.net**

Search Again

If you would like to add another domain, enter it here, and click "G

www. [   ]   com ∨   GO!

Checkout

Click the checkout button to register the
checked domains on your list below.   Checkout   Ca

User Login

New Users

If this is the first time using our registration services -click

Existing Users

Username: [   ]

Password: [   ]

Login

Forgot Your Password?

Enter your email address to have your account information ema

[   ]   Email It!

Check Web Pages in Multiple Browsers

You can open your completed Web page in multiple Web browsers to ensure that it appears as you intended wherever it displays. Most Web browsers display the same Web page with slight differences, depending on how the Web browsers interpret the HTML tags. For example, older Web browsers may not recognize some tags and may simply ignore them.

When you finish composing your HTML document, you should open it in the Web browser that you normally use to ensure that all of your text and images are visible. You can inspect your Web page for common errors, such as an omitted closing tag that can lead to unexpected results.

If possible, check your pages on different operating systems, such as Mac OS and Windows, because the operating system can influence your Web page's appearance.

When you finish inspecting the Web page in the Web browser that you normally use and have corrected any errors, you can open the Web page in another Web browser and repeat your inspection.

Because the Web browser can display local HTML pages that are saved on your computer's hard drive, you can load the pages directly from your hard drive before uploading them to your Web server. However, you should also inspect them after uploading them to the server to ensure that all of the links on the Web page function properly.

Check Web Pages in Multiple Browsers

1. Launch the Web browser that you normally use.

2. In the Address bar, type the location and name of the Web page you want to open.

3. Press Enter or click the button to open the page.

4. The Web browser displays the page.

5. Inspect the page for any obvious omissions or errors.

   ● This example shows a Web page in which an image failed to load and a closing tag was omitted.

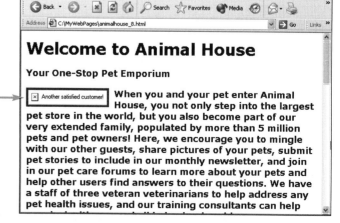

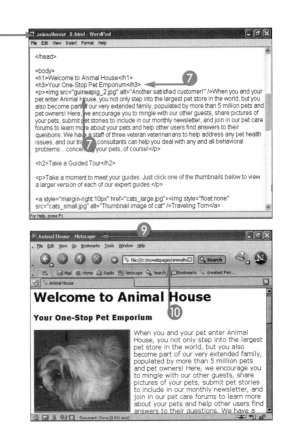

⑥ Open the HTML document in your HTML editor.

⑦ Fix any source code errors.

⑧ Save the document.

⑨ Run a different Web browser.

⑩ Type the location and name of the document and press Enter.

⑪ Inspect the Web page for any obvious errors and any differences in how this Web browser displays the page.

● You may need to adjust the source code to modify the page so that its appearance is acceptable in both Web browsers.

Are Internet Explorer and Netscape Navigator the only Web browsers that I should check?

▼ Internet Explorer and Netscape Navigator represent about 90 percent of the Web browsers that people use to surf the Web, but you can find different versions of each Web browser running on different operating systems. For example, the current version of Internet Explorer is 6, but testing your Web page in version 5 may reveal some problems. If possible, test your Web pages in the current and previous versions of both Internet Explorer and Netscape Navigator. If you have access to another Web browser, such as Opera, you should test it in that Web browser, as well.

Should my page look any different on two computers that both run the same versions of Windows and Internet Explorer?

▼ Your pages may look different if you specified any non-standard fonts. A Web browser can display text in various fonts, as specified in the HTML source code, but only if those fonts are installed on the computer. If a particular font is not installed, the Web browser selects the font that is closest in appearance to the specified font or that the user has specified as their default: serif, sans serif, or monospaced font.

Validate Web Pages

After you complete your Web page and test it in multiple Web browsers, you can validate it. This ensures that the source code complies with the XHTML specification in the document declaration, for example, XHTML 1.0, Transitional. Validating your source code is a simple process of opening it in a validator, which is a utility that checks the source code for errors. You can download these utilities from file repositories, such as www.download.com. Alternatively, you can upload your Web page to a validator online at validator.w3.org.

Validating utilities compare the source code syntax in your HTML document with the accepted specification and show you any syntax errors that they discover in your HTML source code. For example, W3C's XHTML validator verifies that all paired tag sets have an opening and closing tag and that unpaired tags end in />. If the validator discovers a syntax error, it displays the error along with its location, specified as a line number and column number. You can then edit the source code and run the validation check again. The validator does not check for spelling errors; it only checks for source code errors.

Validate Web Pages

1 Launch your Web browser.

2 Type **validator.w3.org** in the Address bar and press Enter.

3 Scroll down to Validate by File Upload.

4 Click Browse.

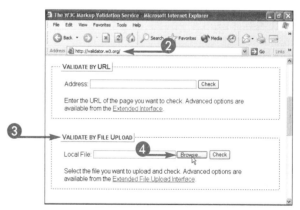

● The Choose File dialog box appears, displaying files and folders on your computer.

5 Navigate to the folder in which the Web page file you want to validate is stored.

6 Click the Web page filename.

7 Click Open.

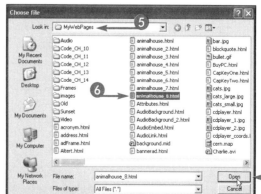

- The location and name of the Web page file appear here.

8 Click Check.

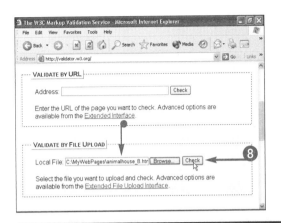

- The validator checks the page and displays any source code errors.

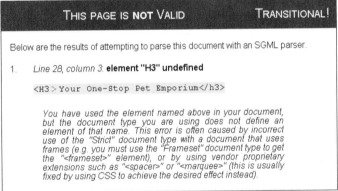

> **THIS PAGE IS NOT VALID**   **TRANSITIONAL!**
>
> Below are the results of attempting to parse this document with an SGML parser.
>
> 1. *Line 28, column 3:* **element "H3" undefined**
>
>   `<H3 > Your One-Stop Pet Emporium</h3>`
>
>   *You have used the element named above in your document, but the document type you are using does not define an element of that name. This error is often caused by incorrect use of the "Strict" document type with a document that uses frames (e.g. you must use the "Frameset" document type to get the "<frameset>" element), or by using vendor proprietary extensions such as "<spacer>" or "<marquee>" (this is usually fixed by using CSS to achieve the desired effect instead).*

What other validation utilities are available?

▼ Many validation utilities are available. Web Design Group (WDG) offers an online XHTML validator, which you can find at www.htmlhelp.com/tools/validator/. Another excellent choice is CSE HTML Validator, which you can find at www.htmlvalidator.com. You can also download and install a standalone version of CSE HTML Validator from www.download.com. Many HTML editors have built-in features that automatically highlight potential errors and may even check your documents for spelling errors and broken links. If you want to validate an external CSS stylesheet, you can use W3C's online CSS validator at jigsaw.w3.org/css-validator/.

Can validation utilities automatically correct errors?

▼ Capabilities vary for different validation utilities. Some utilities can automatically correct certain errors, while others only highlight the errors so that you can correct them. HTML Tidy, which you can access at infohound.net/tidy/, among other Web sites, automatically revises HTML source code for you, providing you with a corrected version of your file. The HandyHTML Studio text editor includes HTML Tidy. When your source code is complete, you can run HTML Tidy to automatically correct errors. Most errors consist of typos and omitted closing tags, so if you use an HTML editor that inserts the tags for you, you can avoid most errors.

Spell Check Your Web Site

Even if you compose your HTML source code in a text editor that does not have a spell checker, you can check your source code for typographical errors and misspellings. You may be an excellent typist and speller, but many typographical errors and misspellings can go unnoticed when you focus on the HTML tags. You should run a spell check on your source code to identify and eliminate these errors.

If you use a text editor that includes a spell checker to edit your source code, you can run the spell check from the text editor. The spell checker may highlight your tags, but you

can easily skip past them. If you use a text editor that does not have its own spell checker, you can copy your source code, paste it into a word processor that does have a spell checker, and run the spell check.

If the spell checker highlights errors, you can take note of the errors and return to your HTML document to correct the errors. This ensures that you do not introduce hidden codes from your word processor into your HTML source code.

Spell Check Your Web Site

① In your HTML editor, open the source code document that you want to spell check.

② Click Edit.

③ Click Select All.

④ Press Ctrl+C to copy the source code.

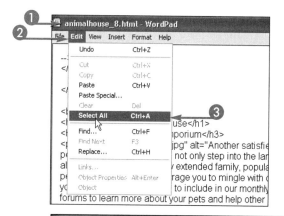

⑤ Open a new document in a word processor such as Microsoft Word.

⑥ Click Edit.

⑦ Click Paste.

● The HTML source code appears within the word processor.

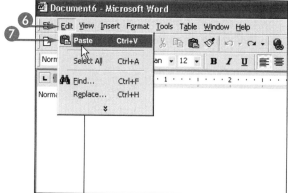

⑧ Click the button to start spell checking the document.

● If the spell checker stops on an HTML tag, click the button to ignore the tag.

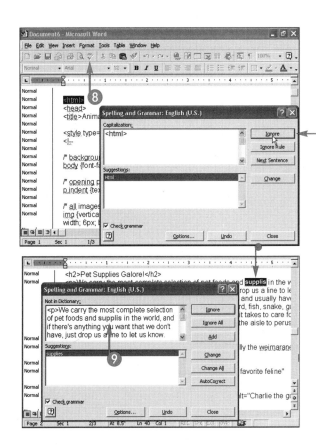

● If the spell checker finds a misspelled word, it highlights it and offers to correct it.

⑨ Take note of the misspelling, so that you can correct it in the original HTML document.

● When the spell check is finished, you should have a complete list of any typos or misspelled words.

Why should I run the spell checker when it become confused with all the HTML tags and attributes?

▼ Misspellings can turn away many users. Make your source code as clean as possible so that it does not distract and annoy visitors.

The spell checker questions tags because they do not match words stored in the spell checker's dictionary. When your spell checker stops on a tag, click Ignore All so that the spell checker questions the tag only once. You can omit the tags from the text by displaying the page in your Web browser and then copying and pasting the text from the Web browser, but if your page contains images, those images are also copied.

Do most HTML editors include a spell checker?

▼ Yes. Most HTML editors include a spell checker that can help you eliminate typographical errors and misspellings from your documents. You should also read your HTML source code carefully for any errors that a spell checker may overlook, for example, missing words or wrong words, such as "their" when you meant to type "there." Have a friend or colleague read over your Web page, as well. When you work on a page for so long, you commonly overlook even the most obvious errors. Remember this standard editing advice: Never proofread your own work.

Check Links

To avoid leading your visitors to a File Not Found message, which commonly appears as Error404, you can check the links in your Web pages to ensure that they open the correct pages or lead to Web sites that actually exist. If you have a relatively small Web site with few links, you can check the links manually by clicking them. You can then note any errors and correct your source code before publishing your Web pages.

Testing links can be tricky, especially if your document contains links to pages that you intend to store in other directories on your Web server. If your document contains

these types of links, you should upload your Web page and any linked pages to the Web server first, as explained in Chapter 18, before testing the links. If your Web page contains only absolute links — links that specify the entire URL of the Web page or other item — or if it contains links to other Web pages that are stored in the same directory on the server, you can test the links on your computer before uploading the files.

Check Links

① Launch your Web browser.

② Type the location and filename of the Web page that contains the links you want to check.

③ Press Enter or click the button to load the page.

● The Web browser displays the page.

④ Click a link you want to check.

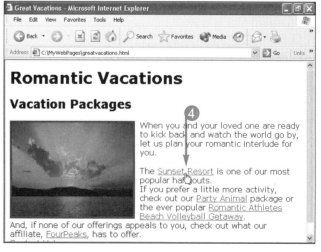

- If the link points to a Web page or Web site that does not exist, an error message appears.

⑤ Take note of any error messages.

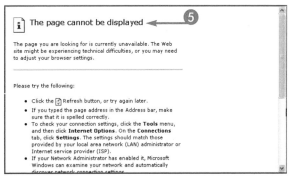

- If the link points to a page or Web site that does exist, the Web browser loads the page.

- You should ensure that the page that loads is the one that you intended to load.

- When you are finished checking links, you should have a list of any errors you need to correct.

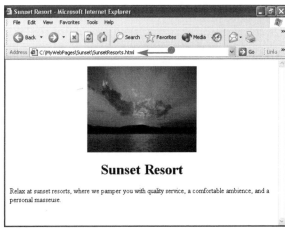

Are any utilities available for automating this process?

▼ Full-featured Web site creation and management programs, such as Microsoft FrontPage, include link-checking utilities. For example, FrontPage can display a schematic diagram showing all the links at your Web site and indicating which links are functioning properly and which are broken. You can also find several link-checking utilities on the Web. You can go to Web Link Validator at www.relsoftware.com/wlv/, or NodeWorks Link Checker at www.nodeworks.com. W3C has its own link checker, which you can use online at validator.w3.org/checklink. Download.com at www.download.com has a complete section for Web site management utilities.

What common errors do I need to be aware of when checking links?

▼ By carefully examining the URL that follows the href attribute, you can usually discover the problem with a link. Some common errors include adding a forward slash at the beginning of a relative URL or adding "http://" before a relative URL, mistyping a Web site address, typing a directory or filename in the wrong case, or typing a backward slash instead of a forward slash. Sometimes users mistake an underscore character (_) for a space, omit a period, or type a period where it is unnecessary.

Choose a Web Host

You can make your Web page accessible to users all around the world by publishing it on the Web. Publishing a Web page consists of uploading your HTML documents and all files associated with them — external style sheets, images, audio clips, and video clips — to a *Web server*. A Web server is a computer that stores Web pages and associated resources and makes them available to other computers, called *clients*, upon request. When you use your computer and Web browser to view a page, your system is acting as the client opening the page from a Web server.

You have four basic choices in Web servers: your Internet service provider's (ISP) Web server, a dedicated Web-hosting service, a corporation's Web server, or your own computer. If you choose an ISP or other Web-hosting service, the steps you take to upload the files vary, depending on the service. In most cases, you can use a program that the service provides to upload the files, although you may need to use FTP software on your computer. This section discusses some of the available options so that you can make an educated choice.

Internet Service Providers

When you subscribe to an ISP for Internet service, your subscription typically includes unlimited Internet access, e-mail, and a limited amount of space on a Web server. Storage space typically ranges from 5MB to 20MB, and the service gives you a 1GB to 2GB monthly file transfer allowance. For example, if you have a Web page that is 100KB in size, including source code and media files, and your ISP provides a 1GB monthly file transfer allowance, users may open the page approximately 10,000 times in a month, which is sufficient for most small Web sites that have a moderate amount of traffic. If you include large video clips or images that people are likely to view, you may find 1GB insufficient, in which case you can pay to have your storage space and file transfer allowance increased.

Few ISPs offer domain name registration, so your Web site's URL typically looks something like http://www.isp.com/~*yourname*.

Free Web-hosting Services

Several Web sites, including Yahoo! Geocities at geocities.yahoo.com, offer free Web-hosting for personal Web sites in exchange for allowing the Web site to display advertising on your page. Free services often feature tools for creating your pages online, so you do not need to upload files. For example, at Yahoo!, you complete a form to specify your preferences and add information to your page. If you decide to compose your HTML source code, the service may provide a form in which you can paste your source code to place it on the server. Some free services provide few resources, while others are more generous. For example, Yahoo! Geocities has 15MB of storage and a 3GB monthly file transfer allowance, which is competitive with what most ISPs offer.

Commercial Web-hosting Services

Commercial Web-hosting services charge you a monthly or annual fee for hosting your Web site. Many services include a one-time fee for registering a domain name so your Web site has an easily identifiable address. Cost varies, depending on the services you want. Some Web-hosting services include: Web design, maintenance, and backup; database management; secure order forms; and Web site statistics for corporations and merchants. They may also offer more affordable plans for individuals and small businesses.

Commercial Web-hosting services typically provide a more generous amount of storage on the Web server and a larger monthly file transfer allowance than either ISPs or free Web-hosting services, but you can expect to pay about five dollars for each additional GB per month. If you plan to maintain or grow your Web site — using it for business purposes, or attracting a great deal of traffic — a commercial Web-hosting service is the best choice, even if it costs a little extra.

Comparing Web-hosting Services

When comparing Web-hosting services, you may be tempted to focus on cost, storage, and the monthly file transfer allowance, but you should consider other features, as well. For example, reliability is a big consideration. If you intend to do business through your Web site, you need a Web-hosting service that maintains its server and keeps it up and running at all times. You should also find out whether the service backs up Web sites regularly.

You also need to know how you can transfer files to the server. For example, do you need to upload files using an FTP server or can you save them directly to the server using some other Web technology, such as WebDAV? If you use FrontPage to create your pages, does the server support file transfers from FrontPage? Does it support FrontPage extensions, which extend the capabilities of HTML? Do you need Common Gateway Interface (CGI) support to process form data? Before you sign up with a Web-hosting service, you should ensure that it offers the features you need.

Hosting Your Web Site on Your Computer

If you have a fairly powerful computer, a constantly active Internet connection such as a cable modem connection, Web server software, and a cooperative ISP, you can host your Web site on your computer. Most operating systems include programs that enable your computer to act as a Web server. For example, Windows XP Pro, Windows NT, and Windows 2000 Server include Microsoft's IIS Web server; Windows ME includes Personal Web Server; and Mac OS X includes the Apache Web Server.

However, because this increases the amount of traffic over your Internet connection, some ISPs do not allow you to use your computer as a Web server. For more information about using your computer as a Web server, see the section, "Host Your Own Web Site."

Obtain a Domain Name

or a fee, you can register a unique, identifiable domain name that users can type in their Web browsers to open pages at your Web site. Without a registered domain name, your Web site uses the domain name that your ISP or hosting service assigns to it, which can sometimes be difficult for users to remember.

When you register a domain name, the name you choose is assigned to a unique IP address — a number that represents your Web site. Every computer on the Internet is assigned an IP address that identifies it. Because remembering a

name is generally easier than remembering a number, domain names enable users to specify locations as names rather than as long strings of numbers. A domain name server, or DNS, interprets the domain name and directs the Web browser to the appropriate IP address.

You can register a domain name, assuming someone else has not yet registered the same name, with any of several domain registrars on the Web. Prices vary, depending on the registrar and on the length of time you intend to keep the name registered. Many Web-hosting services include domain name registration as part of their fees.

Obtain a Domain Name

1 Launch your Web browser.

2 Type the address of a domain name registration service and press Enter.

● This example shows itsyourdomain.com.

3 Type the domain name that you want, omitting the last three letters, such as .com.

4 Click here and click the extension that you want.

5 Click the button that executes the search.

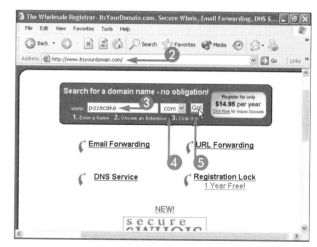

● If the domain name that you requested is already registered, a message appears telling you so.

6 Repeat steps 3 to 5 until you find a domain name that you want and that is also not registered.

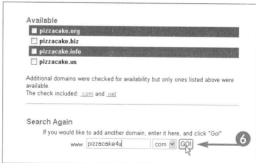

● A list of available domain names appears.

⑦ Select the domain name or names that you want to register.

⑧ Click the button to continue the registration process.

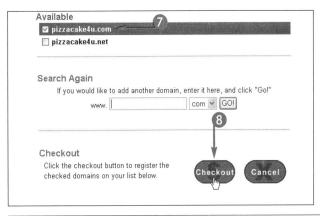

⑨ Follow the on-screen instructions to complete the transaction.

● Your domain name registration is submitted, but the service may need some time to process your registration.

How do I find legitimate domain name registrars?

▼ The Internet Corporation for Assigned Names and Numbers (ICANN) maintains a list of accredited domain name registrars, complete with links to the services. Go to www.icann.org, click the "Registrars" link, then click the "Registrars Listing" link, and then scroll down the page to view the list.

Can I register a domain name if my IP address changes?

▼ If you host your own Web site, your Web server may have a *dynamic* IP address, which your ISP assigns to it. You can use a dynamic DNS service to ensure that your domain name remains linked to your computer's IP address whenever the address changes. For more information, go to TZO at www.tzo.com or another dynamic DNS service.

Do I own rights to the domain name forever?

▼ No. You usually register a domain name for a fixed amount of time, typically in one-year increments. You need to re-register the domain name before your registration expires in order to keep using it. You can register a domain name for up to ten years. If you switch Web-hosting services, you can keep your domain name, but you must perform a transfer to assign a different IP address to the domain name. Most domain name registrars provide a *Whois* option that enables you to look up information about the person or organization that has registered the domain name. For more information, see the domain name FAQ page at www.internic.net/faqs/domain-names.html.

Check Total File Size of Your Web Site

To avoid exceeding your allotted storage space on the Web server, you can check the total amount of storage space that your Web page files require. The easiest way to check the total amount of storage space required is to place all of your Web page files in one main folder, and then check the cumulative size of the folder. The main folder can include subfolders for related files, such as images, external style sheets, audio files, and video files.

If you have previously stored files on the server, you should also check the amount of space those files occupy. You can usually check the file sizes by viewing a list of the files in your folder on the server. See the section, "Set Up an FTP Client" for more information.

If the total storage space exceeds the allotted space, you have two options: You can pay more for additional storage space or you can modify your files in some way so that they require less storage space. For example, you may need to shorten an audio clip or eliminate some large image files. If you eliminate files, then you must also remove any tags in the source code that refer to those files.

Check Total File Size of Your Web Site

① Launch your computer's file management utility.

● This example shows My Computer in Windows.

② Navigate to the disk drive that contains the folder in which your Web page files are stored.

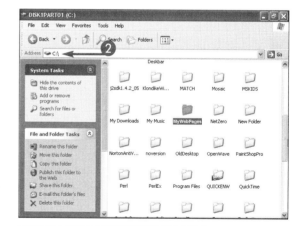

③ Right-click the folder.

④ Click Properties.

● The Properties dialog box appears,
displaying the total storage space that the
folder and its contents require.

⑤ Click OK.

⑥ To check a single file's size, navigate to the
directory in which the file is stored.

● The size of each file in the directory
appears. You may need to change views to
display the file sizes.

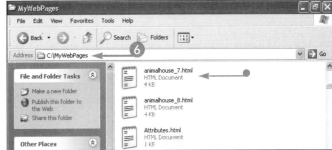

**Can I compress files before storing them on the
server?**

▼ Yes. You can use a file compression utility, such as
WinZip, to compress files that you want to share
with other users. However, compressing your HTML
document, images, or other related files converts
them to a format that a Web browser cannot
display. If you are running low on storage space,
consider deleting media files such as images, video
clips, audio clips, and animations. Compared to
media files, HTML text documents consume little
space. If you do remove media files, make sure you
delete any references to them in your HTML
document.

Can I remove files from the server?

▼ Yes. Most ISPs and Web-hosting services include file
management tools or provide FTP access that
enables you to delete files, create or delete
subdirectories, and move files and directories.

**I have some extra storage space on the server.
Can I use it to store other files?**

▼ Most ISPs allow you to use the storage space in
your folder for any files that you want to store on
the server. However, these files may be accessible to
anyone on the Internet, so do not use the server to
store files that contain sensitive information.

Set Up an FTP Client

With many Web-hosting services, you can upload files from your computer to the Web server using file transfer protocol (FTP). To use FTP, you can run a program on your computer called an FTP client. It connects to the FTP server and typically provides a two-paned window with the contents of your computer displayed in one pane and the contents of the FTP server displayed in the other pane. You can then copy files from one pane to the other to transfer them between your computer and the FTP server.

Before you can upload Web pages to the server, you must set up the FTP client so that it can connect to the server. To set up an FTP client, you need to have the Web site

address, your username, and your password. You can obtain this information from your ISP or Web-hosting service.

You can download and install any of several excellent FTP clients from www.download.com. For example, CuteFTP and WS_FTP are two very popular clients. If you have the Windows networking components installed, you can set up your FTP server as a network place on your computer, and use Windows as your client. The next section, "Upload Pages with an FTP Client," shows you how to transfer files.

Set Up an FTP Client

① Launch your FTP client software.

- This example uses WS_FTP. The steps may differ if you are using a different FTP client.

② Click Connection Wizard.

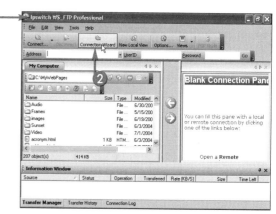

- The Connection Wizard appears, prompting you to type a name for the Web site.

③ Type a name to identify the Web site.

④ Click Next.

- The Wizard prompts you to specify the FTP server's address.

⑤ Type the FTP server's address.

⑥ Click Next.

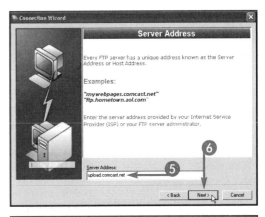

- The Wizard prompts you to type your username and password.

⑦ Type your username.

⑧ Type your password.

⑨ Click Next and follow the on-screen instructions to complete the process.

- When you finish, you have a named connection that you can select to connect to the FTP site.

How do I set up an FTP site as a network place in Windows?

▼ If Windows Networking is not installed, install it from the Windows installation CD. Then click Start and click My Network Places. Under Network Tasks, click the Add a network place link to launch the Add Network Place Wizard. Click Next, then click Choose another network connection. Click Next, and then follow the on-screen instructions to enter the FTP site's address along with your username and password. This creates a folder icon for the FTP site that acts like a folder stored on your computer. To upload files to the FTP server, you can drag them from a folder on your computer to the folder for the FTP server.

I entered the FTP site's address along with my username and password, but I still cannot connect to the server. Why?

▼ In some FTP clients, you must type **ftp://** before the FTP server's address. For example, you must type **ftp://ftp.site.com** rather than just **ftp.site.com**. If you are setting up an FTP server in Windows, you can click the View some examples link on the page that prompts you to enter an FTP server address to see the proper syntax. If you still cannot connect, check your username for typos and re-enter your password. You might also have a firewall installed that prevents you from connecting.

Upload Pages with an FTP Client

fter you connect to your FTP server, you can upload pages from your computer to the server to place your pages on the Web, where others can view them. If you can connect to your FTP server, as explained in the section, "Set Up an FTP Client," uploading files is as easy as copying them from one folder to another on your own computer.

When you connect to your FTP server, the FTP client typically displays a two-paned window that shows the contents of your computer in one pane and the contents of the FTP server in the other pane. In the pane that displays

the contents of your computer, you can navigate to the directory where your Web page files are stored. The pane that displays the contents of the FTP server typically shows the contents of your main directory, in which you want to place the Web document that functions as your home page. In most cases, you can create subfolders for related files, if necessary.

When the source directory on your computer and the destination directory on the FTP server display, you can click files on your computer and then click a button or enter a command to upload them to the server.

① Launch your FTP client program.

- This example uses WS_FTP. The steps may differ if you use a different FTP client.

② Click Connect.

- The Site Manager dialog box appears.

③ Click the Web site to which you want to connect.

④ Click Connect.

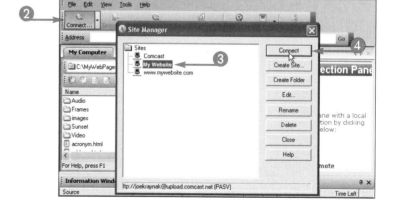

- The FTP client displays the contents of your computer here.

- The FTP client displays the contents of your directory on the FTP server here.

⑤ Navigate to the directory that contains the files that you want to upload.

⑥ Click a file that you want to upload and then Ctrl+click any additional files that you want to upload.

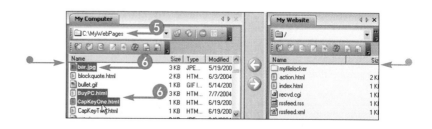

● The selected files appear highlighted.

⑦ Navigate to the directory on the server in which you want to store the files.

⑧ Click the Upload button.

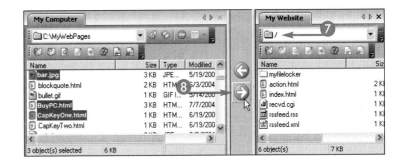

● Your FTP client uploads the selected files to the FTP server.

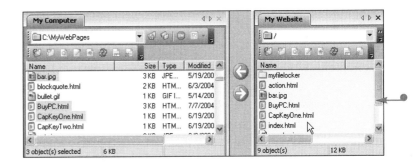

I am using Windows Networking as my FTP client, so how do I upload files?

▼ Change to the folder that contains the files that you want to upload, and select the files. Right-click one of the selected files and click Copy. Click Start, then click My Network Places and double-click the folder that represents your FTP server. Windows connects to the server and displays the contents of your folder on the server. Navigate to the folder in which you want to upload the files, right-click a blank area in the window that displays the folder's contents, and click Paste. You can also display separate windows for your computer and your FTP client and drag and drop files from one window to the other.

Can I copy, or download, files from the FTP server to my computer?

▼ Yes. You can download files or folders from the FTP server to your computer. Select the items that you want to download in the server pane and change to the directory on your computer where you want to place the downloaded files. Then, click the button to start the download. If you created a folder for your FTP server in windows, you can copy files from that folder and paste them into a folder on your computer to transfer them. Most Internet connections are optimized for downloading, rather than uploading, files, so do not be surprised if you can download files much faster than uploading them.

Upload Files with Your Web Browser

I f you do not have an FTP client or you do not want to use another specialized program, you can use your Web browser as an FTP client. Most Web browsers support both HTTP and FTP protocols, so they can manage FTP file transfers.

To access an FTP site, you type **ftp://** in the Web browser's Address bar, followed by the FTP site's domain name. For example, typing **ftp://ftp.microsoft.com** links you to the Microsoft public FTP site. To prevent unauthorized access to files, ISPs and other Web-hosting services password-protect

your directory on the server, so you must enter your username and password to gain access to your directory. Your Web browser prompts you whenever you connect to an FTP site that requires a password.

When you connect to an FTP site, the directories appear as folders and the files appear as icons. You can upload files by dragging and dropping them into the Web browser window. To download files, you can right-click a file's link and click Save Target As or drag the file to a directory on your computer.

Upload Files with Your Web Browser

① Launch your Web browser.

② Type **ftp://** followed by the domain name of the FTP server.

③ Press Enter or click the Go button in your Web browser.

● If your FTP server is secure, your Web browser displays a dialog box asking for your username and password.

④ Type your username.

⑤ Type your password.

⑥ Click Log On.

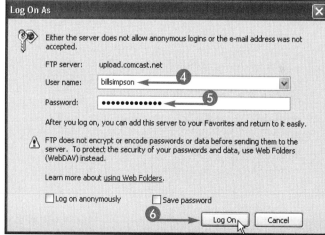

- The Web browser connects to the FTP server and displays the contents of your directory on the server.

⑦ Navigate to the directory in which you want to place your Web page files.

- This example shows the root directory.

⑧ Run your computer's file management utility.

⑨ Navigate to the directory in which your Web page files are stored.

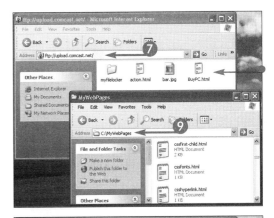

⑩ Select the files that you want to upload to the server.

⑪ Drag and drop one of the selected files from the file manager window into the Web browser window.

- Your computer uploads the files to the FTP server.

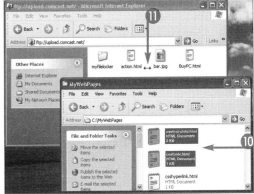

I try to connect to my FTP server, but my Web browser keeps displaying an error message. What should I do?

▼ In Internet Explorer, you simply need to enter the FTP server's domain name, and it prompts you for your username and password. In Netscape Navigator, type **ftp://***username@ftp.site.com* where *username* is the user ID your ISP or Web-hosting service assigned to you and *ftp.site.com* is the FTP server's domain name. Navigator displays a dialog box prompting you to enter your password. Type your password and click OK. You can save some time by typing the password in your entry: **ftp://***username:password@ftp.site.com*.

Can I have my Web browser save my username and password so I do not need to enter it next time?

▼ Yes. Internet Explorer provides an option for saving your username and password. When prompted to enter your username and password, type the requested information, click the Save password option (☐ changes to ☑), and then click Log On. In Netscape Navigator, type your password when prompted, click the Use Password Manager to remember this password option (☐ changes to ☑), and click OK.

Upload Files with WebDAV

If your ISP or Web-hosting service supports WebDAV, you can upload files to your Web server simply by copying them to a Web folder that you set up on your computer. You can even open a document directly from your Web server into your HTML editor, modify it, and then save it to the server just as you open, edit, and save files on your computer.

WebDAV stands for Web-based Distributed Authoring and Versioning, which is a technology that provides one or more users with easy access to files that are stored on Web servers. WebDAV's primary purpose is to enable multiple users to collaborate on projects. However, because it provides such a transparent bridge between the Web server and client, many Web-hosting services also support it for individual users.

If your ISP or Web-hosting service supports WebDAV, you can create a Web folder on your computer that is linked to your folder on the Web server. In Windows, this folder appears in My Network Places. Whenever you want to save or open a file on the Web server, you can go to My Network Places and open the Web folder that you created.

Upload Files with WebDAV

1 Click Start.

2 Click My Network Places.

● My Network Places appears.

3 Click Add a network place.

● The Add Network Place Wizard appears.

4 Click Next.

5 Click Choose another network location.

6 Click Next.

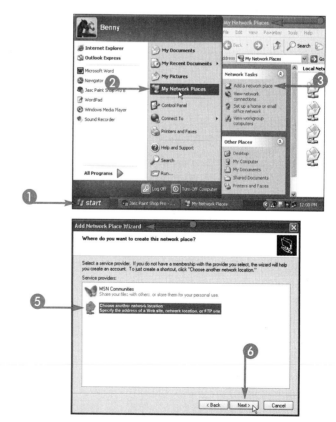

● The Wizard prompts you to type the address of the Web site that the new shortcut will open.

⑦ Type the URL that specifies the location of the WebDAV folder on the server.

⑧ Click Next and follow the on-screen instructions to name the location and complete the process.

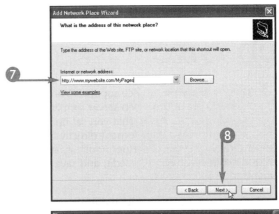

● When you open My Network Places, the new Web folder appears.

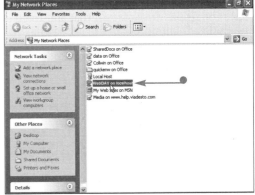

How do I find out the location of the WebDAV folder?

▼ Your ISP or Web-hosting service must set up a WebDAV folder on the server before you can set it up as a Web folder on your computer. Contact your ISP or Web-hosting service to determine if they support WebDAV and to find out the location of your folder.

Can I delete files from the folder?

▼ Yes, a WebDAV folder functions like any other folder on your computer. You can go to My Network Places and double-click your Web folder to view its contents. To delete a file, right-click the file's name or icon and then click Delete.

Can other people modify files in my WebDAV folder?

▼ WebDAV is designed to enable multiple users to collaborate on creating and editing Web pages and other documents safely. You can store your original documents in a separate file that is protected. Other users can open the documents, edit them, and save them to the server without affecting the originals. However, you must set up your Web site properly and configure permissions so that only authorized users have access to your Web site. Contact your ISP or Web-hosting service for additional information and instructions. You can learn much more about WebDAV and its ongoing development by visiting www.webdav.org.

Host Your Own Web Site

With a relatively powerful computer, a broadband Internet connection, and Web server software, you can host your own Web site by making your computer function as a Web server. Web users can then connect directly to your computer to open Web pages stored on its hard drive.

Before you invest the time and effort into hosting your own Web site, contact your ISP to see if they permit you to host your own Web site. Because of the traffic that this may add to your connection, many ISPs prohibit running a Web site over a residential connection. You may need to pay extra or

change to an ISP that supports personal Web site hosting. You should also ensure that the connection is fast and reliable and that your computer has plenty of memory to handle incoming requests.

If you decide to host your own Web site, you must install Web server software on your computer. Windows XP Pro, Windows NET, and Windows 2000 server include Windows IIS, which can handle FTP and HTTP protocols. Mac OS X includes the Apache Server software. After installing the software, you can enable your Web server. This example uses Windows XP Pro to enable and access a Web server.

Host Your Own Web Site

① Copy the Web page files that you want to publish.

② Navigate to the Inetpub/webroot directory on your computer.

● Windows creates this directory when you install Windows IIS.

③ Paste the copied Web page files into the inetpub/webroot directory.

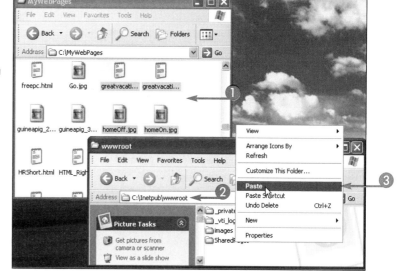

④ Launch your Web browser.

⑤ Type **http://localhost/**_filename.html_ where _filename.html_ is the name of the Web page that you want to open.

⑥ Press Enter or click the button to load the specified file.

● Your Web browser opens and displays the Web page.

7️⃣ Launch My Network Places.

8️⃣ Click View Network Connections.

9️⃣ Right-click the icon for your Internet connection.

🔟 Click Status.

1️⃣1️⃣ In the dialog box that appears, click the Support tab.

1️⃣2️⃣ Note your computer's IP address.

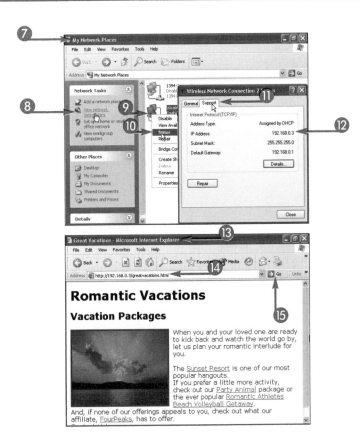

1️⃣3️⃣ Launch your Web browser.

1️⃣4️⃣ Type **http://** followed by the IP address you noted in step 12 and the filename you typed in step 5.

1️⃣5️⃣ Press Enter or click the button to load the specified file.

● Your Web browser loads the Web page using the IP address of your computer.

When I host my own Web site, are my files secure?

▼ When your computer acts as a Web server, it is susceptible to the same security risks as other Web servers. A commercial Web server is more secure because users do not have direct access to any files on your computer.

How can other people open the files on my Web server?

▼ They access your Web site by typing **http://** followed by your Web site's IP address. In Windows IIS, if you name the home page default.htm, it opens automatically when you type the Web site address; otherwise, you must specify a filename. If your computer uses a router you must enable several ports so users outside your network can access the pages. Refer to your router's instructions or help system for more information.

Can I register a domain name for my Web site if I host it myself?

▼ Yes. This works best if your ISP assigns your computer a static IP address — an address that never changes. Most ISPs assign your computer a dynamic IP address that is different each time your computer connects to the ISP, or the ISP may change the IP address every few days. If your ISP uses dynamic IP addresses, you can register with a dynamic DNS service that keeps track of IP address changes and retains the link between your computer and your domain name regardless of the IP address. You also need to install domain name server (DNS) software on your computer. This is usually included with the server software.

HTML Numeric Entity	HTML Name	Octal Number	Symbol	Description
&#032;		40		Space
&#033;		41	!	Exclamatio
&#034;	&quot;	42	"	Quotation
&#035;		43	#	Hash mark
&#036;		44	$	Dollar sign
&#037;		45	%	Percent sig
&#038;	&amp;	46	&	Ampersan
&#039;		47	'	Apostroph
&#040;		50	(	Left parent
&#041;		51	)	Right parer
&#042;		52	*	Asterisk
&#043;		53	+	Plus sign
&#044;		54	,	Comma
&#045;		55	-	Hyphen
&#046;		56	.	Period
&#047;		57	/	Forward sl
&#048;		60–67, 70, 71		
&#058;		72	:	Colon
&#059;		73	;	Semicolon
&#060;	&lt;	74	<	Less-than s
&#061;		75	=	Equals sign
&#062;	&gt;	76	>	Greater-tha
&#063;		77	?	Question m
&#064;		100	@	At sign

Value Format

COLOR You can express colors in the form of a color name or a hexadecimal value. You may also specify colors in RGB form, (r, g, b), where r, g, and b are either numbers or percentages. The color chart included with this book provides hexadecimal values and RGB codes for the 216 Web-safe colors.

LENGTH Lengths may contain an optional plus or minus sign followed by a numeric entity and a unit identifier. Unit identifiers include em (height of the font), ex (height of the letter x), px (pixels), in (inches), cm (centimeters), mm (millimeters), pt (points), and pc (picas).

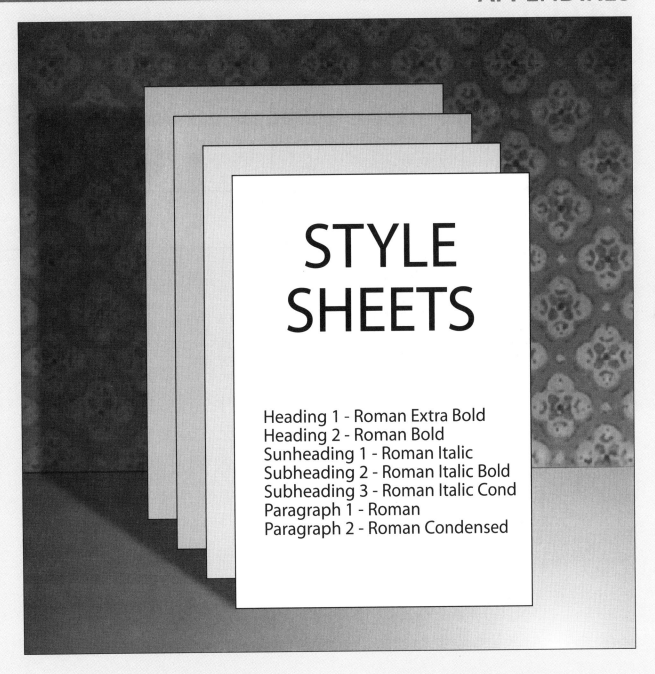

STYLE
SHEETS

Heading 1 - Roman Extra Bold
Heading 2 - Roman Bold
Sunheading 1 - Roman Italic
Subheading 2 - Roman Italic Bold
Subheading 3 - Roman Italic Cond
Paragraph 1 - Roman
Paragraph 2 - Roman Condensed

Special Characters

Y ou can use the following named or numeric entities to add special characters to HTML code. The numeric entities from 160 to 255 all have name equivalents, while most of the entities from 32 to 126 do not. For these entities, you must use the numeric notation. In addition, characters ranging from 127 to 159 are not part of the HTML standard, and the output may vary among operating systems. These entities are marked with an asterisk (*).

To include character entities in JavaScript code, you must use a JavaScript escape sequence (\) with the octal number.

Character Entities

HTML Numeric Entity	HTML Name	Octal Number	Symbol	Description
&#032;		40		Space
&#033;		41	!	Exclamation point
&#034;	&quot;	42	"	Quotation mark
&#035;		43	#	Hash mark
&#036;		44	$	Dollar sign
&#037;		45	%	Percent sign
&#038;	&amp;	46	&	Ampersand
&#039;		47	'	Apostrophe
&#040;		50	(	Left parenthesis
&#041;		51	)	Right parenthesis
&#042;		52	*	Asterisk
&#043;		53	+	Plus sign
&#044;		54	,	Comma
&#045;		55	-	Hyphen
&#046;		56	.	Period
&#047;		57	/	Forward slash
0 to 9		60–67, 70, 71	0–9	Numbers 0–9
&#058;		72	:	Colon
&#059;		73	;	Semicolon
&#060;	&lt;	74	<	Less-than sign
&#061;		75	=	Equals sign
&#062;	&gt;	76	>	Greater-than sign

Character Entities

HTML Numeric Entity	HTML Name	Octal Number	Symbol	Description
&#063;		77	?	Question mark
&#064;		100	@	At sign
A to Z			A–Z	Uppercase letters A–Z
&#091;		133	[	Left bracket
&#092;		134	\	Backslash
&#093;		135	]	Right bracket
&#094;		136	^	Caret
&#095;		137	_	Underscore
&#096;		140	`	Grave accent
a to z		a–z	a–z	Lowercase letters
&#123;		173	{	Left curly brace
|		174	|	Vertical bar
&#125;		175	}	Right curly brace
&#126;		176	~	Tilde
&#133;			…	*Ellipsis
&#134;			†	*Dagger
&#135;			‡	*Double dagger
&#136;			ˆ	*Circumflex
&#137;			‰	*Permil
&#145;			‘	*Left single quote
&#146;			’	*Right single quote
&#147;			“	*Left double quote

continued

PART VII

Character Entities (continued)

HTML Numeric Entity	HTML Name	Octal Number	Symbol	Description
&#148;			”	*Right double quote
&#149;			•	*Bullet
&#150;			–	*En dash
&#151;			—	*Em dash
&#153;			™	*Trademark sign
&#159;			Ÿ	*Capital Y, umlaut
		240		Nonbreaking space
&#161;	&iexcl;	241	¡	Inverted exclamation point
&#162;	&cent;	242	¢	Cent sign
&#163;	&pound;	243	£	Pound sign
&#164;	&curren;	244	¤	Currency sign
&#165;	&yen;	245	¥	Yen sign
&#166;	&brvbar;	246	¦	Broken vertical bar
&#167;	&sect;	247	§	Section sign
&#168;	&uml;	250	¨	Umlaut
&#169;	&copy;	251	©	Copyright sign
&#170;	&ordf;	252	ª	Feminine ordinal sign
&#171;	&laquo;	253	«	Left angle quote
&#172;	&not;	254	¬	Not sign
&#173;	&shy;	255	-	Soft hyphen
&#174;	&reg;	256	®	Registered trademark sign
&#175;	&macr;	257	¯	Macron accent
&#176;	&deg;	260	°	Degree sign
&#177;	&plusmn;	261	±	Plus or minus sign
&#178;	&sup2;	262	2	Superscript 2
&#179;	&sup3;	263	3	Superscript 3
&#180;	&acute;	264	´	Acute accent
&#181;	&micro;	265	µ	Micro sign
&#182;	&para;	266	¶	Paragraph sign
&#183;	&middot;	267	·	Middle dot
&#184;	&cedil;	270	¸	Cedilla

Character Entities

HTML Numeric Entity	HTML Name	Octal Number	Symbol	Description
&#185;	&sup1;	271	¹	Superscript 1
&#186;	&ordm;	272	º	Masculine ordinal
&#187;	&raquo;	273	»	Right angle quote
&#188;	&frac14;	274	¼	One-quarter fraction
&#189;	&frac12;	275	½	One-half fraction
&#190;	&frac34;	276	¾	Three-quarters fraction
&#191;	&iquest;	277	¿	Inverted question mark
&#192;	&Agrave;	300	À	Capital A, grave accent
&#193;	&Aacute;	301	Á	Capital A, acute accent
&#194;	&Acirc;	302	Â	Capital A, circumflex
&#195;	&Atilde;	303	Ã	Capital A, tilde
&#196;	&Auml;	304	Ä	Capital A, umlaut
&#197;	&Aring;	305	Å	Capital A, ring
&#198;	&AElig;	306	Æ	Capital AE ligature
&#199;	&Ccedil;	307	Ç	Capital C, cedilla
&#200;	&Egrave;	310	È	Capital E, grave accent
&#201;	&Eacute;	311	É	Capital E, acute accent
&#202;	&Ecirc;	312	Ê	Capital E, circumflex
&#203;	&Euml;	313	Ë	Capital E, umlaut
&#204;	&Igrave;	314	Ì	Capital I, grave accent
&#205;	&Iacute;	315	Í	Capital I, acute accent
&#206;	&Icirc;	316	Î	Capital I, circumflex
&#207;	&Iuml;	317	Ï	Capital I, umlaut
&#208;	&ETH;	320	Ð	Capital eth, Icelandic
&#209;	&Ntilde;	321	Ñ	Capital N, tilde
&#210;	&Ograve;	322	Ò	Capital O, grave accent
&#211;	&Oacute;	323	Ó	Capital O, acute accent
&#212;	&Ocirc;	324	Ô	Capital O, circumflex
&#213;	&Otilde;	325	Õ	Capital O, tilde
&#214;	&Ouml;	326	Ö	Capital O, umlaut
&#215;	&times;	327	×	Multiply sign

continued

HTML Numeric Entity	HTML Name	Octal Number	Symbol	Description
&#216;	&Oslash;	330	Ø	Capital O, slash
&#217;	&Ugrave;	331	Ù	Capital U, grave accent
&#218;	&Uacute;	332	Ú	Capital U, acute accent
&#219;	&Ucirc;	333	Û	Capital U, circumflex
&#220;	&Uuml;	334	Ü	Capital U, umlaut
&#221;	&Yacute;	335	Ý	Capital Y, acute accent
&#222;	&THORN;	336	Þ	Capital thorn, Icelandic
&#223;	&szlig;	337	ß	SZ ligature
&#224;	&agrave;	340	à	Small a, grave accent
&#225;	&aacute;	341	á	Small a, acute accent
&#226;	&acirc;	342	â	Small a, circumflex
&#227;	&atilde;	343	ã	Small a, tilde
&#228;	&auml;	344	ä	Small a, umlaut
&#229;	&aring;	345	å	Small a, ring
&#230;	&aelig;	346	æ	Small ae ligature
&#231;	&ccedil;	347	ç	Small c, cedilla
&#232;	&egrave;	350	è	Small e, grave accent
&#233;	&eacute;	351	é	Small e, acute accent
&#234;	&ecirc;	352	ê	Small e, circumflex
&#235;	&euml;	353	ë	Small e, umlaut
&#236;	&igrave;	354	ì	Small i, grave accent
&#237;	&iacute;	355	í	Small i, acute accent
&#238;	&icirc;	356	î	Small i, circumflex
&#239;	&iuml;	357	ï	Small i, umlaut
&#240;	&eth;	360	ð	Small eth, Icelandic
&#241;	&ntilde;	361	ñ	Small n, tilde
&#242;	&ograve;	362	ò	Small o, grave accent
&#243;	&oacute;	363	ó	Small o, acute accent
&#244;	&ocirc;	364	ô	Small o, circumflex
&#245;	&otilde;	365	õ	Small o, tilde
&#246;	&ouml;	366	ö	Small o, umlaut

Character Entities

HTML Numeric Entity	HTML Name	Octal Number	Symbol	Description
&#247;	&divide;	367	÷	Divide sign
&#248;	&oslash;	370	ø	Small o, slash
&#249;	&ugrave;	371	ù	Small u, grave accent
&#250;	&uacute;	372	ú	Small u, acute accent
&#251;	&ucirc;	373	û	Small u, circumflex
&#252;	&uuml;	374	ü	Small u, umlaut
&#253;	&yacute;	375	ý	Small y, grave accent
&#254;	&thorn;	376	þ	Small thorn, Icelandic
&#255;	&yuml;	377	ÿ	Small y, umlaut

Cascading Style Sheet Reference

The CSS Properties table lists the Cascading Style Sheet properties defined in the Level 1 specification as well as key Level 2 positioning properties. Support for Level 1 and Level 2 style properties varies from Web browser to Web browser, so you must ensure that you adequately test CSS style sheets on a variety of Web browser versions. Some online resources also provide CSS

compatibility charts that you can use as a reference. The W3C's CSS home page at www.w3.org/Style/CSS/ provides a list of online resources.

Although some CSS properties accept only certain keyword values, others can take values such as colors, lengths, and percentages. The CSS Values table defines the correct formatting for these values.

CSS Values

Value	Format
COLOR	You can express colors in the form of a color name or a hexadecimal value. You may also specify colors in RGB form, (r, g, b), where r, g, and b are either numbers or percentages. The color chart included with this book provides hexadecimal values and RGB codes for the 216 Web-safe colors.
LENGTH	Lengths may contain an optional plus or minus sign followed by a numeric entity and a unit identifier. Unit identifiers include em (height of the font), ex (height of the letter x), px (pixels), in (inches), cm (centimeters), mm (millimeters), pt (points), and pc (picas). If the value of the length is zero, you may omit the unit identifier.
NUMBER	A number may contain an optional plus or minus sign followed by the number.
PERCENT	Percent values may contain an optional plus or minus sign, followed by a number and the percent sign.
URL	For properties that accept URL values, use the keyword url, followed by the URL enclosed within single or double quotes and parentheses, for example, url("http://www.mysite.com").

CSS Properties

Property	Possible Values	Default Value	Description
background			Shorthand property for defining values for the other background properties, listed in any order.
background-attachment	scroll | fixed	scroll	Fixes the background image to the window, or allows it to scroll with the document.
background-color	COLOR | transparent	transparent	Sets the background color of an element.
background-image	URL | none	none	Sets an image for the background of an element.
background-position	PERCENT | LENGTH | top | center | bottom | left | right	0% 0%	Defines initial position of the background image. Paired values correspond to x and y coordinates.
background-repeat	repeat | repeat-x | repeat-y | no-repeat	repeat	Specifies how the background image should be tiled.
border			Shorthand property to set all four borders of an element. May include one or more COLOR values, a value for border-width and a value for border-style.

CSS Properties

Property	Possible Values	Default Value	Description
border-bottom			Defines the bottom border of an element. May include COLOR, a value for `border-bottom-width`, and a value for `border-style`.
border-bottom-width	LENGTH | thin | medium | thick	medium	Defines the width of the bottom border.
border-color	COLOR		Defines the color of all four borders.
border-left			Defines the left border of an element. May include COLOR, a value for `border-left-width`, and a value for `border-style`.
border-left-width	LENGTH | thin | medium | thick	medium	Defines the width of the left border.
border-right			Defines the right border of an element. May include COLOR, a value for `border-right-width`, and a value for `border-style`.
border-right-width	LENGTH | thin | medium | thick	medium	Defines the width of the right border.
border-style	dashed | dotted | double | groove | inset | none | outset | ridge | solid	none	Defines the style of all four borders.
border-top			Defines the top border of an element. May include COLOR, a value for `border-top-width`, and a value for `border-style`.
border-top-width	LENGTH | thin | medium | thick	medium	Defines the width of the top border.
border-width	LENGTH | thin | medium | thick	medium	Defines the width of all four borders.
bottom	LENGTH | PERCENT | auto	auto	Defines the bottom offset for positioned elements where position is other than static.
clear	both | left | none | right	none	Moves an element down until it is clear of the specified margin.
clip	SHAPE | auto	auto	Defines what portion of an element's content should be visible. The only SHAPE currently available is `rect` where the top, bottom, left, and right offsets are defined as either LENGTH or `auto`.
color	COLOR		Defines the color of an element.
display	block | inline | list-item | none	block	Sets the display type of an element.
float	left | none | right	none	Sets whether an element should float to either the left or right.

PART VII

continued

Property	Possible Values	Default Value	Description
`font`			Shorthand property that defines all of the font-related properties in the following order: `font-style`, `font-variant`, `font-weight`, `font-size`, `line-height`, `font-family`.
`font-family`		font names	Defines the fonts for a particular element.
`font-size`	`xx-small` | `x-small` | `small` | `medium` | `large` | `x-large` | `xx-large` | `larger` | `smaller` | LENGTH | PERCENT	medium	Sets the font size.
`font-style`	`normal` | `italic` | `oblique`	`normal`	Sets the font style.
`font-variant`	`normal` | `small-caps`	`normal`	Sets the font to small caps.
`font-weight`	`normal` | `bold` | `bolder` | `lighter` | NUMBER	`normal`	Defines the weight of the font. When numbers are used, they must be in multiples of 100 and may range from 100 to 900.
`height`	LENGTH | `auto`	`auto`	Defines the height of an element.
`left`	LENGTH | PERCENT | `auto`	`auto`	Defines the left offset for positioned elements where position is other than static.
`letter-spacing`	LENGTH | `normal`	`normal`	Defines the amount of space between letters.
`line-height`	LENGTH | NUMBER | PERCENT | `normal`	`normal`	Sets the height of a line of text.
`list-style`			Shorthand property to define the style of a list. May include values for `list-style-image`, `list-style-position`, and `list-style-type`.
`list-style-image`	URL | `none`	`none`	Sets an image to use as a list bullet.
`list-style-position`	`inside` | `outside`	`outside`	Sets the indentation of list items.
`list-style-type`	`circle` | `disc` | `square` | `decimal` | `lower-alpha` | `lower-roman` | `upper-alpha` | `upper-roman`	`disc`	Defines a list marker for ordered or unordered lists.
`margin`	LENGTH | PERCENT | `auto`	`auto`	Sets all four margins of an element.
`margin-bottom`	LENGTH | PERCENT | `auto`	0	Sets the bottom margin.
`margin-left`	LENGTH | PERCENT | `auto`	0	Sets the left margin.
`margin-right`	LENGTH | PERCENT | `auto`	0	Sets the right margin.

CSS Properties

Property	Possible Values	Default Value	Description
margin-top	LENGTH | PERCENT | auto	0	Sets the top margin.
overflow	visible | hidden | scroll | auto	visible	Determines how overflow content should be handled.
padding	LENGTH | PERCENT		Sets the padding on all four sides of an element.
padding-bottom	LENGTH | PERCENT	0	Sets the bottom padding.
padding-left	LENGTH | PERCENT	0	Sets the left padding.
padding-right	LENGTH | PERCENT	0	Sets the right padding.
padding-top	LENGTH | PERCENT	0	Sets the top padding.
position	static | absolute | relative | fixed	static	Defines the type of positioning of an element.
right	LENGTH | PERCENT | auto	auto	Defines the right offset for positioned elements where position is other than static.
text-align	center | justify | left | right	left	Defines how text should be aligned.
text-decoration	blink | line-through | none | overline | underline	none	Defines any special text decorations.
text-indent	LENGTH | PERCENT	0	Defines the amount of indentation for the first line of text.
text-transform	capitalize | lowercase | none | uppercase	none	Transforms the text contained within the element.
top	LENGTH | PERCENT | auto	auto	Defines the top offset for positioned elements where position is other than static.
vertical-align	PERCENT | baseline | bottom | middle | sub | super | text-bottom | text-top | top	baseline	Controls the vertical positioning of an element.
visibility	visible | hidden | inherit	inherit	Determines whether positioned elements are visible or transparent.
word-spacing	LENGTH | normal	normal	Sets the amount of space between words.
white-space	normal | nowrap | pre	normal	Defines how white space within an element should be handled.
width	LENGTH | PERCENT | auto	auto	Defines the width of an element.
z-index	auto | INTEGER	auto	Sets the stacking index of an element.

PART VII

A

INDEX

continued

INDEX

D

`Date()` constructor, 222
`<dd>` tags, 58
debugging, 180
`defaultStatus` property, 189
definition lists, 58
`<del>` tags, 45
`delete` operator, 173
`<description>` tags, 348, 349
DHTML (Dynamic HTML), 100–101
digital video editors, 291
disk cache, 26
`<div>` tags, 69, 81
`<dl>` tags, 58
`document.close()` method, 168
`document.cookie` property, 220, 221, 225
`document.images` property, 214, 215
`document.lastModified` property, 194, 195
Document Object Models. *See* DOMs
`document.open()` method, 168
Document Type Definition. *See* DTD
`document.write()` method
    add, 175
    arguments, 169
    call, 169
    defined, 168
    using, 173
    in Web page generation, 168
domain name server software, 381
domain names
    available, list, 369
    registrars, 369
    registration, 366, 368–369, 381
    rights ownership, 369
DOMs (Document Object Models)
    array grouping, 210
    consistency, 211

    defined, 161
    reference, 210–211
    support, 160
    version numbers, 211
draw
    circles, 307
    lines, 307
    objects, 306–307
    shapes, 307
    text objects, 306
drawing tools
    Brush, 306
    Lasso, 308, 309
    Pen, 307
    Pencil, 307
    Selection, 308, 309
    Subselection, 309, 310
`<dt>` tags, 58
DTD (Document Type Definition)
    defined, 11, 38
    frameset, 38, 39
    public line, 38
    specification omission, 39
    specify, 38–39
    strict, 38, 39
    transitional, 38, 39
Dynamic HTML. *See* DHTML

E

elements
    control, 101
    default stacking order, 99
    flow around, 97
    layer, 98–99
    name, 101
    overlap, 98
    position, 96–97
    `z-index` property and, 98–99

continued

continued

INDEX

continued

continued

continued

continued